Contextualizing Missionary and National Identity

A Study of Czech Protestant Missionary Identity
Among Slavs in the Western Balkans

David Symon

Langham
ACADEMIC

© 2025 David Symon

Published 2025 by Langham Academic
An imprint of Langham Publishing
www.langhampublishing.org

Langham Publishing and its imprints are a ministry of Langham Partnership

Langham Partnership
PO Box 296, Carlisle, Cumbria, CA3 9WZ, UK
www.langham.org

ISBNs:
978-1-83973-970-5 Print
978-1-78641-290-4 ePub
978-1-78641-291-1 PDF
DOI: https://doi.org/10.69811/9781839739705

David Symon has asserted his right under the Copyright, Designs and Patents Act, 1988 to be identified as the Author of this work.

All rights reserved. No part of this publication may be reproduced, stored in a retrieval system or transmitted, in any form or by any means, electronic, mechanical, photocopying, recording or otherwise, without the prior written permission of the publisher or the Copyright Licensing Agency.

Requests to reuse content from Langham Publishing are processed through PLSclear. Please visit www.plsclear.com to complete your request.

Scripture quotations are from The Holy Bible, English Standard Version® (ESV®), copyright © 2001 by Crossway, a publishing ministry of Good News Publishers. Used by permission. All rights reserved.

Unless otherwise stated, photos tagged "Photo diary" are © David Symon.

British Library Cataloguing-in-Publication Data
A catalogue record for this book is available from the British Library

ISBN: 978-1-83973-970-5

Cover & Book Design: projectluz.com

Langham Partnership actively supports theological dialogue and an author's right to publish but does not necessarily endorse the views and opinions set forth here or in works referenced within this publication, nor can we guarantee technical and grammatical correctness. Langham Partnership does not accept any responsibility or liability to persons or property as a consequence of the reading, use or interpretation of its published content.

Backed up by rich empirical evidence, conversant with contemporary scholarly discussion, and guided by a sound methodology for interdisciplinary research, David Symon offers the reader a volume that has a great potential to make a significant contribution to the field of mission studies. The author does not shy away from even such complex issues as identity, culture, or nation. Rather, he addresses them in their multifacetedness to offer a solid framework for constructive discussion on the ways of interaction among various agents engaged in Christian missionary endeavours. *Contextualizing Missionary and National Identity* by David Symon will be greatly appreciated by all those interested in intercultural mission, whether academicians or reflective practitioners.

Pavol Bargár, PhD
Protestant Theological Faculty,
Charles University, Czechia

David Symon has carried out detailed work on the issue of identity in intraslav Christian mission, neatly combining flexible use of theory with excellent field work. Although there are several basic categories of identity, David focusses on the national identity of the missionaries. His work confirms how ethnocentrism might become a barrier for missionary work, yet displays how, on the other hand, awareness and proper situational use of the national identity facet could serve to advance it. The book *Contextualizing Missionary and National Identity* sheds new light on modern mission from the Czech Republic and into the former Yugoslavia but clearly has implications for mission situations in which those who proclaim and who hear the gospel are positioned along linguistic, cultural, or religious continua.

Paul Woods, PhD
Theological Educator at Large,
OMF International, UK

Dedication

I dedicate the thesis to my four daughters.

Contents

Abstract xv

Acknowledgments xvii

Chapter 1 1
Introduction
    1.1 Background and research questions 1
        1.1.1 Background 1
        1.1.2 Research questions 3
    1.2 Introducing the region 5
        1.2.1 Former Yugoslavia and former Czechoslovakia –
             geopolitical terms 5
        1.2.2 Two Communist regimes 8
        1.2.3 Two break-ups 10
        1.2.4 Negotiating spatiality within Europe 13
    1.3 Thesis structure 17

Chapter 2 21
Theoretical Framework for the Study of How Czech Missionaries Negotiate Their Identity in the Former Yugoslav Countries
    2.1 Introduction 21
    2.2 Identity 22
        2.2.1 Definition 22
        2.2.2 Multiple identity facets and identity salience 24
        2.2.3 Social identity complexity 26
        2.2.4 National identity facet 31
        2.2.5 Christian identity facet 34
    2.3 Culture 35
        2.3.1 Definition 35
        2.3.2 Christian anthropological view of Christ
             transforming cultures 37
        2.3.3 Missionaries' contextualization in local culture 39
        2.3.4 Cross-cultural comparison in missiological perspective ... 42
    2.4 Mission 44
        2.4.1 Definition 44
        2.4.2 Mission from the Czech Republic 47
        2.4.3 Religious identity in the Czech Republic 51
        2.4.4 Religious identity in former Yugoslav countries 54
    2.5 Chapter summary 56

Chapter 3 59
  Methodology
    3.1 Research framework...59
      3.1.1 Introduction 59
      1.1.1 Case study..60
    3.2 Scope and primary sources 62
      3.2.1 Research scope 62
      3.2.2 Primary sources 63
      3.2.3 Complementary primary sources 67
    3.3 Research ethics...68
      3.3.1 The positionality of the researcher...68
      3.3.2 Ethics and risk assessment 70
    3.4 Methods 71
      3.4.1 Data gathering methods 71
      3.4.2 Methods of data analysis 74
    3.5 Procedure 76
      3.5.1 Performing the interviews...76
      3.5.2 Interview circumstances..78
      3.5.3 Other procedural steps in data gathering and analysis 80
    3.6 Chapter summary..83

Chapter 4 85
  Cross-cultural Dimensions for Czech Missionaries in Former Yugoslav Countries
    4.1 Chapter framework 85
      4.1.1 Models for cross-cultural comparison...85
      4.1.2 Approach to cross-cultural comparison in this chapter.....88
    4.2 Rules vs. people orientation 90
    4.3 Achievement vs. ascription 96
    4.4 Individual vs. communitarian culture 104
    4.5 Openness vs. closeness 111
    4.6 Temperament differences 116
    4.7 Discussion of cultural differences and similarities 119
    4.8 Chapter conclusions..124

Chapter 5 127
  Czech Missionaries' Czech Identity Salience and Suppression in Their Interaction with Slavs in Former Yugoslav Countries
    5.1 The matter of national identity facet salience and
        suppression...127
      5.1.1 Situational identity salience and suppression...................127

  5.1.2 National identity negotiation 129
 5.2 Czech Identity Salience of Czech missionaries 131
  5.2.1 Encountering artefacts 131
  5.2.2 Interaction with other Czechs, Slovaks, and other
   nationals 135
 5.3 Czech identity suppression of Czech missionaries 139
  5.3.1 Interaction with non-Czechs 139
  5.3.2 Czech language suppression 141
  5.3.3 Czech identity suppression in adjustment to the
   local culture 150
 5.4 Simultaneous salience and suppression of Czech
  missionaries' Czech identity facet 153
 5.5 Chapter conclusions 157

Chapter 6 161
Discussion of Czech Identity in Mission in Former
Yugoslav Countries
 6.1 National identity in mission 161
 6.2 Czechs and Westerners in mission in former Yugoslav
  countries 164
  6.2.1 Czechs' ambiguous spatiality 164
  6.2.2 Western – American? 166
 6.3 Czech identity salience in mission 168
  6.3.1 Situational utilisation of Czech identity salience 168
  6.3.2 Acceptance of Czechs by former Yugoslavs 173
  6.3.3 Favourable factors for Czech missionaries in former
   Yugoslav countries 177
 6.4 Religious identity facet and its missiological implications 181
  6.4.1 Challenges of ethnoreligious identity for Czech
   Protestant missionaries 182
  6.4.2 Protestants' challenge of contextualization 188
  6.4.3 Towards a dialogue concerning ethnoreligious
   identity 191
 6.5 Chapter conclusions 194

Chapter 7 203
Czech Missionaries Negotiating Multiple Identity Facets
 7.1 Introducing identity facets of Czech missionaries 203
 7.2 Human nature 206
  7.2.1 Male or female 206
  7.2.2 Family member 207

- 7.3 Personality 209
  - 7.3.1 Personality traits holder 210
  - 7.3.2 Interest group member 213
  - 7.3.3 Worker 214
- 7.4 Culture 219
  - 7.4.1 Christian 219
  - 7.4.2 Missionary 222
  - 7.4.3 Someone with regional or supranational identity 226
  - 7.4.4 Another national 230
- 7.5 Chapter conclusions 235

Chapter 8 237
Interrelations of "Czechness" with Other Identity Facets: Discussion of Social Identity Complexity
- 8.1 The four social identity complexity interrelations as the analysis framework 237
- 8.2 Intersection 243
- 8.3 Dominance 245
- 8.4 Compartmentalization 250
- 8.5 Merger 255
- 8.6 Chapter conclusions 260
  - 8.6.1 Critical evaluation of social identity complexity concept 260
  - 8.6.2 Missiological implications of social identity complexity 266

Chapter 9 269
Conclusion
- 9.1 Introduction 269
  - 9.1.1 Thesis summary 269
  - 9.1.2 Returning to research questions 270
- 9.2 Contribution to knowledge 272
- 9.3 Missiological findings and implications for mission practice 277
  - 9.3.1 Central argument 277
  - 9.3.2 Implications for "Czechness" in mission in former Yugoslav countries 279
  - 9.3.3 Mission to former Yugoslavs and to Czechs 282
- 9.4 Further research 284

Appendix A 291
    Interviewees' Detailed Profiles
Appendix B 297
    Informed Consent for Research
Appendix C 301
    List of Semi-structured Interview Questions
Appendix D 305
    Interview Transcript Example
Bibliography 309

List of Figures

Figure 1: Western, Eastern, and Southern Slavs 5

Figure 2: Multiple ingroup representations 27

Figure 3: Type and length of Czech missionaries' commitment 65

Figure 4: Geographical positions of current, returned, and periodic Czech missionaries in former Yugoslav countries 66

Figure 5: Data collection and analysis diagram 73

Figure 6: Illustrative NVivo word cloud frequency from interview transcripts .. 82

Figure 7: Diffuse vs. specific cultures 113

Figure 8: The levels of language 148

Figure 9: Three levels of uniqueness in mental programming. 204

Figure 10: Multiple ingroup representations 238

Abstract

This thesis is a multiple case study and explores how contemporary Czech Protestant missionaries negotiate their national identity in the culturally proximal context of working with Slavs in Bosnia and Herzegovina, Croatia, Kosovo, Montenegro, North Macedonia, Serbia and Slovenia. The issue that I explore is the Czech identity facet of the missionaries, in the light of the social identity complexity concept with focus on interrelations of multiple identity facets. The research process makes use of in-depth interviews and personal diaries for data collection, followed by thematic analysis.

The argument begins by delineating areas of cultural differences to help understand situations when Czech identity facet of missionaries tends to become salient or suppressed. The thesis proceeds with examining implications of Czech identity salience and suppression for mission practice, and describes the single identity facets, which are of significance for Czech missionaries. Finally, the thesis focuses on how these identity facets interrelate and argues for their more integrative treatment in order to advance the intercultural work.

The present study emphasizes that awareness and proper utilisation of missionaries' national identity facet leads towards reducing prejudice and more effective contextualization. In this perspective, my research could benefit mission practitioners who negotiate their identity in the quest for self-identification in mission, and their counterparts in the mission fields.

The discoveries of my thesis contribute to missiological studies on missionaries' identity, adding particular findings to missiology with a focus on Central and Eastern Europe. This thesis primarily makes a contribution to the critical discussion on the concept of social identity complexity, the adequacy of which this qualitative study examines.

Acknowledgments

My first thanks go to God as a deep appreciation of who He is and of the ways He is weaving my life's path, including studies at OCMS. When in February 2020 I was diagnosed with acute leukaemia, I underwent medical treatment and praise God, not only did I survive, but I continued to press on with my studies. A substantive part of the data was analysed in a hospital room while receiving chemotherapy, and much writing continued through successive maintenance medication. Thanks to Him and to everybody around me for moral and prayerful support in these uneasy times!

Perhaps the best way to commence expressing my gratitude to specific people is with Czech missionaries and my other respondents, because without them this research would not have existed. Thank you for spending time with me and opening up to me. I want to express my deep appreciation for the input of my two supervisors, Pavol Bargár and Paul Woods, who helped shape my research focus and guide me on the long-lasting journey. Thank you both, for your approach and for your friendship. I am thankful for the OCMS community, and especially thankful for David E. Singh, my house tutor, who helped me improve my writing skills and kept encouraging me. Thank you also, Damon So, Bill Prevette, Stuart Judge, Paul Bendor Samuel and all others who have provided scholarly input, together with the prayers of the OCMS staff and scholars.

I am grateful for the OCMS alumnus Dejan Aždajić, who, together with our common friend in Bosnia and Herzegovina Deron Bauer, helped me to start the research journey and pointed me to OCMS. I appreciate scholarly input from Jiří Bukovský, who pointed me to Czech authors and leaders, including Peter Cimala from Comenius Institute in Prague who has become my mentor during the years of the PhD journey. Thank you, Andrew Funka, for the language editing that was an immense help.

My appreciation goes to those who have provided funds or helped me in practical ways to study at OCMS: The Kemptons for accommodation in the initial five weeks at Oxford, supporters of our ministry, church and denomination leaders, especially Tomáš Süss, Stanislav Bubik and Radek Smetana, for giving me space to study, along with fulfilling my other obligations, together with material and moral support.

Last, but not least, my family. There are not enough words to express my gratitude, I have appreciated everyone in my family, they were all very supportive. My in-laws provided great help to my wife when I was away. I am thankful for our little ones, and I look forward to when my children read some of my work and will finally be able to say something beyond "Daddy works on the computer." I would like to thank my wife for being always supportive of my decisions, including this research. I love you, Irena.

CHAPTER 1

Introduction

1.1 Background and research questions

1.1.1 Background

I was born in Czechoslovakia, and when I started to attend primary school in our quarter of Prague in 1989, we were obliged to say "Comrade teacher" until November. After that, we were instructed to switch the address to "Mrs. teacher." Communism fell and, suddenly, many things changed in the country overnight. Other transformations, including the breakup of Czechoslovakia into the Czech Republic and Slovakia, have come during the course of time. A definite instant change was freedom to proclaim the Christian gospel, as well as the ability to travel abroad without restrictions. This led, among other things, to a gradual rise in international missions from the Czech Republic – at first mainly to the former Soviet Union, particularly Ukraine, and to the former Yugoslav countries.

Historically, missions from Czech territory have deep roots, whether these were the disciples of Cyril and Methodius expelled from the Sázava monastery (Eastern church missions); St. Adalbert of Prague (Catholic missions); or the pre-reformers of the fourteenth and fifteenth century, including John Hus, and the Moravian[1] brothers (Protestant missions). Despite a relatively rich history, the contemporary Czech Republic is often considered

---

1. These were predominantly Germans exiled from Moravia (currently the eastern part of the Czech Republic) and received by Count Zinzendorf on his estate at Herrnhut (Neill, *History of Christian Missions*, 202). They were sent to various parts of the world and played a formative role in future Protestant missions endeavours (Tennent, *Invitation to World Missions*, 251).

a mission field[2] rather than a missionary sending country. Still, the mission activity has increased, particularly in the last decade, as Czech missionaries[3] are being sent with the help of more than ten mission agencies or directly as church initiatives.

With my background in an atheist family, I started to believe in Christ at the age of eighteen and almost immediately became involved in international missions. After finishing university studies, I worked in Bosnia and Herzegovina for eight years. Therefore, the research interest in the Czech missionaries' identity originates from my personal experience as a mission practitioner and from questions arising from previous studies in sociolinguistics and practical theology. The desire to learn more, and the attempt to discover how findings from literature and from Czech mission practice could inform each other, directed me to go deeper in my reflection and evolved into a PhD research project. To be more specific, several particular issues gave rise to the topic of this research project, which is entitled "Czech Mission: Identity of Czech Protestant Missionaries in Their Interaction with Slavs in former Yugoslav Countries."

The first was the realization of the limited degree to which the newly emerging missions from the Czech Republic are accompanied by relevant missiological literature. In my initial literature search, I was challenged when faced with the lack of attention given to international mission in the Czech academic milieu and that international missiology seems largely unfamiliar with Czech mission.[4] I also noticed the undervalued significance of certain sociological concepts in mission studies. These are concepts which relate to negotiating sameness and otherness, salience of identity in various circumstances, and mutual negotiating of various identities – parts of one's identity. While crafting the research proposal together with my tutor, as I reflected on mission, on the Czech context, and on the former Yugoslav context, I realized missionaries' identities are truly complex. In the process of the literature

---

2. Statistically, Czechs are less than fifteen per cent Christian (Škrabal, "*Religious Faith of Inhabitants*," 5).

3. While "missionary" can be broadly understood as "anyone who communicates the gospel in a cross-cultural setting" (Hiebert, *Anthropological Insights for Missionaries*, 28), the scope will be specified further in the work.

4. The literature review is found in 2.4.2.

search, an article on social identity complexity[5] emerged and this theoretical concept, together with other related theoretical elements from social psychology and missiology, helped to locate my research within the broader work.

Another area of concern and curiosity was aspect of national identity among Czech missionaries. This again originates from missionary practice and from the observation of how other colleagues function. I realized that the negotiation of one's national identity is highly relevant in regard to the ambiguous nature of Czech national identity and to the specifics of the region which I focused on.[6] Czechs continue to negotiate their spatiality in Europe between East and West;[7] they are neither strongly Catholic nor Protestant;[8] it is ambiguous whether language, birth in the country, citizenship or other marks should be considered the main characteristics of "Czechness."[9] They often recognize the national identity facet fully for the first time when they move abroad, and even more so as missionaries. Then they are prompted to engage the "other" with the goal to pass the Christian gospel on, and yet still retain their cultural elements. To add to that, it can be easily anticipated that events of the recent war and current tensions among Slavs in the Western Balkans imply that it is precisely national identity which is highly significant for the former Yugoslav region.[10] It will be further discussed that it is particularly the fusion of national and religious identity that presents itself as a crucial factor both for the local nations and for the missionaries involved.[11]

Out of an interest in the more general question, "What does it mean to be a Czech missionary to Slavs in former Yugoslav countries?", I found a PhD project emerged.

1.1.2 Research questions

The central research question is: "How is the identity of contemporary Czech missionaries negotiated in their interaction with Slavs in former Yugoslav countries?" The British social anthropologist of Czech origin Ladislav Holý

---

5. Roccas and Brewer, "Social Identity Complexity."
6. See the introduction in section 1.2.
7. Holý, *Little Czech*.
8. Hošek, *It Is Our Story*.
9. Vlachová, "Significant Others."
10. Volf, *Exclusion and Embrace*; Goodwin, *Fractured Land*; Kuzmič, "Journey from War."
11. In (2.4.4).

uses the very term I adopted – "negotiation."¹² According to him, "what constitutes Czech identity must be conceptualised not as timeless and unchangeable attributes of the Czech nation, as Czechs themselves conceptualise them, but as constructions perpetually re-created and modified."¹³ This aspect of the constant negotiating of one's identity is in accordance with social identity theorists' conclusions.[14]

The main research question is elaborated into sub-questions:

1. To what extent can the Slavic Czechs working with their fellow Slavs in former Yugoslav countries be considered cross-cultural?
2. How and in what circumstances does the Czech identity of Czech missionaries become salient or suppressed?
3. How does the missionaries' "Czechness" interact with their other identity facets?

In order to investigate the topic, it was essential to bring in these subordinate auxiliary research questions which are linked to theoretical concepts. This research on Czech missionaries' identity negotiation in their interaction with Slavs in former Yugoslavia aims to critically approach components of the theoretical concept of social identity complexity.[15] Together with this, the goal is to contribute to enhancing missiological reflection in the Czech Republic, which appears to be understudied. Apart from the desired theoretical contribution, the parallel purpose of this research is to inform mission practice, since missionaries' competencies in their inter-cultural work can be connected to their progress in negotiating their identity. My findings can help Czech missionaries, and hopefully others as well, navigate their national identity in various circumstances in their interactions with others, in ways that will enhance their missionary impact.

Even though the impact of this research cannot be entirely predicted and measured, I expect the research on identity negotiation of Czech missionaries to contribute significantly to the body of knowledge. The issue of identity and

---

12. Holý, *Little Czech*, 328. Holý's work, based on ethnographic observation in the years 1992–1993, is entitled "The Little Czech and the Great Czech Nation: National Identity and the Post-Communist Transformation of Society." The title depicts internal contradictions of Czech national traits (See also Uherek and Bryson, "Ladislav Holý").

13. Holý, 201.

14. Tajfel, *Human Groups*; Turner, "Towards Cognitive Redefinition."

15. Roccas and Brewer, "Social Identity Complexity."

mission is discussed in anthropology of mission, in practical missiology, and in the sociology of religion.[16] Yet, as will become evident from the reviewed literature, there is no discussion on applying the social identity complexity concept in the culturally proximal context such as the encounter of Western and Southern Slavic nations. Furthermore, this is a pioneer work on Czech mission after 1989, since there is little written on international mission from the Czech Republic. And while this, in the context of global mission, may seem a particular and regional phenomenon, its exploration may lead towards more research on identity in connection with mission from Central and Eastern Europe.

1.2 Introducing the region

1.2.1 Former Yugoslavia and former Czechoslovakia – geopolitical terms

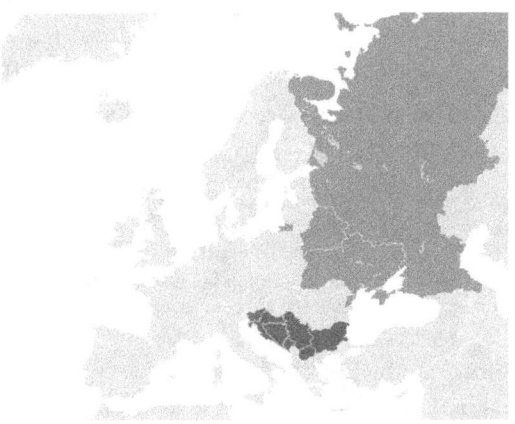

Figure 1: Western, Eastern, and Southern Slavs

Several geopolitical terms, as used in this research, need to be clarified. To start with, perhaps the most noticeable is former Yugoslavia or former Yugoslavs. The name "Yugoslavia" – the land of Southern Slavs (*jug* or *jye* means "south") builds upon the concept of "yugoslavism" which originated

---

16. This research, with its focus on missionaries' national identity and its negotiation in the cultural proximal context, extends beyond missiology by its interdisciplinary reach.

in the nineteenth century. It was not politically realized until the Kingdom of Yugoslavia came into being in 1929, having replaced the former Kingdom of Serbs, Croats and Slovenes. During the Communist regime of Tito,[17] the transnational Yugoslav identity was introduced[18] and a specific national category "Yugoslav" was created in the census of 1961.[19] Still, only a minority of the population identified with the Yugoslav nationality and "yugoslavism" has never been fully realized, remaining only as "yugonostalgia," an overly optimistic picture of the past.[20]

"Former Yugoslavia" refers chiefly to the legacy countries of the Socialist Federal Republic of Yugoslavia, which successively broke apart in 1991 (Slovenia, Croatia), in 1992 (Bosnia and Herzegovina, North Macedonia), in 2006 (Montenegro, Serbia), and in 2008 (Kosovo). Being aware of different cross-cultural challenges of former Yugoslav communities in this work, instead of listing all the nations or using alternative general or inexact terms, the term "former Yugoslavs"[21] is being used. Here it refers to Slavs[22] whose heritage is rooted in one of these countries. Specifically, these are: Bosniaks,[23] Croats, Macedonians, Montenegrins, Serbs, and Slovenes.

Another state named by a different composite word, "Czechoslovakia," on the other hand, consisted of only two nations, and hardly any reference to "former Czechoslovaks" can be found. Czechoslovakia was created in 1918

---

17. Josip Broz "Tito" (1892–1980) was the most influential Western Balkan statesman in the twentieth century. He was the head of the Yugoslav antifascist movement and the president of the Socialist Federal Republic of Yugoslavia.

18. Toró, "Compatibilities and Incompatibilities," 48.

19. Tomić, "From 'Yugoslavism,'" 277.

20. "Yugonostalgia" (*jugonostalgija*) is linked with disillusionment with nationalist politics of the legacy Yugoslav countries (Tomić, 287).

21. It has not been fully realized, yet the term "ex-Yugoslavs" or "former Yugoslavs" in a non-national sense has been widely used in the academy and it proves to be both economic and sufficiently exact.

22. Even though Albanians (of Kosovo, of Ulcinj region in Montenegro, of the Preševo region in Serbia, and elsewhere), are technically former Yugoslavs as well, together with minorities of Roma, Hungarians and several others, this research focuses on former Yugoslavs – Slavs.

23. The word "Bosniak" (*Bošnjak*) was coined under the Austro-Hungarian administration in the nineteenth century, originally aspiring to include all three ethnic groups in the occupied territory. It did not take root, yet the term was resurrected in the 1990s (Greenberg, *Language and Identity*, 140). The difference between "Bosniaks" ("*Bošnjaci*") and "Bosnians" ("*Bosanci*") remains a hot topic, since Bosnian Serbs and Croats also refer to themselves, or are labelled as such when they come to Serbia or Croatia, as Bosnians (Žeželj and Pratto, "What Identities," 176).

after World War One, with the goal of constituting a Slavic majority over the German and Hungarian component in the newly created state. Czechs accepted the common identity more than the Slovaks.[24] After 1989, the issue of the country's name was highly disputed in the so called "Hyphen war." Slovak deputies insisted on "Czecho-Slovak Republic" and a compromise, "Czech and Slovak Federal Republic" was accepted.[25] Czechs and Slovaks split in 1993 and the Czech Republic and the Slovak Republic (or Slovakia) were formed.

In the Czech milieu, there is a certain terminological ambivalence between the usage of "the Czech Republic," with the connection to the republican constitutional arrangement, and the shorter more recently officially recognized version "Czechia."[26] The Czech Republic and Czechia both have the goal to incorporate all the three historical regions: Bohemia (*Čechy*), Moravia (*Morava*) and Silesia (*Slezsko*). Czechs are rather divided on the issue of the country's name subjectively: they either use the accustomed longer version or they prefer Czechia, the popularity of which has grown in recent years, particularly in the public sphere, trade, and the academy.[27] In my writing I use them interchangeably, and when the research participants refer to their country, I follow their statements: it can be "the Czech Republic" (*"Česká republika"*), often is "Czechia" (*"Česko"*) and alternately a rather inaccurate labelling connected to the dominant historical land "Bohemia" (*"Čechy"*).[28]

In the former Yugoslavia region, similarly, there has been an ongoing discussion on names of particular countries. Due to the limited space for deeper introduction, only a few examples can be given: Macedonia, after a long phase of the official name "Former Yugoslav Republic of Macedonia," reached an agreement with Greece and, since February 2019, the country

---

24. Plecitá, *National Identity*, 13; Kubiš et al., "Czech Republic: Nation Formation," 146

25. Holý, *Little Czech*, 190.

26. "On 17 May 2016 the Permanent Mission of the Czech Republic to the United Nations informed the UN that the short name to be used for the country is Czechia." (United Nations, "United Nations Member States"). To be noted, it is not a new name for the country, rather an addition to an already existing one, a short version.

27. Compare with Čižmárová, "History and Popular Attitudes"; Krejčí, "Don't Be Afraid"; Pabian, "Czech Christianity"; Drbohlav et al., "Czech Republic on its Way."

28. Nevertheless, it is quite common in Europe that a country's name is derived from one of its regions (e.g. Austria (Lower and Upper Österreich)), Switzerland (the canton of Schwyz), Poland (Greater and Lesser Poland).

uses the new official name North Macedonia. Bosnia and Herzegovina is one country with two names in the title, these are geographical-historical parts of Bosnia (north) and Herzegovina (south), yet these are not strictly delineated. Instead, the country consists of two political entities: The Federation of Bosnia and Herzegovina and the Republic of Srpska.[29] Next, the name of the Republic of Kosovo is derived from the Serbian word *Kosovo polje* ("field of blackbirds"), and even though it is nowadays inhabited by a majority of Albanians, the Serbian word is used for the country's name, and specifically the ending -o in the English version.[30]

1.2.2 Two Communist regimes

The Communist regime in former Yugoslavia differed in many ways from the one in Czechoslovakia or in other countries in the Eastern European region. Yugoslavia was unique in the sense that it was not the Red Army, but local Communist freedom fighters (*partizani*) who liberated the country from the Nazis, and it was independent of the Soviet Union.[31] The regime was of a gentler nature than in the Soviet bloc, yet the initial purges in 1945 and in 1948, after Tito's split with Stalin, surpassed the persecution in some Soviet satellite countries, such as in Czechoslovakia in the 1950s. Since 1948 Yugoslavia pursued a unique self-managed socialism[32] and throughout the Cold War period was in the leading position of the "Non-Alignment Movement." Connected to that, Yugoslavs were allowed to travel to the West, unlike Czechoslovaks, who were restricted in travel and even for holidays in Yugoslavia needed special exit permission in their passport.[33]

---

29. The Republic of Srpska (*Република Српска*) is not to be confused with the Republic of Serbia; it is a Serbian dominated political entity within Bosnia and Herzegovina. Connected to this, a precise usage is to refer to people in proper Serbia as "Serbians," and to the ethnic group members as "Serbs." It is analogous for "Croatians" and "Croats."

30. The Albanian version is *Kosova* (Britannica, "Kosovo: Self-Declared"). Another example of when the English version uses a non-native language is *Montenegro*, which is the Italian "Black Mountain" version of the local *Crna Gora*.

31. Malesevic, *Identity as Ideology*, 170.

32. The Communist ideologists in Yugoslavia strove for a genuine expression of the political system more in tune with the original Marxist doctrine and "hence more just, free and equal to all its citizens as well as its constitutive units than its Soviet . . . counterparts" (Malesevic, 169).

33. Vlachová, "Significant Others," 6.

In Czechoslovakia, until 1948, the Communist Party's intention was to promote a specifically Czechoslovak form of Communism based on the local democratic tradition. When Czechoslovakia became more anchored in the Eastern bloc, under Stalin's influence, the mild Czechoslovak experience with Communism was replaced by political repression in the 1950s.[34] In the "Prague Spring" of the 1960s the country experienced a loosening of the strict regime, and it was stopped by the Warsaw Pact armies' invasion in 1968. The 1970s, on the other hand, witnessed hard-line Communist "normalisation."

The fall of Communism in both Yugoslavia and Czechoslovakia was connected to, and followed by, a break-up of the country in the early 1990s along ethnic lines. In Yugoslavia, the organisation[35] of republics and autonomous areas within the country after World War Two had its impact on national self-identification in the early 1990s.[36] Two important factors in this self-identification process proved to be religion[37] and language. Macedonian and Slovenian differ linguistically from the Serbo-Croat[38] language – which as

---

34. Blaive, "Czechs and Their Communism."

35. Macedonia and Montenegro were instituted as republics, while Vojvodina, the northern part of Serbia, and Kosovo as autonomous areas. The first violent clashes at the end of the 1980s happened in Kosovo.

36. In their historical narratives after 1991, each nation "symbolically reinvented itself and its past" (Tomić, "From 'Yugoslavism'", 279) and engaged elements of myth (Goodwin, *Fractured Land*, 24).

37. Religious identity of single former Yugoslav nations is addressed in the following chapter.

38. See Comrie, *World's Major Languages*, 330–346. Novi Sad Agreement in 1954 labelled this southern Slavic language *srpskohrvatski ili hrvatskosrpski* ("Serbo-Croatian or Croato-Serbian"). For more on the difference between the Serbian and Croatian variant, on the language history and on its dialects Compare Greenberg, *Language and Identity*, 20–31; 33; 47). When avoiding uneasy situations local speakers refer to the language often as *domaći jezik* (domestic language), "*naš jezik* or *naški* (our language)" (Tomić, "From 'Yugoslavism'", 287).

a consequence of the political break-up, split into four variants: Serbian,[39] Croatian,[40] and newly coined Montenegrin[41] and Bosnian.[42]

1.2.3 Two break-ups

Czechoslovakia split peacefully, yet the break-up of Yugoslavia was accompanied by the most violent conflict in Europe since World War Two.

Reasons for the violent disintegration of Yugoslavia have been heavily disputed. The popular view of why "the powder keg of Europe" exploded again attempts to find its causes in the proverbial age-long ethnic hatred, connected with the renaissance of religion which strengthened the awakened national movement, after having been suppressed on behalf of "brotherhood and unity"[43] under the regime of Tito. This view has been heavily critiqued, predominantly by authors from the Balkans, while different factors of the break-up have been added to the discussion. The historian Maria Todorova brings attention to how the break-up of Yugoslavia tends to keep being exhibited as a Balkan crisis, where ancient Balkan enmities, ghosts and cultural patterns come to the surface.[44] The mixture of rationality and emotions, myths,

---

39. Serbian, as the "heir" of the Serbo-Croatian language, remained the most permissive of the four: It uses two variants, Eastern ekavian and Western ijekavian, and it actively uses two alphabets: Cyrillic and Latin (Symon, "Studies of Contemporary Student Slang," 45–47).

40. Croatian linguists in particular were active in creating new vocabulary replacing foreign terms and they worked hard to distinguish their language from its Serbian counterpart as much as possible, which can be documented by Brodnjak's, "The Dictionary of the Difference between Serbian and Croatian Language," published in Zagreb (Brodnjak, *Dictionary of the Difference*).

41. The linguist Greenberg comments on the language situation in Montenegro: "The Serbs and some Montenegrins categorically deny the existence of a separate Montenegrin language" (Greenberg, *Language and Identity*, 15).

42. The recognition of Bosnian language by Serbs and Croats is an unfinished process. "Had Bosniacs called their language by the 'ethnic name' (Bosniac language), rather than the 'regional term' (Bosnian language), they would have weakened their link to Bosnia, their geographical and spiritual homeland. However, it ignores Bosnia-Herzegovina's Serb and Croat communities, who might share with the Bosniacs a spiritual affinity for the region of Bosnia . . . Simultaneously, the Bosniacs could accept neither Croatian nor Serbian since such an acceptance would have signalled the Bosniac assimilation into either the Croatian or Serbian ethnic spheres" (Greenberg, *Language and Identity*, 15).

43. This phrase was a hallmark of the Yugoslav regime. This brotherhood was not without inequalities, for "it was built out of the formal distinction between peoples (*narodi*), or titular nations of each republic, and nationalities (*narodnosti*), or groups, which belonged to a non-titular Yugoslav nation" (Tomić, "From 'Yugoslavism,'" 276).

44. Todorova, *Imagining the Balkans*, 186.

ethnic cleansing,⁴⁵ all of these are, according to her, not unique to the Balkan context only.⁴⁶

According to political scientist Dejan Jović, what might have led to the disintegration of Yugoslavia was the identity crisis of the specific Yugoslav version of Communism. It constructed itself in opposition to two "others": the representative democracy of Yugoslavism between the world wars on one side, and Soviet-style communism on the other.⁴⁷ In the second half of the 1980s⁴⁸ the Soviet "other" ceased to exist and liberalism entered Yugoslav society, coming hand-in-hand with nationalism. The sociologist Siniša Malešević targeted different phases⁴⁹ of Yugoslavia's decentralisation in order to explain what led to the break-up and he highlighted the key moment when, after Tito's death in 1980, the federal party delegated power more to republic parties' leaderships.⁵⁰ The historian Đorđe Tomić comes to a similar conclusion when he states that it was the conservative communist elite who used nationalism to demobilize their reformist political opponents.⁵¹ Other significant factors were of economic and ethnoreligious nature. The more developed republics of Slovenia and Croatia considered themselves held back by the obligation to contribute to the federal budget to support economically weaker fellow-republics. And the re-emergence of nationalism was no surprise after Tito's suppression of old wounds from the Second World War. Turkish scholar Peri Pamir calls it the "deep freeze effect," pointing out that these "were merely kept frozen only to resurface when authoritarian structures which imposed

---

45. The vocabulary of "ethnic cleansing" and "genocide" came to wide usage in the 1990's proceeding from the ethnic conflicts, especially in Bosnia and Herzegovina and in Rwanda, and can be defined as "the creation of ethnically homogenous areas through the mass expulsion of other ethnic populations" (Giddens, *Sociology*, 686).

46. Todorova, *Imagining the Balkans,* 186. Todorova quite straightforwardly complains about the Western double lens approach and briefly compares Nagasaki and Sarajevo, Vietnam and Bosnia. Compare Hatzopoulos *Balkans beyond Nationalism*, 176, who challenges nationalism as the ordering principle of Balkan history.

47. Jović, "Communist Yugoslavia and Its 'Others,'" n.p.

48. The Soviet Union ceased to exist in 1991, yet the Soviet other had already ceased to exist for the Yugoslavs in the second half of the 1980s under Gorbachev's reforms.

49. He outlines these phases as between the years 1948–1974, 1974–1987 and 1987–1991 and notes that "decentralisation was used as an ad hoc mechanism for decreasing the pressure from 'below'" (Malesevic, *Identity as Ideology*, 183).

50. Malesevic, 183.

51. Tomić, "From 'Yugoslavism,'" 279.

an artificial homogeneity disintegrated."⁵² Generations changed, yet ethnic passions never disappeared. Ernest Gellner depicts the operation of the "three generations law" when "the grandson tries to remember what the son tried to forget."⁵³

While the fall of Communism and happenings in the early 1990s meant horrific war for most regions of former Yugoslavia, Czechs and Slovaks in 1989 after the "Velvet Revolution" on 1st January, 1993 experienced a "Velvet Divorce." The era of freedom, economic improvement, unrestricted travelling – including possibilities for international mission work – began. The early 1990s were characterized by the return to the European West and the internationalism of civic society.⁵⁴ Czech citizens voted in a referendum and the country joined the EU in 2004. Gradually, the complete openness westwards was replaced by a certain dose of caution, if not opposition, and a split arose between Euro-optimists and Euro-sceptics. This conflict is best depicted by the debate of the two Václavs, the last Czechoslovak (and the first Czech) president Václav Havel and his successor Václav Klaus, who held the presidential office between 2003 and 2013.⁵⁵

Czechs and Slovaks split in peace and have kept an above average relationship and cultural ties.⁵⁶ Slovaks are Czechs' closest Slavic others, and the languages are similar: their speakers understand each other, can read books, listen to music and watch films or TV shows in the neighbour's language. "Slovaks often study or work in the Czech Republic, Slovak students are still allowed to take exams in their native language, and it is not rare to

---

52. Pamir, "Nationalism, Ethnicity and Democracy," n.p.

53. Gellner, *Thought and Change*, 163. Describing the behaviour of immigrants into America, he claims it operates everywhere. Likewise, it can be applied for the Yugoslav case of remembering the atrocities of the war forty years ago – when the ethnic passions were swept "under the carpet," leaving conflicts unresolved.

54. Krejčí, *Czechness and Europeannes*, 19; Holý, *Little Czech*, 151.

55. The cosmopolitan Havel, who emphasized civic society, responsibility, and involvement, was definitely a Euro-optimist (Havel et al., *Briefly Please*, 217), while Klaus, himself an economist, was very pragmatically focused on national interests and approached the EU cautiously (See Auer, "After 1989," 411).

56. Chalániová, "Cultural Diplomacy and Stereotypes," 27. The newly elected presidents of Slovakia and the Czech Republic pay their first international visits to Prague or Bratislava. The two countries are political and commercial partners. There are mutual artistic productions, research projects, visits or friends and family, and associations for both Czechs and Slovaks abroad (Chalániová, 4).

overhear a two-language conversation."[57] The generally warm relationship is not without stereotypes[58] and a certain dose of prejudice. Nevertheless, Slovaks remain Czechs' most appreciated and accepted significant other.[59] The split of Czechoslovakia on 1st January, 1993, happened out of political will, the majority of inhabitants wished to stay together in the common state. The "self-evident" nature of the independence,[60] when the Czech Republic "just happened," is commemorated by the "celebration" of a national holiday. The anniversary falls on 1st January, the day after the New Year celebration, and practically no Czech celebrates it as national holiday. Instead, 28th October, the day of the birth of Czechoslovakia, is widely celebrated as the Independence Day.[61]

1.2.4 Negotiating spatiality within Europe

1.2.4.1 Western, Central or Eastern Europe?

Historically, the Czech territory was evangelized both from the East by Cyril and Methodius, and from the West by Latin monks.[62] The twentieth century witnessed both Western (German Nazis) and Eastern occupations (USSR-led Warsaw Pact armies). The division after World War Two was situational and conditioned politically,[63] and the forty years of Communism, when the country's orientation was towards the East, is considered by Czechs as a rare

---

57. Chalániová, 4.
58. "Stereotypes" can be defined as "popularly shared (mis-)conceptions, common beliefs and general characteristics of groups" (Chalániová, 1) or "fixed and inflexible characterizations of a social group" (Giddens, *Sociology*, 668).
59. Burjanek, "Xenophobia among the Czech Population," 57.
60. Vlachová and Řeháková, "Identity of Non-Self-Evident Nation," 258.
61. Interestingly, the events on 28th October, 2018 that marked the 100-year anniversary of the independent Czechoslovak Republic were in the Czech Republic commemorated by a whole spectrum of celebrations and were advertised as "The Past Century Together – national celebrations of 100 years of the Republic" (See Radosta, *Czech and Slovak Century*) without explicitly claiming the "Czechness" of the event as it focused on the Czecho-Slovak common history.
62. Neill, *History of Christian Missions*, 72.
63. Osamu Leda from Slavic-Eurasian Research Centre of Hokkaido University concludes that the division of Europe between East and West was artificial: "The East-West division of Europe was constructed by the imperialist view of politics in the Cold War. Geographically or historically, we have no categorical reasons to separate" (Ieda, "Regional Identities," 65).

time in history. The historian Kenney stresses that due to the experience of the past, especially with the Soviets, "Eastern" is considered backward by Czechs.[64]

The term "Europe" in its usage appears to function almost as a synonym with the European West and alternatively with the European Union. The Polish scholar Jerzy Kłoczowski has noted that the history of Europe is characterized by the fact that "it has sometimes been treated as the true 'European Europe' in opposition to the European East."[65] In connection with this, the view of the Czech Republic as part of Eastern Europe is nearly non-existent in Czech scholarship.[66] "Eastern Europe" has a political connotation. West-East geopolitical spatiality still points to the legacy of the Cold War period and therefore has its limitations.[67] Along with that, the term "Post-Communist" Europe does not seem fitting either, since a historical period of time is to be labelled as "post" only temporarily.[68]

Instead, two prevailing views are present: the Czech Republic as part of the West and the Czech Republic as part of Central Europe – the self-perception of Czechs is often linked to its supposedly balanced central location between the cultural spheres of East and West.[69] The term "Mitteleuropa"[70] was reintroduced by Czechoslovak, Polish and Hungarian intellectuals as a tool of "return to Europe," namely escaping Eastern Europe.[71] According to the political scientist Ondřej Slačálek, the Czech Republic is clearly Western. In his fierce argumentation he says that it is not a "bridge" between East and West. It represents a West that was merely "kidnapped."[72] In other words,

---

64. Kenney, *Burdens of Freedom*, 1.

65. Kłoczowski, *East-Central Europe's Position*, 13. My translation; original: "*On la traitait parfois comme une vraie "Europe européenne" opposée à "l'Est" européen.*"

66. The anthropologist Ladislav Holý concludes that Czechs detest "being classified as Eastern Europeans and are quick to point out that Prague is west of Vienna" (Holý, *Little Czech*, 151).

67. Todorova, *Balkan Identities*, 15.

68. Zrinščak, "Anonymous Believers," 69.

69. Vlachová and Řeháková, "Identity of Non-Self-Evident Nation," 258.

70. This term was first introduced by the German politician Friedrich Naumann (1860–1919) in 1915 as the endeavour for an economic federation in the German speaking lands and was later adopted by Hitler. Owing to its ideological poisoning and to the division of Europe by the Iron Curtain into the West and the East, the term was dormant for decades (Teponen, "Czech Destiny," 22–23).

71. Holý, *Little Czech*, 151; Teponen, "Czech Destiny," 23.

72. Slačálek, "Postcolonial Hypothesis Notes," 41.

the Czech Republic can be considered in a certain way "no more Eastern, but not yet Western."[73] The reflection of a similar in-between position can be observed with scholars from other countries in the region, for example by the Polish writer Czesław Miłosz, who in his autobiography, "Native Realm: A Search for Self-Definition," delineates the complexity of the relationship of Poles towards East and West.[74]

The positionality of the Czech Republic, in-between North and South, is related to the East-West discussion. Even though Czechoslovakia was not directly involved in colonial history, a form of Czech colonialism could be the "'development' of the Balkans in the time of Austro-Hungary . . . and first of all the administration of Sub-Carpathian Ruthenia between 1919 and 1939."[75] Albeit not being a Western country – a former colonizer – the present-day Czech Republic by its import and export politics shares an indirect responsibility for unequal trade conditions. By admitting that and by meeting the criterion of belonging to donors of international development aid, and not to receivers, it confirms its belonging to the global North.[76]

I do not consider it justified to use any of the terms: "Western," "Eastern," "Central," nor "Post-Communist." Instead, a compromise term is being used in this work, "Central and Eastern Europe." It is in the usage of the EU documents[77] which deal with these countries and it also is used in missiological literature focusing on this area as a whole.[78]

---

73. Ieda, "Regional Identities," 62.

74. The Polish author from today's Lithuania meditates on his homeland and its areal specifics, depicting the mutual hatred of Poles and Russians and the uneasy interrelation of contempt for Germans (Miłosz, *Native Realm*, 118–121). He considers himself as someone who "cannot be fitted into stereotypes like the German *Ordnung* or the Russian *âme slave*" (Miłosz, 7).

75. Horký-Hlucháň and Profant, "Reflection of the Global North," 19. My translation; original: "'*Rozvoj' Balkánu v době Rakousko-Uherska . . . a zejména správu českými a slovenskými guvernéry Podkarpatské Rusi mezi lety 1919 a 1939.*" Compare Holubec, *We Haven't Made It Yet*, 249.

76. Horký-Hlucháň and Profant, 17–18, 27.

77. Publications Office of the European Union, "EU Vocabularies."

78. Klingsmith, *Missions Beyond the Wall*, Kool, "Missiologist's Look."

1.2.4.2 The Balkans or Southeastern Europe?

The historical-geographical term "the Balkans"[79] might evoke a similar notion for the people in this part of Europe as the term "Eastern Europe" for Czechs, as it is at times connected with backwardness. The history of the usage of the term "the Balkans" and its etymology[80] point towards diversified approaches, the main debate being between those who embrace the term and those who disassociate themselves from it, preferring the term "Southeastern Europe."

The former stance is represented by the classic work of the Bulgarian historian Maria Todorova, "Imagining the Balkans."[81] Todorova considers that labelling the Balkans "Southeastern Europe" is an initiative "from above," namely from Western Europe, to create a neutral name fitting the region, and she argues that its usage is not appropriate for the reason that, similarly to *Mitteleuropa*, the term *Südosteuropa* witnessed a discrediting when becoming "an important concept in the geopolitical view of the Nazis."[82] Others, such as Nada Švob-Đokić from the Zagreb Institute for International Relations, who acknowledges that the term was indeed used first by German historians in the nineteenth century[83] and in the 1990s was reintroduced "through the direct political, diplomatic and military involvement of European countries and the USA"[84] opt for this term. "Southeastern Europe" (SEE) is a preferred term particularly in the countries of Slovenia[85] and Croatia[86] with strong links to

---

79. "Balkan" is used in English as an adjective. In most Slavic languages, it is the singular name referring to the peninsula and its political formations, opposed to the English plural form "the Balkans" (Todorova, *Imagining the Balkans*, 31).

80. The word *"Balkan"* comes from Turkish, and it means a mountain range, formerly Haemus in Greek and presently Stara Planina in Bulgaria (Todorova, 26). It was first used to refer to the peninsula by the German geographer August Zeune who "was convinced that the mountain of Balkan was spread all over the region" (Švob-Đokić, "Balkans Versus Southeastern Europe," 35).

81. Todorova, *Imagining the Balkans*. The book, originally published in 1997, develops the concept of Balkanism, inspired by and not dissimilar from Edward Said's Orientalism.

82. Todorova, 28.

83. The term *Südosteuropa* was coined at the Berlin Congress in 1878 by the German geographer Theobald Fischer (Švob-Đokić, "Balkans Versus Southeastern Europe," 36).

84. Švob-Đokić, 40. This term was supposed to "make people forget the ethnic, national and religious wars on distribution and deployment of economic means in the 1990's" (Komlosy and Hofbauer, "Identity Construction," 12).

85. Slovenia has been an EU member since 2004.

86. Croatia has been an EU member since 2013. Croatia especially finds itself in the geo-historical crossroads of the regions of Central Europe, Mediterranean, and former Ottoman Turk dominated lands (Skoko, *Croatia and Its Neighbours*, 188).

the West and the EU institutions and the desire to delineate from the Balkan "other" in order to modernize what is considered a periphery of Europe. The SEE proponents critique "the Balkans" for its meaning as a "unified entity"[87] in their desire to include the region's differences in a more neutral way and not a clearly defined whole. Todorova, as well, agrees that "there has never been a common Balkan identity,"[88] yet she does not see it as an obstacle for the terminological usage of "the Balkans." It can be anticipated, regarding the internal fragmentation of the region, that the disunity in terminology will prevail.

In my work I do not avoid the term "the Balkans," yet being aware of its ambiguity and with regards to the scope of this research, I prefer the usage of a more precise term "former Yugoslav countries." Along with it, as a reminder, I use "former Yugoslavs," "Central and Eastern Europe" and both "the Czech Republic" and "Czechia." In sum, Czechs and former Yugoslavs, in spite of their differences, find similar traits in self-identification in spatiality – in (a.) naming their countries and in (b.) negotiation of establishing themselves geopolitically within Europe, as laid out in the preceding two passages. The above are perhaps the most widely used geopolitical terms throughout the thesis, and they require this initial clarification.[89]

1.3 Thesis structure

The structure of the thesis is as follows. Chapter 2 reviews the literature in order to lay out theoretical framework for the research. Sections 2.2, 2.3, and 2.4 focus on three theoretical realms connected to Czech missionaries' identity negotiation in the culturally proximal former Yugoslav context: identity, culture, and mission. Sections 2.4.1 and 2.4.2 continue the introduction in chapter 1 of the two contexts with focus on religious identity and its implications for Protestant mission work. Chapter 3 "Methodology" describes technical aspects on how the research was carried out. Section (3.1) illuminates the overall research framework used in this work – a multiple case study. In

---

87. Švob-Đokić, "Balkans Versus Southeastern Europe," 38; see also: Hatzopoulos, *Balkans beyond Nationalism*, 156.

88. Todorova, *Balkan Identities*, 9.

89. Comprehension and utilization of other terms, especially those linked to theoretical concepts, is presented in chapter (2.).

3.2, scope and primary sources are thoroughly defined, which is necessary for understanding the limitations of the research. In brief, the focus is on (a.) Czech, (b.) long-term (resident or periodically returning), (c.) Protestant (d.) missionaries who have worked with (e.) Slavs in former Yugoslav countries (f.) since 1989. In section 3.3 on ethics, the essential measures of methodological rigour are introduced, personal bias and preconceptions are taken into consideration, together with assessing possible risks and benefits this research might bring to its participants. In 3.4, two kinds of methods are expounded – methods of data gathering and methods of data analysis. A major source of data are semi-structured interviews, and they are supported by personal diaries. These are subsequently approached by the means of thematic analysis. The final section 3.5 explains specifically how the primary sources were approached and what the individual steps in acquiring the data and generating the evidence were.

Chapters 4, 5, 6, 7 and 8, form the main part of the thesis as they comprise the analysis. These chapters are designed in alignment with the overall aim of the central research question and the three complementary research questions: "To what extent can the Slavic Czechs working with their fellow Slavs in former Yugoslav countries be considered cross-cultural?" – chapter 4; "How and in what circumstances does the Czech identity of Czech missionaries become salient or suppressed? – chapters 5 and 6; "How does the missionaries' "Czechness" interact with their other identity facets?" – chapters 7 and 8.

Chapter 4, relates to the first sub-question on the cultural proximity issue and introduces the topic of missionaries' Czech identity negotiation in the former Yugoslav context. Another two chapters are joined to the second sub-question – chapter 5 looks at circumstances of Czech identity salience and suppression and chapter 6 focuses specifically on particular situations related to mission work, and they both include missiological outcomes. The last two analysis chapters focus on multiple identity facets of Czech missionaries 7 and their interrelation with their Czech identity 8. Even though each chapter contains its findings and certain conclusions, there is a clearly specified gradation in the logic behind the way the chapters are organized. Chapter 4 is linked to the following two chapters, since one has to first entertain basic aspects of the two cultural contexts without aspiring for a broader comparative cross-cultural study, in order to be able to recognize what the situations could be for the Czech identity salience or suppression. Similarly, chapters 5 and 6, which are already based in social identity theory and identity theory, create a bridge to chapters 7 and 8 which focus on specifics of the social identity complexity concept. And lastly, with the help of the introduced individual identity facets of Czech missionaries in chapter 7, chapter 8 arrives at four interrelations of multiple ingroup representations[90] and the main argument of the thesis, which is summed up in the conclusion, chapter 9.

---

90. Roccas and Brewer, "Social Identity Complexity."

CHAPTER 2

Theoretical Framework for the Study of How Czech Missionaries Negotiate Their Identity in the Former Yugoslav Countries

2.1 Introduction

The main research question, "How is the identity of contemporary Czech missionaries negotiated in their interaction with Slavs in former Yugoslav countries?", entails a multi-dimensional literature review which in this chapter addresses three theoretical realms: identity (in 2.2), culture (in 2.3) and mission (in 2.4). In the missiological perspective, these three are interconnected, as aptly expressed by the theologian Timothy Tennent:

> The gospel, like the Incarnation itself, must become embodied within culture. An acultural gospel cannot be inserted into a culture from some neutral vantage point. Those who communicate the gospel do so from within their own identity, and those who receive it do so from within their own identity.[1]

Indeed, to comprehend one's mission action, a person's identity needs to be explored, and aspects of culture of origin investigated. Added to that,

---

1. Tennent, *Invitation to World Missions*, 186.

on the other hand, one's identity is being moulded by the mission experience and by exposure to other cultures. Through the reading on my research topic, I have been continuously redirected to one of three terms: "identity," "culture" and "mission." These, therefore, in the literature review constitute theoretical pillars for the research on Czech missionaries' identity negotiation in the cultural proximal context of former Yugoslav countries. Still, each of the three[2] terms can be consulted only to the necessary extent caused by the limitation and focus of this study, largely based in missiology.

2.2 Identity

2.2.1 Definition

A fitting definition would seem like a proper commencement of the discussion on identity. Yet, identity is hard to approach as something definite. Some scholars seem to prefer to move from what identity is to how it is formed.

> "Self" is a determinant as much as a product of interaction. That most private of human possessions is also the one most dependent on human sociality . . . It is in interaction with others that the awareness of "having a self" or indeed of "being a self" dawns upon us and the life-long labour of building and rebuilding identities is conducted.[3]

Sociologists Bauman and Reid maintain it is in society where one's identity is constructed and continuously reconstructed, which is an object of inquiry of social psychology. Identity in this work is treated along this line as negotiating self in dependence on outer circumstances, the way it is outlined by social identity theorists. Its examination here focuses less on the individual[4]

---

2. The three terms in their variants appear multiple times in the interviews: culture 391 times as the seventh most repeated word; mission 170 times, missionary 267 times; and identity or identities 167 times. The utilisation of such quantitative elements by NVivo is, nevertheless, limited in this research since (a.) the transcripts were translated to English and (b.) the counting incorporates the transcribed interviewer's questions along the way. Still, it is notable and suggests confirming the focal point in these three terms – identity, culture, mission.

3. Bauman and Raud, *Practices of Selfhood*, 55.

4. This is certain delineation in focus and scope from the research on personal identity which "is concerned with behaviour that is typical of a person and distinguishes that person from others" (Berry et al., *Cross-Cultural Psychology*, 86).

aspect and more on the social. To help introduce it, in the following overview certain features of identity theory[5] and social identity theory[6] are discussed.

Identity theory as a sociological framework draws from the symbolic interactionism of G. H. Mead and his work, "Mind, Self and Society" (1934), on the reciprocal relationships between self and society. In identity theory, one's self is an occupant of a role and the role, associated with its performance, is the basis of identity.[7] The identity is behavioural and is based on what one does as the role implementer and how one in that role interacts with others.

While identity theory focuses on role-based identities, social identity theory's focus is on who is as a group member – on group category-based identities.[8] Henri Tajfel, the founder of social identity theory, introduced it to help explain intergroup behaviour, to reduce intergroup bias, and to contribute to conflict resolution. He claimed about social identity: "It is created out of social realities, it changes with them, it always includes views about 'others.'"[9] The identity in social identity theory is based on belonging to a group and on outgroup comparison. Outlined initially by Tajfel,[10] followed by his colleague John Turner who developed self-categorization theory,[11] it evolved into the social identity theory of intergroup behaviour[12] where "groups, as collections of people sharing the same social identity, compete with one another for evaluatively positive distinctiveness."[13]

---

5. Identity theory is represented by Stryker, Burke and Stets.
6. Social identity theory is represented by Tajfel, Turner, Hogg and Abrams.
7. Burke and Stets, *Identity Theory*, 225.
8. Stryker and Burke, "Past, Present, and Future," 289.
9. Tajfel, *Human Groups*, 226.
10. His original publication presenting human identity in social behaviour and intergroup conflict was called "Human Groups and Social Categories: Studies in Social Psychology" (Tajfel, *Human Groups*).
11. The self-categorization theory investigates the determinants when people start perceiving themselves as a group (i.e. "how individuals are able to act as a group at all") (Turner, *Rediscovering the Social Group*, 42). One aspect of enthusiasm for groups within this theory is disputable: Turner asserts that membership of a group frees human beings from restrictions and "allows them to be more than just individual persons" (Turner, 67). To object to this, behaviour of groups in a crowd can be perceived as regression to more irrational forms of behaviour (as experienced in World War Two, and again in atrocities of the 1990s in Yugoslavia and in Rwanda).
12. Tajfel and Turner, "Social Identity Theory."
13. Hogg et al., "Social Identity Perspective," 248.

Identity theory and social identity theory and their interrelation continue to be debated in scholarship, which entails (a.) variations[14] within both theories, (b.) critique[15] of a group of scholars of the other theory, and interestingly, also (c.) a gravitation towards the strengthening of the two theories' bonds.[16] Despite social identity theory and IT differing in their conceptualization of groups,[17] they both address the issue of multiple identities and identity salience, which is of significance for the research on Czech identity of the missionaries and is outlined in the following sub-section.

2.2.2 Multiple identity facets and identity salience

The term "identity" carries with itself both stability and limitation. Similarly, the term "identity construction" might mislead in the sense that identity can be constructed once for all. Instead, it appears to change together with social realities out of which it is created[18] as it is being constantly "negotiated."[19] The social anthropologist Richard Jenkins noted: "One's social identity – indeed one's social identities . . . – is never a final or settled matter."[20] In his work, he uses the plural to stress his conclusion there is no single final identity.

---

14. It is, in the case of social identity theory, the social identity complexity concept which will be introduced in the following section. Stets and Burke (Stets and Burke, "Sociological Approach to Self," 133–135) offer a good outline for identity theory variations, compare with their more recent book, "Identity Theory" (Burke and Stets, *Identity Theory*).

15. Social identity theory was critiqued by identity theory proponents for its presumably strong focus on a group's homogeneity (Stets and Burke, "Identity Theory and Social Identity Theory," 236) and neglect of intergroup roles relationships (Stets and Burke, "Sociological Approach to Self," 133). Others have suggested an application of social identity theory not exclusively on macrosocial intergroup relations but use its value for small interactive groups (Hogg et al., "Social Identity Perspective," 268).

16. See Stryker and Burke, "Past, Present, and Future," 289. Those calling for a merger of identity theory and social identity theory argue that the differences are a matter of emphasis and that processes of self-categorization into groups (social identity theory) and identification into roles (identity theory) are analogous (Stets and Burke, "Sociological Approach to Self," 145). This is met with disapproval by the social identity theory theorists whose stance is that while identity theory is useful in its domain with mostly individualistic emphasis on interpersonal social interactive contexts, social identity theory is useful with its emphasis on intergroup relations (Hogg, Terry and White, "Tale of Two Theories," 267).

17. In a social identity theory, a group is a collective of similar persons all of whom identify with each other and see themselves in contrast to outgroups, in contrast to the identity theory view of a group as a set of interrelated individuals (Stets and Burke, "Identity Theory and Social Identity Theory," 227–228).

18. Tajfel, *Human Groups*, 226.

19. Holmberg, "Understanding Christian Identity," 29.

20. Jenkins, *Social Identity*, 4.

Turner agrees with the plural as he describes social identity as "the sum total of the social identifications used by a person to define him- or herself."[21] The mission anthropologist Hiebert also acknowledged these, according to him, "multiple statuses" which are associated with a particular social context.[22] Social scientists Bodenhausen and Kang, who in their article, in their focus on multiracialism, examined both challenges and opportunities for perceiving and experiencing multiple identities.[23] They emphasized that identity ambiguity is a current issue in modern society and noted that "demographic trends defy the preference for simple structure."[24]

Evidently, one's social identity is complex, and individuals are members of various groups to which they belong at the same time[25] – starting with the prominent identities of gender, family, class, occupation, religion and ethnicity.[26] Sometimes these are differentiated between ascribed (assigned), e.g. ethnicity and gender; and achieved (chosen), e.g. sport clubs.[27] Even though the terms slightly differ, in this work, "identity facets" and "ingroup memberships" of Czech missionaries are used interchangeably.[28] Furthermore, "identity facets" is preferred to "identities," due to the possible connotation of an unstable and internally split personality that "identities" could evoke.

"Identity salience" is used in alignment with its general understanding by social identity theorists as the activation of an identity in a situation.[29] Salience of individual identity facets is realized in various settings and situations[30] and

---

21. Turner, "Towards Cognitive Redefinition," 18.
22. Hiebert, *Anthropological Insights for Missionaries*, 257. He goes on to explain: "Most individuals occupy a number of different statuses at any one time in life. A person may be a teacher, a Presbyterian, a Democrat, a wife, and a mother at the same time. Each of these statuses is associated with a particular social context." (Hiebert, 257) The wording "most individuals" can be objected to, since all individuals supposedly possess such multiple statuses.
23. Bodenhausen and Kang, "Multiple Identities," 215.
24. Bodenhausen and Kang, 559.
25. Roccas et al., "Toward a Unifying Model," 294; Smith, *National Identity*, 4.
26. Esler, "Outline of Social Identity Theory," 24.
27. Knifsend and Juvonen, "Role of Social Identity Complexity," 623.
28. Along the common practice in social identity theory, where scholars abundantly use "identity" when talking about societal ingroups and outgroups (Roccas and Brewer, "Social Identity Complexity"), I perceive that group membership provides a person with social identity.
29. Stets and Burke, "Identity Theory and Social Identity Theory," 229.
30. Stryker and Burke, "Past, Present, and Future," 286.

while in identity theory is the behavioural[31] notion of identity salience, in social identity theory these are the moments when a person's belonging to one group becomes salient over belonging to the other. Hogg and his colleagues point out that the current debate is whether the multiple identities can be simultaneously salient or whether they are "hydraulically related to one another so that the more one identity prevails, the less others do."[32] On the other side of an imaginary identity negotiation spectrum can stand "identity suppression" – as another significant term for negotiation of identity facets used in this work. This, in contrast, is not a widely used term.[33] If identity salience was defined as the likelihood the identity facet is activated in a given situation,[34] identity suppression could analogically be understood as the likelihood the identity facet is deactivated in a given situation. "Suppression" is a bit problematic and might evoke negative connotations, yet in this work it is used as a rather technical and aggregate term referring to situational moments of intentional (and unintentional) deactivating, silencing, turning down, overshadowing, and placing into the background of one of the individual identity facets or identities.

Turner admits that the functioning of these multiple social identities is not yet fully understood.[35] Social psychologists Sonia Roccas and Marilynn Brewer pursued the social identity theory findings and in 2002 introduced the new theoretical concept of social identity complexity.

2.2.3 Social identity complexity

The concept of social identity complexity addresses situational identity salience and "refers to the nature of the subjective representation of the multiple ingroup identities."[36] The starting point is that individuals are members of multiple groups and hold multiple ingroup identities which interrelate. These interrelationships are subjectively represented from least to more

---

31. People acting in multiple roles, (e.g. a "person may work on the weekend while another may spend time with the children, although both may have a 'parent' role identity") (Hogg, Terry and White, "Tale of Two Theories," 258).
32. Hogg et al., "Social Identity Perspective," 268.
33. See, for example: Marschburn and Knowles, "White Out of Mind."
34. Stryker and Burke, "Past, Present, and Future," 292.
35. Turner, "Towards Cognitive Redefinition," 21.
36. Roccas and Brewer, "Social Identity Complexity," 88–89.

complex and categorized by the authors into the following four multiple ingroup representations, as shown in the table below: intersection, dominance, compartmentalization and merger.[37]

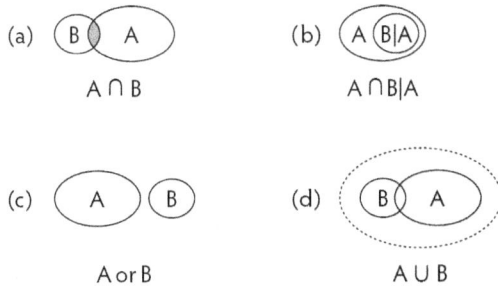

Figure 2: Multiple ingroup representations[38]

(a) Intersection is a unique identity as an outcome of larger categories from which it is derived and it is distinct from them. (b) Dominance means that other potential identifications are subordinated to one primary group identity. (c) Compartmentalization is the identity representation when context is important – social identities are activated in a specific situation and realized in the process of differentiation and isolation. (d) Merger, as the most inclusive form of social identity, is the sum of all combined ingroup identifications.

On a continuum from low to high complexity the authors situate intersection and dominance as relatively low, while compartmentalization and merger appear in general as high social identity complexity.[39] Roccas and Brewer conclude that higher social complexity, when more individuals are perceived as ingroup members, is to be embraced as it can help reduce intergroup prejudice.[40]

The four interrelations are part of the matter the proponents of the social identity complexity construct discuss. The general idea of social identity complexity is "subjective representation of the overlap between an individual's multiple identity groups; higher social identity complexity (less overlap) is

---

37. Roccas and Brewer, 90–91.
38. Roccas and Brewer, 90.
39. Roccas and Brewer, 93.
40. Roccas and Brewer, 104.

associated with intergroup advantages."[41] More particularly, it engages two distinct complexity types in overlap: shared ingroup characteristics and shared memberships across ingroups. The former aspect (overlap of group characteristics) takes into consideration the perceived similarity of prototypical values, norms, forms of behaviour and other characteristics, the later aspect (overlap of group membership) is the perceived extent of shared memberships across ingroups.[42] Further, the authors outline the antecedents of a person's complex social identity, which according to them[43] are experiential factors,[44] situational factors,[45] personal attributes[46] and conclude the article with the study of ingroup threat and outgroup tolerance by a survey among students in the USA (n=122) and Israel (n=99), which results in their thesis that "awareness of ingroup diversity provides an effective formula for reducing intergroup prejudice."[47]

Roccas, Brewer and their colleagues continued[48] with their research of social identity complexity and other scholars followed up with the investigation of multiple identity interrelations as well.

Marilynn Brewer summed up the development of the theoretical concept since 2002 and in "Social identity complexity and acceptance of diversity" (2010) clearly set the primary goal of the construct – to provide an effective tool for policy makers in multicultural societies. She noticed two extremes in pluralistic societies: assimilationist ideology with one majority dominant

---

41. Bodenhausen and Kang, "Multiple Identities", 559.

42. Roccas and Brewer, "Social Identity Complexity," 94.

43. Roccas and Brewer, 95–99.

44. These societal experiences are, according to Roccas and Brewer, living in multicultural or in stratified society (Roccas and Brewer, 96–97).

45. Four such situations are outlined by the social identity complexity proponents: When in minority and appearing as distinct, when doing multiple tasks concurrently and requiring attention capacities, when being under stress, when facing ingroup threat (Roccas and Brewer, 98–99).

46. Roccas and Brewer present two types of attributes: "Persons who are certainty-oriented use ingroup-outgroup distinctions to maintain clarity and avoid uncertainty, whereas uncertainty-oriented people are more tolerant of unclear ingroup boundaries." (Roccas and Brewer, 98)

47. Roccas and Brewer, 104.

48. The works, "Social Identity Complexity and Outgroup Tolerance" (Brewer and Pierce), "Toward a Unifying Model of Identification with Groups: Integrating Theoretical Perspectives" (Roccas et al., "Toward a Unifying Model"), and "Social Identity Complexity: Its Correlates and Antecedents" (Miller, Brewer and Arbuckle), engaged with even more primary sources and added to the discussion.

group and multicultural ideology where cultural differences are institutionalized, monolithic essentialized perceptions of cultural groups may be encouraged, and people might still face segregated living and discrimination.[49] According to her, pluralistic societies do not imply high social identity complexity per se, but only provide the potential for complex multiple identities. Brewer argued that that "the key is to capitalize more effectively on our capacity for multiple social identities,"[50] and suggested adopting cross-cutting identities when making policies in diversified nations such as the USA or Israel.

The application of social identity complexity can be found across diverse disciplines[51] connected with this concept of social psychology. There are nevertheless alternative variations and approaches to social identity complexity as defined by the concept protagonists. Social psychologist Galen V. Bodenhausen comes to the same conclusion, that high complex identity is beneficial in accepting the diversity within the ingroup and in tolerance for the outgroup,[52] yet defines only three models of "multiple identity management": dominance, compartmentalization and integration.[53] The social identity complexity perception is not dissimilar from findings in identity theory. A recent identity theory study on role-related identity of adult women in the USA,[54] concludes with four[55] identity facet interrelations (like social identity complexity), and adds a fifth one.[56] Their multiple identity facets

---

49. Brewer, "Social Identity Complexity and Acceptance."

50. Brewer, 29.

51. These are, for example, migrant studies (Verkuyten and Martinovic, "Social Identity Complexity and Immigrants' Attitude"; Schmid, Hewstone and Al Ramiah, "Neighborhood Diversity"; Prati et al., "Encouraging Majority Support"), child studies (Knifsend and Juvonen, "Role of Social Identity Complexity"), political science (Augoustinos and De Garis, "Too Black"), international relations (Maloku et al., "Stimulating Interethnic Contact"), business (Meyer, "Social Identity Complexity and Sports"), and theology (Kok, "Social Identity Complexity Theory").

52. Bodenhausen, "Diversity," 11–12.

53. Bodenhausen, 4–8.

54. Graham, Sorell and Montgomery, "Role-Related Identity."

55. These are, according to Graham, Sorell and Montgomery, 255; 261–264: (a.) hierarchical, when one role predominates and other roles are subordinate; (b.) lateral/holistic, with multiple equally integrated and balanced roles; (c.) multi-role structure which is characterized by inseparable role combinations and intertwining; (d.) unembedded structure when role-related identity is subordinated to the sense of ego identity and when there is resistance to identify with any role, rather to perceive him- or her-self as an integrated person.

56. In addition to that, their own study, which included sixty in-depth interviews, added a fifth category of identity in transition: someone not having clearly structured identity, unhappy

categorization evokes the social identity complexity categories of dominance, compartmentalization, intersection, and merger. These authors do not directly refer to the social identity complexity concept but admit that role-related identity interacts with the domain of social identity,[57] so their work confirms how certain findings of identity theory and social identity theory overlap.

My research, based on the in-the-field situation, offers a fresh insight into Slavic Czech missionaries' identity negotiation in the proximal southern Slavic context by the utilization of four social identity complexity interrelations which imply the following innovations and possible contributions: Firstly, as social identity complexity is situated, by Roccas, Brewer and the vast majority of authors who followed them, it uses quantitative analysis and draws its data from surveys. This research distinguishes itself from others utilizing this methodological approach since it is qualitative and interview-based.[58] Secondly, since the vast majority of studies utilizing social identity complexity are performed in the West, a reflection from the Central-Eastern part of Europe, together with studies from Asia and elsewhere, could be beneficial.[59] Thirdly, scholars who apply social identity complexity across various disciplines predominantly focus on the negotiation of low versus high complexity. In accordance with the original social identity complexity thesis that "awareness of ingroup diversity provides an effective formula for reducing intergroup prejudice,"[60] they aim to confirm that high social identity complexity relates to positive intergroup attitudes.[61]

---

and wishing for a change (Graham, Sorell and Montgomery, 264).

57. Graham, Sorell and Montgomery, 252.

58. Examples of several social identity complexity qualitative works are the discourse analysis of presidential candidate speeches in the USA (Augoustinos and De Garis, "Too Black"), the in-depth interview-based research of online gamers' identity in Australia (O'Connor et al., "Sense of Community"), and narrative interviews and focus groups on Georgians' ethnic identity (Gamsakhurdia, "Quest for Ethnic Identity").

59. The majority of these studies appear in a multicultural and multi-ethnic Western society, which differs from typical contexts of the former Communist European countries. Most recently, several studies utilizing the social identity complexity concept have appeared in non-Western contexts, e.g. in China (Xin, Xin and Lin, "Effect of Trustors"), in Georgia (Gamsakhurdia, "Quest for Ethnic Identity") and interestingly partially also in Serbia (Levy et al., "Complex Social Identities").

60. Roccas and Brewer, "Social Identity Complexity," 104.

61. These are conclusions of migrant studies in Italy (Prati et al., "Encouraging Majority Support," 429), in Germany and in the UK (Schmid, Hewstone and Al Ramiah, "Neighborhood Diversity", 141), of child and adolescent studies in the USA (Knifsend and Juvonen, "Role of

These current studies do not focus on analysing the four[62] categories of multiple ingroup (or identity facet) interrelations in more detail. While the main goal of social identity complexity can be considered constructing policy implications in multicultural societies,[63] it is also clearly helping individuals negotiate their multiple identity facets in various circumstances.[64] Therefore, I consider it justified to utilize the social identity complexity concept for helping Czechs negotiate their national identity in situations of mission in former Yugoslav countries and also to inform both Czechs and former Yugoslavs on implications of high or low social identity complexity in their respective societies. My research attempts to examine these four interrelations in detail and therefore aspires to provide original insight into how to utilize social identity complexity in an innovative way and how to approach it critically.

2.2.4 National identity facet

According to sociologist Anthony Giddens, ethnicity is one of the primary and most significant group identities.[65] The focus in this work is on the "Czechness" of the missionaries, and for this reason the theoretical introduction entails discussion of ethnic and national identity. The next sub-section, then, depicts its relation to religious, particularly to Christian, identity.

The complex debate about whether ethnicity is immutable (primordial) or unsettled (situational) or something in-between was initiated by the anthropologist Fredrik Barth, who in his work, "Ethnic Groups and Boundaries" (1969), argued for the changeable nature of ethnicity, especially with the possibility of assimilation.[66] Jenkins follows on Barth's original argument when he claims that "identity is always a dialectic between similarity and difference"[67] and adds that groups and group boundaries should not be per-

---

Social Identity Complexity", 623), of international studies by authors from Dutch and Belgian universities (Maloku et al., "Stimulating Interethnic Contact").

62. Intersection, dominance, compartmentalization and merger are, according to social identity complexity, "four alternative forms of identity structure that reflect different ways in which the relationships among multiple ingroups can be subjectively represented" (Roccas and Brewer, "Social Identity Complexity," 89–90).
63. Brewer, "Social Identity Complexity and Acceptance," 28.
64. Roccas and Brewer, "Social Identity Complexity," 103–104.
65. Giddens, *Sociology*, 35.
66. Barth, *Ethnic Groups and Boundaries*, 22–23.
67. Jenkins, *Rethinking Ethnicity*, 169.

ceived as given, but rather continuously under construction.[68] Barth's colleague Thomas H. Eriksen similarly points at the fluid and ambiguous aspects of ethnicity negotiation, which can be to a certain degree manipulated by the identity carriers and admits that the degree of manipulation in social situations is not indefinite.[69] Barth's theoretical position that the ethnic group is defined by the sense of "group-ness" led the theologian Kuecker to suggest that Barth's understanding of ethnicity might relate to social identity theory: "The Barthian constructivist view ultimately suggests that ethnic identity is formerly based on an evaluative comparison with the outgroup."[70] The social anthropologists' debate on ethnic identity as such relates to national identity.

There are two basic models of looking at the concept of nation: nation as a given reality (ethnos: an ethnic community) and nation as a construct (demos: nation state).[71] A more post-modernist view claims that nation belongs to the invented and constructed world.[72] Its prominent representative, Benedict Anderson, authored "Imagined Communities: Reflection on the Origin and Spread of Nationalism." According to him, nations are "imagined" because in the mind of each member of a particular nation there is only an image of the communion with other members; he will never meet most of his co-nationals.[73] Another significant scholar, Ernest Gellner,[74] argued in this matter

---

68. Jenkins, *Being Danish*, 3.

69. "The coastal Sami would usually be prone to play down the importance of ethnicity in interaction with the dominant Norwegians – or they might try, in a negotiating approach, to present themselves as carriers of a Norwegian identity . . . one cannot ascribe any identity to somebody by claiming, say, that an Irish person is 'really' a Jamaican" (Eriksen, *Ethnicity and Nationalism*, 38). Or as stated more expressively: "I cannot awake one morning and suddenly decide to be a Hutu" (Castells, "Globalisation and Identity," 63; see also Jenkins, *Rethinking Ethnicity*, 173).

70. Kuecker, "Ethnicity and Social Identity," 67.

71. Vlachová and Řeháková, "Identity of Non-Self-Evident Nation", 255. It needs to be added that there is a spectrum of other views and that both of these theories, which do not represent a recognized binary, have their adherents and critics.

72. Bekus, *Struggle over Identity*, 15.

73. Anderson, *Imagined Communities*, 6.

74. Ernest Gellner (1925–1995), a prominent United Kingdom based political scientist and theorist of nation, came originally from a German speaking Jewish family in Prague.

similarly that nation, nationalism[75] and nation-state[76] are products of modern development, whose origins lie with the Treaty of Westphalia in 1648 and the eighteenth-century French and Industrial revolutions.[77] For Gellner, nationalism is primarily a political principle[78] and nation was constructed as a requirement of nationalism: "Nationalism is not the awakening of nations to self-consciousness; it invents nations where they do not exist."[79]

On the other hand, the representative of primordialism, Anthony Smith, the author of "National Identity,"[80] acknowledges that historical territory, legal-political community and the civic equality of its members are all components of the standard Western model of the nation.[81] He goes further and critiques the constructivist view by claiming that it is the non-Western ethnic conception of nation which is the valid model.[82] According to Smith, these are the attributes of nation as an ethnic community: "collective proper name, a myth of common ancestry, shared historical memories, one or more differentiating elements of common culture, an association with a specific "homeland," a sense of solidarity for significant sectors of the population."[83] Similar to Smith, the Czech political theorist Miroslav Hroch considers that nation is a "constituent of social reality of historical origin."[84]

---

75. The prominent sociologists Bauman and May describe nationalism as "the superiority of its own nation, of its national culture and character" (Bauman and May, *Thinking Sociologically*, 143). According to Smith, nationalism can signify different things: 1. the process of forming and maintaining nations; 2. a consciousness of belonging to the nation; 3. a language and symbolism of a nation; 4. an ideology and prescriptions for the realization of national aspirations; 5. a social and political movement to achieve the goal of the nation (Smith, *National Identity*, 72; compare Gellner, *Nations and Nationalism*, 88–109).

76. Nation-state could be defined as "a state dominated by an ethnic group, whose markers of identity (such as language or religion) are frequently embedded in its official symbolism and legislation" (Eriksen, *Ethnicity and Nationalism*, 119).

77. Gellner, *Nations and Nationalism*, 8–52; see also Giddens, *Sociology*, 958.

78. Gellner, 1.

79. Gellner, *Thought and Change*, 168.

80. Smith, *National Identity*.

81. Smith, 9–11.

82. Smith, 11.

83. Smith, 21.

84. Hroch, *Social Preconditions*, 3. In his book which was first published in 1969 he examined which social circumstances were favourable for the rise of patriotic feelings among various non-dominant ethnic groups, that he used in his case study, for example, Estonians, Flemish, Finns, Czechs. Hroch suggested the following phases in this national awakening process: "Phase A (the period of scholarly interest), Phase B (the period of patriotic agitation) and Phase C (the rise of a mass national movement)" (Hroch, 22).

I am aware of a certain dichotomy,[85] as I work with both conceptions of nation – but these can often be reconciled and situationally both be true for certain people groups in certain time periods.[86]

2.2.5 Christian identity facet

Christian identity as part of religious identity is closely linked with national identity and the topic of Czech Protestant Christian missionaries. Religion as "a unified system of beliefs and practices relative to sacred things"[87] aspires to supply "existential answers to individuals' quests for security providing a picture of totality, unity, and wholeness"[88] and hence to provide identity to individuals and society.

The literature search for "Christian identity" leads in the first place to theologians who focus on the first century differentiation from Jewish identity as they study the Pauline New Testament letters, which is thoroughly summarized by Bengt Holmberg in his "Understanding Christian Identity."[89] Kathryn Tanner noted that a distinctively Christian identity was not formed in that period and that "it arose in a step-by-step process of engagement with particulars."[90] Judith Lieu agreed with the existence of a tendency to impose an idea of unity out of rich diversity on the creation of Christian identity: "Christian identity is not something which appears clearly as such at a given moment."[91] William Campbell, the expert on Pauline letters, affirmed that Christian identity is still under construction or reconstruction and urged

---

85. Czechs themselves are not united on the issue, as historical debates demonstrate in polemics of Václav Havel with the prominent writer Milan Kundera (Havel, *About Human Identity*, 187–200) or in the claims of Jan Patočka: "The continuity does not exist . . . Philosophy of history based on national character, allegedly creating a historical continuum, or on ideology motives, has always proved to be a pure construction" (Patočka, "Philosophy of Czech History," 462). My translation; original: "*Tato kontinuita neexistuje . . . Filosofie dějin založená na národním charakteru, domněle vytvářejícím dějinné kontinuum, nebo na motivech ideových se pokaždé ukázala jako čistá konstrukce.*"

86. An example from the region of study can be the supposed primordial origin of the Macedonian nation, versus the year 1945, when the Socialist Republic of Macedonia, within Yugoslavia under Tito's regime, was constructed.

87. Durkheim, *The Elementary Forms* (quoted in Storm, "Secular Christianity as National Identity," 22)

88. Kinnvall, "Globalization and Religious Nationalism," 759.

89. Holmberg, "Understanding Christian Identity."

90. Tanner, *Theories of Culture*, 117.

91. Lieu, *Neither Jew nor Greek*, 25.

for its review in the social, cultural, and theological dimensions.⁹² An establishment of Christian identity will indeed remain an unresolved issue, and additionally the question arises: "If Christian, then which Christian?"

Understanding of Christian identity in this work is based on responses of the Protestant Christian missionaries, along the perception of Christian identity as an active "Christ-follower" identity, when faith in Christ is connected with deeds that follow.⁹³ Tanner adds to this that Christian identity is based on a common person, not on common practices and rituals,⁹⁴ and what unites Christians as Jesus followers is the concern for true discipleship.⁹⁵ Christian identity here is therefore not linked to any particular denomination, since it is precarious even for the Protestants themselves to agree on a "Christian identity" comprehension.

The section on identity aimed to clarify utilization of the terms, "identity," "identity salience," and "multiple identity facets," bearing in mind the focus of this research on national identity. The following sections 2.3 on culture and 2.4 on mission develop the discussion on Christian identity in transforming cultures and on the specifics of religious identity of Czechs and of Slavic nations of former Yugoslavia, where national and religious identity facets often merge.

2.3 Culture

2.3.1 Definition

"Culture," with the original meaning *colere* in Latin,⁹⁶ is presently understood differently across disciplines in social science. Sociologist Anthony Giddens defines culture as "values, norms, habits and ways of life characteristic of a

---

92. Campbell, *Paul and the Creation of Christian Identity*, 2.
93. Campbell, 12.
94. It can be noticed, nevertheless, that there are two ceremonial – and biblical – sacraments, baptism and communion, emphasising certain communal aspects of Christian identity.
95. Tanner, *Theories of Culture*, 152.
96. The classicist perception of *colere* (to cultivate or instruct) included a sophisticated way of acting and value judgements of good and bad cultures. This has widely been abandoned for the more universally accepted empiricist perception of culture where no culture is better than another (Seee Bevans and Schroeder, *Constants in Context*, 47).

coherent social group."⁹⁷ While society is the group of people itself, culture can be understood as characteristics of that group, and society can be comprised of multiple cultures.⁹⁸ In the symbolic framework of anthropologist Clifford Geertz, where symbols construct public meaning, culture is understood as webs of significance. According to him, culture is "a system of inherited conceptions expressed in symbolic forms by means of which men communicate, perpetuate, and develop their knowledge about and attitudes toward life."⁹⁹ Recent publications of missiological research apprehend culture similarly, as a "symbolic system by which meanings are expressed in both tangible (e.g. art, gesture, rituals) and intangible (e.g. speech) forms that are socially acquired, learned behaviours and transmitted intergenerationally."¹⁰⁰ It needs to be added that the tangible and intangible distinction appears precarious for culture.

Anthropological studies have become increasingly significant for practical theology and missiology, and missional anthropology¹⁰¹ has emerged as one of the missiology subdisciplines. The theologian Robert Schreiter noticed: "When it comes to defining culture, everyone is aware of the notorious difficulty of the task."¹⁰² Still, theologians, missiologists and Christian anthropologists often tend to view culture rather inclusively. Lesslie Newbigin understands culture as "the sum total of ways of living developed by a group of human beings and handed on from generation to generation."¹⁰³ David Hesselgrave considers that culture "takes into account linguistic, political, economic, social, psychological, religious, national, racial, and still other

---

97. Giddens, *Sociology*, 995.
98. See Hiebert, *Cultural Anthropology*, 32–33.
99. Geertz, *Interpretations of Cultures*, 89.
100. Gilbert, Johnson and Lewis, *Missiological Research*, 312.
101. According to Tennent, Christian anthropologists differ from anthropological understanding of culture in four areas: (a.) God is the source and sustainer of culture; (b.) Christians affirm the reality of sin and its personal and collective implications; (c.) God has revealed himself within human culture; (d.) Christians believe that the eschatological culture of new creation has broken into the present (Tennent, *Invitation to World Missions*, 171–174).
102. Schreiter, "Communication and Interpretation," 230.
103. Newbigin, *Foolishness to Greeks*, 3. He considers language to be central to culture and around that centre he groups visual and musical arts, technologies, law and social and political organization. He further finds sets of beliefs, experience and practices, including religion, to be part of culture.

differences."[104] Carver Yu, in his theological perspective on the understanding of Karl Barth, perceives culture highly inclusively – culture is humanity.[105] Missiologists Lingenfelter and Mayers position culture more pragmatically, for them it is "a set of conceptual tools and social arrangements that people use to adapt to their environment and to order their lives."[106] The Christian anthropologist Hiebert defines culture as an "integrated system of learned patterns of behaviour, ideas and products characteristic of a society."[107] Catholic missiologist Stephen Bevans similarly recalls three aspects of culture when he points to previous scholarly work:[108] ideational culture, culture as performance, and material dimension.[109]

The overall understanding of culture in this research, therefore, complies with the perception of culture as a non-clear-cut unit, and particularly national culture, for example Czech or Serbian culture, as rather overlapping and multidimensional in essence. Due to the missiological focus of this research, these topical concepts are briefly introduced in the subsequent three sub-sections: A Christian anthropological view of Christ transforming cultures; missionaries contextualization in local culture; cross-cultural comparison in missiological perspective.

2.3.2 Christian anthropological view of Christ transforming cultures

Many scholars consider Richard Niebuhr's, "Christ and Culture"[110] to be a key book that sparked the debate on the Christians' approach to culture. Niebuhr proposed a typology with five views of the relationship of Christ and culture: Christ against culture, the Christ of culture, Christ above culture,

---

104. Hesselgrave, *Communicating Christ Cross-Culturally*, 99.
105. Yu, "Culture from Evangelical Perspective," 82.
106. Lingenfelter and Mayers, *Ministering Cross-Culturally*, 112.
107. Hiebert, *Cultural Anthropology*, 25. In this perspective, products are artefacts of material culture, behaviour signifies actions and customs, and ideas are understood as "systems of shared concepts by which people carve up their worlds, of beliefs by which they organize these concepts into rational schemes, and of values by which they set their goals and judge their actions" (Hiebert, 28).
108. "Robert Schreiter, following Jens Loenhoff, proposes a definition that includes three aspects or dimensions." (Bevans and Schroeder, *Constants in Context*, 47)
109. Bevans and Schroeder, 47.
110. Niebuhr, *Christ and Culture*.

Christ and culture in paradox, and Christ as Transformer of culture.¹¹¹ His classic work has been critiqued for assuming a Christendom framework and monoculture.¹¹² Even the definition of culture as an "artificial secondary environment which man superimposes on the natural"¹¹³ evokes more of a monolithic and dichotomous understanding. Culture, instead, tends to be more recently viewed as a diverse phenomenon with multidimensional elements.¹¹⁴ Nevertheless, despite the deficiencies,¹¹⁵ Niebuhr's typology is exceedingly beneficial, and many contemporary Christian scholars proceed in elaborating it.¹¹⁶

Niebuhr's "Christ transforming cultures" is found to be most helpful by many evangelical authors.¹¹⁷ Hesselgrave asserts: "In Christ, humanity is redeemed, and culture can be renewed so as to glorify God."¹¹⁸ Yu explains this theological connection in detail: "Christ then may be regarded as the crown of what every culture is striving for . . . A culture confronted by Christ does not need to be a clean empty page."¹¹⁹ Cultures, according to conclusions found in the Evangelical statement on mission in the Cape Town Commitment,¹²⁰

---

111. On one side of the spectrum can stand Christ against culture (counter-cultural type) and on the other Christ of culture (accommodative type), the three other positions placed in between (the synthetic position with good elements of culture, yet placing Christ above; dualist position with the stress on temporality of culture; and the conversionist position). Niebuhr provides space for opting for any of the five, "because they are related to the fragmentary and frail measure of our faith" (Niebuhr, 235).

112. Tennent, *Invitation to World Missions,* 163–167.

113. Niebuhr, *Christ and Culture,* 32.

114. See Clifford Geertz's webs of significance to be analysed in an interpretative search for meaning (Geertz, *Interpretations of Cultures,* 5) or Kathryn Tanner's concept of culture being under development and its relational identity accentuated (Tanner, *Theories of Culture,* 115).

115. Niebuhr himself admits that it is hard to conform the complexity to a type, since "type is always a construct" (Niebuhr, *Christ and Culture,* 45).

116. An example to be highlighted is Bevans' six models of encounter of Christian faith and culture (Bevans and Schroeder, *Constants in Context,* 48).

117. See Tennent, *Invitation to World Missions,* 162. This is more complex, as Moreau says: "While Bevans and Schroeder accurately catalogue the majority of Evangelical models under the descriptors 'translation' and 'countercultural,' these two descriptions alone do not adequately convey the myriad approaches used by Evangelicals" (Moreau, *Contextualization in World Missions,* 44).

118. Hesselgrave, *Communicating Christ Cross-Culturally,* 116.

119. Yu, "Culture from Evangelical Perspective", 85.

120. The Cape Town Commitment (2010) is, together with the other two texts, the Lausanne Covenant (1974) and the Manila Manifesto (1989), the third major evangelical statement on missionary belief and practice produced by the Lausanne movement.

involve two concurrent elements: appreciation and the need for transformation: "We love the world of nations and cultures ... Ethnic diversity is the gift of God in creation and will be preserved in the new creation, when it will be liberated from our fallen divisions and rivalry."[121] In the light of this, there are no "better" cultures than others, as the professor Thomas Schirrmacher emphasizes: "There should be no claim to superiority on the part of one's own culture above another culture."[122] In this perspective, cultures are affirmed, yet certain elements within cultures are encouraged to change. Hiebert adds:

> We, indeed, must learn to appreciate deeply the cultures of other peoples, and this appreciation in us is born only out of a love for them as human beings. On the other hand, we cannot deny them their right to change by forcing them to live in human zoos.[123]

This discussion is connected to the following section on how to approach other cultures in practical mission work.

2.3.3 Missionaries' contextualization in local culture

The Catholic theologian José M. De Mesa summed up the consequences of Vatican II (1962–1965): "Different terms like 'radical adaptation' to the culture, 'indigenization,' 'localization,' and 'inculturation' have been proposed to indicate the meaning and the process involved in integrating gospel and culture in a particular setting."[124] He added that "today the term 'contextualization' is at times regarded as synonymous and proposed as more suitable"[125] and indeed, it builds upon these earlier terms.[126] "Contextualization" was first used in 1972 at the World Council of Churches by Taiwanese reflective practitioner Shoki Coe, whose concern was contextual[127] theology: "His

---

121. "Cape Town Commitment," 64, point 7b.

122. Schirrmacher, *Biblical Foundations*, 44. In his book, he proposes sixty-nine modern theses in light of Luther's ninety-five and links the Reformation with twenty-first century missiology.

123. Hiebert, *Cultural Anthropology*, xvi.

124. De Mesa, "Mission and Inculturation." 230.

125. De Mesa, 230.

126. See Bosch, *Transforming Mission*, 447; Tennent, *Invitation to World Missions*, 345.

127. Local theologies, as underlined by the missiologist Knud Jørgensen, mark the difference from The Edinburgh Missionary Conference: "1910 still believed that Western theology was universally valid and based on the ecclesiastical confessions. Contextualization implies learning through the experimental nature of all theology and through an ongoing

approach was to allow the text (Scripture) to provide the vocabulary and the perspective needed to wrestle with a changing context."[128] "Contextualization" has been widely accepted, especially in Evangelical circles. Hesselgrave defines this missional endeavour as: "The attempt to communicate the message of the person, works, word, and will of God in a way that is faithful to God's revelation, especially as it is put forth in the teachings of Holy Scripture, and that is meaningful to respondents in their respective cultural and existential contexts."[129]

Moreau describes it as a process of adapting Christian faith in diverse cultural settings.[130] Tennent uses the term in his work yet critiques its focus on the context. Instead, he prefers "translatability" as a more suitable word, since it considers both the source and target of missions.[131] When arguing that "not only is the gospel linguistically translatable, but the gospel also is culturally translatable,"[132] Tennent refers to the architects of the concept of mission as translation, among whom can be considered Andrew Walls, Kwame Bediako, and Lamin Sanneh.[133] The central thesis of Sanneh's book, "Translating the Message: The Missionary Impact on Culture," was that Christianity identified itself with the need to translate out of Aramaic and Hebrew and it does its mission by translation.[134] So, even though I treasure the concept of mission as translation, I use the verb to "contextualize" and the term "contextualization," aligning with the current use in Protestant missiology, being aware of its limitations.

---

dialogue between text and context" (Jørgensen, "Introduction: Mission as Learning," 8). The missiologist Dean Gilliland underlined the usefulness of the focus on the local context: "Contextualization guards against the imperialism of theology" (Gilliland, "Contextual Theology as Incarnational Mission," 13).

128. Wheeler, "The Legacy of Shoki Coe," 79. For Coe (1914–1988), it specifically meant the changing context of Taiwan, where ethnic differences, urbanization, and political situations influenced the church structure, often conflicting with its mission (Wheeler, 79).

129. Hesselgrave, *Communicating Christ Cross-Culturally*, 143.

130. Moreau, *Contextualization in World Missions*, 46.

131. Tennent, *Invitation to World Missions*, 352.

132. Tennent, 86. "Translation" in missiology comes from translation studies, which acknowledges not only the original text for translation, the context to be translated to, but also the agents of translation (See also Prince and Kikon, "Mission as Translation," 259).

133. Haney, "Mapping Mission as Translation," 148.

134. Sanneh, *Translating the Message*, 36.

It may be true that Protestant missionaries desire to see that the gospel is embodied and embedded in all cultures[135] and, grounded on the understanding of the biblical verses in 1 Corinthians 9: 19–23,[136] they are aware that Christians "are obligated, out of love, to adapt to the culture of others."[137] On the other hand, as the missiologist Lesslie Newbigin noticed, missionaries tend to base their belief and practices on their home culture, and they perceive cultural differences as ungodly.[138] Sociologists similarly hold that those of a certain culture tend to alter culture of the other, and in that sense "culture can become a proselytizing activity."[139]

Therefore, instead of no contextualization or minimal contextualization on one side, and excessive contextualization, when culture is given priority over the universal claims of the Christian message, on the other side, it seems there is an alternative in missiology called "critical contextualization." It, in brief, "seeks a balanced approach in which missionary interaction with societies is both true to the Bible and sensitive to the cultures of the particular people groups."[140]

The missiological term "contextualization" can be associated with the socio-psychological notion of "identity suppression," which has been briefly introduced.[141] To avoid misunderstanding, in chapter 5 on suppressing one's identity in relation to mission work in a different culture, a broader, yet admittedly somewhat vague, term of cultural "adjustment," or alternately "adaptation,"[142] is employed.

---

135. "Cape Town Commitment," 64.

136. "For though I am free from all, I have made myself a servant to all, that I might win more of them . . . I have become all things to all people, that by all means I might save some. I do it all for the sake of the gospel, that I may share with them in its blessings." (ESV) In these verses, the apostle Paul calls for adjusting to others in sharing the good news about Christ.

137. Schirrmacher, *Biblical Foundations*, 47.

138. Newbigin, *Foolishness to Greeks*, 21. In his book, Newbigin lists several characteristics of Western culture and its influence from the Enlightenment (Newbigin, 15–34) and suggests how to engage it with the Gospel (Newbigin, 134–149).

139. Bauman and May, *Thinking Sociologically*, 134.

140. Hiebert, "Gospel in Human Contexts," 100.

141. To contextualize in a new environment entails suppression of one's own cultural, national, or even denominational or organizational identity.

142. Adaptation to other cultures, in the words of intercultural psychologists, "refers to the long-term ways in which people rearrange their lives and settle down into a more-or-less satisfactory existence" (Berry et al., *Cross-Cultural Psychology*, 369). Further on, "acculturation," in contrast to "enculturation" and "socialization" (to one's own culture), entails the meaning

2.3.4 Cross-cultural comparison in missiological perspective

An adequate contextualization requires a proportionate familiarization with the two (or more) cultural contexts relevant for mission. Missiologists notice the challenge of accessing the cross-cultural comparison. Several models exist and they are usually linked to the strategic tools used to determine which cultures to send missionaries to. In 1974, missiologist Ralph Winter[143] addressed the Lausanne Congress for World Evangelism and talked about the urgency of world evangelizing shifting attention from countries as political units to individual nations as ethnic units.[144] In order to mobilize the church to reach the "unreached people groups,"[145] Winter introduced the strategic tool of E-scale[146] taxonomy. In his definition, "E" stands for evangelism, "E-1" means our own culture, "E-2" close culture, "E-3" far culture, in the cultural and not in the geographical sense.[147] Having followed the observation that most missionaries are being sent to "reached" people groups,[148] Winter argued for sending missionaries to E-2 and E-3 cultures until E-1 churches are established.[149] Another missiological contribution to the dialogue on cross-culturality was provided by Hesselgrave, who having been aware of the E-scale, introduced a seven-dimensional diagram to measure "the extent of cultural distances

---

of "the form of transmission experienced by individuals that results from contact with, and influence from, persons and institutions belonging to cultures other than their own" (Berry et al., 21).

143. Ralph Winter (1924–2009) was a missionary to Mayan Indians in Guatemala for ten years and a founder of Frontier Mission Fellowship which gave birth to the US Center for World Mission.

144. Barnet and Martin, *Discovering the Mission*, 295–296.

145. At the beginning, Winter considered the "unreached" to be a group that is less than twenty per-cent practicing Christian (Winter, "Frontier Mission Perspectives," 60). Initiatives that followed, such as the Joshua project or International Missions Board, count as such peoples who are less than two per-cent Evangelicals (Tennent, *Invitation to World Missions*, 364–368).

146. Along with the E-scale which "measures the linguistic and cultural distance missionaries must cross for effective evangelism to take place" (Barnet and Martin, *Discovering the Mission*, 468), Winter developed the P-scale which is the distance a "non-believer must travel to find the church" (Winter, "Frontier Mission Perspectives," 64).

147. Winter, "New Macedonia," 352. This scale is based on the interpretation of the biblical text of Luke 1:8 where Jesus sends his disciples to be his witnesses in Judea, Samaria and the ends of the earth (Winter, 350–351).

148. Winter and Koch, "Finishing the Task," 543.

149. "Until every tribe and tongue have a strong, powerfully evangelizing church in it, and thus, an E-1 witness within it, E-2 and E-3 efforts coming from outside are still essential and highly urgent." (Winter, "New Macedonia," 350)

between any two cultures."¹⁵⁰ This diagram consists of seven areas¹⁵¹ and is assessed on a scale from "one" (completely different) to "ten" (the same); the higher the score, the more the cultures are similar.¹⁵²

Missiological efforts, such as the E-scale, Hesselgrave's seventy points assessment or others, are useful strategic tools which, nevertheless, with their emphasis on numbers come with limitations both for mission studies and for cross-cultural studies. Hesselgrave admits that "a quantitative analysis of cultural difference seems to be premature (with potential for the future) and might appear misleading and subjective, since standards of comparison are hard to set."¹⁵³ Similarly, the reality is more complex than as outlined by the three Es. Even though Winter himself acknowledges in-between numbers (e.g. E-2.5¹⁵⁴), cross-cultural mission might not be drawn as a linear picture of a sending culture on one side of the spectrum, of a receiving culture on the other, and of several points on this straight solid line in-between. More likely, it resembles an uneven diagram in which various subcultural influences and unique individual experiences must be considered and included. Missionaries' personal culture, caused by familial and societal background, needs to be taken into consideration as well, and also the occurrence of tripleculture or multiculture.¹⁵⁵ The certain "biculture"¹⁵⁶ or, perhaps better expressed, "intermediate culture"¹⁵⁷ missionaries obtain, enables them to compare certain cultural traits. Still, as Wijsen points out, "one cannot simply oppose two cultures as if they are monolithic entities."¹⁵⁸

---

150. Hesselgrave, *Communicating Christ Cross-Culturally*, 169.

151. These areas are: worldview, cognitive process, linguistic form, behavioural pattern, social structure, media influence, motivational resources (Hesselgrave, 171).

152. Hesselgrave provides this diagram with the empirical study of an American missionary to France, who scored forty-nine, and to the Philippines, who scored thirty-three (Hesselgrave, 172).

153. Hesselgrave, 173.

154. Winter, "Frontier Mission Perspectives," 65.

155. "Triple-" or "multi-" culture is understood as situations when a missionary deals with more than two cultures, for example, those of mixed marriages, those who work in international teams, or those who encounter more host cultures.

156. See Hiebert, *Anthropological Insights for Missionaries*, 228.

157. "Missionaries experience that they are no longer at home in their own culture and not yet at home in the host culture . . . they constitute an intermediate culture." (Wijsen, "Intercultural Theology," 228)

158. Wijsen, 225.

The more modern perspective of intercultural psychologists Trompenaars and Hampden-Turner admit this very actuality: "Culture is not a 'thing,' a substance with a physical reality of its own. Rather, it is made by people interacting, and at the same time determining further interaction."[159] Still, intercultural or cross-cultural psychology[160] and cross-cultural management studies generate tools to measure cultural differences (or "dimensions of national culture," or "cross-cultural personality traits"). Such models differ in delineation of categories and in their number: For example, there are six in Hofstede model,[161] five in NEO-PI-3,[162] nine in GLOBE,[163] seven in Trompenaars' culture dimensions model.[164] So again, although these comparison tools are useful, there is no normative "culture," and therefore it is precarious to compare similarities and differences in a cross-cultural case study, as will become clear from the engagement with some of the models in the analysis chapter 4.

2.4 Mission

2.4.1 Definition

Since "mission" has a "broad range of acceptable meanings,"[165] it needs to be clarified how this term is used in this study. First, being aware that the usage of the terms "mission" and "missions" is not completely unified, I use it in compliance with scholars who consider "missions" in plural to be a multitude of activities that God's people can engage in order to participate in the total

---

159. Trompenaars and Hampden-Turner, *Riding the Waves of Culture*, 24.

160. "Cross-cultural psychology is the study: of similarities and differences in individual psychological functioning in various cultural and ethnocultural groups; of the relationships between psychological variables and socio-cultural, ecological and biological variables; and of ongoing changes in these variables." (Berry et al., *Cross-Cultural Psychology*, 3)

161. Hofstede Insights, "Six Dimensions of National Culture."

162. McCrae, Costa and Martin, "The NEO–PI–3." NEO-PI-3 as the third edition of Personal Inventory, enhanced NEO-PI and NEO-PI-R (revised).

163. Globe Project, "Overview of the 2004 study."

164. Trompenaars and Hampden-Turner, *Riding the Waves of Culture* (first published in 1989, published for the fourth time in 2020). See also THT Consulting, "Culture for Business."

165. Moreau, "Mission and Missions," 636. "Mission" is not found explicitly in the Bible, it is derived from the Greek *apostello* and its Latin translation *mitto*. Originally, "mission" referred to the sending aspect within the Trinity and until the introduction of Catholic mission by Ignatius of Loyola in the sixteenth century the church used other terms for what we mean by mission today (Moreau, 636).

biblical assignment – the mission of God.¹⁶⁶ This understanding is linked with the concept of *missio Dei*,¹⁶⁷ when Christians join in God's initiative in mission. Tennent quotes the biblical text from Matthew 28:18 where Jesus says: "All authority in heaven and on earth has been given to me," and emphasizes that "missions begins with who God is; only then can it be cast as specific duties or responsibilities of the church in the world."¹⁶⁸

Second, the holistic¹⁶⁹ aspect of mission is acknowledged and applied. While some tend to view relief and development work as a bridge or as a consequence of evangelism, others perceive them as complementary partners.¹⁷⁰ Theologian Christopher Wright considers the Bible to provide a warrant for holding the two together and critiques the, according to him, "artificially created dichotomy."¹⁷¹ Instead of one or the other holding primacy, he opts for the view of "centrality" when both hub (evangelism) and rim (social action) constitute a wheel of mission.¹⁷² This view of holistic mission is perceived as a suitable model in this research.

Third, "mission" in this work refers to international or intercultural mission, yet does not consider it something theologically separate from the mission in the home country, as the missiologist David Bosch stated: "The difference between home and foreign missions is not one of principle but of scope."¹⁷³ The classic distinction between cross-cultural "missions" and "evangelism" in one's own culture has been challenged, yet it would be useful if certain boundaries between the broad and narrow definition of mission

---

166. Wright, *Mission of God's People*, 25; see also Peters, *Biblical Theology of Missions*, 11.

167. "*Missio Dei* was first used in a missionary sense by the German missiologist Karl Hartenstein in 1934. He was motivated by Karl Barth's emphasis on the *actio Dei* ("the action of God"), over against the human-centred focus of liberal theology at that time" (McIntosh "Missio Dei," 632).

168. Tennent, 488. In his Trinitarian perception of mission, the Father is the sender and Lord of the harvest, the Son is the model of embodiment, and the Holy Spirit is the empowering presence for all of mission (Tennent, 75).

169. Also referred to as "integral mission" or "mission as transformation" (Samuel and Sugden, *Mission as Transformation*).

170. Tennent, *Invitation to World Missions*, 392.

171. Wright, *Mission of God's People*, 276. He reacts by providing examples of Bible reading and praying as part of the discipleship process, or of breathing and drinking water, both as integral parts with none having primacy.

172. Wright, 277–278.

173. Bosch, *Transforming Mission*, 10.

were kept. Stephen Neill noted: "If everything is mission, nothing is mission,"[174] i.e. if mission is defined too broadly then it gets complicated to define what mission actually is, since not all church action can necessarily be labelled mission.[175] Tennent similarly argues that "the distinction must be retained, but we have to separate it from its long association with geography."[176] Wright suggests a correction to Neill's statement: "It would seem more biblical to say, 'If everything is mission – everything is mission.'"[177] He dislikes the evangelism-mission division and argues that even though not everything is a cross-cultural evangelistic mission, all Christian action should be missional as it participates in God's mission.[178]

Winter argues that there remains a genuine need for intercultural missionaries,[179] first of all due to the lack of local Christian workers.[180] Besides that, the dynamics of foreign and local workers labouring together can be very beneficial – the intercultural workers might help the local workers discover blind spots and vice versa.[181] The argument for the legitimacy of international mission could be followed further and expanded, yet it is outside the scope of this study. Tennent reflects on the developments of the twenty-first century, including the decline of Christendom in the West, with the collapse of the "West-reaching-the-rest" paradigm; and argues for "multidirectional missionary movement."[182] This mission from everywhere to everywhere,[183] when "the church on every continent is simultaneously sending missionaries and

---

174. Neill, *Creative Tension*, 81.
175. Moreau, "Mission and Missions," 636.
176. Tennent, *Invitation to World Missions*, 24.
177. Wright, *Mission of God's People*, 26.
178. Wright, 26.
179. Even though all Christians, not just a group of professionals are to be missional (Tennent, *Invitation to World Missions*, 126), in this study the Christian intercultural workers are referred to as missionaries (See Wright, *Mission of God*, 23).
180. Winter, "New Macedonia," 350–353.
181. See Wachsmuth, "Missional Insights," 76.
182. Tennent, *Invitation to World Missions*, 33.
183. Wright points out that there are no "ends" of the earth which is a globe and even though many people still live in fairly monocultural societies, "from a missional perspective, the 'ends of the earth' are as likely to be found in your own street as far across the sea" (Wright, *Mission of God's People*, 286).

receiving missionaries,"[184] includes contemporary missions from the Czech Republic as a modest contribution to the global mission movement.

2.4.2 Mission from the Czech Republic

The topics and concerns of contemporary Czech missiological literature focus in the vast majority on cases of domestic mission in the Czech Republic. Major areas addressed are: (a.) ecumenism as means of mission; (b.) dialogue with the irreligious majority society; (c.) the relationship between foreign missionaries and local Czech workers. The prominent Czech author in the field Pavel Černý[185] touches on all of these areas, including ecumenism and the unity of Christians. The interrelation of mission and ecumenism is tackled by another Czech scholar, Catholic author Robert Svatoň, who finds this bond supposedly leads to a testimony to the nations.[186] The recent publication, "A Czech Perspective on Faith in a Secular Age,"[187] edited by Tomáš Halík[188] and Pavel Hošek,[189] aimed at developing a corresponding missiological approach for the church's dialogue with contemporary seekers. Hošek himself has published two useful books where he argues for a better understanding of Czech identity to help contemporary seekers re-embrace the Christian faith.[190]

The dynamics of cooperation of foreign missionaries and Czech local workers has been a topic of reflection since the 1990s, after the initial influx of Western missionaries to Czechoslovakia and the Czech Republic. This

---

184. Tennent, *Invitation to World Missions*, 493.

185. Černý comes from the Brethren Church and could be labelled as one of the pioneers of Czech missiology, both as an author and missiology teacher. His fields of interest are ecumenism (Černý, "One Lord") and interreligious dialogue (Černý, "Practice of Christian's Dialogue"), the relationship between theology and practical missiology (Černý, "Response to Paul Negrut"; Černý, "Christ's Work"; Černý, "Mission Form"; Černý, "Relationship of Theology and Missiology"), and missiology in the secular environment of the Czech Republic (Černý, "Mission of the Contemporary Church"; Černý, "Mission in the Czech Republic").

186. Svatoň, "Unity and Mission," 79.

187. Halík and Hošek, *Czech Perspective on Faith*.

188. Halík, the Templeton Prize winner in 2014, is a leading Czech scholar of religion. The influence of this Catholic author, priest and sociologist can be seen in the generation of younger authors, such as Hošek.

189. Pavel Hošek is a leading Czech Protestant scholar of religion.

190. In, "Gods Return: Religious Changes in the Postmodern Time" (Hošek, *Gods Return*), he looks at specifics of Czech identity and how to approach a contemporary Czech person with the Gospel. In, "Islam as a Challenge for Christians" (Hošek, *Islam as a Challenge*), he depicts how Islam can serve as a mirror to Czech believers and non-believers and how it might help them understand who they are or who they are not.

was at first addressed in 1997 by theologian Dan Drápal[191] in, "Will We Survive Western Missionaries? Reflections of a Czech Pastor on Meeting the Western Missionaries."[192] The next decade witnessed two similar works, master's theses,[193] by theologians David Novák and Daniel Fajfr. They both, Novák briefly[194] and Fafr in his whole work,[195] address the tension and need for cultural understanding between Czech workers and foreign missionaries.

The debate on mission in the Czech Republic is in its infancy. Czech authors only to a minor degree refer to international mission originating from their country. In one of his conference papers Černý appeals to the Czech Christian community: "It is time that Czech churches get involved in international mission. Sending mission workers develops evangelism and deaconry in the world and immensely enriches and strengthens the local church."[196] It needs to be remembered that this "mission in reverse"[197] is supposed to function rather as a side effect of the international mission work. Drápal seems to begin to see the connection between western missionaries in the Czech Republic and the challenges of Czech missionaries to be sent: "We can make experience both ways. I realized that I can easily become condescending when meeting Christians from the Ukraine or Albania."[198]

Whereas contemporary Czech mission to other countries from Protestant churches has been arguably understudied, some literature exists as far as the Catholic church in the Czech Republic is concerned. Josef Dolista's,

---

191. Drápal is a remarkable person with regards to the spiritual awakening which started in 1980s and spanned to 1990s. In 1991 he was one of the founders of the Christian Mission Society (*Křesťanská misijní společnost – KMS*), a Czech-originated and Czech-led mission society. After 1989, the first Czech Protestant long-term missionaries were sent by KMS – to Croatia – and they are included in this study.

192. Drápal, *Will We Survive*. In his work, he portrays a disparity in Christian foreign missionaries: those who ask locals what to help with or those who come with their own agenda (Drápal, 39).

193. They both graduated from International Baptist Theological Seminary (IBTS). Before it was relocated to Amsterdam, the Prague location (1997–2014) helped produce several Czech graduates, among them Fajfr and Novák.

194. Novák, "Critical Examination of Mission," 37; 65–66.

195. Fajfr, "Critical and Evaluative Study."

196. Černý, "Mission Form," 10. My translation; original: *"Je na čase, aby se české církve více zapojovaly do zahraniční misie. Vysílání misijních pracovníků rozvíjí evangelizaci a diakonii ve světě a nesmírně obohacuje a posiluje místní církev."*

197. Escobar, *New Global Mission*, 162.

198. Drápal, *Will We Survive*, 40.

"The Mission Effort of the Church,"[199] which is based on a Catholic theology of mission,[200] is noteworthy as the only missiology textbook by a Czech author until now. Contemporary author Stanislav Balík in his chapter, "Christianisation from the Czech Lands, especially in the second half of the 20th Century,"[201] analyses contemporary Catholic mission and concludes that international mission has been an "unprocessed topic."[202]

In connection with that, there are several foreign and local theologians and missiologists who reflect on mission from countries of similar contexts in Central and Eastern Europe. Anne-Marie Kool[203] distinguishes three time periods so far for mission in Central and Eastern Europe: 1. 1989–1998, 2. 1999–2009, 3. Since 2009. She considers the first decade dedicated to importing the western mission paradigms or re-introducing paradigms of the past. The second decade was, according to her, a period of disillusionment. The last decade lasting till now is supposedly a time of "new innovative and creative mission paradigms re-emerging."[204] Her colleague Scott Klingsmith, similarly, recognizes the search for an authentic mission from Central and Eastern Europe. In his cross-case analysis of international mission from Poland, Romania and Hungary after 1989, "Missions Beyond the Wall: Factors in the Rise of Missionary Sending Movements in East-Central Europe,"[205] he points out the challenges and the advantages for missionaries from Central and Eastern European countries in contrast to Westerners.[206] Other Western

---

199. Dolista, *Mission Effort*.

200. While approaches differ within the Catholic church (Bevans and Schroeder, *Constants in Context*), mission is officially promoted. This is due to encyclicals and exhortations of the three recent popes, "especially Evangelii nuntiandi by Paul VI and Redemptoris missio (about the permanent validity for missionary work) by John Paul II and Evangelii Gaudium by Francis" (Černý, "Mission in the Czech Republic," 611).

201. Balík, *Christianization from the Czech Lands*.

202. Balík, 329.

203. Missiologist Anne-Marie Kool helped establish the Central and Eastern European Association for Mission Studies (CEEAMS) in 2002 in Budapest.

204. Kool, "Revolutions in European Mission," 213. Kool in a commendable, yet slightly problematic, way to support indigenous mission distinguishes two types of mission (Kool, 14): "The Enlightenment paradigm" portrays individuality and the focus on success of the West, while the ideal "biblical paradigm" models the emerging mission from Central and Eastern Europe which resembles the original mission from the Antioch church (Kool, 22).

205. Klingsmith, *Missions Beyond the Wall*.

206. These are, according to him, language adaptability, experience of persecution under Communism, visa situations, stronger sense of relationships, and living standard expectations (Klingsmith, 133–134, 146).

scholars offer only limited insight into mission from these countries,[207] yet local authors are reflecting more and more on mission practice – in which especially Romanians are taking the lead.[208]

It truly is beneficial to gain a broader perspective from related literature, yet it becomes clear that literature on international mission from the Czech Protestant churches is meagre and needs to be enhanced. Klingsmith ends his study on Polish, Hungarian and Romanian mission by suggesting further research – pointing to the need for studying Ukrainian mission, followed by the statement: "In addition, the Czech Republic needs to be studied."[209] This theme has been engaged to a certain degree, "albeit more at a level of practical ministry[210] rather than that of theological or missiological reflection."[211] The review of Czech mission in this chapter section thankfully refers to useful missiological works, especially by Černý, Bargár, and Kool and Klingsmith, yet I conclude that international Czech mission is understudied. Publications are focused on mission to Czechs, and as for literature on mission from the Czech Republic, there seems to be a gap. Therefore, this research on Czech missionaries' identity is substantiated and aims to become a contributive piece of work. Before moving to the next rather technical chapter, I need to address one particular issue related to intercultural encounters and mission – religious identity in both geopolitical contexts.

---

207. One of them is the missiologist Malcolm Clegg who in his MA thesis, "Understanding the Times – Research into the Impact and Direction of Christian Mission in Post-Communist Central and Eastern Europe at the Turn of the Century" (Clegg, "Understanding the Times"), in spite of a rather ambitious title, admits certain limitation of the results – only twenty-three out of one hundred twenty-five returned the questionnaires and moreover, about sixty per-cent of respondents are from one country only (Poland).

208. See Vlasin, "Twenty-Five Years of Mission"; Rițișan and Constantineanu, "APME – A Case Study."

209. Klingsmith, *Missions Beyond the Wall*, 195.

210. Stories of missionaries and popular articles on mission have been regularly published in several Christian magazines, the most popular "Life of Faith" (*Život víry*) which is published by the already mentioned Christian Mission Society (Christian Mission Society, "Life of Faith") Or in another magazine which focuses solely on mission "Nehemia Info" (Endowment Fund Nehemia, "Nehemia Info Magazine").

211. Bargár, "Mission in the Czech Republic," 290.

2.4.3 Religious identity in the Czech Republic

In the 2011 census 10.4 per cent of Czechia's population was Catholic, 1.1 per cent Protestant, 54 per cent other or unspecified and 34.5 without confession.[212] On the basis of this count, less than fifteen per cent of the population is Christian, both practising and nominal, and Czechs are popularly proclaimed to be one of the most atheist nations in the world. Atheism is, nevertheless, a minority worldview: the census statistics[213] and prominent sociologists of religion are in accord that Czech society is not majority atheist.[214] "We could locate most of today's inhabitants of the Czech Republic in the 'grey zone' between a distinctive, reflected, practised religious faith and explicit atheism."[215] They would label themselves as "without confession."[216] Czechs, lacking an orienting focus,[217] can be labelled as "something-ists."[218] The majority of society holds an anti-religious[219] sentiment or is lukewarm in its relationship with any institutionalized faith. Both the Catholic church and mainline Protestant churches struggle with decreases in membership, although several smaller Protestant denominations and other minority

---

212. Škrabal, "Religious Faith of Inhabitants", 5.

213. The data on religion based on the census in 2011 are available at the Czech Statistical Office (Czech Statistical Office, "Religious Faith of Inhabitants").

214. Zdeněk Nešpor admits that Czechs are among the least religious in Europe and in the world (Nešpor, *Too Weak in Faith*, 187), yet he concludes: "Czechs refuse the Christian God. But they do not cease to believe in something" (Nešpor, 188). His colleague David Václavík notices that the non-religious Czechs actually identify themselves with a religious interpretation of the world (Václavík, *Religion and Modern Czech Society*, 215). Czechs are believers in their own way (See also Hamplová and Nešpor, "Invisible Religion," 586; Rattay, "Atheism in the Czech Republic," 22).

215. Halík, "Catholic Church in the Czech Republic," 145. My translation; original: *"Většinu dnešních obyvatel České republiky bychom nejspíše mohli zařadit do určité "šedé zóny" mezi vyhraněnou, reflektovanou a praktikovanou náboženskou vírou a výslovným ateismem."*

216. Václavík, *Religion and Modern Czech Society*, 213.

217. Hošek, "Discerning the Signs," 29.

218. It was Halík who introduced this term and Hošek further described "something-ists" as "adherents of the more or less clearly articulated conviction that there most probably is 'something' above us" (Hošek, "Discerning the Signs," 26). According to him, Czech society is characterized as: "post-rationalist, post-ideological, post-individualistic, post-traditional, post-optimistic and post-materialistic" (Hošek, 32–41).

219. Rather than "anti-religious," Czech scholars prefer to use the more exact term "anti-clerical" (Hošek, "Towards a Kenotic Hermeneutics"; Václavík, *Religion and Modern Czech Society*) to stress the deep-rooted distrust to any institution (Hošek, *Gods Return*, 95; Nešpor, *Too Weak in Faith*, 188). The person in authority can either be a secular clerk or a clergyman.

religious bodies[220] are experiencing growth.[221] There is a rise in interest and growth in alternative religious movements, such as Hare Krishna, esotericism, eastern philosophy, or new paganism.[222]

Nešpor concludes that, "contemporary Czechs are among the least religious in Europe and in the world."[223] This raises the question, what is causing this phenomenon? Arguably, the current state is not only the legacy of forty years of Communism, there are deeper historical influences that predate the Communist coup d'état in 1948; they reach back to the time of re-Catholization after 1620 and the following centuries in the Habsburg Empire.[224] Most scholars agree on the nineteenth and twentieth century factors that led to the anti-religious Czech society of today:[225] 1. Urbanisation, industrialisation and liberalisation in the Czech lands, the industrial centre of the Austro-Hungarian empire; 2. events of the anti-German and anti-Catholic Czech national revival; 3. anti-clerical interpretations of Czech history after 1918;[226] 4. the shift of a large segment of the population to leftist ideology after the First World War and in later periods; and 5. relocation of lower social class settlers to Sudetenland after 1945, when replacing the expelled Germans who were mostly Roman Catholics; 5. widespread secularism, similarly to the situation in the Western part of Europe, where church is perceived to be irrelevant. In addition, understandably, one important factor was Communism

---

220. This is firstly the Orthodox church and in a lesser scale Islamic centre (Nešpor, *Too Weak in Faith*, 139). Islamic faith is fairly new to the Czech context, while Orthodoxy is more historically rooted; a tiny Czech Orthodox community started at the turn of the nineteenth and twentieth century and the contemporary upswing of Orthodoxy is the result of immigrants from the former Soviet Union (Nešpor and Vojtíšek, *Encyclopaedia of Small Christian Denominations*, 18).

221. Škrabal, "Religious Faith of Inhabitants", 5–6.

222. Nešpor, *Too Weak in Faith*, 118. The reason for the trend, in spite of the lack of non-adherence to institutionalized faith, is that "Czech people are generally quite interested in non-materialist interpretations of reality" (Hošek, "Towards a Kenotic Hermeneutics," 1).

223. Nešpor, 187. My translation; original: *"Současní Češi patří mezi nejméně náboženské národy Evropy a světa."*

224. Hošek, *Gods Return*, 87; Hošek, "Discerning the Signs," 14.

225. Bargár, "Mission in the Czech Republic", 272; Černý, "Mission in the Czech Republic," 603; Hošek, "Discerning the Signs," 15–20.

226. After 1918, the religious picture of the country changed completely. 1.5 million people out of 13.5 million left the Catholic Church, and only half of them found a new religious affiliation, others chose atheism or non-affiliation (Hamplová and Nešpor, "Invisible Religion", 591). Most of those who stayed were faithful only on the formal level.

itself, especially the anti-church politics of the 1950s and the "normalisation" of the 1970s.[227]

The Czech religious situation differs from other neighbouring countries that also experienced a Communist regime – Eastern Germany, Slovakia and Poland – where statistics show a more positive attitude to religion.[228] The religious situation in the Czech Republic more closely resembles that of countries such as France, rather than that of its immediate geographical neighbours.[229] Czechs are generally resistant to or suspicious of institutionalized faith, they perceive dogmas and firm beliefs to be a harmful form of fanaticism and often are ready to fight against it. Yet, Czechs "have strong religious 'memory chains' maintained by socialization and education"[230] – and Christianity is their carrier, as the largest official religion which is historically linked to the country. The Czech society is nevertheless split; if Christianity, then which one? Pavel Hošek in his theological essay on Christian values in Czech culture analyses traditions[231] linked to Czech Catholicism and Czech Protestantism and responds to the claims for the genuine Czech Christian roots by arguing against the division by calling the historical narrative "our story": in his perception, all the traditions can be embraced and incorporated in forming a contemporary Czech national identity based on Christian values of the past.[232]

Based on the material above, noting that Czechs are in their majority neither strong Catholics nor Protestants, it can be concluded that the

---

227. After the Communists came to power in 1948, church property was "nationalized," and it was not until 2013 that a law on the restitution of the property was passed.

228. Hošek, "Towards a Kenotic Hermeneutics," 2.

229. "In both the Czech Republic and France, modernistic and nationalistic ideologies led to conflict with the dominant Catholic confession, ideologies which were only strengthened as the result of strong socialist movements . . . Moreover, both countries have witnessed the forced suppression of certain Protestant minorities." (Hamplová and Nešpor, "Invisible Religion", 593; seee also Halík, "Catholic Church in the Czech Republic", 144)

230. Vlachová, "Significant Others", 11. These are: celebrating Easter and Christmas, familiarity with biblical stories and major characters of Christian faith and numerous, widespread usage of popular sayings in Czech which originate from the Bible.

231. Specifically, these are the traditions of Saint Wenceslas (Catholic), of Jan Hus and the Brethren (Protestant), of Saint John of Nepomuk in Baroque (Catholic), and of the National Revival and Masaryk (Protestant). He involves the tradition of Cyril and Methodius, and traditions of the relationship to paganism and to Judaism, both complementary to the development of Christian faith in the specific Czech context.

232. Hošek, *It Is Our Story*, 174–177.

Czech national identity, including the identity of Czech missionaries, is not ethnoreligious.[233]

2.4.4 Religious identity in former Yugoslav countries

While in the Czech case, religious identity seems relatively unimportant, Smith points out that most religious communities coincide with ethnic groups and in his list he includes examples of Serbs and Croats.[234] The corresponding ethnoreligious matching for Slavs of former Yugoslavia emerges according to the following key: Bosniaks – Muslims; Croats – Catholic Christians; Macedonians – Orthodox Christians; Montenegrins – Orthodox Christians; Serbs – Orthodox Christians; Slovenes – Catholic Christians.

Even though the religious identity of individuals might significantly vary,[235] in agreement with the scholars' consensus,[236] it can be asserted that the identity of nations of former Yugoslavia is of an ethnoreligious nature, due to its geopolitical location. In this territory, the Western and Eastern Christian traditions meet, together with Islam having come from the southeast. Ottoman Turks, particularly, impacted the region with their "completely different concept of nation. The Turkish word for nation was *millet*, which denoted religious affiliation."[237]

The American scholar of religion with roots in contemporary Croatia and Serbia, Paul Mojzes, notices that this connection of nation and religion is perceived to be unchanging, and anything that challenges the homogeneity of

---

233. The term "ethnoreligious" was described by Anthony Smith as the situation when religious communities are closely related to ethnic identities (Smith, *National Identity*, 7).

234. "The Armenians, Jews, Monohysite Amharra offer classic instances of this coincidence . . . Poles, Serbs and Croats, Maronites, Sikhs, Sinhalese, Karen and Shi'i Persians are among the many ethnic communities whose identity is based on religious criteria of differentiation." (Smith, 7)

235. "Rather than approaching religious identity as constant across groups, consideration of varying religious ideologies could reveal important differences concerning both individual and intergroup processes." (Ysseldyk, Matheson and Anisman, "Religiosity as Identity," 65)

236. Authors writing on the former Yugoslavia religious situation, in their work, sooner or later tackle the religious aspect connected to the nation. For example, Goodwin, *Fractured Land*, 24 (on national identity of the three nations of Bosnia and Herzegovina); Bellamy, *Formation of Croatian National Identity*, 74 (on the relation of the Catholic church to the party HDZ in Croatia); Parushev, "Mission as Established Presence," 70 (on the role of the Orthodox church in the societies in Eastern Europe).

237. Foteva, *Do the Balkans Begin*, 12.

the ethnoreligious identity is perceived as a threat to group survival.[238] Peter Kuzmič, the leading Protestant theologian from the region,[239] comments that national ideologies replaced Communism[240] and he considers this rediscovering of national religious identity to be harmful: "This powerful synthesis of ethnicity, religion and culture became one of the most dangerous enemies of the progress and peaceful transformation of Post-Communist nations."[241] The sociologist of religion Siniša Zrinščak agrees with this when he explains that "higher religiosity is provoked by social processes but does not mean any real changes in religious orientation."[242] Kuzmič argues that Catholic, Protestant and Orthodox churches of Europe are themselves a complex mission field where nominal Christians need to be awakened – those who are indifferent to their faith and those "who have found false security in a superficially sacramentalistic, cultural and/or nationalistic . . . Christianity."[243] Miroslav Volf, Kuzmič's countryman and distinguished colleague,[244] agrees and to underline the approach in this European context, he uses the metaphorical phrase, "washing the face of Jesus," in understanding that Jesus Christ is already present in every culture, even though he may not yet be recognized or worshiped.[245]

Therefore, in the Protestant Evangelical view, mission means to reach out to all nations.[246] Nonetheless, in contexts of more established traditional

---

238. Mojzes, "Proselytism in the Successor States," 232.

239. Peter Kuzmič himself in his personal life represents a true international person of Yugoslavia (Kuzmič, "Journey from War," 223): Kuzmič is a Slovenian who lived in Serbia, Bosnia and Herzegovina and Croatia, where he founded the Evangelical Theological Seminary in Osijek.

240. Kuzmič, "Christian Mission in Europe," 23.

241. Kuzmič, "Journey from War," 225.

242. Zrinščak, "Anonymous Believers," 77.

243. Kuzmič, "Christian Mission in Europe," 22.

244. This scholar from the Balkans with Croatian, Czech and German ancestors authored a significant book on identity, "Exclusion and Embrace: A Theological Exploration of Identity, Otherness, and Reconciliation" (Volf, *Exclusion and Embrace*) where he argues that we need each other's culture in order to shape us and help us focus on God (Volf, 52–53) who can teach us that "the only alternative to violence is self-giving love, willingness to absorb violence in order to embrace" (Volf, 295).

245. Volf, "Fishing in the Neighbor's Pond," 28.

246. Proclaiming the Gospel message to all, regardless of the jurisdiction, makes the relationship of Evangelical Protestants with traditional ecclesial bodies difficult (Mojzes, "Proselytism in the Successor States", 236) – since their mission is focused inwardly on the believers in diaspora and on preserving the national identity (Parushev, "Mission as Established Presence", 72).

Christian frameworks, genuine effort in evangelism is often considered an unwelcomed proselytism. There is a disagreement between the older and newer churches on what it means to be a Christian:

> The historic Christian churches throughout the former Yugoslavia tend to maintain that baptism and membership in their churches is the mark of being a Christian . . . The evangelical churches in the successor states of former Yugoslavia tend to ask whether persons believe they have an active relationship with Jesus Christ, whether they regard the Bible as the word of God, and whether they are filled with the Holy Spirit. If they are not, such persons are to be evangelized.[247]

Macedonian theologian Kosta Milkov considers the problem of proselytism as a problem of mutual ecclesial exclusivity.[248] Furthermore, the former Yugoslavs share aversion to proselytism because it reminds them of past pressures and fear that it might weaken "the fabric of society, which is held together by ethnoreligious glue."[249] And it is especially in this vulnerable time of reasserting political autonomy that religious identity plays a stronger role.[250] For most former Yugoslavs, national and religious identity are interconnected and, as such, unchangeable. This, on the other hand, entails a challenge and has serious implications for the work of Protestant missionaries, including those coming from the Czech Republic.

2.5 Chapter summary

This chapter was divided into three parts: 2.3 identity, 2.4 culture and 2.5 mission, which have introduced key terms, principal authors and major

---

247. Mojzes, "Proselytism in the Successor States", 236

248. Milkov makes the point by asking: "Should (the Evangelicals) consider the infant baptism of the Orthodox converts valid when the official view of the Orthodox is that they are not really a Church?" (Milkov, "Roots of Proselytism," 102)

249. Mojzes, "Proselytism in the Successor States", 242. Mojzes outlines the specific bad experiences with proselytism the former Yugoslavs have had in the past: 1. one former Yugoslav nation attempting to rebaptize the other during World War Two and the war in the 1990s; 2. proselytism of Communists towards Marxism-Leninism; 3. recommitment to national religious institutions of its own people (Mojzes, 222). Compare with the understanding of proper evangelism and proselytism in the Cape Town Commitment ("Cape Town Commitment," 71).

250. Schreiter, "Communication and Interpretation", 230.

academic discussion in the respective fields, all in consideration of and in connection with the research question and sub-questions of this study on Czech missionaries' identity in interaction with Slavs in former Yugoslav countries. Significantly, this chapter helped illuminate concepts, such as multiple identity facets, identity salience and social identity complexity, which are all pivotal in terms of proceeding towards the main argument throughout the subsequent chapters. The next chapter 3 focuses on the methodology of the research project.

CHAPTER 3

Methodology

3.1 Research framework
3.1.1 Introduction
This research on identity negotiation of Czech missionaries is interdisciplinary. The study of cultural proximity connected to mission work belongs to cultural anthropology and missiology; the concept of social identity complexity is related to social identity theory and belongs to social psychology. Beth Grant in, "Interdisciplinary Research: Challenges and Pitfalls," emphasized the need to balance "the depth of disciplinary research with the breadth of interdisciplinary research."[1] It truly is a challenge to present a study that is deep enough, yet not too absorbed in the specifics.

The study of the Czech identity of Czech missionaries is field-based research, and as a reminder, its main research question is: "How is the identity of contemporary Czech missionaries negotiated in their interaction with Slavs in former Yugoslavia?" The sub-questions are as follows: 1. To what extent can the Slavic Czechs working with their fellow-Slavs in former Yugoslav countries be considered cross-cultural?" 2. "How and in what circumstances does the Czech identity of Czech missionaries become salient or suppressed?" and 3. "How does the missionaries' 'Czechness' interact with their other identity facets?"

---
1. Grant, "Interdisciplinary Research," 24.

1.1.1 Case study

The selected research approach is case study. The prominent author on case study Robert Yin presents it as a preferred strategy when the focus is on a contemporary phenomenon within a real-life context, when "how" and "why" questions are being posed.[2] Other scholars elaborate on its attributes: case study "involves the in-depth exploration of a specific bounded system"[3] and aims to understand in detail a case in order to "shed light on the wider phenomenon of which that case is an example."[4]

Case study is not without criticism, especially due to small sample size and lack of representativeness, limitations in generalization, difficulty representing the results numerically, a tendency to subjectivity, and potential for researcher bias.[5] Nevertheless, the issues from this brief list can also be conspicuous problems in any sociological study.[6] As a matter of fact, case study is characterized by variegated positive features, such as: helping understand complex inter-relationships, being grounded in lived reality, producing more detailed information, putting emphasis on context and human factors and facilitating conceptual and theoretical development.[7] Case study is therefore very apt for this research, as it is found helpful for connecting practices of Czech missionaries to theoretical concepts.

Concerning the issue of case study generalization and replicability, some scholars opt for a theory-before-research approach, while others follow a pattern of theory-after-research and argue that case studies can be used to generate theory.[8] The moments when some case study researchers attempt to secure a wider application of the data can in some instances resemble grounded theory framework where theory arises from the data.[9] In grounded

---

2. Yin, *Case Study Research*, 1.
3. Chmiliar, "Multiple Case Designs," 582.
4. Johnson, "Case Studies," 123.
5. See Johnson, "Case Studies", 125–126.
6. Hamel, Dufour and Fortin, "Conflict of Methods," 24
7. See Johnson, "Case Studies", 125–126.
8. Berg, *Qualitative Research Methods*, 319–320.
9. And even though theory may be derived from the data, it does not entail it always concerns "grounded theory." Bryman notices that "Sometimes the term is employed simply to imply that the analyst has grounded his or her theory in data" (Bryman, *Social Research Methods*, 541).

theory, theory can, according to some, be built from cases as well.[10] This can be done especially by employing multiple case strategy. Connected to this, the term "induction" is proposed as a useful tool to suggest how other similar cases might operate.[11] Other scholars, on the other hand, find the value in understanding the case itself.[12] The sociologist Tim May says that case study is "valuable in its own right. Theoretical development is not the primary aim, but generalization remains possible."[13]

In this research on Czech missionaries, it might, on one hand, seem problematic to draw broader conclusions – either by suggesting that what worked for Czechs in former Yugoslav countries in the thirty years following 1989 would work again in subsequent decades (repetition), or by assuming it would also work for Poles in Bulgaria during the same period (replication).[14] On the other hand, it is desirable to aim for general conclusions. This involves both conclusions for mission practice and principally conclusions which may contribute to existing theoretical literature beyond the studied topic. The goal of this research, which engages theory beforehand and is organized along the three research sub-questions, is to contribute to elements of the existing theoretical concept of social identity complexity and to critique it.

Additionally, the question of single versus multiple case study arises. Czech missionaries and their "Czechness" can be perceived in two ways. They can either be considered as one case – one community, group of people,[15] and one phenomenon specific to time and space.[16] Or they can be treated as individual personal cases, resulting in a multiple case study, alternatively called

---

10. Eisenhardt, "Building Theories," 546–647.

11. "By induction we can conclude from facts in a case a rule that actually is operative, and probably is operative, in similar cases." (Johansson, "Case Study Methodology," 9)

12. See the article by John E. Moriceau, "Generalizability" (Moriceau, "Generalizability," 419). Gomm and the collective of authors add on this: "Some case studies researchers suggest that the goal of their work is not the production of general conclusions, and that this does not detract from its value" (Gomm, Hammersley and Foster, "Case Study Methods," 99).

13. May, *Social Research*, 225.

14. Moriceau mentions several specific forms of generalizability, such as linear or circular generalizability, uncovering causal powers, recognizing the experience in the natural world, imagining a hologram, reoccurring repetitions with dissimilar features (Moriceau, "Generalizability", 420–421).

15. Thomas, *How to Do Your Research Project*, 150.

16. Johansson, "Case Study Methodology", 5.

cross-case study, comparative case study, or contrasting case study.[17] In this research, the common denominator, Czech identity of the missionaries, could imply the single case study approach. The problem might appear that even though Czech missionaries in former Yugoslav countries may form a specific embedded group, it is highly debatable to what extent they could function as one unit.[18] Therefore, multiple case perception is chosen for this research. According to Yin, a case study with many cases can break down each case into a set of common variables.[19] These individual variables can be clustered along commonalities and thematically analysed. Added to this, multiple case study, as utilized in this research, does not entail the comparison typical for cross-case studies. The responses from individual cases are not systematically compared or numbered, yet instead a more synthetic method, led by the three research sub-questions, is chosen for the data analysis.[20]

3.2 Scope and primary sources

3.2.1 Research scope

This multiple case study involves twenty-two missionaries and nine other respondents, thirty-one participants in the research altogether. My initial goal was to involve thirty respondents which was accomplished. Primary respondents were Czech nationals who were or had been long-term missionaries residing in or periodically returning to former Yugoslav countries. Together with that, complementary respondents (senders, colleagues and local people) were involved.

I focus on (a.) Czech (b.) long-term (c.) Protestant (d.) missionaries working with (e.) Slavs in former Yugoslav countries (f.) since the year 1989. Each of the aforementioned limitations in scope call for clarification:

(a) By "Czech" I do not mean people sent by Czech Republic-based churches or Czech citizens, but ethnic Czechs, which is necessary

---

17. Berg, *Qualitative Research Methods*, 326.
18. They come from diverse family, church and regional backgrounds, and they have worked in differing former Yugoslav contexts in various time segments.
19. Yin, *Case Study Research*, 139.
20. The specifics of data analysis are outlined in sections 3.4 and 3.5.

Methodology

in order to evaluate their Czech identity in interaction with other Slavs.

(b) The designation "long-term" is understood here as those who have left their homes and lived in former Yugoslavia for at least one year.[21] Adding to this, the designation "returning" refers to those who have been repeatedly returning to a former Yugoslav country, for instance annually for two weeks over a ten-year period.

(c) I cherish both Catholic and Orthodox tradition, yet I choose to concentrate on those from the Protestant Church.[22]

(d) The category "missionary" refers to a Christian worker in a cross-cultural context ministering to people in another ethnic group.[23]

(e) I focus on Czech missionaries who work with Slavs in the countries of former Yugoslavia – Bosnia and Herzegovina, Croatia, Kosovo, Montenegro, North Macedonia, Serbia and Slovenia. This does not involve ministry to the respective nationals in diaspora, only to those within the area of former Yugoslavia.[24]

(f) The year 1989 was chosen as it was the breakpoint for Czech and Slovak history when the Communist regime ended.[25]

3.2.2 Primary sources

The sample size was defined with the help of on-field circumstances. The interview[26] respondents were accessible to me as a researcher, some in the Czech Republic and others in the former Yugoslav countries during my field

---

21. Admittedly, this usage is at variance with the way "long-term" is most often used in mission practice.

22. To clarify, I aimed to cover all Protestants, yet as the matter of fact, with one exception (Erika 1), the respondents came from various Evangelical and Pentecostal denominations and from independent churches, rather than from the more historical two mainline Protestant churches – the Czechoslovak Hussite Church and the Evangelical Church of Czech Brethren.

23. See Wright, *Mission of God*, 23.

24. There are two factors to this decision. First, I consider it important to involve all former Yugoslav countries, since they are interconnected – often one national group lives in the territory of multiple states. Second, I believe it is achievable to focus on this region as a whole, in accordance with the research scope.

25. This point in history resulted among other things in unrestricted international travelling which meant that also Czech cross-cultural workers could freely go abroad.

26. Specifics on data collecting methods, including semi-structured interviews, can be found further below in the chapter.

trips. The sources encompassed resident missionaries, periodically returning missionaries and supporting or complementary respondents who were linked[27] to one of the missionaries. The following paragraphs and figures briefly introduce these selected primary sources.[28]

Leading primary sources were missionaries who have been staying or stayed in a former Yugoslav country, n=13. I aimed to interview all the residing Czech missionaries in former Yugoslav countries who were in residence or who had returned. The sending initiatives of Czech missions can be, due to their rather small size, quite easily tracked down. Therefore, all of the residing Czech missionaries, with several exceptions,[29] who were active in former Yugoslav countries in between 1989 and 2019, were included in the sample. Similarly, a major part of Czechs who return periodically to former Yugoslav countries could be found due to the relatively small size of the church sending body, yet in this category there were others who could be potentially incorporated in the sample as well and were missing. As for the complementary primary sources, they were composed of a rather heterogeneous collection of interviewees. Still, they were consistent with the research goals, and included sending pastors, leaders of mission agencies, and colleagues in a local team. The following table introduces this sample: (a.) residing missionaries; (b.) periodically returning missionaries; (c.) complementary sources.

---

27. Eventually consisting of n=9, these were either Czechs (senders, friends and supporters), former Yugoslavs (local leaders and co-workers), or international teammates (members of mission organisations).

28. Apart from this, an alphabetical list of the interviewees can be found in Bibliography under Primary sources.

29. A wife of one missionary did not participate and most of the missionaries' children were not included in the sample. Also, those who left in 2021 and later were not part of the research.

Primary sources: Czech missionaries	n
1–2 years	2
2–10 years	2
10–20 years	3
20–30 years	6
Total residing missionaries	13
Total periodically returning missionaries	9
Total long-term missionaries	**22**
Supporting primary sources	9
Total sample	**31**

Figure 3: Type and length of Czech missionaries' commitment

The representativeness of this sample is supported by its diversity.[30] Out of the thirty-one respondents, there were twenty-one males and ten females, there were two respondents aged 20–30, eight 30–40, thirteen 40–50 and eight 50–60. There were Czechs, Bosniaks, Croats and Serbs in the sample. There were three respondents from Serbia, two from Bosnia and Herzegovina, one from Croatia, one from Slovenia and one from South Africa. As for the historical regions of the Czech Republic,[31] there were fourteen from Bohemia (out of these, nine were from Prague), seven from Moravia and two from Silesia.

The missionaries' locations were as follows in the figure below: Bosnia and Herzegovina (five), Serbia (five),[32] Croatia (seven), Slovenia (four), Kosovo (one). In the overall respondents' statistics, the countries of North Macedonia and Montenegro were mentioned only marginally. Then, one missionary was involved in Kosovo and one missionary family in Slovenia. In Bosnia and Herzegovina there was one residing missionary and several returning ones.

---

30. An alphabetical list of the interviewees is under primary sources in the bibliography. For their detailed profiles, including the interview dates, see Appendix A.

31. As a reminder, the Czech Republic, or Czechia, is comprised of three historical regions: Bohemia (*Čechy*), Moravia (*Morava*) and Silesia (*Slezsko*) and of fourteen administrative districts, with the capital Prague (*Praha*) as one of them.

32. Despite the separate colouring on the map, the Vojvodina autonomous province is counted as part of Serbia.

Croatia and Serbia, the biggest former Yugoslav republics, were also the most represented countries in this research sample.

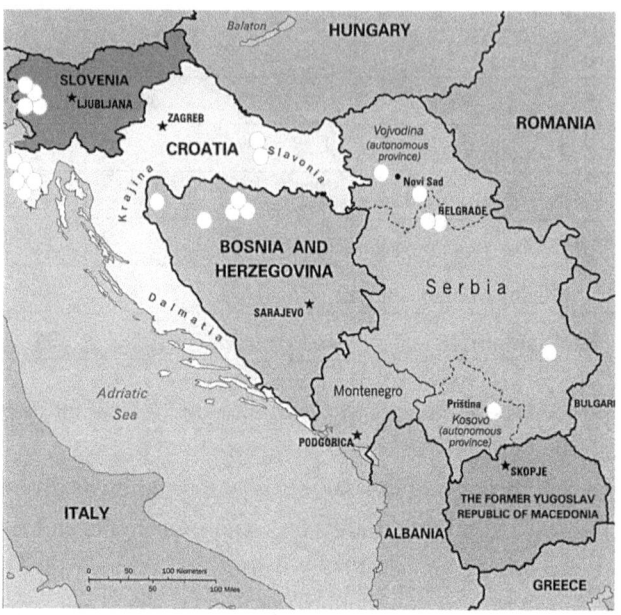

Figure 4: Geographical positions of current, returned, and periodic Czech missionaries in former Yugoslav countries[33]

Because I was able to interview nearly all the known Czech Protestant missionaries in former Yugoslav countries, I can be confident my study is without selection bias. There were two streams of primary sources: I engaged missionaries of differing mission lengths, and supplementary sources that added to the credibility of the findings. My approach was not triangulation[34] per se, but rather a support and an augmentation of the data credibility.

---

33. https://www.mapsland.com/europe/yugoslavia/detailed-political-map-of-yugoslavia-1996. CC BY-SA 3.0

34. The methodological approach of triangulation intends to "decrease, negate, or counterbalance the deficiency of a single strategy, thereby increasing the ability to interpret the findings" (Thurmond, "Point of Triangulation," 253).

3.2.3 Complementary primary sources

Besides the field notes taken directly when interviewing respondents (n=4), I found it immensely helpful to include ethnographic elements, such as diary notes, and photos in this study.[35] Admittedly, these all originate from an authentic, yet limited experience, mainly from Bosnia and Herzegovina – the photos were taken between 2003 and 2018 and the diary notes refer to relevant logs of myself as mission practitioner (n=4) and records of other mission workers between 2008 and 2019 (n=4 as well, provided by three sources). Nevertheless, it appears justifiable to include these personal diaries as a valid source of primary data. Tim May points out that accounts of events provided by the research participants might be inaccurate, he says that "accounts might be accurate but there were circumstances which surrounded these that the interviewee was not aware of."[36] This implies that the subjectivity level of the interviewees' responses may equal the credibility of the personal diary notes. This cannot be asserted with certainty about personal photos – their utilization may indeed occur as problematic.[37] I recognize that while some scholars readily embrace personal diaries as a valid source of data, others struggle with it, and that I have a need to resolve the issue for the sake of this research. It would perhaps be most useful to consider this source of data not on the same level as the direct engagement with Czech missionaries and other respondents, yet to include them in the study as valuable complementary sources in the effort of sense-making. In addition the photographs serve as helpful illustrative points. In summary, the primary sources are:

1. Interviewees from period 2018 to 2019
   (a) Czech Protestant missionaries in former Yugoslav countries
   - Residing (one year or more)
   - Returning periodically

---

35. It needs to be highlighted that this is not participant observation as such, with the researcher as a participant taking field notes, since it would be highly problematic to establish myself as a legitimate observer of processes which were taking place prior to the commencement of this research in 2016.

36. May, *Social Research*, 158.

37. The photos' plausibility can be put under question due to the shift in perspective – the photographer's view was different from the one of the researchers who tend to discover new meanings in a retrospective reflection of themes, in the light of this research.

(b) Supplementary sources related to a particular missionary
   - Czech respondents
   - Former Yugoslavs or other nationals
2. Field notes
3. Personal diaries
   (a) Diary notes from period 2008 to 2019
   (b) Photo diary from period 2003 to 2018

3.3 Research ethics
3.3.1 The positionality of the researcher

It is important to acknowledge that I as the researcher am also a participant in this research process. According to social scientists Bauman and May, qualitative researchers "cannot break off completely from the knowledge that they seek to comprehend."[38]

I realize that my perspective on the research is influenced by my worldview, cultural background and life experience. May affirms that "values and experiences are not something to be bracketed away as if ashamed by their entry in the process."[39] Indeed, it is not uncommon that researchers are relationally involved with those they are studying.[40] I approach the study with a theocentric[41] understanding of the world as an Evangelical/Pentecostal Christian and as an ethnic Czech and a former student of Slavic studies in Prague who has an affiliation to the Czech nation and to Slavic nations in general. Adding to this, I approach the study as someone who has been involved in cross-cultural missions since 2002 and lived in Bosnia and Herzegovina for eight years. I have a warm relationship with former Yugoslav nations and owing to my wife's ancestry, my children were able to obtain citizenship of Croatia, Bosnia and Herzegovina and of the Republic of Srpska.[42] I live in the Czech Republic, yet I am continuously and deeply engaged in former Yugoslavia.

---

38. Bauman and May, *Thinking Sociologically*, 7.
39. May, *Social Research*, 69.
40. Gilbert, Johnson and Lewis, *Missiological Research*, 66.
41. It is mentioned to acknowledge the realisation of personal bias and the Christian worldview where God is in the centre, as opposed to anthropocentrism. The presupposition here is that the larger cosmos or particular cultural realities cannot be properly understood apart from the triune God (See Tennent, *Invitation to World Missions*, 175).
42. For the difference between the Republic of Serbia and the Republic of Srpska see section 1.2.1.

This personal bias of intellectual and emotional attachment to the research topic might have affected the relevance of the on-field investigation and of the data analysis. Some research participants might have adjusted their responses to me as someone similarly involved and someone acquainted with their location. Additionally, other perils common in qualitative research might have appeared, such as the Hawthorne effect when people change their behaviour "because an interest is being taken in them,"[43] or they might have responded with the goal "to give a positive view of themselves in public."[44] I, as a researcher, needed to be constantly aware of the gap that tends to evolve between what the respondents perceived and what I perceived they had perceived. Geertz voiced it even more distinctively: "What we call our data are really our own constructions of other people's constructions"[45] and there certainly are pertinent elements in the statement.

On a more positive note, any of these personal attachments serve not only as weaknesses, but as strengths as well,[46] since possessing both the inside and outside view can be advantageous.[47] According to educational consultant Estelle Phillips, a researcher's involvement is a factor which provides dedication and helps with time management.[48] Moreover, research out of one's life experience can prove to be very fruitful, as illustrated by example of the major scholarly figure Henri Tajfel, whose "interest in social identity and inter-group dynamics was born from his own life-experiences as a European Jew."[49] While I met some of the respondents for the first time, with others I have maintained a long-lasting friendship or at least an acquaintance over the years – which helped to initiate the interviews. A beneficial factor is that none of the interviewees are subordinate to me in terms of work, which probably helped reduce some bias. And as already mentioned, personal diaries as subsidiary data help supplement the main data from the respondents.

This research on Czech missionaries in former Yugoslav countries by a Czech missionary in a former Yugoslav country is not and cannot be in its nature completely neutral and objective. This is acknowledged by my critical

---

43. Thomas, *How to Do Your Research Project*, 141.
44. Roberts, *Biographical Research*, 66.
45. Geertz, *Interpretations of Cultures*, 9.
46. Thomas, *How to Do Your Research Project*, 21.
47. See Bauman and May, *Thinking Sociologically*, 7.
48. Phillips, *How to Get a PhD*, 145.
49. Horrell, "Becoming Christian," 5.

realist position which accommodates the view that facts are not value-free and that a preliminary faith for the purpose at the beginning of an epistemological enterprise is accompanied with passion and the value judgement of a scientist.[50]

3.3.2 Ethics and risk assessment

During my research, I applied the highest standards of ethics, in accordance with the principles of research at the Oxford Centre for Mission Studies, which follow the recognized United Kingdom standards of research ethics.[51] I was committed to operate carefully with the data and to honour the trust given to me by the respondents. The basic principle was not to harm the participants and to be honest with data collection and analysis.[52]

My research did not involve more than a minimal risk. Czech missionaries in the Balkans are presumably not endangered by this type of research. Possible risks could have involved maintaining their privacy, since it is challenging to remain in anonymity, for example, a reader might be able to work out the identity of a Czech missionary in Slovenia. Missionaries were offered anonymity in the research process by not mentioning their name or the country of service. The country could be introduced as a former Yugoslav republic with Christian Orthodox, Catholic, or Muslim majority.[53] Nonetheless, even though a certain level of anonymity could have been ensured by, as Thomas suggests, changing participants' names, omitting information on the church and organisation they work with or by broadening the region of their operation,[54] I am afraid that in the case of Czech missionaries it might still be difficult to remain in anonymity, at least for the audience which is acquainted

---

50. Newbigin, *Foolishness to Greeks*, 77.

51. In particular, with Ethical Guidelines for Educational Research, fourth edition (BERA, "Ethical Guidelines").

52. Basic ethical rules are outlined as follows: "Do not harm participants, maintain their privacy, bring them available benefit, inform them about the research, involve them only voluntarily, ensure research of good quality, be honest with data and reporting" (DeRoche and DeRoche, "Ethics," 337).

53. In the case of majority Orthodox, these would point to three countries: North Macedonia, Montenegro and Serbia. In the case of majority Catholic countries, these would narrow down to two countries, Croatia and Slovenia, and such would also be the case of majority Muslim countries, Bosnia and Herzegovina and Kosovo.

54. Thomas, *How to Do Your Research Project*, 47.

with contemporary Czech missions.[55] In this research, for the text to read well and provide a basic level of anonymity, a nickname for each respondent is used. Several missionaries shared a nickname, therefore the primary sources list involves, for example, Ema 1 and Ema 2.

I am aware that my research, which focuses on identity, might have been pertinent to certain personal and sensitive matters. For this reason, the participants were fully informed in advance about the research's goals, together with possible benefits and risks that come along with it. Since this was not a large-scale research endeavour, each missionary was accessed personally and asked for approval. Along with that, they were also required to approve complementary respondents who would share information about them. The advantage of such approval prior to an interview is that it helps participants to know what exactly is expected from them, including the purpose of the study, expected benefits, possible harm, and information about how the data will be published and kept and for how long.[56] At the same time, it protects the researcher from later potential charges and for all the above reasons a formal signed consent is considered the best.[57] The interviewed missionaries in this research were thus provided with a document, "Informed consent for research,"[58] which all of them signed. From other peripheral participants, such as are those whose notes are quoted or those whose faces are distinctively visible in the foreground of photographs, only an oral or informal written consent was required. The participants' involvement was totally voluntarily, and they were all able to express their will to take part in my work.

3.4 Methods

3.4.1 Data gathering methods

Case study as a research framework might involve various data gathering methods, ranging from quantitative to a combination of methods to solely

---

55. Clandinin notices that the respondents "could be recognized by other members of that subcommunity, no matter how well we 'disguise' them" (Clandinin, *Handbook of Narrative Inquiry*, 554).

56. Thomas, *How to Do Your Research Project*, 49; see also Seidman, *Interviewing as Qualitative Research*, 63–80.

57. DeRoche and DeRoche, "Ethics", 339.

58. See Appendix B.

qualitative research. For the purpose of my research, a lot of information from a relatively small sample needed to be retrieved. So, some approaches, such as survey, would have indeed been limiting.

In this qualitative research it seemed most reasonable to gather material by semi-structured interviews. People possess the "ability to symbolize their experience through language."[59] This sense making, as expressed by language, is perceived by the interviewer, together with non-verbal signals rising from the interaction. Berg defines "interview" as "conversation with a purpose"[60] and adds that "the purpose is to gather information."[61] In this way, a semi-structured interview provides both space for flexible interaction and allows the conversation to cover the designated topics.[62] Within the interviews, elements of narrative inquiry[63] are used: the individual sections of interview questions start with: "Could you tell me your story?", or a similar open-ended invitation. I found it crucial to provide space for the narrative of the interviewees and to utilize strengths which are associated with semi-structured interviews: "greater understanding of the subject's point of view"[64] and "freedom to follow up points as necessary."[65]

Along with the interviews one on one, focus groups were involved in this data gathering method, both as planned sessions and as group interviews led by circumstances. At times it was more natural to hold an interview with a missionary couple, or together with their colleagues. The condition for focus group participants is that they "should possess shared knowledge or experience that connects them with the discussion topic"[66] and it supposedly "uses synergistic group interaction to illuminate informants' attitudes, values,

---

59. Seidman, *Interviewing as Qualitative Research*, 8.
60. Berg, *Qualitative Research Methods*, 101.
61. Berg, 101.
62. Morris in his book, "A Practical Introduction to In-Depth Interviewing," develops in detail the features of an ideal semi-structured interview which is a "free-flowing interaction in which the interviewer allows the interviewee a good deal of leeway. However, the interviewer also directs the conversation as discreetly as possible so as to ensure that the interviewee conveys as much relevant information as possible" (Morris, 3).
63. See Clandinin, *Handbook of Narrative Inquiry*, 5; Webster and Mertova, *Using Narrative Inquiry*, 19.
64. May, *Social Research*, 136.
65. Thomas, *How to Do Your Research Project*, 198.
66. Koeshall, "Focus Group Interviews," 145.

and assessments of a topic or issues."[67] Usage of focus groups can serve as a useful complementary method to the classical interviews, especially the higher possibility for the moderating researcher to observe the participants' body language, emotional reaction and level of involvement in the discussion.

In summary, the data was extracted from multiple primary sources, and the methods of the data retrieval in this research were equally multifaceted. The section (3.2) introduced one major and one complementary data source: respondents[68] (of all three sorts) and personal diary. This diagram illustrates the organisation of the data collection and analysis in this research:

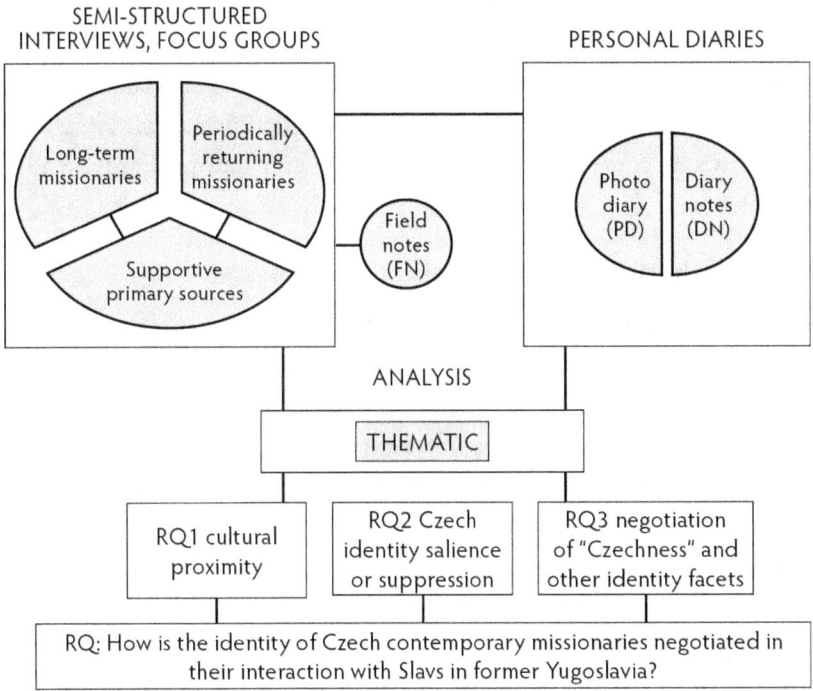

Figure 5: Data collection and analysis diagram

---

67. Koeshall, 145.

68. Respondents of all three categories introduced earlier: Czech residing and returning missionaries and complementary sources – individuals connected to a particular Czech missionary.

The data was gathered specifically from:
1. Semi-structured interviews:
    - Long-term missionaries
    - Returning missionaries
    - Complementary sources
2. Field notes from the interviews (Field notes)
3. Personal diary:
    - Diary notes
    - Photo diary

This outline demands highlighting the emphasis that data retrieved from the interviews was prioritized with the supporting data from field notes and personal diaries. Nevertheless, these were still found to be a suitable complementary method to support the data acquisition from semi-structured interviews, all contributing towards the development of the argument in this research.

3.4.2 Methods of data analysis

The most fitting method of data analysis for this research is thematic analysis. The material was coded[69] and organized into themes in connection to my research sub-questions.[70] The process of coding was performed using hard copy of interview transcripts and a software program as a useful tool.[71] Coding was part of the inductive process which was both analytic – focusing on single interview transcripts – and synthetic – juxtaposing multiple accounts of the respondents and adding the supplementary primary data. Scholars point at possible perils of the thematic analysis coding process: reducing participants' responses and arranging them into themes carries a danger of leaving out the context of the data[72] and the focus might shift

---

69. Coding in this work is understood as "closely inspecting text to look for recurrent themes, topics, or relationships" (Lapadat, "Thematic Analysis," 926), or as "identifying major themes and concepts and their relationship running through the data" (Gilbert, Johnson and Lewis, *Missiological Research*, 312).

70. Morris reminds those who chose this method: "The themes you select should reflect what you think are the important and salient topics and associated data required to answer the research question/s posed" (Morris, *Practical Introduction to In-Depth Interviewing*, 128).

71. The exact procedure of the data analysis is described in detail in section 3.5.

72. Lapadat, "Thematic Analysis", 927.

from the in-depth case study to a more surface level tendency for drawing comparisons.[73] Therefore, to help preserve the context and unique responses of particular missionaries' narrative,[74] analysis elements are found in this research. This may specifically mean including a brief respondent introduction or allowing space for several lengthy passages of the interviewees' statements.

Significantly for this data analysis layout, themes were not organized as they emerged, with the goal to create a theory grounded in the collected material. Rather, underlining the case study approach, themes were generated being cognizant of the three[75] research sub-questions: Initially, missionaries' Czech national identity negotiation in the interaction with Slavs in former Yugoslavia, as perceived by the respondents, were analysed. Then, themes of salience and suppression of the Czech identity of Czech missionaries in the former Yugoslavia were drawn from the data. And finally, the themes of how the missionaries' "Czechness" interrelates with their other identity facets emerged. All emerging themes were arranged in organizing themes, which were subsequently divided into sub themes.[76] Within each chapter, a grid based on theoretical literature was employed:

In chapter 4, the adjusted Trompenaars and Hampden-Turner model of cultural dimensions was applied to help thematically organize the material on cultural differences and similarities, in order to proceed to discuss them in the light of the missiological concept of the E-scale. In chapter 5, first identity salience[77] was taken as an organizing theme for situational negotiation of missionaries' "Czechness." The second organizing theme was suppression of Czech missionaries' Czech identity and simultaneous identity salience and suppression emerged as a third organizing theme in this chapter. Chapter 6 followed the same grid of identity salience and suppression, with special

---

73. May, *Social Research*, 233.

74. The thematic and narrative analysis combination is quite common and a legitimate approach in qualitative research (Bryman, *Social Research Methods*, 554).

75. For reminder, the research sub-questions are: 1. "To what extent are the Slavic Czechs working with their fellow-Slavs in former Yugoslav countries cross-cultural?", 2. "How and in what circumstances does the Czech identity of Czech missionaries become salient or suppressed?" and 3. "How does the missionaries' 'Czechness' interact with their other identity facets?"

76. This approach is used in qualitative research on social identity complexity in O'Connor et al., "Sense of Community."

77. These signify moments when one person's belonging to a group becomes salient over belonging to the other.

regard for the mission work context, as it aimed to arrive at missiological conclusions. The remaining two analysis chapters constituted the culmination of the thesis' focus on missionaries' identity. Here, a specific concept from social identity theory – social identity complexity[78] – created the analysis framework. And more specifically, it was the four interrelations of ingroup memberships representations as particular elements of the social identity complexity theoretical concept. In chapter (7.), the organizing themes were single identity facets of Czech missionaries, while in chapter (8.) the social identity complexity interrelations of intersection, dominance, compartmentalization and merger constituted the four organizing themes.

3.5 Procedure
3.5.1 Performing the interviews
This section commences by describing the interview process which was in progress between June 2018 and December 2019. The total number of the interviews was twenty-five and noticeably, this number is lower than the research participants number (thirty-one). The reason for this is that some respondents were interviewed individually and then in a focus group, while others were interviewed solely within a focus group. Focus groups were spontaneous, rather than planned, in this research. They consisted mainly of married couples and were as follows: Josef 1 and Klára (Croatia), Josef 2 and Renata (Croatia), Vratislav and Denisa (Croatia), Roman 1 and Ema 2 (Serbia), Roman 2 and Erika 2 (Bosnia and Herzegovina), Patrik, Ema 1 and Šimon (Slovenia). At other occasions, wives of returning missionaries (namely Radek, Josef 2 and Roman 2), who have themselves been only one or two times in the Balkans, were present at the interviews.[79] They featured as silent observers with an occasional comment, and only one of them, Erika 2, wife of Roman 2, became more actively involved and eventually was included in

---

78. Roccas and Brewer, "Social Identity Complexity."

79. Due to the circumstances on the field and certain level of informality of semi-structured interviews, other persons at times happened to be present during the interviews as observers. To be precise, these were: my wife during interviews with Vratislav (Croatia) and Denisa (Croatia), Jakub 1 (Bosnia and Herzegovina), Bethany (Erika 1 Bosnia and Herzegovina), a co-worker of Roman 1 (Serbia) and Ema 2 (Serbia), who did not understand Czech, and Daniel (Slovenia) was present at the interview with Patrik (Slovenia).

the research as the thirty-first respondent, in which only thirty participants were originally planned. This proved suitable for the reason that, regrettably, the wife of Jonatán (Croatia) was unable to provide an interview and also because I struggled whether to include several respondents, especially Prokop (Marek Kosovo), in the sample.[80]

Out of the twenty-five interviews, two were performed in English, three in Serbian and twenty in Czech. The missionaries were interviewed exclusively in Czech, and complementary sources required three language options for the interview questions: (1.) Czech, (2.) English and (3.) a language understandable to most former Yugoslavs. The western *ijekavica*[81] variant of the Serbian language was chosen to be suitable for a mutual smooth understanding with native speakers of Bosnian, Montenegrin, Croatian and Serbian languages.[82] It was advantageous for the research that I as the interviewer possess knowledge of this language and therefore local people could be approached directly, without a translator or mediating language.

The interview questions[83] were organized according to research sub-questions into three blocks.[84] Based on the thematic/narrative dynamics outlined earlier, there were two kinds of questions for each of the three blocks: (a.) an initial one opening up the topic and (b.) follow-up complementary questions.[85] It needs to be mentioned that these three blocks were not always pursued chronologically, along the research sub-question one, two and three, yet rather as they emerged from the conversation. The content was significant, not the

---

80. Marek (Kosovo) was included because he had some experience with the Slavic population, despite his main focus being on Albanians. His sending pastor, Prokop (Marek Kosovo), was the only one in the sample who has not been to former Yugoslavia area, yet some of his remarks on Czech identity in relation to their church's first missionary were found helpful for the purpose in this research. In addition to that, a seeming challenge occurred when Jakub 1 during the interview declared that he recently was baptized into the Orthodox church. Still, until May 2018 he organized mission teams to the former Yugoslav countries as a Protestant, so he fits the sample.

81. Serbian uses two variants, Eastern *ekavian* and Western *ijekavian*, and it actively uses two alphabets: Cyrillic and Latin (Symon, "Studies of Contemporary Student Slang", 45–47).

82. And at the same time, it is comprehensible by a majority of the population in Slovenia and North Macedonia as well, even though Macedonian and Slovenian differ linguistically from the Serbo-Croat language system.

83. The list of the semi-structured interview questions in English can be found in the Appendix C.

84. These were labelled: Missionary's Czech identity negotiation in the interaction with Slavs in former Yugoslav countries, Czech identity salience, Multiple identity facets negotiation.

85. Bryman, *Social Research Methods*, 557.

order of the responses. The set of questions prepared for the complementary primary sources was slightly different from the one the missionaries themselves were asked, yet still related to the same research questions.[86] Besides that, at the beginning of each interview, missionaries' backgrounds were investigated to a basic extent. The initial set of questions started with the opening question resembling this one: "Could you tell me something about yourself and how did you get involved in the mission work in . . . [one of the countries of former Yugoslavia]?" It was then followed by questions about the respondents' name, age, town, region, church denomination, mission organisation, location and type of mission work, role in the team, partner church or organisation.

3.5.2 Interview circumstances

Most interviews were approximately forty-five minutes long. Interviews of varying lengths were performed in various circumstances; they were both interrupted or continuous, and they were recorded in different locations – both ideal or loud environments: at our home, at other peoples' homes, or on "neutral ground" – a church building, mission office, cafés and on one occasion, online.

During the interviewing process I faced diverse accompanying conditions and challenges. Some supporting sources were rather cautious, while in contrast others demonstrated a rather overtly wishful approach and highlighted missionaries' positive points. Matěj is an example of the former, when he, quite understandably, gave an account of the three couples his organisation sent to Croatia, and included sensitive matters where he chose to be diplomatic. Eldina, who displayed an affirming certitude in positively evaluating Erika 1, exemplifies the latter.

> Excellent team member, a person that everybody would like to work with, that's how I see her, I would always work with Erika, always.
>
> —Eldina, f (female), supervisor and team leader (Erika 1 Bosnia and Herzegovina)

---

86. The interview questions for complementary primary sources are part of Appendix C as well.

> I think she was definitely a person you could trust, she was a person who was capable – her relationship with God was so evident in everything she did.
>
> —Bethany, f, teammate (Erika 1 Bosnia and Herzegovina)

Erika 1 worked on two teams, Bosnian student mission (Eldina as team leader) and church city team (Bethany as teammate). Eldina's comment, as one of those who were present throughout the interview with her, appears as uncritical and perhaps conditioned by Eldina's favour for Erika 1 and by good memories of the work together in Bosnia and Herzegovina, yet it needs to be added that others, such as Bethany, gave similar accounts. The issue of personal involvement, as discussed in (3.3.1), indeed mattered at times in the interview process, and I had to pay close attention to it when it came to the analysis.

Connected to this, the interviews seemed to have led missionaries towards action steps to (a.) reconsider their ministry, (b.) start something new, and (c.) have at times a direct therapeutic effect.

> It is a question whether the work survives if we go back to Bohemia. . . . It is not a successfully planted church if it is still a mission station. It needs to proceed from local people, it always is different when it is someone local than a so-called "missionary."
>
> —Patrik, m (male), 20–30 years in Slovenia

> You have encouraged me in this, because I have laid aside evangelism in a drawer for some time.
>
> —Radek, m, returning to Serbia

(a.) Patrik, during the two interviews I performed with him, and especially the second one, used the opportunity to reflect on himself as a Czech missionary in Slovenia, and more specifically on the lasting fruit of his family's church planting effort. Radek explicitly admitted he needed to refocus and perhaps plan another trip to Serbia in a near future. These interviews, thus, provided space for the interviewees to reflect on their current ministry.

> So, I think Czechs should be missionaries everywhere . . . Not the saying "a Czech – a musician," yet instead "a Czech – a missionary."
>
> —Roman 1, m, 2–10 years in Serbia

(b.) The statement of Roman 1 makes sense only in context. Having reflected on positive traits of Czech mission, he adjusts a popular saying in Czech, underlining the universal ability to play musical instruments, to underline the potential he alleges. Roman 1 was inspired to encourage Czechs to mission and launched a side ministry by creating a new web site which is devoted to the "Czechness" of mission. Together with him, Jakub 1, who also was prompted to reflect on, "What does it mean to be a Czech missionary?", initiated a similar project.

> And when we got there [went to Croatia in summer 2019], I realized that everything is solved, that nothing lives in me, that it is only in the memories, in past which is stored somewhere. . . . Interesting. This year – a healing. And now I talk to you about these things.
>
> —Jonatán m, 10–20 years in Croatia

Several interviewees were noticeably appreciative they could talk about events of the past, about which it was less easy to share with people in the Czech Republic with no international mission experience. The interview with Jonatán, Josef 2, Renata and perhaps also more respondents seemed to have had some level of therapeutic effect. In other occasions, the interviews entailed reconnecting to old colleagues and friends or making new acquaintances and friendships. In some cases, also helping the missionary reconnect to the Czech environment and engaging in a common project (Kristýna, Erika 1). This is all to underline the personal involvement which, again, with a dose of precaution, I was able to turn from perilous to beneficial.

3.5.3 Other procedural steps in data gathering and analysis

The process of data gathering from personal diaries was, timewise, largely parallel to the engagement with missionaries and other respondents in the interviews, taking place throughout 2018 and 2019. Diary notes and photo diaries were assembled mostly throughout 2018 and 2019 as well. Compared to the interviews, there is not such a need to describe in detail the process of data gathering of the diary notes and the photo diaries. The diary notes were taken as seemed relevant from credible contributors acquainted with the context of Czech Protestant mission in former Yugoslav countries. The photographs originate from a personal photo gallery and were taken either by me or a person in my presence.

Analysis of both the personal diary and interviews is accompanied by a corresponding reference system. When quoted, respondents' names and brief accompanying information are used, for example, Josef 3, m, returning to Bosnia and Herzegovina.[87] When integrated in the text, only Josef 3 is mentioned. Field notes and personal diaries analysis follows a similar shortcut system to the interview analysis, for example, Field notes/Diary notes-SN-2018-07 Sarajevo, Bosnia and Herzegovina (Field Notes/Diary Notes, initials of anonymous informant,[88] date, place) and, for example, Photo diary-2015-11 Skopje, North Macedonia (Photo Diary, date, place).

After a year and a half of field work (June 2018 – December 2019), a careful overall analysis of the interviewees' responses, together with field notes and personal diaries, followed during 2020 and more intensely in 2021. The interview data analysis was executed in three elementary phases: (1.) Respondents were interviewed, recorded and then field notes (Field notes) were made during or immediately after the interview; (2.) the records were transcribed[89] and, (3.) the transcriptions were read and the data organized and coded, with the help of computer-assisted qualitative data analysis software NVivo 12. The programme was used rather as an organizing tool keeping all the data compact[90] and helping to allocate individual quotes to single categories or emerging themes.

---

87. The complete alphabetical list of participants can be found under primary sources in the Bibliography.

88. I realized the need to keep the qualitative research humane, yet regarding these additional personal diaries, for whoever did not sign a written consent, I decided to use only name initials.

89. See interview transcript examples in Appendix D.

90. All the sources of data obtained – interview transcripts, interview notes; and other complementary diary notes and photos – were imported to NVivo.

Figure 6: Illustrative NVivo word cloud frequency from interview transcripts

The analysis was conducted for each primary source individually, according to the single research sub-questions. The data from each individual primary source was subsequently juxtaposed with the data from other primary sources and supplemented with the data from personal diaries: (a.) Photo diary and (b.) Diary notes. The analysis consisted of (a.) sorting the personal photo gallery archive, which was thoroughly searched, with the goal to retrospectively[91] assign appropriate single photographs to the emerging themes within the framework of this research. It also consisted of (b.) making sense of journal logs and linking remarks of eligible people to the three research sub-questions. Ultimately, after the completion of the coding process, all the data was read in parallel and the analysis elaborated in chapters 4, 5, 6, 7 and 8. Even though every analysis chapter interacts with primary sources, and each has its conclusions, some are stronger in bringing forth evidence. There is a sense of culmination in the thesis, and while chapters 4 and 6 lead to certain missiological conclusions, it is chiefly chapter 8 which wraps up the thesis in its central argument and the theory critique.

---

91. Potential perils of this approach are already discussed in (3.2).

3.6 Chapter summary

The necessary methodological foundations for the research project are laid out. To sum up, this research is a multiple case study on Czech Protestant missionaries in the former Yugoslav countries since 1989, who were or have been in residence for at least a year or who have been repeatedly returning. It engages primary sources, missionaries themselves and others engaged on the sending and the receiving side, in semi-structured interviews, followed by case study thematic data analysis. The interview data was supported by the data from personal diaries. Each of the upcoming chapters approaches the data in thematic analysis, attempting to answer the central research question, "How is the identity of contemporary Czech missionaries negotiated in their interaction with Slavs in former Yugoslavia?" Chapter 4 starts by engaging the first research sub-question.

CHAPTER 4

Cross-cultural Dimensions for Czech Missionaries in Former Yugoslav Countries

4.1 Chapter framework

The first analysis chapter 4 attempts to answer the initial research sub-question, "To what extent are the Slavic Czechs working with their fellow-Slavs in former Yugoslav countries cross-cultural?" The thematic analysis in chapter 4 looks at the comparison of the two cultural environments, yet it does not entail a whole-scale comparative cross-cultural study. This chapter's goal is to investigate what could be the areas of cultural difference leading to the circumstances of Czech identity of the missionaries becoming salient or suppressed – which is the focus of chapters 5 and 6.

4.1.1 Models for cross-cultural comparison

Some of the currently most utilized scales of cross-cultural comparison have already been mentioned in chapter 2.[1] Perhaps the most renowned are the five cross-cultural "personality traits" (NEO-PI-3), the six "dimensions of national culture" (Hofstede), and the nine (GLOBE) or seven (Trompenaars) "cultural dimensions." There is not much space to go into detailed description of each scale, yet it seemed useful to at least compare the categories in order to

---

1. For more models see Berry et al., *Cross-Cultural Psychology*, 52–71; 89–96.

notice the certain overlap.² Personality psychologist Robert McCrae organizes the many specific traits of NEO-PI in terms of five factors: neuroticism (N), extraversion (E), openness to experience (O), agreeableness (A), and conscientiousness (C).³ Geert and Gert Jan Hofstede enlist the six-dimensional model of national culture: power distance index (PDI), individualism vs. collectivism (IND), masculinity vs. femininity (MAS), uncertainty avoidance index (UAI), long term vs. short term orientation (LTO), and indulgence vs. restraint (IVR).⁴

Authors of the GLOBE Project distinguish between nine cultural dimensions: assertiveness, future orientation, humane orientation, institutional collectivism, in-group collectivism, gender egalitarianism, power distance, uncertainty avoidance.⁵ Fons Trompenaars and Charles Hampden-Turner, in their focus on how cultural differences affect the process of doing business and managing, identify seven fundamental dimensions of culture: universalism vs. particularism, communitarianism vs. individualism, neutral vs. emotional, diffuse vs. specific, achievement vs. ascription, attitude to time, attitude to environment.⁶ The enlisted models follow five basic categories of "values orientation theory"⁷ which argues that in any culture there is a limited set of preferred value orientations.⁸

Wide distribution, clear structure and organisation – these are undeniable strengths of these classifications, due to the usage of quantitative methods. These models, applied in management and cross-cultural leadership, nevertheless contain certain weaknesses. NEO-PI-3 with its Big Five model, for example, is critiqued that "it does not explain personality function – it only

---

2. In addition, most of the categories are self-explanatory.
3. McCrae, Costa and Martin, "The NEO–PI–3." To add, "NEO" stands for "Neuroticism-Extraversion-Openness."
4. Hofstede Insights, "Six Dimensions of National Culture."
5. Globe Project, "Overview of the 2004 study." GLOBE stands for Global Leadership and Organizational Behavior Effectiveness.
6. Trompenaars and Hampden-Turner, *Riding the Waves of Culture*, 10–29.
7. Kluckhohn and Strodtbeck, *Variations in Value Orientations*.
8. The five problems people in different cultures face are according to this theory: relationship of the individual to others (relational orientation), temporal focus of human life (time orientation), modality of human activity (activity orientation), human being's relation to nature (man-nature orientation), character of innate human nature (human nature orientation), see Trompenaars and Hampden-Turner, *Riding the Waves of Culture*, 16.

describes these individual differences."⁹ In other words, it merely states to which category they belong, and does not explain why people differ on traits or how the traits become manifest in their behaviour.[10]

The next question is whether translations of these instruments are equivalent and relevant across various cultures. In the third version of NEO-Personal Inventory new items are shorter and more up to date.[11] Still, McCrae, while arguing for the model's universality, recognizes this peril with regards to the questionnaires.[12] Recent research of over seventy thousand participants from sixty-two countries showed that personality differences across countries and cultures are surprisingly small relative to individual variations within the cultures.[13] According to these researchers, "accurate ranking of countries on all personality traits is difficult to establish."[14]

Another issue is that cultures constantly change and are not clear-cut units which can be compared as monolithic entities.[15] Cross-cultural comparison can be problematic specifically in Central and Eastern Europe where, as pointed out by the regional scholar Akos Jarjabka, who compared the cross-cultural comparison models, the situation is complicated by the constant change after the economic and social transition.[16] Slovenian scholars, who focused on the Hofstede model, similarly critiqued the functionalist view that values of national cultures are determined by national borders.[17]

---

9. McCabe and Fleeson, "Are Traits Useful?", 289.

10. McCabe and Fleeson, 289.

11. McCrae, Costa and Martin, "The NEO-PI-3", 268. NEO stands Neuroticism, Extraversion, and Openness to Experience.

12. McCrae, "Cross-Cultural Research," 9.

13. Allik, Church and Ortiz, "Mean Profiles of the NEO," 3.

14. Allik, Church and Ortiz, 3. They base this conclusion on findings such as this one example from the region of interest: "It is also surprising that Bulgaria is closer to these Anglophonic and Nordic countries than other Slavonic nations such as Serbia" (Allik, Church and Ortiz, 9).

15. See Wijsen, "Intercultural Theology", 225. With regards to that, this is a useful characterization of culture: "Culture is man-made, confirmed by others, conventionalised and passed on for younger people or newcomers to learn" (Trompenaars and Hampden-Turner, *Riding the Waves of Culture*, 24).

16. The Hungarian social scientist compared GLOBE, Hofstede and Trompenaars and concluded that there is no single "best" method and that it is important to develop a differentiated cultural management method for each culture. (Jarjabka, "Organizational Culture," 34–35).

17. Prašnikar, Pahor and Vidmar Svetlik, "Are National Cultures," 2. The authors claim that corporate cultures will still continue to be influenced by the national cultures of the countries

The perception of cultures on a dual axis map, with its supposedly mutually exclusive categories, has been under critique, among others by the proponents of the Trompenaars model.[18] These authors attempt to regard beyond that and perceive cultures as circles with preferred arcs joined together as they "dance from one preferred end to the opposite and back."[19]

In sum, cross-cultural comparison in quantitative models may run the risk of being descriptive, inaccurate and static. In addition to this, and perhaps even more in the case of qualitative approaches, it may be liable to personal bias and preconceived stereotypes.[20] Trompenaars and Hampden-Turner say that a stereotype, first, "exaggerates and caricatures the culture observed and, unintentionally, the observer. Second, people often equate something different with something wrong."[21] Hiebert calls attention to this general human disposition when "people everywhere seem to look on their own culture as most suitable or best"[22] and observes the tendency for ethnocentrism[23] when comparing cultures. Evaluators, including the participants of this research, thus tend to assign value statements to cultural differences. They perceive the differences as deficiencies, as it seems best to them from the viewpoint of their own most suitable, in this case Czech, culture.[24]

4.1.2 Approach to cross-cultural comparison in this chapter

Another deficiency of the models is their shortage of data for former Yugoslav countries.[25] This is precisely the reason, together with the embedding of

---

of their origin (Prašnikar, Pahor and Vidmar Svetlik, 23). Compare the differences of national cultures in European Values Study (European Values Study, "EVALUE").

18. Trompenaars and Hampden-Turner, *Riding the Waves of Culture*, 27.

19. Trompenaars and Hampden-Turner, 27.

20. "Using extreme, exaggerated forms of behaviour is stereotyping. It is, quite understandably, the result of registering what surprises us, rather than what is familiar." (Trompenaars and Hampden-Turner, *Riding the Waves of Culture*, 26). Giddens defines it as "fixed and inflexible characterizations of a social group" (Giddens, *Sociology*, 668).

21. Trompenaars and Hampden-Turner, *Riding the Waves of Culture*, 26.

22. Hiebert, *Cultural Anthropology*, 38.

23. He understands ethnocentrism as a "feeling of cultural superiority" (Hiebert, *Anthropological Insights for Missionaries*, 98).

24. Berry et al., *Cross-Cultural Psychology*, 8.

25. Usually, only Serbia, Croatia, or Slovenia, are covered, and sometimes Bosnia and Herzegovina, while there is often no data available from North Macedonia, Montenegro and Kosovo.

this qualitative research on Czech missionaries' identity in the discipline of missiology and partially social psychology, that none of these models can be utilized as a hermeneutical tool. Instead, an adapted version of cultural dimensions from the Trompenaars and Hampden-Turner model are applied as a reference point in my thematic analysis of the material on cultural differences. This helps briefly discuss cultural similarities, adding a sense of orientation, while not applying the model as such. Again, no model is perfect and even the Trompenaars and Hampden-Turner model categories tend to be mutually exclusive,[26] yet they seemed best to encompass emerging themes from the responses of my research participants.

Instead of the seven[27] categories of Trompenaars and Hampden-Turner, I decided to work with five. The authors differentiate between the five categories of "Relationship with people" and "Attitudes to the environment" and "Attitudes to time" as sixth and seventh dimensions of culture.[28] In my research, the two lastly mentioned were not listed as separate categories for the reason they both relate to people as well: I assigned attitudes to time to the category of task vs. people orientation (universalism vs. particularism) and attitudes to the environment to the discussion on individualism vs. communitarianism.[29] The Trompenaars and Hampden-Turner model categories here are further rearranged and partially renamed. Therefore, this is the designation and the section structure in this chapter: 3.2 rules vs. people orientation, 3.3 achievement vs. ascription, 3.4 individual vs. communitarian, 3.5 openness vs. closeness, 3.6 temperament differences.

Again, the goal of the chapter is to explore the areas of cultural difference for Czech missionaries in former Yugoslav countries which could lead to salience or suppression of Czech identity in missionaries' circumstances. Measuring cultural differences between Czechs and single former Yugoslav nations is not the central part of the thesis. It does not aim at comparing similarities and differences of both respective cultural settings. Instead, such

---

26. The authors, whose model is used primarily for consulting and training in business across cultures, admit: "Western thinking based on Cartesian logic which forces us to describe something as either one thing or the other, rather than entertaining several possibilities at once or seeing how one thing can lead to another" (THT Consulting, "Culture for Business").

27. Trompenaars and Hampden-Turner, *Riding the Waves of Culture*, 8–10

28. Trompenaars and Hampden-Turner, 8–10.

29. Both attitudes to time and environment in this perspective are related to human behaviour.

comparison serves as a preparation for Czech identity facet salience and suppression in the former Yugoslav cultural environment and especially for the later discussion on Czech identity facet's interrelations.

Lastly, several notes to the interviewing process for this chapter follow. The first[30] set of interview questions[31] opened by asking: "To what degree, according to you as a Czech, is the work with Slavs in former Yugoslavia cross-cultural?" After that, variations of these supplementary inquiry questions followed: "How do you perceive differences and similarities between the Czech and... [former Yugoslav] culture?", "How do Bosniaks, Croats, Macedonians, Montenegrins, Serbs and Slovenians respond to you as a Czech missionary?", "Could you recall a moment when they were accepting you and listening to you because of that, or when they rejected you, or when they were indifferent?"

4.2 Rules vs. people orientation

The first adapted category is orientation to rules and tasks, as opposed to people.

> Czechs have everything organized in categories... There [in Slovenia], they are not strict, they don't follow procedures.
>
> —Daniel, m, returning to Slovenia
>
> The arrangements that were agreed on are often not valid, it is more on the line of relationships than obligations.
>
> —Matěj, m, leader of sending mission agency (Josef 1 Croatia)
>
> I think Czechs hold the upbringing more firmly. Do you know when the children went to sleep when they were little? And kids here go to sleep at ten or eleven.... Looser rules.
>
> —Kristýna, f, 20–30 years in Serbia

---

30. The first set of questions' section on cultural similarities and differences was proceeded by a preparatory set of questions focused on the exploration of the missionary's background.

31. It needs to be noticed that the set of questions prepared for the complementary primary sources was slightly different from the one the missionaries themselves were asked, yet related.

In the Trompenaars and Hampden-Turner model of cultural dimensions, the universalist dimension of culture assumes that one good way must always be followed, while the particularist reasons that friendship coming with its special obligations is supposedly always to be prioritized.[32] Organized and strict (Daniel), obligations (Matěj) and a firmer way of raising children (Kristýna) stand in contrast to a looser following of procedures and focus on relationships. These responses are limited in range and there is room to fill spaces in-between the two seemingly opposite poles – and this is valid for each cultural dimension category as the analysis proceeds. Order, following rules and procedures vs. certain spontaneity is related to social behaviour regarding the management of time.

> There is more of a structure. I think Erika comes to mind in the way she was so structured in everything . . . And sometimes the culture here is very like: "You know, let's meet whenever." So, I think time is one way of thinking, a difference.
>
> —Bethany, f, teammate (Erika 1 Bosnia and Herzegovina)
>
> They are focused on relationships, it is important to build relationships and simply to be together. We Czechs are focused on that something is happening, that things have a flow and move forward, to see some results.
>
> —Erika 1, f, 1 year in Bosnia and Herzegovina
>
> We were shocked when we moved here that everything is slow paced here, cup of coffee, we had to learn to slow down.
>
> —Klára, f, 20–30 years in Croatia

The South African missionary, who has been in the country for over twenty years highlighted the challenge of negotiating the need for structure of Erika 1. The following interview extract from the Czech respondent herself indicates she has recognized the difference and progressed in the negotiation of stress on rules, results and activities versus on relationships. Klára's response similarly refers to the initial stage of hers and her husband's mission stay. In Bosnian, Croatian, Montenegrin and Serbian there is a phrase "*samo polako*" ("take it easy") which literally means "only slowly," and it underlines

---

32. Trompenaars and Hampden-Turner, *Riding the Waves of Culture*, 8.

the time management style when "instead of the efficiency of getting from A to B in the shortest possible time, there is the effectiveness of developing closer relationships long-term."[33] For example, while Czechs would perhaps enjoy chatting on the way walking to some goal point, former Yugoslavs, enjoy walking back and forth in *čaršija* (the main pedestrian street), as the picture below illustrates. They prefer going to the same location, and perhaps meeting a familiar person.

Photo diary-2003-08 Struga, North Macedonia

Time management is unavoidably connected to efficiency and attitudes to work.

> In the Balkans you say: "We'll start at 8 a.m.," so, first we get coffee, a cigarette, a relaxed time.... It means we meet at eight, but first we rest and so on. In Bohemia it means the lights are on, we have the tools, and we are working, starting at eight.
>
> —Daniel, m, returning to Slovenia

Daniel, like many Czechs predominantly from Bohemia, inaccurately uses here the term of one of the Czech Republic historical regions "Bohemia" ("*Čechy*") instead of a more encompassing term "Czechia" ("*Česko*"). In his

---

33. Trompenaars and Hampden-Turner, *Riding the Waves of Culture*, 135.

response, he points out that Czechs in former Yugoslav countries might at first learn to adjust to the rhythm of the local affairs. Work itself first entails the fellowship with co-workers, and there often is no sharp rule that work starts at 8 a.m. The following two responses refer to anecdotes from similar life situations linked to differing perception of time.

> They are different, they say: "We will come at 7 a.m.," and they come at 9, you would kill them, as we say. Until you get used to that 7 is 9, I got angry a couple of times at one brother, he would say: "I will come in ten minutes," and he came in half an hour. I said: "So, why the heck do you say that?" Tell me: "I don't know when I can come." And I got angry at him a couple of times and then he was crushed and apologized to me. So, I say that we are kind of Germans, 7 is 7 and not 11. And I made breakfast and he came for a late lunch, I prepared eggs and told him: "You will eat it cold."
>
> —Radek, m, returning to Serbia
>
> We are taught by the German mentality that we like to keep the terms and when we make a deal it needs to be valid. Here it is negotiated and almost always it is different than how it was agreed. When you order a plumber on Wednesday at five, then you are literally shocked when you see him on Wednesday at five, mostly he does not come. Mostly he comes on Thursday and in April (laugh).
>
> —Josef 1, m, 20–30 years in Croatia

Radek who periodically travels to Serbia, narrated in a very expressive way in his central Moravian accent this story of how he made breakfast for the local pastor. Even though he might have uttered this still in some sort of remaining frustration, there was a tone of amusement in his voice. Josef 1, actually together with his wife was the first Czech missionary sent out after 1989 who has remained in the target country; he takes these matters with humour where he has adjusted. Both referred to Germans, and they were not alone. Other respondents made similar comments, recalling here the introduction on the West versus East geopolitical spatiality of Czechia in chapter 1. Czechs share the longest common history with Germans who used to constitute about one third of the country's population before the expulsion in 1945.[34] Czech-German relations are generally looked upon as a history of conflict, as they are regarded with envy, suspicion and readiness to resist.[35] On the other hand, to expound the rather ambiguous perception, Germans are often admired as an economic model and as an example in diligence.[36]

> It is known that Czechs are half-Germans, so they like the order, regularity, so when the train leaves on time, when things are in their place, when opening hours agree with what is written on the store – and that does not sometimes happen in a foreign country where it may be written: "I'll come immediately."

—Jakub 1, m, returning to Bosnia and Herzegovina

Photo diary-2009-01 Mostar, Bosnia and Herzegovina

---

34. "Out of 10 million inhabitants of the Czech lands (in 1921) it was 67.7 per cent Czechs, 30.6 per cent Germans and 1 per cent Poles" (Drbohlav et al., "Czech Republic on its Way", 8). "During the years 1945–1947 some 2,820,000 Germans were transferred and expelled from Czechoslovakia to Germany or Austria in three, organised as well as spontaneous, waves" (Drbohlav et al., 8).

35. Auer, "After 1989", 413; Vlachová, "Significant Others", 9.

36. See Pynsent, *Questions of Identity*, 184.

The photograph illustrates Jakub's observation at the end of the statement on the difference of more fixed vs. flexible rules. It says "open" ("*otvoreno*"), on a locked door where a phone number and a person name are provided. To expound on Jakub's assertion, it is highly questionable that Czechs are half-Germans. It is definitely not something widely "known," yet the respondents repeatedly related to the proverbial German punctuality as a reference point in the comparison of Czechs and former Yugoslavs. This perspective is present in contemporary Czech scholarship as well, theologian Petr Činčala asserted "the Czechs are ethnically Slavs, but they are less Slavic than other Slavs."[37]

> The difference that I see that Czechs are harder workers than Bosnians in some way, I mean, there are Bosnians who are also hard workers but Bosnians also like to rest and relax I think more than Czechs. . . . I see Czechs and Dutch very close concerning being active, but far from us (laugh).
>
> —Eldina, f, supervisor and team leader (Erika 1 Bosnia and Herzegovina)
>
> Our view is that they [Slovenes] are much closer to us than other Yugoslav nations, to have a party for three days, it is not here. They are hardworking people, dutiful, more similar to us, apparently and that is my theory, more mixed up with German element than the others, like Czechs. So, in this they are much more similar to us, you don't have to argue with them in that, some "punctuality" [in Slovenian], or how you say it in Czech, is here, some degree of organisation, even though the Balkans influences them.
>
> —Patrik, m, 20–30 years in Slovenia

Eldina and other non-Czech[38] participants in this research, together with Czech respondents, such as Patrik, while attempting to engage in cross-cultural comparison, speak of their limited experience. It probably is valid

---

37. Činčala, "Theoretical Proposal for Reaching," 86.

38. Eldina figures as one of the non-Czech interviewees of this research whose competency to respond on this is based on multiple years that Czech missionaries have worked alongside them, together with other teammates from other, mostly Western, countries. In addition, all of those involved in this research have visited the Czech Republic at least once.

that Czechs are more active and hard-working than Bosnians in some areas. And Slovenes certainly do differ in many cultural traits from other former Yugoslavs.[39] Certainly, for some cultures, "doing" seems to play a more important role: "We must keep busy. To be idle is laziness – one of the key sins of our culture."[40] Still, it could seem simplistic to mark certain cultures as task-oriented, and other as people-oriented, since all of us are involved in tasks.

4.3 Achievement vs. ascription

> It is very interesting to see how Czech missionaries desire that their mission work is successful. . . . Kristýna is focused on finishing things, she is not fatalistically oriented. In our culture it is like if things happen, they happen, or don't happen, fatalistic. She is a person who is very hardworking and takes responsibility into her hands and knows that she can change results by participating in things.
>
> —Vladan, m, pastor and team leader (Kristýna Serbia)

While achievement means that the status depends on what a person has accomplished, ascription means that status is attributed by birth, kinship, gender, age or connections.[41]

Vladan's perception of Kristýna as an achiever in contrast to his view of Serbian culture as more driven by fate introduces this category of cultural dimension and at the same time it implies how these dimensions are in fact interconnected. The seemingly delineated terms like "rules," "achievement," or "individualism" may function as part of a larger unit, as there are no sharp edges to the categories. The Hofstede model for the similar cross-cultural traits separates "masculinity" versus "femininity," where the high (masculine) score indicates that the society is driven by competition, achievement and success and low (feminine) score indicates that "quality of life is the sign of

---

39. See (4.3). Patrik further developed on the contemptuous ethnic Slovenes' attitude to immigrant Slavs from other former Yugoslav republics: "They are Slovenes, Europeans, they despise *južnjaki* (southerners)" (Patrik, m, 20–30 years in Slovenia).

40. Hiebert, *Anthropological Insights for Missionaries*, 121.

41. Trompenaars and Hampden-Turner, *Riding the Waves of Culture*, 135.

success and standing out from the crowd is not admirable."[42] In this country comparison, the Czech Republic scores 57 as masculine, while Bosnia and Herzegovina (48 points), Montenegro (48 points), North Macedonia (45 points), Serbia (43 points), Croatia (40 points), and Slovenia (19 points) score as "relatively feminine societies."[43] It needs to be stressed that the data for Bosnia and Herzegovina, North Macedonia and Montenegro are only estimates, furthermore, Kosovo is not included in the study at all. The results for Slovenia call for vigilance, since Slovenia usually is on the other side of such scales. A recent wide scale study comparing behaviour of businesspeople from Slovenia, Serbia and Russia, oppose these particular findings.[44] Regardless of the differences of cultural traits between single former Yugoslav countries, it seems there is a moderate difference between their cultures and Czech culture.

> Jonatán: I don't believe humour of the type of Jára Cimrman [Czech fictional hero] would spread there (laugh), it is totally boring.
>
> Interviewer: Well, where would the Jára Cimrman humour spread?
>
> Jonatán: Quite easily to England, they have a dry humour. . . . But the dry Balkan humour is crueller. A big measure of situational spontaneity, some things sprout out as a fountain of a situation and it is natural for them. It seems to be they make fun of each other, about Montenegrins, about Bosnians.
>
> Interviewer: But Jára Cimrman he makes fun of himself, of Czechs.
>
> Jonatán: They don't know that, I don't think so. Of course, there are always exceptions.
>
> —Jonatán, m, 10–20 years in Croatia

---

42. Hofstede Insights, "Six Dimensions of National Culture."

43. Hofstede Insights, "Hofstede Insights – Country Comparison." Only four entries are allowed at a time on the interactive webpage.

44. This study unfortunately does not contain the cross-cultural appliance of the Hofstede model (this is applied only to Slovenian managers), yet the Trompenaars and Hampden-Turner model results for achievement versus ascription speak clearly: Slovenia scored 54.6 and Serbia 46.2 (Prašnikar, Pahor and Vidmar Svetlik, 16).

> I have a feeling when talking to Serbs here, they look for identity in history, what belonged to them, what area of land, that we Serbs or Slavic nations are very old, and they keep talking about that... I have never met this in Bohemia, here people refer to that a lot and they try to find their identity in this – at one point of history they were great and then someone took them over.
>
> —Roman 1, m, 2–10 years in Serbia

One area related to the issue of status is certainly the humour. While former Yugoslavs abound with humour on the account of Bosnians (that they are supposedly unintelligent) and Montenegrins (that they are supposedly lazy), Czechs, who of course make fun of others, especially Germans and Austrians, often address their own failures in a specific indirect humour. Perhaps the best example of this is the most translated Czech novel, "The Good Soldier Svejk: And His Fortunes in the World War,"[45] about a Czech soldier in the Austrian army pretending to be simple minded and foolish. The figure of Jára Cimrman[46] was invented by a group of artists in the 1960s and since then became very popular and even attempted to participate in the competition "The greatest Czechs" in 2005.[47] He seemed to excel in everything, alluding to Czech patriotism and at the same time mocking Czech powerlessness under the Austrian empire.[48] This is the reason Jonatán, in his response, was not sure whether a similar type of humour, embodied in the person of Jára Cimrman, would arise in former Yugoslav countries. There, Roman noticed, to place history as an object of humour is highly problematic. In addition to that, it can be said that history seems to play a more intense role perhaps also due to fresh memories of the war which accompanied the disintegration in 1990s. Status here can thus be considered threatened when one makes fun of himself and questions historical issues related to neighbouring countries.

---

45. Hašek, *Good Soldier Švejk*. This novel on a soldier who pretended was first published in the years 1920–1923.

46. The surname refers to its original German version Zimmermann, alluding to the fact that a huge percentage of Czechs have German surnames.

47. O'Connor, "Jara Cimrman."

48. See Holý, *Little Czech*.

In cultures of former Yugoslav nations, seemingly more than in Czech culture, status, whether acquired or ascribed, needs to be manifested:

> They wear nice looking clothes, brands, and Czechs look like – it is incomparable. We were considered by them as those who wear socks in the sandals.
>
> —Renata, f, 10–20 years in Croatia

> Some Czechs wear socks in sandals, that is more of a funny reference than something serious, but we had a lecture by Czech lector recently about that. One thing that was said that here in Czechia there are people who have money and don't need to manifest it, while those are very few in Serbia. Because there you should show that you have certain status in society and property.
>
> —Miroslav, m, acquaintance and director of Czech minority association in Belgrade Serbia (Kristýna Serbia)

> Here it is not important what kind of suit you have, but in Serbia it is important it is expensive, branded, so it is obvious there is some money behind it. I had a friend who went out in the evening and he had clothes on for seven hundred Euro. And I know he was unemployed.
>
> —Miroslav, m, acquaintance and director of Czech minority association in Belgrade Serbia (Kristýna Serbia)

> If there is a birthday you need to look like you have more money.
>
> —Renata, f, 10–20 years in Croatia

Renata and Miroslav refer to a rather amusing stereotype of Czechs that former Yugoslavs often utter as they notice Czechs' comparatively lower taste in clothing, which is highlighted by the socks.[49] In his second response, Miroslav expands on this by providing an example of pride in appearance, even though this could well relate to some Czechs who tend to show off as well. The significance of external appearance is, according to these respondents, connected to the need to display it. People in former Yugoslavia value abundance in hospitality and celebrate in a fancier way. The occasions could

---

49. The socks are related to practicality which is addressed later in the analysis.

be, for instance, a birthday party for children (Renata's example) or a wedding (in the picture).

Photo diary-2012-09 Novo Čiče, Croatia

In the realm of weddings, and other formal public events, former Yugoslavs prefer more structure than Czechs who adhere to informality.[50] This is connected to Hofstede's power distance and even though the Czech Republic with its 57 points scored "relatively high" among cultures accepting hierarchical order, the numbers for other countries are much higher: Slovenia 71, Croatia 73, Serbia 86, Montenegro 88, Bosnia and Herzegovina 90, North Macedonia 90.[51]

This means former Yugoslav cultures, viewed through the lens of this culture dimension, are less egalitarian and status is more ascribed than achieved. Unsurprisingly, the matter of hierarchy and the stress on ascribed status and prestige seems to be more obvious as one moves southwards[52] from central European areas. As already introduced by Miroslav and Renata, one such indicator is clothes:

---

50. In Czech culture, there is no one "ascribed" way to organize a wedding (and a huge percentage of the population do not wed at all), celebrate Christmas or perform a funeral. This differs in southern Slavic cultures when these moments are usually linked to a specific religious tradition.

51. Hofstede Insights, "Hofstede Insights – Country Comparison."

52. Think of for example, Scandinavia vs. southern Italy.

Czechs would go in a swimsuit to the bank. . . . Here, in the church, when you are a pastor or a leader you need to dress nicely. To preach in a sweater or in a pulled-out T-shirt like in Czechia, that is not appropriate.

—Josef 2, m, 10–20 years in Croatia

So, in order to preach or to lead people, we needed to learn to dress nicely, wives need to be dressed well, children too and if there is one stripe missing on your sweatpants, you stitch it there.[53]

—Josef 1, m, 10–20 years in Croatia

The interviewee said off the record that the locals took pity on him, and he was given a pair of nice jeans and branded clothes to wear.

—Field notes-DS-2018-10 Prague, Czech Republic (Marek Kosovo)

Other objects of material culture,[54] apart from clothes, which display status may be fancy cars, huge houses, or excess of food and drinks in hospitality. An anecdote says how a Bosnian disgraced his village – while all others would drive Mercedes or BMW, he came back from Germany in a Škoda Superb. It may sound a bit exaggerated, yet the point is that in certain cultures if one has resources, he is supposed to show it off. Sometimes it is in order not to put the family to shame, and it might be intentional or unintentional, simply imparting the values:

Huge houses where several generations lived together, that's what we noticed.

—Erika 2, f, 30–40, returning to Bosnia and Herzegovina

The observation of Erika 2 points to all the three parts of Hiebert's definition of culture as an "integrated system of learned patterns of behaviour, ideas and products characteristic of a society":[55] Houses in Bosnia and Herzegovina are big in comparison to Czech houses (material culture); they are built that

---

53. The interviewee is referring to the Adidas brand with three stripes.
54. See Hiebert, *Cultural Anthropology*, 33.
55. Hiebert, 25.

way because children, usually sons, remain living there and take care of their family (behaviour); the reason why generations live together is the family is of value (ideas).

Trompenaars and Hampden-Turner presented results of a questionnaire on the percentage of respondents who disagree that respect depends on family background. For Serbia it was sixty per cent, while for the Czech Republic it was eighty-seven per cent.[56] The strong sense of allegiance to family and friends is connected to the topic of nepotism and corruption in work ethics:

> They get on my nerves and some of the Serbian characteristics I don't like because I have tried to start business there and I got angry several times because "we talked, we talked and there was nothing" [in Serbian]. So, a year went by (laugh), the Lord God probably didn't want that, we tried several times, in different companies, but everyone wanted a commission fee from it.
>
> —Radek, m, returning to Serbia

> Here, people are more turned to each other, because they depend on finances, they have lower incomes, and depend on each other.
>
> —Stojan, m, husband (Kristýna Serbia)

> Ok, a good thing in Serbian culture, the individualism – when people do not have opportunity to be independent, when they don't have material goods they can rely on to solve their everyday problems, they rely on people. We don't have material resources, but we have resources in social relationships, so we always lean on one another.
>
> —Vladan, m, pastor and team leader (Kristýna Serbia)

> Nepotism always looks like a negative thing, the relationship in that structure, looks as negative for those out of that culture, it looks like nepotism. For us, who are from this culture, it does not look like nepotism, it looks like a machine that moves society, it does not have to be positive, neither negative, simply, that's how things work, you can tell me positive things, or negative things. It depends what kind of person you are, if you build it on biblical

---

56. Trompenaars and Hampden-Turner, *Riding the Waves of Culture*, 106.

ground, knowing that this is not a Western culture, but honour and shame culture, that "patronage" [in English] exists . . . So, it is a habit and here it functions that we take care for each other.

—Vladan, m, pastor and team leader (Kristýna Serbia)

In Serbia and most other former Yugoslav contexts, there are situations when Czechs' approaches, such as Radek, end in collision. They learn that it is not sufficient to appear on the scene and prove they are good in a certain area (achieved), yet instead they need to know someone (ascribed) – and if they do not, they may be expected to provide an alternative (to pay). This is certainly not connected to specific cultures, but rather systems, especially in the whole post-Communist world. Still, the necessity of a connection[57] to achieve various important or even everyday matters, as Radek was learning, is valid in former Yugoslav countries perhaps in a bigger scale than in the Czech Republic. His frustrated response on work ethics linked with nepotism stands in contrast to Vladan's explanation of positives of the work based on relationships.

Vladan, together with Stojan, clarifies the matter from an insider perspective: in hierarchical cultures, such as seems the Serbian opposed to the Czech, nepotism is not necessarily something negative. The historical and current political and economic predispositions compel people to lean on each other – the system fails, yet family and friends can take care of themselves. There is much strength in such comprehension, as Vladan highlights, yet the side effect is that it unfortunately discourages individual efforts for achievement, and many young people emigrate to make fortunes in the West.

Hiebert adds that in largely Western-oriented cultures people are expected to take care of themselves, while in other cultures such self-reliance behaviour marks a loner – someone who is antisocial.[58] With this in mind, the discussion traverses to the following cultural dimension of individualism versus communitarianism.

---

57. Besides the standard word "veza," there is a specific slang version "štela" in Bosnian, Croatian, Montenegrin and Serbian.

58. Hiebert, *Anthropological Insights for Missionaries*, 124.

4.4 Individual vs. communitarian culture

In measuring cultural differences, people regard themselves primarily as individuals or primarily as part of a group.[59] A group of Czech short-term missionaries from my home church in Prague under Daniel's leadership came to order a hamburger-like grilled spicy meat, with various side dishes at a fast-food booth in a Bosnian town in October 2019:

> When we were ordering *pljeskavica*, each one of them was asking: "What is this, what is that?" And I was directing them to what is considered the standard.
>
> —Daniel, m, returning to Slovenia

Daniel is, due to his family heritage (he was born in Croatia to Croat father and Czech mother), familiar with the local culture, was "directing them to what is considered the standard." He was trying to simplify it to the waiter (and to himself) and was explaining to the group that there is only a limited number of options and that they cannot continue reconsidering the side dishes – or later in a café to expect to find coffees with various flavours fitted to a personal taste.[60] Instead, they should for a moment forget their individual requests and simply get what everybody gets, have the order prepared in advance and stick to it.

The difference between the individual and communitarian results in Hofstede's model were: The Czech Republic scored as a more individualist society by 58 points, while the southern Slavic countries were considered collectivist: Croatia 33, Slovenia 27, Serbia 25, Montenegro 24, Bosnia and Herzegovina 22, North Macedonia 22.[61] This is manifested in a close commitment to the member group, in most cases the family:

> Here [in the Czech Republic], we are more individualistic and in Bosnia it is the family. They are together and what others think, what society thinks, it all plays a very important role.
>
> —Erika 1, f, 1 year in Bosnia and Herzegovina

---

59. Trompenaars and Hampden-Turner, *Riding the Waves of Culture*, 8.

60. I was present with him and the group as similar situations occurred during breakfasts and at cafés.

61. Hofstede Insights, "Hofstede Insights – Country Comparison." Again, the results for Bosnia and Herzegovina, North Macedonia and Montenegro are only estimates.

> I was surprised a lot by the homelessness, it is very different than here in our country. . . . Even poor people had homes in Bosnia and Herzegovina.
>
> —Josef 3, m, returning to Bosnia and Herzegovina

The communal aspects the respondents notice, such as the significance of the opinion of others, taking care of one another, or simply the value of spending time together, is typical for communitarian cultures. When describing the category, Hofstede adds that such loyalty often "overrides most other societal rules and regulations."[62] Josef 3 pointed out the comparative lack of homelessness, which is certainly lower in comparison to the Czech Republic, thanks to the values of family honour in a more collective culture, and perhaps also due to a less efficiently functioning system of state social care, so people are compelled to take care of each other and function as a community.

Another two respondents provide a Serbian perception of Czech culture with regard to individualism and communitarianism.

> Hm, similarities: Czechia is Slavic, the fellowship among people, seeing each other more often. Instead of the Western idea "I can do it by myself," but it is more like: "I need fellowship, I need friends, I need to invest in my friends." . . . And people are more relaxed compared to people in the West.
>
> —Miodrag, m, colleague (Kristýna Serbia)

Opposed to what Miodrag stated, his team leader Vladan classified Czechs as individualists:

> Whenever I come up to Czechia, the Western individualistic influence is there. Our influence is more Eastern, collectivist. Here, your identity gets expressed by what other people think about you, rather than I am an individual for myself. Differences are not supported here, they don't get encouraged, while in the West up in Czechia, through all that I saw, it is totally OK to be different. Here it is not at all OK, it is encouraged to be the same as others. So, the differences are very big and it is very important to understand that the culture which is in Serbia,

---

62. Hofstede Insights, "Hofstede Insights – Country Comparison."

Bosnia, Croatia, is a so called "honour and shame" [in English] culture which comes from the East.

—Vladan, m, pastor and team leader (Kristýna Serbia)

Interestingly, Miodrag and Vladan differ in their perspectives, which might be due to the generational difference or the fact that Miodrag goes to Czechia more regularly to visit a partnering organisation, spends more time there with his young peers and moreover has learned to speak basic Czech. Vladan used the word "up" ("*gore*") which often does not refer only to the geographical direction, and can be applied in the sense of looking up to Czechia – as part of the European West. They both in their comparison engage another outgroup, the Westerners, which would in their case be predominantly the English, since their teammates, apart from Kristýna, are English, including the pastor's wife. Vladan noted that "differences are not supported here" and truly, in more collectivist cultures, individuals are not encouraged to stand out. Being distinct from the collective is connected to the sub-theme of practicality:

> When I think of Erika I also remember her little bag she was carrying with a little food in it and I don't know whether it's something in Czech culture that you have to make sure that you have the food with you.
>
> —Bethany, f, teammate (Erika 1 Bosnia and Herzegovina)
>
> So, the differences that come to mind are coming in summer and sort of into the fall and wearing socks and sandals (laugh).
>
> —Bethany, f, teammate (Erika 1 Bosnia and Herzegovina)
>
> Certainly, with winter, outside, with coffee, doing nothing, grilling, I didn't feel "at ease" ("*v pohodě*"), we were sitting outside, freezing, and it was dark, and they put a bulb above us. They wanted to grill for us, but in a very unacceptable environment. If I was grilling, I would place nice seats, nice lights, make it nice.
>
> —Josef 3, m, returning to Bosnia and Herzegovina

Bethany's first response refers also to Erika eating a raw carrot as a snack while walking on the street or unpacking a 10 a.m. refreshment during a team meeting, which appeared as something very foreign. In her second response, she jokingly points at the socks in sandals as a cultural difference, which was already mentioned as a certain stereotype of Czechs' lesser stress on outer appearance.[63] It refers to individualism as well, in the sense of taking care of one's personal comfortable space and is connected to the value of *pohoda* (contentment), which is mentioned by Josef 3. *Pohoda*, as addressed by Czech and Slovak social scientists, best translates as "ease," "peace," "comfort" or "contentment."[64] Even though it implies "not being in a hurry, not being disturbed by others and enjoying relaxed approach to life,"[65] therefore it is partly corresponding to *polako* (slowly) or *ćeif* (enjoyment) in southern Slavic languages, the Czech[66] word *pohoda* is still very specific.[67] In order to reach this *pohoda*, Czechs are ready to behave as individualists and equip themselves with sufficient food or drinks and get fittingly dressed for a specific kind of weather.

While Croatia, Serbia and Slovenia score about fifty, Czechs have according to Hofstede's scale a high score of seventy, a pragmatic culture where people "show an ability to adapt traditions easily to changed conditions, a strong propensity to save and invest, thriftiness, and perseverance in achieving results."[68] Another theme linked to practicality and to pragmatism in individualism (vs. communitarianism) is handling money.

> The worst thing you can be in this culture is stingy, if I have money, I want to share. . . . We don't talk about money, how much this costs, how much that costs. If you have money, pay for it.
>
> —Diary notes-JV-2018-07 Sarajevo, Bosnia and Herzegovina

---

63. This footwear seems very practical and comfortable – the foot can breathe, and no dust dirties it thanks to the socks – yet it tends to be viewed with contemptuous smiles, no matter whether the socks are trendy and regardless the possibly high price of the sandals in a specialized outdoor shop.

64. For example, Brodský, "Czech Identity," 15; Činčala, "Theoretical Proposal for Reaching," 98; Dumetz and Gáboríková, "Czech and Slovak Republics," 10; Rattay, "Atheism in the Czech Republic," 23.

65. Dumetz and Gáboríková, "Czech and Slovak Republics," 10.

66. It needs to be stressed that Czechs and Slovaks perceive it nearly the same, the Slovak language includes *pohoda* as well.

67. Alongside this, it refers to an attitude of peace and a search for non-conflict relationships when an excess of one extreme over another is evaluated negatively. This is related to Czechs' popular unofficial code of "middle golden way" (*zlatá střední cesta*) which is applied to various areas of life (See Holý, *Little Czech*, 182).

68. Hofstede Insights, "Hofstede Insights – Country Comparison."

Stojan: There are correct things, and incorrect things. For example, in Czechia it is normal to split paying of the bill, here it is unimaginable, for years you talk about it, there is more pride than Czechs have.

Interviewer: Or more generosity.

Stojan: Yes, but generosity is when I later do not remind you that. If I every time remind you: "Look, who you are that you don't pay," it is not my generosity, but pride.

—Stojan, m, husband (Kristýna Serbia)

Photo diary-2018-07 Sarajevo, Bosnia and Herzegovina

To follow up on the previous discussion, the Czechs drive for practicality is again manifested in this area – in their economic thinking, they tend to ensure they are spending the right amount of money for the quality of the goods or services expected. The picture above illustrated this very occurrence where Czech short-term missionaries count off the money on the street according to their individual expenses. This contrasts with a more spontaneous way of dealing with money in former Yugoslav cultures, where it is more connected with shame and honour. "Economical thinking" as a value for most

Czechs can by contrast be perceived as being too thrifty and too concerned for how much one can save. An American missionary colleague who spent twelve years in Sarajevo, instructed a Czech short-term mission team during a session on orientation to culture on this mentality: "when you have money, treat others." This can be an expression of privilege and hospitality, yet on the other hand, Stojan clarifies that it may in fact lead to a certain legalism, taking pride in paying for someone or expecting to be treated next time in return.

After focusing on money matters, another theme within this individualism versus communitarianism section is attitudes toward nature.

> I think in the way she loved nature and being outside, that's very Czech (laugh). And I loved that about her, I mean I love it about you guys, that's very inspiring.
>
> —Eldina, f, supervisor and team leader (Erika 1 Bosnia and Herzegovina)
>
> When I started to hike somewhere people were wondering why I go alone, that I have no fear, that the country, the forest is wild and so on.
>
> —Erika 1, f, 1 year in Bosnia and Herzegovina

As Erika's case documents, Czechs would often go off beaten paths to nature (and travel elsewhere) individually or in self-organized groups, whereas former Yugoslavs tend to prefer comfort when travelling, for example, visiting European cities as a group. There is of course no hard and fast rule, and Hošek clarifies in connection with Czech national identity and the relationship with nature, that Czechs enjoy experiencing nature both individually and together through staying in cabins and cottages.[69]

According to Trompenaars and Hampden-Turner, there are cultures which see the world as more powerful than individuals and people should go along as man is part of nature, while other more inner-directed cultures incline toward controlling the nature.[70] Instead of a clear dualistic delineation, cul-

---

69. Hošek, *It Is Our Story,* 139.
70. "They either believe that they can and should control nature by imposing their will upon it, as in the ancient biblical injunction 'multiply and subdue the earth'; or they believe that man is part of nature and must go along with its laws, directions and forces." (Trompenaars and Hampden-Turner, *Riding the Waves of Culture,* 10)

tures should be viewed as inclining towards one or the other side. The attitude toward the control of nature is linked to individual responsibility in recycling.

Photo diary-2009-03 Sarajevo, Bosnia and Herzegovina

The picture depicts a container for recycling waste in the middle of Miljacka river in the Bosnian capital Sarajevo. Notwithstanding the fact that the river is filthy at all times, this example presents a rather extreme illustration of a comparatively poorer awareness of nature protection and ecology than what is the case in the Czech Republic.[71] This is tightly linked to a more individualist stance of "How can I help recycle?" versus "Everyone should do it" (and hardly anyone does). As observed, in Bosnia and Herzegovina for instance, people highly value cleanness inside and around their house, yet streets and common places are not that well-kept. This contrasts with a more communal responsibility in this matter in the Czech Republic.

To close this section, where the sub-themes, such as family, money, clothes, nature and ecology were thematically arranged as aspects of individualism

---

71. In many regions of some former Yugoslav countries, waste is often thrown within the vicinity of people. Luckily, nature still remains clean, due to the fact there are large uninhabited areas. On the other hand, in the more densely populated Czech Republic, nature is more strongly protected.

and communitarianism, Czech culture can be, in line with Hofstede's model, considered more individualistic than former Yugoslav cultures. There are nevertheless individual elements in southern Slavs and collective elements in Czech culture. Brewer and Chen critique the classical studies of comparison of the West and the East between individualistic and collectivist cultures; they claim that in all societies, individuals are collectivistic and call for a multi-layered attribute of cultures.[72] The geographical differences within such a small country as the Czech Republic confirm that, the more one moves east from Bohemia in the West towards Moravia, the more communality, hospitality, folklore, traditions and institutionalized faith can be observed.[73] In conclusion, there is an internal struggle between communal and individual dimensions for both Czech culture and the cultures of former Yugoslav nations.

4.5 Openness vs. closeness

I think they are very cordial, they are hospitable, very cordial.

—Erika 2, f, returning to Bosnia and Herzegovina

They are more cordial, they are closer to Slovaks in this way. . . . I don't know, I think we are different, they become friends faster, they are hospitable, and wilder.

—Radek, m, returning to Serbia

Slovenians are more open. When you come to a doctor people talk: "Why are you here, what's wrong?" Or when in the lift, I debate with people a lot.

—Šimon, m, 20–30 years in Slovenia

Perhaps the biggest thing I have seen in Croatia and now even more deeply in Serbia is that people are more open, more sociable. When you meet someone in Bohemia on the street, when we were evangelizing and said: "Let's go for coffee, we will discuss it there," – this has not probably happened in our life [in

---

72. Brewer and Chen, "When (Who) are Collectives," 134–136.
73. Činčala, "Theoretical Proposal for Reaching", 93.

Czechia]. And I've grown up in church and I was involved in different outreaches, also on the street. And here it happens to us, it was happening in Croatia, so I think the Balkans people are more sociable.

—Ema 2, f, 2–10 years in Serbia

This set of responses refers to situations where Czech missionaries perceived certain openness, or in other words, cordiality or sociability, in former Yugoslavs. Being able to start a conversation immediately (Šimon, Ema 2), becoming friends faster (Radek) and enjoying the hospitality (Erika 2) signifies the openness people from former Yugoslav cultures display more than Czechs. All of these responses might, nevertheless, refer only to the initial level of openness.

> The differences are in that Czechs go for deep water, Croats scratch the surface and it takes long until you get deep in the relationship.
>
> —Josef 1, m, 20–30 years in Croatia

To elaborate on his statement, Josef 1 says that for Czechs the first contact might take more time, yet then they often open up, while Croats become friends faster, yet it often is a struggle to deepen the relationship. This helps illuminate the discussion on the ambiguity of openness and closeness later in this section.

As another category of cultural dimensions, Trompenaars and Hampden-Turner define "diffuse versus specific," sometimes also labelled low and high context cultures. As the diagram below portrays, the context refers to the degree of the content one has to be acquainted with before effective communication can occur.[74]

---

74. Trompenaars and Hampden-Turner, *Riding the Waves of Culture*, 86–90.

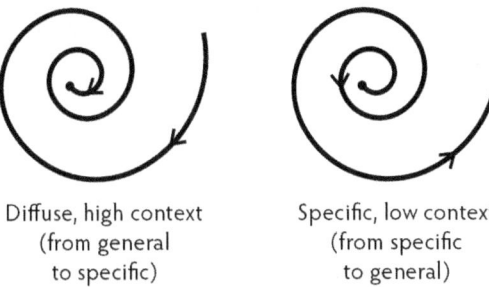

Diffuse, high context	Specific, low context
(from general	(from specific
to specific)	to general)

Figure 7: Diffuse vs. specific cultures[75]

It would be helpful to keep this diagram in mind as I proceed in the analysis of the following two missionaries' responses:

> Yes, the culture is different. It looks open and sharing, but in reality it is a false openness, because the real things remain hidden and hidden to the closest persons. . . . This directness was not wanted. But in our understanding, when you have a problem with something, let's talk about it openly, relaxed, in grace and let's name it, for if we don't name it, how can we get rid of it, if we don't define it. And there it was that a big concern was how someone will feel.
>
> —Josef 2, m, 10–20 years in Croatia

> Josef was rebuked because he was too direct, that he is too truthful and direct and that he offends people by being direct. In Bohemia, it was all right when he called things by their name and it is even today, it is the gift from the Lord, that he can see the root of a problem. And there suddenly he was not sensitive enough, that what he thinks of himself, he needs to change the approach.
>
> —Renata, f, 10–20 years in Croatia

These themes were recurrent in the interview with this married couple, who worked in Croatia for fourteen years. Their critique of Croatian openness

---

75. Trompenaars and Hampden-Turner, 89.

originates in the burn-out Josef 2 and Renata admitted as they struggled with cultural differences which is underlined by yet another statement:

> In cooperation with the hypocritical culture that is there, that they appear open, and in fact they are not. They appear to share, but in fact they do not share about things truthfully. In cooperation with that you have to play their game, like: "How are you?", "I am fine." [in Croatian]
>
> —Josef 2, m, 10–20 years in Croatia

Here, Josef 2 rather harshly labels Croatian culture "hypocritical" which might have been connected to what was said earlier about the dissimilar degree of openness, or it might well have originated in his and Renata's personal expression of faith.[76]

To interpret this more clearly, it would be helpful to return to the Trompenaars and Hampden-Turner model of cultural dimensions which distinguishes between specific cultures, where work and private life are separated, and diffuse cultures, where ideas are not separated from people themselves.[77] For the latter, a direct confrontational speech might prove insulting due to the importance of avoiding loss of face. Paul Hiebert, who focused primarily on the North American cultural context, acknowledged that instead of avoiding confrontation, "we tend to be direct, even confrontational in our relationships. When faced with a problem, we want immediately to get to its source."[78] This quote resonates with the understanding of Josef 2 who certainly does not exemplify the whole Czech missionary sample, since others seemingly opt for more accommodating approaches.

To draw this section gradually towards the conclusion, it seems that each time it depends on the type of social behaviour and the topic discussed. For instance, Josef 1 responded on directness which is not appropriate in the Czech context:

---

76. As part of the background information, they shared during the interview how they became believers in the 1990s and how they have always valued small groups. There, they would confess sins to one another and the level of mutual accountability and openness was incomparable to the praxis they experienced and perceived in Croatia in the first decade of the new millennium.

77. Trompenaars and Hampden-Turner, *Riding the Waves of Culture*, 85–86.

78. Hiebert, *Anthropological Insights for Missionaries*, 129.

> To ask directly about financial questions like: "How much you earn, how much you spend for the rent, what was the price of your car?" is quite normal here.
>
> —Josef 1, m, 20–30 years in Croatia

Josef 1 underlines that there certainly are issues that are appropriate to be direct within one culture and vice versa. The presumed openness of the proverbial warm-hearted southern Europeans, including Slavs of former Yugoslavia, and the supposed closed Western Slavs is often marked with some sort of stereotyping.[79] Another stereotype, linked to this, is beer drinking vs. coffee drinking:

> Maybe you like to go for a beer, but Bosnians are more kind of a coffee type or *rakija* [fruit brandy].
>
> —Eldina, f, supervisor and team leader (Erika 1 Bosnia and Herzegovina)

Again, in more specific cultures, according to the Trompenaars and Hampden-Turner model of cultural dimensions,[80] work and private life are separated, and this example points to an accustomed practice where beer is usually drunk in the evening after work. On the other hand, in more diffuse cultures a substantial amount of work is often done over a cup of coffee. And still, both are seemingly open in the sense of society. Therefore, based on the responses in (4.5), instead of finding either Czech or former Yugoslav cultural dimensions to be strictly direct or indirect, or opened or closed, it seems reasonable to entertain the idea that they are in fact both open and closed, in their own way.

---

79. In observation, the general stereotype is that *sjevernjaci* (pejorative term for northerners in former Yugoslavia) are cold and closed, in contrast to the presumed hospitality, directness, and openness of the southern nations. On the other hand, Czechs use pejorative phrases such as *horká hlava* (hot head) or *jižní krev* (southern blood), taking pride in their supposedly detached reasonableness in contrast to the perceived excessive emotionality.

80. Trompenaars and Hampden-Turner, *Riding the Waves of Culture*, 85–86.

4.6 Temperament differences

> They are different in that they are of fuller temperament.
>
> —Erika 1, f, 1 year in Bosnia and Herzegovina
>
> Czechs are less emotional, Bosnians are more expressive, particularly the showing of anger. We called our teammate Czech-irritated, because we didn't know whether he was angry.
>
> —Diary notes-JV-2018-07 Sarajevo, Bosnia and Herzegovina

The category for this differentiation in the Trompenaars and Hampden-Turner model is named "neutral versus emotional." It asks: "Should the nature of our interactions be objective and detached, or is expressing emotion acceptable?"[81] It refers to certain national temperament traits on the introversion-extroversion spectrum. And even though ways emotions are expressed differ, emotional attachments remain present. The interviewees' responses include emotions in their value judgements as well:

> Croats are Slovaks let free of chains: of full temperament, warm hearted, corrupted, nationalistic, superficial in their way. . . . Czechs are distant emotionally, sour, bitter, ironical, strange, appearing intellectual, but on average they are not. Very cynical, superficial.
>
> —Jonatán, m, 10–20 years in Croatia

In order to understand the rather expressive "Slovaks let free of chains" (*Slováci utržení ze řetězu*), it would help to remember the observation, stated earlier in (4.4), that the further east supposedly the more temperamental in the sense of extraversion occurs: from Bohemia to Moravia, then via Western Slovakia towards the more eastern regions, all the way to Ukraine. Jonatán, who has been exposed to multiple Slavic cultures,[82] attempts here in brief to compare Croatian and Czech culture – and he critiques them both as superficial. Jonatán's usage of "superficial" might have served for him as a substitute for a certain inadequacy of both cultural contexts – earlier in the interview

---

81. Trompenaars and Hampden-Turner, *Riding the Waves of Culture*, 9.

82. Jonatán has a partial Slovak family heritage and currently the company he works for has many Serbian, Bosniak and Macedonian clients.

he admitted to both the struggles, adjusting with his family to life in Croatia and hardships in the ongoing process of reintegration to Czech culture. It seems that regarding temperament, the respondents were not able to avoid uttering strong opinions and general stereotypes.

> Or one more Croatian, or commonly Balkan, problem comes to my mind that people are split and have disagreements and it's infiltrated in churches. . . . Some people had disputes with others and they left and brought with them part of the people. It is an unhappy characteristic of the Balkan mentality.
>
> —Matěj, m, leader of sending mission agency (Josef 1 Croatia)
>
> I think here in the Czech Republic, the identities of people are rather adjustable. Even though people have individual requests, they tolerate each other, they are like: "I tolerate your individual requests, you tolerate mine and we function," because we are all different. And in the Balkans, it is connected to what you asked before, people are mostly similar or the same, so to say, and it is hard to adjust to the others.
>
> —Daniel, m, returning to Slovenia

It often seems that in their cross-cultural comparison attempts, Czechs tend to view themselves uncritically, in a peaceable self-perception, as if splits and disagreements did not apply to them. On the other hand, the national character of former Yugoslavs is, as Matěj's and Daniel's responses point out, frequently stereotyped as rather adversarial and linked to "balkanisation."[83] Todorova advocates that the "Yugoslav" (not the "Balkan," she emphasizes), crisis in the 1990s and its aftermath ought to cease to be explained in terms of proverbial Balkan enmities and cultural patterns.[84] Matěj and Daniel both allude to this accustomed perception, as they sat next to each other the presumed non-tolerating firmness of former Yugoslavs, as opposed to seemingly

---

83. "Balkanization" was coined at the end of World War One and it refers to "the process of nationalist fragmentation of former geographic and political units into new and problematically viable small states" (Todorova, *Imagining the Balkans*, 32).

84. Todorova, 186. Instead, it should be approached by rational criteria such as: "Issues of self-determination versus inviolable status quo, citizenship and minority rights, problems of ethnic and religious autonomy, the prospects and limits of secession, the balance between big and small nations and states, the role of international institutions" (Todorova, 186).

refined and polished Czech manners. Their responses might, nevertheless, contain perceptibly valid elements in the relationship of emotions to national temperament. According to these respondents and the others above in this section 4.5, former Yugoslavs tend to open up more than Czechs in their expressions of joy, of sorrow, of anger, or of national pride – which is the last sub-theme within this category.

> I am a moderate patriot, I don't like the exaggerated nationalism that is in Serbia, but it depends where, it is linked to Orthodoxy, and they have bumper stickers: "I am a 100 per cent Serb" (in Serbian).
>
> —Radek, m, returning to Serbia

Photo diary-2017-05 Prijedor, Bosnia and Herzegovina

The extroverted expression of national pride is widespread in former Yugoslavia in comparison to the Czech Republic. For instance, flags can be seen not only at sport events, but also on churches or mosques, at weddings and other occasions (in the picture is a Bosnian Serb wedding). Czechs, who are often patriotic as well, and sometimes even nationalistic, find themselves perplexed by this kind of former Yugoslav firm self-confidence which is often in an emotional way linked in their national temperament to their religion. The responses on the relationship between nation and religion as a cultural difference to the Czech cultural context were plentiful, and since they are connected to moments when the Czech[85] identity of the missionaries became salient (and often suppressed at the same time) it is addressed in the following chapter 5.

Finally, even though Czechs tend to be more "neutral," and former Yugoslavs more "emotional,"[86] I find it delicate to assess the interviewees' responses on emotions. The findings do point out that there are certain differences in national temperament, yet it probably always depends on one's personal predisposition.

4.7 Discussion of cultural differences and similarities

In the analysis up to this point, I have investigated areas of cultural dimension differences between Czechs and former Yugoslavs. The cultural differences have been the main focus, yet the interviewees perceived many similarities, or simultaneous differences and similarities. Therefore, before proceeding to answer the first research sub-question, "To what extent is the Slavic Czechs working with their fellow-Slavs in former Yugoslav countries cross-cultural?", more extracts from primary sources follow.

> A lot of similarities, I think from our point of view as Czechs, Slovenes are central Europeans, they are tidy, hard-working, their mentality is relatively easy going.
>
> —Patrik, m, 20–30 years in Slovenia
>
> I'm thinking about the biggest features, because when you compare on one hand for example Norwegian mentality with the Balkan one, you find many things, Czechs' mentality on the other hand more. . . . The Czech and the Croat, the southern, mentality, is very similar, we are Slavs.
>
> —Daniel, m, returning to Slovenia

---

85. To be more precise, apart from Czech, also their Protestant, and their missionary, identity.
86. Trompenaars and Hampden-Turner, *Riding the Waves of Culture*, 9.

> The cultures are more similar than different (The respondent makes comparison of Czechs to Dutch and to American teammates).
>
> —Eldina, f, supervisor and team leader (Erika 1 Bosnia and Herzegovina)

Henry Tajfel outlined that the way social identity functions always includes views about the "other" as ingroup members compare themselves to the outgroup.[87] While Daniel's and Eldina's response explicitly involve other Europeans, and when compared to them, Czechs and former Yugoslavs indeed seem to be more similar than different. Patrik's outgroup is more implicit. In his value judgement of Czechs and Slovenes being "hard-working" and "tidy," which can be questionable, the outgroup he aligns them with are probably Germans, or even Austrians, who are located geographically in-between Slovenia and the Czech Republic, or on the other side he perhaps brings into comparison the more south-eastern former Yugoslavs. Cross-cultural comparison is often treacherous since it contains subjective value judgements and each time it depends on who one compares to. Here it was Europeans, on other occasions the respondents integrated non-Europeans as the outgroup:

> I think there are definitely many things they have in common which makes it easier for someone coming from the Czech Republic to adapt to the culture here, because there is not as big of a jump as from a Western culture maybe.
>
> —Bethany, f, teammate (Erika 1 Bosnia and Herzegovina)

> At the same time when one goes out of Europe he can see how similar we are, in what ways we are the same. So, I think when one does not leave Europe it is different, but when he leaves Europe then it is not that much different.
>
> —Erika 1, f, 1 year in Bosnia and Herzegovina

In Bethany's "Western culture," other Europeans, Americans (the prevailing missionary force in the country), and possibly also herself as South African, might have been included. Erika 1, after one year in Bosnia and

---

87. Tajfel, *Human Groups*, 226.

Herzegovina, has become a missionary to a South Asian country and was able to bring to the interview a quite self-evident perspective – in comparison to non-Europeans, Czech culture and former Yugoslav cultures do not differ substantially.

Major themes that emerged during the engagement with the respondents, as far as cultural similarity, were (1.) language and (2.) history. I attempted to narrow down the responses to represent how best, according to the interviewees, the two cultural contexts are similar, yet different in their specific way.

> The shock for me was certainly the language, we thought that we could communicate in Russian or Ukrainian, but it ended up at about thirty per cent during the first visit and I was glad.
>
> —Josef 3, m, returning to Bosnia and Herzegovina
>
> People in ex-Yugoslavia and in the Czech Republic I think they still have lot of things in common and the language is very similar, it's Slavic, so these things make us closer to each other.
>
> —Eldina, f, supervisor and team leader (Erika 1 Bosnia and Herzegovina)

When addressing first of all language, an integrated part of people's behaviour and material culture, some respondents found it surprisingly different – Josef 3 supposed he could utilize his knowledge of other Slavic languages. Others, like Eldina, on the contrary accentuate the similarity and consider the Western Slavic Czech and southern Slavic languages as a uniting factor. I noticed that it was primarily belonging to the Slavic language group that caused respondents to contemplate more subtle aspects in cross-cultural comparisons:

> The first impression is very good, that we are brother Slavs. So, this is positive and also when you mutually spend more time, the differences come up.
>
> —Josef 2, m, 10–20 years in Croatia
>
> I think the only thing we have is the language. So, the same thing is the Slavic language, and all other is very, very different.
>
> —Vladan, m, pastor and team leader (Kristýna Serbia)

It is obvious that there is a sense of gradability in moving from similarities to differences. Josef 2 who, again caused by certain disillusionment, evaluates single elements of culture as positive versus negative. He finds the Slavic heritage a principal visible pointer to the cultures' connection. Vladan, nonetheless, considers that the connecting component to be precisely the Slavic language, while otherwise the cultures differ. In spite of this claim, later during the interview he pointed out several commonalities in behaviour and more cultural similarities.[88]

The second area of cultural similarities (and differences) which emerged was history.

> The mosques and minarets, that made me realize we live in a completely different place.
>
> —Erika 2, f, returning to Bosnia and Herzegovina
>
> They [Slovenians] subconsciously nostalgically don't want to be Yugoslavs in their head, but in the heart, or I don't know where, they live out of the Yugoslav heritage. . . . Everyone says: "Yes, during the time of Tito." So, that's the biggest difference that we notice here somehow, that is not in mentality, but in history. Our forty years and theirs is so different and it is apparent till today. Our heritage that we were under pressure, and their heritage that they were open to both sides and resourcing advantages from the West and the East, it still is here.
>
> —Patrik, m, 20–30 years in Slovenia
>
> We are not burdened by the elements of war.
>
> —Josef 3, m, returning to Bosnia and Herzegovina
>
> Sometimes it is not about two hundred Euros monthly more, but people have often told me, the Czech Republic is a functioning country.
>
> —Miroslav, m, acquaintance and director of Czech minority association in Belgrade Serbia (Kristýna Serbia)

---

88. See section 6.4.1.

These selected quotes represent the location of four various historical periods: (a.) Ottoman Turks (from fourteenth to twentieth century A.D.); (b.) the Communist regime (1948–1991); (c.) the war of 1991–1995 (and 1999); (d.) the time of transition after 1991, connected to the economic development.

(a) Erika 2 in her first visit, noticed an unfamiliar scene[89] – Islamic sacral buildings connected to the Ottoman era. This is different, yet similar – nations in both cultural spheres were in substantial historical timeframes subdued, Czechs by the Austrian Habsburg dynasty, most former Yugoslavs by the Ottoman Turks.[90]

(b) Patrik found the biggest difference in the contemporary consequences of the former regime. Communism was present in both countries, yet Czechoslovak and Yugoslav Communism differed significantly, due to the fact that the Yugoslav president Tito split from Stalin in 1948 and led his own international politics, while Czechoslovakia was one of the satellite states of the Soviet Union.[91]

(c) The brief, yet significant, comment of Josef 3 refers to the war in the 1990s. Both Czechoslovakia and Yugoslavia disintegrated, and while Czechs and Slovaks in 1993 experienced a "Velvet divorce" after the "Velvet revolution" in 1989, the break-up of Yugoslavia was accompanied by the most violent conflict in Europe since World War Two.[92]

(d) Miroslav's statement relates to the economic advancement after the fall of Communism until now. While all the post-Communist countries have undergone the transition, its level varies. Jakub 2 adds: "There [in former Yugoslav countries] you can find a certain defeatism and the memory of the past good times" (Jakub 2, m, returning to Serbia). The economy is often connected to a certain sense of national pride, and this can still be felt when former Yugoslavs relate to former Czechoslovaks. During the Tito era, Czechoslovaks were seen as inferior, because of the worse economic conditions as one of the satellite states of the Soviet Union. Yet since the 1990s

---

89. In the Czech Republic, only a few small mosques are in use, and they have no minarets.

90. Slovenia, parts of Croatia, Serbia and in one particular time Bosnia and Herzegovina as well were occupied by Austro-Hungary – which again is a similarity, together with the impact of the apostles to the Slavs, as one of the respondents noticed: "The common history is partially here, Cyril and Methodius, Austro-Hungarian empire" (Renata, f, 10–20 years in Croatia).

91. See section 1.2.2.

92. See section 1.2.3.

former Yugoslavs have started to consider Czechs and Slovaks to be more advanced. Miroslav, in the response above, wishes to stress that what perhaps matters more for those who emigrate is not always necessarily a higher monthly income, but quality of life in a functioning civic society.

4.8 Chapter conclusions

In this chapter, apart from the theme of cultural similarities 4.7, five areas emerged as themes from the interviews with Czech missionaries and other respondents. These five areas of cultural differences were: 4.2 rules vs. people orientation, 4.3 achievement vs. ascription, 4.4 individual vs. communitarian, 4.5 openness vs. closeness, 4.6 temperament differences, and they were grounded largely in the Trompenaars and Hampden-Turner model for cross-cultural comparison.[93]

The partial findings of this qualitative perspective on the juxtaposed Czech and former Yugoslav cultures made me realize how leaning on one specific cross-cultural comparison model can be precarious and how it is almost impossible to rely on a determined definition of culture. For instance, the Hiebert's three-fold[94] integrated system of culture as products, behaviour and ideas,[95] can prove insufficient. His own work contains self-critique: the

---

93. Trompenaars and Hampden-Turner, *Riding the Waves of Culture*.

94. Trompenaars and Hampden-Turner, similarly to Hiebert, locate three layers of culture: (a.) the outer layer – explicit products, the middle layer – norms and values, the core – assumptions about existence (Trompenaars and Hampden-Turner, *Riding the Waves of Culture*, 21–24). Their perception, nevertheless, differs from Hiebert's regarding behaviour – its expressions belong to the outer, while values on how to behave to the middle layer.

95. Hiebert, *Cultural Anthropology*, 25.

three categories tend to overlap,[96] the number of categories may differ,[97] such categories change, since cultures change.[98]

I opted for the Trompenaars and Hampden-Turner model of cultural dimensions to help direct the thematic analysis in sections 4.2 to 4.6, yet neither Trompenaars' and Hampden-Turner's cultural dimensions, Hofstede's model, GLOBE, NEO-PI-3, or other could possibly answer completely the initial research question, "To what extent can the Slavic Czechs working with their fellow-Slavs in former Yugoslav countries be considered cross-cultural?" The initial five sections concentrated mostly on the areas of differences (and covered similarities along the way), and the previous sub-section 4.7.1 expanded more on similarities. In sum, Czechs, Bosniaks, Croats, Macedonians, Montenegrins, Serbs and Slovenes live in a diverse, yet not too distant geopolitical space; they share several common historical epochs; they speak related Slavic, yet distinguished languages; their appearance is similar, they dress like average Europeans; they eat, drink and use similar products. They resemble each other, yet significantly differ in values and behaviour, including in the areas of: orientation to rules vs. relationships 4.2, achievement vs. ascription 4.3, evincing signs of individual vs. communitarian ways of life 4.4, being "open" or "closed" 4.5, and in their national temperament 4.6.

Therefore, even though it is admittedly quite vaguely worded, the answer to the question would be: they are similar, yet different. The extent of cultural similarity or difference was, nevertheless, found to be problematic to measure. According to the missiological tool of E-scale, introduced in 2.3.4, for this sort of cross-cultural setting, which involves crossing "the frontier constituted by

---

96. Hiebert also acknowledges that the relationship of behaviour to the realm of ideas is complex: people do not always live up to their beliefs and values, and on the other hand, they often acquire behaviour patterns without learning their meaning (Hiebert, 29).

97. Hiebert further in a later publication perceives culture as a partially integrated system which is composed of only two categories, one internal and one more externally expressed: "ideas, feelings, and values encoded in learned patterns of behaviour, signs, products, rituals, beliefs, and worldviews shared by a community of people" (Hiebert, "Gospel in Human Contexts," 18). This alludes to the Trompenaars and Hampden-Turner model understanding of the core or middle layer of culture which manifests itself in the outer layer (See Trompenaars and Hampden-Turner, *Riding the Waves of Culture*, 21–24).

98. Hiebert himself emphasized: "Cultures constantly change as new meanings are assigned to existing behavioural forms or as old meanings are forgotten" (Hiebert, *Cultural Anthropology*, 29).

insignificant differences of language and culture,"[99] Czech and either of the studied southern Slavic cultures could be classified as E-2 (i.e. as a "closed" culture).[100] This might have been anticipated beforehand, yet the evidence of this concise cross-cultural probe allows us to claim with more firmness that when Czechs missionally interact with Slavs in former Yugoslav countries it can be designated E-2 mission. Individual perceptions can of course differ, depending on the region of former Yugoslavia that missionaries work in, or on the expertise and experience of every missionary – Czechs might assess whether they have moved not too far culturally from Central and Eastern Europe to Southeastern Europe, or whether they have transferred to the dissimilar, somewhat exotic, Balkans.

An alternative response to, "To what extent is the Slavic Czechs working with their fellow-Slavs in former Yugoslav countries cross-cultural?", would be: "To the extent that their Czech identity is activated (or becomes salient) in certain situations." Some of the situations were already consulted here in chapter (4.), especially the five differing areas of behaviour caused by various elements of Czech and single former Yugoslav national cultures. The next two research questions help evaluate what those situations are and how the missionaries' "Czechness" interrelates with their other identity facets. This chapter of initial analyses sought to provide a substantial basis for the following chapters 5 and 6 and the discussion on Czech identity salience and suppression. In order to realize what those circumstances in ministry and everyday life in the region are, this familiarity with basic elements of both cultural environments is required.

---

99. Winter, "New Macedonia," 351. For comparison, E-1 involves crossing the frontier between the church and the unbelieving world, and E-3 the frontier of monumental cultural differences (Winter, 351).

100. Winter, 357.

CHAPTER 5

Czech Missionaries' Czech Identity Salience and Suppression in Their Interaction with Slavs in Former Yugoslav Countries

5.1 The matter of national identity facet salience and suppression

5.1.1 Situational identity salience and suppression

The current chapter and the following chapter 6 address the second research sub-question, "How and in what circumstances does the Czech identity of Czech missionaries become salient or suppressed?" In chapter 2 I established that identity is unstable and complex. Turner says that social identity is "the sum total of the social identifications used by a person to define him- or herself."[1] Individuals are members of various groups to which they belong at the same time[2] and their identities or identity facets are constantly being "negotiated."[3] Situational identity salience and suppression are essential constituents of such identity facet negotiation.

---

1. Turner, "Towards Cognitive Redefinition," 18.
2. Roccas et al., "Toward a Unifying Model," 294; Smith, *National Identity*, 4.
3. Holmberg, "Understanding Christian Identity", 29.

"Identity salience," or more precisely "social identity salience," is defined as "the probability that an identity will be invoked across a variety of situations, or alternatively across persons in a given situation."[4] When the authors say "identity," they mean it is one of the multiple identities or identity facets which becomes salient. The utilisation of "salience" corresponds to its usage in identity theory and social identity theory.[5] It is, nevertheless, more problematic to define "identity suppression." It can be understood in contrast to the salience – "likelihood that these identities will be activated"[6] – as the likelihood that these identities will be deactivated in given situations. Again,[7] "suppression" in this work is used as a rather aggregate term referring to the situational moments when one's single identity facet is deactivated, turned down, silenced, overshadowed or placed in the background. The term as such evokes a notion of intentionality, yet it can comprise of both intentional and unintentional moments, as will be clarified from the evidence in this chapter.

Next, it seems necessary to explicate what is meant by "situational." Richard Jenkins says about ethnic identity: "Its salience, strength and manipulability are situationally contingent,"[8] and later on he adds: "Identity is produced and reproduced during interaction, and interaction is always situated in context."[9] Together with him, Roccas and Brewer seem to use "situation" and "context" interchangeably: "Social identities are context specific or situation specific."[10] Context is defined by the Cambridge Dictionary as "the situation within which something exists or happens."[11] It might be helpful to further clarify that I differentiate between the context as a broader term for setting and context for particular situations. Namely, for Czech missionaries this broader context of geopolitical location in time and space is after 1989 in one of the former Yugoslav countries, while the other understanding of context refers to moments and situations Czech missionaries find themselves in at times. These

---

4. Stryker and Burke, "Past, Present, and Future", 286.

5. The former theory focuses on the inner, role-related, perception of one's identity, while the latter to the person's belonging to one group over another.

6. Stryker and Burke, 292.

7. See section 2.2.2.

8. Jenkins, *Rethinking Ethnicity*, 49.

9. Jenkins, 65.

10. Roccas and Brewer, "Social Identity Complexity," 90.

11. Cambridge Dictionary, "Meaning of Context in English."

include location in time and space, and also the interaction with people – their "Czechness" becomes salient (or suppressed) situationally. This delineation is the reason I do not refer to "contextual," but rather "situational" identity salience and suppression, which seems more precise and is in line with the relevant literature on social identity complexity.

5.1.2 National identity negotiation

Based on the material from primary sources, three organizing themes arose in this chapter: 5.2 Czech identity salience, 5.3 Czech identity suppression, and 5.4 simultaneous salience and suppression of the Czech identity facet.[12] The topic of Czech national identity salience and suppression is linked to the earlier discussion on varying perceptions of nation as *ethnos* or *demos*.[13] Nation as a societal construct[14] contrasts with the idea of nation as a primordial ethnic community.[15] As Jenkins concludes in "Rethinking Ethnicity," the ethnic communities themselves are limited both in their fixity and plasticity: "Somewhere between irresistible emotion and utter cynicism, neither blindly primordial nor completely manipulable, ethnicity and its allotropes are principles of collective identification and social organization."[16]

In 2017, the European Values Study focused, among other things, on the perception of nationality.[17] More than ninety per cent of respondents across Europe viewed nationality in the sense of speaking national languages, yet the results differed in other areas. Viewing nationality in connection with the importance of political institutions and laws was slightly higher in Western Europe, while the perception of nationality as having ancestors in the country or nationality who were born in the country was more prominent in Eastern Europe. This might indicate a difference between more immigrant and more emigrant countries. There is not a clear-cut difference between the Western and Eastern parts, yet the survey results could be partly connected to a general

---

12. The third section is significant as Czech identity and placing its "salience" and "suppression" beside each other is not to be viewed through a bilateral lens, yet rather as a multidimensional pattern.
13. See section 2.2.4.
14. Anderson, *Imagined Communities*.
15. Smith, *National Identity*.
16. Jenkins, *Rethinking Ethnicity*, 173.
17. European Values Study, "EVALUE."

tendency towards a more ethnic perception of nation in the more eastern countries, and nation as citizenship in the West.[18]

These are surely limited results and outcomes, within each nation there is always pressure from both sides and a vibrant internal discussion. Czechs, among others, have certainly not been united on the issue and have continuously negotiated their "Czechness" in history. A pivotal book from the first Czechoslovak president, T. G. Masaryk, "the Czech Question,"[19] has been an influential work, yet it has also received much criticism, such as from his contemporary, historian Josef Pekař,[20] who did not find the Gothic and Baroque epochs in Czech history to be a dark period. Masaryk's findings were opposed also by the philosopher of history Jan Patočka who did not perceive that a national character could be built upon a historical continuum reaching as far as legends of prehistoric Czechs and to the Middle Ages.[21] The polemics of Milan Kundera and Václav Havel follow up on the earlier differences and demonstrate the historical divide of Czechs between primordialist and constructivist approaches.[22]

The first Czech president, Havel, has been an icon of the fall of Communism and of the new democracy and, although very respected and renowned, continues to be critiqued for being soft on Communism[23] and for stressing the civic[24] principle over the ethnic national principle.[25] Havel saw "nation as a cause of misfortune, animosity, hatred and violence."[26] He disliked manifestations of Czech nationalism, in his speeches preferring the words "this

---

18. It needs to be added that in some of the EU, southern Europeans often evince similar results to the European East. Furthermore, several countries are not included in the survey altogether.
19. Masaryk, *Czech Question*. First published in 1895.
20. Pekař, *Meaning of Czech History*.
21. Patočka, "Philosophy of Czech History", 462; compare Kundera, "Czech Destiny."
22. Havel, *About Human Identity*, 187–200.
23. The Communist Party was not abolished in 1989. It was allowed to remain as one of the democratic options for voters and it continues its influence to this day. In parliamentary elections in 2017 the Communists gained more than seven per cent of the votes. In 2021, with the result of 3.6% of the votes, they ended up with no representation in parliament.
24. "Civic nationalism defines nationhood in terms of citizenship and political participation." (Bekus, 28)
25. See Kenney, *Burdens of Freedom*, 108–109.
26. Kučerová, "End of Czech Identity," 221.

country" or "the republic" instead of "the Czech Republic" or "Czechia"[27] and often critically addressed what he saw as negative Czech features.[28]

If one intended to simplify the complex matter of national self-identification, this could be outlined: Czechs either possess Czech identity because they have got it (by birth and ancestry), or they have decided for it (they are citizens of the state and they speak Czech). The issue of whether the essentialist or the constructivist perception of nation and national identity is more fitting for the Czech context does not have to be resolved at this point.[29] Instead, this has opened a more profound understanding of the complexity before the analysis of the situational Czech national salience and suppression of contemporary Czech missionaries commences.

Before turning to the analysis itself, these were the flexible questions the interviewing process was comprised of: This interview section opened by asking "Could you tell me about how important for you is to be Czech in . . .?" Auxiliary questions followed: "To what extent do you feel Czech?", "Were there any situations where you really felt very Czech?", "How did you feel, were you happy, proud or was it embarrassing?", "Can you recall moments when your Czech identity stepped to the foreground?", "Were there any situations where you abandoned your "Czechness" and you identified more with former Yugoslavs? How was it?"

5.2 Czech Identity Salience of Czech missionaries

5.2.1 Encountering artefacts

An artefact suggests something tangible which can be for example the bus in the picture. While Czechia-produced Škoda cars are so widespread, that they are hardly noticed in connection to one's "Czechness," other brands such as Zetor (tractors), Tatra (lorries) or Karosa (buses) are not that common. In personal diaries I recall a moment when our international team held a children's

---

27. Kučerová, 221.
28. Brodský, "Czech Identity", 19.
29. A recent survey confirms the ambiguous situation of Czech national identity. Seventy-four per cent of the sample of n=1909 stated it was highly important to speak Czech, sixty percent to have Czech citizenship, fifty-four to feel as a Czech, forty-nine to live in Czechia for most of their life, forty-eight to be born in Czechia, thirty-six to have Czech ancestry, sixteen to be Christian (Vlachová, "Significant Others", 7).

programme in a Serbian enclave village in Kosovo. Tomáš and I were the only Czechs on the team and at one point we spotted an old Karosa with the typical blue stripes. It was rebuilt with iron bars in order to safely transport the villagers through the majority Albanian territory. We were so excited to see this both familiar and unfamiliar sight, "our bus," in this remote place.

Photo diary-2007-07 Gojbulja, Kosovo

The artefacts in this section refer mainly to material things and objects as tangible elements of culture, and they are usually noticed in the initial phase of missionaries' adjustment in the country:

> The time I felt different was for example in the style of clothing (laugh). I had a feeling that people look at me. Or, here in Prague one can walk barefoot (laugh) or have freedom. So, people there looked and commented.
>
> —Erika 1, f, 1 year in Bosnia and Herzegovina
>
> They eat a lot meat and drink yogurt, but they go that far that they eat salami pizza and drink yogurt with that. And see, when you see this first time as a Czech, you say: "Barbarism." Then we have learnt it and we also do it.
>
> —Roman 1, m, 2–10 years in Serbia

> In Montenegro, normal Christian ladies smoke while reading the Bible.
>
> —Radek, m, returning to Serbia

Erika's "Czechness" became salient as her clothing made her feel different in the eyes of her surroundings. Apart from Roman 1, food differences were noticed by several other respondents of the sample, yet evaluated positively, since various meals such as *ćevapi*[30] or *ražnjići*[31] originate in former Yugoslavia and have become popular in Czech cuisine as well. Smoking, on the other hand, which was similarly repeatedly mentioned by other respondents, mostly entailed negative connotations – Radek was astounded that even Protestant Christians smoke.[32]

These experiences are connected to what missiological literature usually refers to as culture shock; Hiebert describes it as a "period of confusion and cultural disorientation."[33] Erika 1, together with everyone around her, was "shocked," and so was Roman 1 astounded by food and Radek by cigarettes. This "shock" may, nonetheless, appear as a one-time event and therefore intercultural psychologists prefer to label this phenomenon "acculturative stress," emphasizing that the psychological conflict involves a process of learning.[34] They further argue "acculturative" is more precise since the source of the stressful experience lies in the interaction between cultures, and by using "culture" it is possible to misidentify the root of the difficulty.[35]

Coming back to the salience of "Czechness," the respondents were often asked the same question, yet they often took time to answer it in a narrative

---

30. *Ćevapi* is a grilled dish of minced meat.

31. *Ražnjići* is a grilled meat on a skewer.

32. In the Czech context, smoking used to be more widespread, yet nowadays it is generally considered harmful and unmodern – and this is observable in sections of former Yugoslav society as well.

33. Hiebert, *Cultural Anthropology*, 39. In addition to that, the cultural shock of re-entry is a certain disorientation in the culture of origin caused by changed circumstances in the homeland and altered relationships with people (See Hiebert, *Anthropological Insights for Missionaries*, 39).

34. This acculturative stress is defined as "a response by individuals to life events (that are rooted in intercultural contact), when they exceed the capacity of individuals to deal with them" (Berry et al., *Cross-Cultural Psychology*, 362).

35. Berry et al. 362.

or avoided it completely. Erika 1 and Kristýna responded immediately with what first came to their mind:

> Interviewer: Were there any situations where you felt you are simply Czech, during the year that you were there, when it came out to the surface somehow?
>
> Erika 1: Well, the situations with garlic when simply (laugh), when we came to the meeting and a colleague said: "You were eating garlic again, am I right?" and she was offering us a bubble gum.
>
> —Erika 1, f, 1 year in Bosnia and Herzegovina
>
> Interviewer: Were there any moments when you felt strongly that you are Czech or were there any moments where you wanted to suppress it?
>
> Kristýna: When there is ice hockey, you say: "Yes, we are playing today." And people give you a weird look, because hockey is not played here.
>
> —Kristýna, f, 20–30 years in Serbia

We already saw that encountering particular artefacts, such as clothing accessories (Erika 1), meal ingredients (Roman 1), or cigarettes (Radek), may situationally come to the foreground in the sense of "I am Czech, I do not wear this, I do not eat this, I do not smoke." These are differing elements of material culture manifested in behaviour. In contrast to that, the mentality "I am a Czech, therefore this is the thing I do" is present as well as Erika 1 and Kristýna stated. To clarify, garlic is an essential part of Czech cuisine, with foods such as potato-garlic pancakes, garlic soup and other meals which are not enjoyed by or familiar to Bosnians and other former Yugoslavs; Czechs excel in ice-hockey which is considered to be a national team sport.

At this stage, in continuity with the preceding sets of responses on salient moments of the Czech identity facets, it must be stressed that a significant overlap kept reappearing in the data analysis process – a thin line of identity in what it is to be Czech and what it is simply to be a foreigner in former Yugoslav countries. Many moments of situational salience of missionaries' "Czechness" could have referred to another national identity facet of other nationals, for example, Swedes play ice hockey, or Dutch like the outdoors. Therefore, as Czech missionaries subjectively perceived the salience of their Czech identity, these were moments both of their "Czechness," and simultaneously the more general "foreignness."

5.2.2 Interaction with other Czechs, Slovaks, and other nationals

First, the Czech identity facet becomes salient when Czech missionaries encounter other Czechs.

> A thing that I see as an encouragement for myself is the cooperation with churches from the Czech Republic. Because still, I am from that culture, I am from Bohemia, I like Czechia, I like Czech language. Two years ago, people from Bohemia started to come, and it is for me not only a spiritual encouragement, but a more personal one.
>
> —Kristýna, f, 20–30 years in Serbia

> There is a Baptist church that was started from zero by Czechs, here in Belgrade. So, when I come somewhere and say: "I am a Czech," and realized that this [church] I am a part of was founded by Czechs one hundred fifty years ago, I say: "Hey, I am not a stranger actually, I am all of sudden at home." So, it makes me joyful when there are links to Czech missionaries.
>
> —Roman 1, m, 2–10 years in Serbia

Apart from small Czech minorities,[36] there are not many Czechs who permanently live or frequently travel to less attractive regions of former Yugoslavia as tourists.[37] These are usually people who visit, as Kristýna highlighted. Recently, together with multiple short-term mission teams from

---

36. More significant numbers of Czech minorities are located in the Daruvar region in Croatia and the Bela Crkva region in Serbia.

37. The travels of Czech tourists are usually limited to the months of tourist summer season, most visit Adriatic coast or the mountains for hiking. So, through the year, and in the other areas not frequented by tourists, it is rare to encounter another Czech.

elsewhere, teams from Czechia[38] have started to come to her town. It was a not only a personal encouragement of her faith, or moral support by a visit from Kristýna's home country, but it also meant that her Czech identity facet was activated. The response of Roman 1 reveals that the salience of "Czechness" may occur as the result of an encounter with other Czechs in person, yet also even retrospectively.

Second, when Czech missionaries encounter Slovaks, their Czech identity facet usually becomes salient.

> The town looks like somewhere in central Slovakia, you know, the houses. It is rather a mixture, the Slovak environment is balkanized over the two hundred fifty years, they are of course Slovaks, but they mix the language and their Slovak is funny. At the beginning I didn't understand them and they didn't understand me. We speak Slovak there because they don't understand Czech.
>
> —Radek, m, returning to Serbia
>
> A Vojvodina Slovak gave a guided tour to our international group of which I was the only Czech and my national identity got activated – the two of us spoke together in Czech and Slovak.
>
> —Diary notes-DS-2015 Bar, Montenegro

The Czech identity facets become salient in the most distinguishable way when Czechs start to speak Czech, which often is not without complications, as Radek's statement emphasizes, since the Slovak minority of Vojvodina, the northern Serbian province, are not as used to hearing Czech as Slovaks in Slovakia are. Czech and Slovak are similar languages, there have mutual cultural ties and a generally warm relationship.[39] And, despite certain stereotypes, Slovaks are the Czechs' most appreciated and accepted other nationality (and vice versa).[40]

---

38. Noticeably, Kristýna, and similarly Roman 1, Patrik and others, who are from the western part of the Czech Republic (or Czechia) refer interchangeably to their homeland as "Bohemia."
39. Chalániová, "Cultural Diplomacy and Stereotypes", 27.
40. Burjanek, "Xenophobia among the Czech Population", 57.

Third, apart from Slovaks, when Czechs encounter other nationals their Czech national identity facet may rise to the foreground.

Interviewer: So, you as a Czech, how were you accepted at school?

Šimon: Well, I didn't care, and even when they called me "Czech," it was not pejorative. When they would say to someone: "You are Bosnian," it was pejorative. When they called me "Czech" it was my nickname, he is "Czech."

—Šimon, m, 20–30 years in Slovenia

Interviewer: To what degree did you feel Czech?

Marek: Quite a lot. I thought it even before but didn't believe in it so much. I think it's better, there are more people from the same culture going to mission. When I saw missionaries, who had relationships with people from their own culture, they were altogether more prepared to see Kosovo as their home, rather than when they went there as lone runners. And I had the desire to share with someone my culture.

—Marek, m, 1 year in Kosovo

The Czech identity facet often becomes salient simply for the reason of being in the country as a Czech (Šimon's response). There are moments when "Czechness" emerges as the result of being in a foreign (former Yugoslav) country, sometimes as the only Czech in the surrounding area. Apart from the case of three families in Croatia in one particular period of time in the same place (Josef 1, Josef 2 and Jonatán with their families), Czechs have constituted a minority in international church or ministry teams.[41] For Marek, the encounter with American teammates and German families who led the ministry in another town meant the realisation of his own Czech background. For me, the friendship with my Finnish teammate (in the picture), with whom I went to sauna, followed winter sports online, watched a Finnish TV show, listened to Finnish music and ate Finnish food, meant primarily comradeship and spiritual encouragement, yet also led me to appreciation of his culture and prompted me to think about my own identity as a Czech.

---

41. The returning missionaries who work with local churches directly do not fall into this category.

Photo diary-2009-04 Banja Luka, Bosnia and Herzegovina

Here [in Croatia] I realized our "Czechness," how we think more about why things don't work, rather than to think how to make them work. Some kind of mentality for us in Bohemia, but here people know it's difficult and look for ways to do it. They are able to satisfy themselves with a half-result or an imperfect result. And we – if we don't have the perspective that it definitely will turn out well and that it will be perfect, we don't want to go for it.

—Josef 1, m, 20–30 years in Croatia

The response of Josef 1, who reflects on the Czechs' more elaborate sense of perfectionism in his perception, indicates that apart from mere realisation of one's "Czechness" due to the encounter with other nationals (and certainly also with other Czechs, or with "brother" Slovaks) and the appreciation of certain cultural traits, one can as well turn critically to the Czech national identity facet. This critical stance, along with the perceived need of cultural adjustment, can be one of the factors leading to the delineation from Czechness, the Czech national identity facet (i.e. to its suppression).

5.3 Czech identity suppression of Czech missionaries

5.3.1 Interaction with non-Czechs

> And what formed him I think towards the mission was not our church, but because he spent – and I am not sure – three or four years in England.
>
> —Prokop, m, sending pastor (Marek Kosovo)

> We went to Berlin for Bible school, we absorbed there and started to get built up.
>
> —Patrik, m, 20–30 years in Slovenia

> When I preach I often use examples from Ukraine, they mind it probably, because there are many stories for these twenty years, and many Ukrainian pastors are still for me an example, as for the ministry in faithfulness, perseverance, determination, and my wish is that this could come to Croatia.
>
> —Vratislav, m, returning to Croatia

Meeting other nationals can, apart from the salience discussed in the previous section, result in suppression of the Czech identity facet. It can either be subtle in nature on the level of influence, such as were the respondents' intense encounters with English, Germans, or Ukrainians. Or, it may be a formative contact, either prior to the mission experience while still in the Czech Republic or during the mission stay in their former Yugoslavia target country.

> During the preparation it was important for me to meet with one missionary from America.
>
> —Erika 1, f, 1 year in Bosnia and Herzegovina

> Josef 1: They influenced us, they had seminars in Prague about mission.
>
> Interviewer: They are from America or?
>
> Josef 1: Yes. An older married couple, they were many years in missions. They were teaching how to prepare to go to missions and published a booklet.
>
> —Josef 1, m, 20–30 years in Croatia

> I somehow came into contact with S., a Korean missionary who influenced me because there were pressures on finances and on proving to the church that supports you that you serve, and it brings fruit. . . . So, there was the influence of Koreans and I was touched by that we were in Korea and I brought something into the mission work. They are very active as missionaries, I liked that.
>
> —Josef 2, m, 10–20 years in Croatia

The responses to the question, "Who of any other nationals have influenced you?", differed in the level of influence. Sometimes it was a mere encounter (Erika 1), at other times an influence in one particular area (Josef 1, Vratislav), yet often it was the matter of major influence, a long-term exposure leading to Czech identity facet suppression (Marek). The latter, which is the focus of this section, was manifested mainly during a missionary's stay in their respective former Yugoslav country. As was already mentioned, Czech missionaries, apart from the three families and those who work directly in a church environment, work in international teams and some of the other nationals become significant influencers.

> Concerning the influence, with all humility, no one had a fundamental influence on us during our stay.
>
> —Josef 2, m, 10–20 years in Croatia

> I will say it honestly, there were some tensions coming from the leader of OM [mission organisation] saying "no" to three Czech families in one place. . . . There were various pressures and of course it was connected to money as well and I admit that the American found one half of our expenses so that we could be there.
>
> —Josef 2, m, 10–20 years in Croatia

> Basically, after a half year of this work, we had an American couple join us, one pastor and his wife. He already was a pastor, so he took over the work. And we had another couple with a baby with us, so we were the team of six and a baby.
>
> —Roman 1, m, 2–10 years in Serbia

Josef 2, on one hand, denied any influence, yet later during the interview, he recalled that the American team leaders were significant for them. It is the very town with more Czechs on the team. Still during the initial years, under the American leadership within an international organisation, Czechs were led to suppress their "Czechness." Roman 1, even though he spent a longer time at the location, had to conform to an American leader who was perhaps more experienced as a pastor, yet less experienced as a missionary in Croatia. The situation he described resembles the one of Josef 2, yet Roman 1 did not consider it a problem, since he and his wife worked under an American church planting movement, with specific internal rules.

The debated connection of influence and identity suppression, as is already becoming clear and as will be clearer from the content of the chapter 6, is often interconnected in a missionaries' experiences in the field. It refers to patterns which may be adopted from the culture of the team leaders or from whoever constitutes a majority in the team. Often, even though they appear as equals, one particular style of mission is pushed forward, for example, an American ministry or reporting paradigm, and the certain element of "Czechness" in mission, whatever it could signify, appears to be as suppressed. This may be painful for a missionary, yet it needs to be admitted that Czechs are objectively not that experienced in the contemporary cross-cultural mission work and often are in the position of learners. Additionally, Czechs seem not to be assertive and in the encounter with other Western nationals, suppress their "Czechness" to the "international," which is most often American, identity dynamics related to mission performance.

5.3.2 Czech language suppression

For Czechs, language has historically played a significant role in national self-identification.[42] It certainly is not unique to Czechs that when the language becomes suppressed, a substantial part of national identity is suppressed along with it. The concerned languages in this research were Bosnian, Croatian, Serbian and Slovenian, yet before approaching the concise inter-lingual

---

42. Czechs and Germans in the Austrian Empire shared the same confession – most were Catholic, the minority Protestant (Václavík, *Religion and Modern Czech Society*, 65). The Czech national movement of the nineteenth century was based on the Czech language – it was "a basic identifying hallmark of the Czech ethnic group" (Kubiš et al., "Czech Republic: Nation Formation", 138).

analysis of these languages and Czech, I would like to briefly focus on English. This continues the discussion from the previous section on the influence of other foreign nationals, taking into consideration that Czech hardly ever functions as the common communication language of an international mission organisation branch or a church ministry team. It usually is English, and the background information of the Czech missionaries revealed a differing approach in using English in their work in their former Yugoslav countries:

1. No necessity to use English (Denisa, Daniel, Ema 1, Jonatán, Jakub 2, Josef 1, Josef 2, Kristýna, Klára, Renata, Patrik, Radek, Šimon, Vratislav).
2. English used for communication and ministry
    (a) English utilized as a team communication language (Erika 1, Marek)
    (b) English utilized occasionally by periodically returning missionaries who are not fluent in the local language (Jakub 1, Josef 3)
    (c) English utilized regularly as ministry language (Erika 2, Ema 2, Roman 1, Roman 2)

(1.) The first group of missionaries worked in local teams or in teams where other nationals also speak the language. Jonatán, Josef 1, Josef 2, Klára and Renata have mastered Croatian. Daniel is a native speaker of Croatian. Ema 1 and Patrik have mastered Slovenian, their son Šimon has grown up in Slovenia. Jakub 2, Kristýna and Radek have mastered Serbian. Most of these respondents speak English very well yet did not need to use it for mission work with former Yugoslavs. (2.) Other missionaries utilized English to varying extents and most appreciate English as they begin to learn the local language as a starting point of ministry. English seems to serve well as a lingua franca for missionary communication and to have such an intermediate language surely is beneficial, yet it may imply in some cases double suppression of Czech. Newbigin complains that "all the dialogue is conducted in the languages of Western Europe, and this in itself determines its terms."[43] Still, as exemplified by the following statement, missiologists ordinarily support the value of learning local languages: "If one wants to communicate Christ

---

43. Newbigin, *Foolishness to Greeks*, 9.

to a people, he must know them. The key to that knowledge has been, and always will be, language."[44] So, even those in the third sub-group (2.c) for whom English plays a more vital role as the primary language of ministry, learn to some degree, in their case, Serbian. As a result, as observed in the mission field, most Czech missionaries normally have to learn the local language and English.

Now, to turn specifically to former Yugoslav languages. If one learns the language fast, excels in it, and even starts to think in it, due to long-term exposure, it all may lead to a certain suppression of "Czechness":

> She learnt the language quickly, she also blended with students quickly and you couldn't tell she was Czech when you just looked at her, you know, because she spoke the language and she was really faithful in learning the culture.
>
> —Eldina, f, supervisor and team leader (Erika 1 Bosnia and Herzegovina)

> I learnt the language fast, I have a talent for that, I can't learn it at school, but when I am with someone, it gets soaked into me naturally, like music . . . They see it, the dialect, diction, gestures, I have switched to another temperament, and I am somewhere else.
>
> —Jonatán, m, 10–20 years in Croatia

As Eldina observed Erika 1, in her perspective language and culture seem to be intertwined. When she said that Erika 1 "blended" and "you could not tell that she was Czech," that evokes a relatively high degree of Czech identity facet suppression. Jonatán went even further in his statement when he said he was "somewhere" else, which in Czech refers to, in the context of speaking about his original national and another national temperament, being a different person, being someone else. They both mention speed of language learning, which admittedly depends on personal predisposition, yet the fact is that the two Slavic languages are related.[45] Mutual language intelligibility of Southern Slavic languages with the Western Slavic Czech is high even though

---

44. Hesselgrave, *Communicating Christ Cross-Culturally*, 355.
45. Compare with section 4.7.2 "Similar, yet different."

for a Czech speaker it is difficult to grasp certain features of Croatian (and therefore also Bosnian, Montenegrin and Serbian) phonology, morphology and syntax.[46]

The following responses may appear a bit non-homogeneous at first, yet they are interlinked as they refer to language suppression from a different angle than the preceding unreserved and seemingly unproblematic embrace of the foreign language.

> Interviewer: Have you started to learn any Serbian or do you plan to?
>
> Roman 2: Not at all.
>
> Erika 2: Not at all.
>
> Roman 2: As for me, the language was quite understandable for me, because I speak English, German and a bit of Polish, so one adapts to another language surroundings, one has an idea where the linguistics is heading in Serbian, so you can catch a few things and understand. But to study it with an aim, I don't have a talent for it, nor time, nor energy, nor a wish. So, like this. We've learnt how to say "hello" and then we successfully forgot it. God bless [*Bog blagoslav*], something like that, I don't know ...

—Roman 2, m, returning to Bosnia and Herzegovina

> Erika 2: When I was there we prepared songs in their language, we had worship songs, and then we merged all together, that was nice (laugh).

—Erika 2, f, returning to Bosnia and Herzegovina

> When I worked in Ukraine, I really was a Ukrainian. And they were saying: "You have to change this and that." And I said: "No, leave this with me, this is me." So, I was speaking Czech-Ukrainian-Russian. I created a specific dialect and what was the best, when I was listening to a sermon of pastors whom I ministered to, they were using my words, my sentences in their sermons and some people were completely off, because they

---

46. Golubović and Gooskens, "Mutual Intelligibility," 369.

didn't know what they were saying. But those who did experience me, the strange language I created, they knew about it, they were laughing.

—Vratislav, m, returning to Croatia

This indeed was a surprising answer of Roman 2 and Erika 2, followed by the realisation that the two returning missionaries did not even recall how to say "hi" in Serbian. Even though the couple later in the interview shared that they learned the words of several Serbian worship songs, they otherwise openly expressed that they do not plan to learn the language for their future trips. This approach sharply contrasts with other periodically returning missionaries, for example, Jakub 2 or Radek who have deeply engaged with the language. Other examples of such partial denial are Roman 1 and Ema 2 who shared in the interview that they deliberately settled for a basic level of Serbian which they use for more informal ministry in personal evangelism or basic communication in the city they live in, while for the ministry of teaching and preaching they use English.[47]

The already sketched elements of reluctance to learn the local language properly can be underlined by Vratislav's response. The example is from Ukraine, where the respondent kept coming for over twenty years, yet it refers to his last years in Croatia as well – his use of Croatian follows the same model. In the rather perplexed response, when he claims he was really a Ukrainian – yet did not speak clear Ukrainian nor Russian – Vratislav wilfully decided to keep some of his Czech, no matter the consequences.[48] In addition to that, he does not speak any English either, so this supra-Slavic language he created has served him as the means of communication and mission work, formerly in Ukraine and now "enhanced" by a fourth Slavic language in Croatia.

This "in-between language" refers to inter-lingual language hybridization. Vratislav has employed it intentionally, yet it often occurs unintentionally, simply due to the long-term exposure to the other language. The linguist

---

47. This certainly is connected to the fact they both studied at an American Bible school and work for an international church planting movement, based in the USA.

48. Vratislav and his wife Denisa speak very limited Croatian, yet they serve in a town with a significant Czech minority, so they can function. They moved to Croatia in 2021 permanently, so the language circumstances may change.

Christina Sanchez-Stockhammer defines language hybridization as: "A process whereby separate and disparate entities or processes generate another entity or process (the hybrid), which shares certain features with each of its sources, but which is not purely compositional."[49] This occurs within particular languages, yet it also is the result of interaction of multiple languages as is the case for Czech missionaries.[50] The concise linguistic analysis of the following extracts further explores this phenomenon.

> We like the country as it is, with all "mistakes" [in Croatian] and mistakes. Otherwise, we would not have been living here for twenty years.
>
> —Josef 1, m, 20–30 years in Croatia
>
> They started coming to Croatia in 1993, and they have lived there since 1996. Josef 1 still has a rich vocabulary in Czech, he is very eloquent.
>
> —Field notes-DS-2019-07 Velika Gorica, Croatia (Josef 1 Croatia)
>
> I think we are "inhabitants of God's kingdom" [in Serbian], I don't know any more how to translate this to Czech.
>
> —Kristýna, f, 20–30 years in Serbia
>
> After the interview, the respondent finished making lunch and prayed over the meal in Serbian. She said: "It is my primary language of communication with God."
>
> —Field notes-DS-2019-06 Niš, Serbia (Kristýna Serbia)

Perhaps the most common hybridization of Czech and former Yugoslav Slavic languages is in (A.) lexicon, together with nuances in syntax and phraseology. Missionaries, such as Kristýna and Josef 1, who have spent over twenty years in either Serbia or Croatia, through the interview at times struggled to find Czech words to express themselves. Josef 1 used both *manama* and *chybama* (in Croatian and in Czech "mistakes" – the plural noun in instrumental case), and Kristýna simply replaced the Czech equivalent with the Serbian.

---

49. Sanchez-Stockhammer, "Hybridization in Language," 135.

50. These hybrids are formed by speakers who will usually belong more to one linguistic community than to another, the results of such processes will presumably be integrated into the stronger language (Sanchez-Stockhammer, 141).

They employed words in these languages to help them express themselves faster. This was certainly aided by the factor that I as the interviewer am a speaker of Croatian and Serbian myself and could "fill in the blanks" for them. Another hybridization, mainly for those active in former Yugoslavia for more than a decade, was in (B.) morphology and in (C.) accent, pronunciation and speech melody.

> These are pressures that you have, in Bohemia you don't have it. Here, you don't know whether you will be able to stay another year.... I can just connect with the place, with the people, I "connect" [*povážu se* – a word formation in between Czech and Croatian] and then you might have to leave because you didn't get your visa.
>
> —Josef 1, m, 20–30 years in Croatia
>
> His pronunciation of the vowel "e" is in many instances according to the Slovenian phonic system.
>
> —Field notes-DS-2019-07 Velika Gorica, Croatia (Patrik Slovenia)
>
> She pronounces the consonants "ž" and "š," which exist in both Slavic languages, not softly, but rather in the harder, Serbian variant.
>
> —Diary notes-DS-2019-06 Niš, Serbia (Kristýna Serbia)

The infinitive of the highlighted reflexive verb in the first extract is in Croatian *povezati se*, and first person singular *povežem se*. In Czech this can be translated approximately as *spojím se*, or alternately as *navážu kontakt*. This resembles Croatian, yet it is not reflexive and requires a following direct object in accusative. In his response, Josef 1 joins the two languages together, using the Croatian root word and the Czech suffix. It is a vivid example of the speaker's morphological creativity which expresses a certain suppression of Czech – and salience of Croatian.

The next area where the long-term missionaries' Czech is influenced by local languages is their pronunciation, namely the phonological shift in their usage of vowels and consonants and their accent. Czech has one accent on the first syllable, similar to how it is in German, while the southern Slavic languages in the studied area are more diversified in this regard, for example, Bosnian/

Croatian/Montenegrin/Serbian have four accents. Czech has a softer pronunciation of consonants, and vowels are pronounced with a difference of length (a-á, e-é, i-í/y-ý, o-ó, u-ú/ů), with no major differentiation of closed vs. opened vowels. The greater or lesser shift in the accent and speech melody becomes apparent after a while when Kristýna and Patrik speak, and the nuances in pronunciation are as well noticeable with attentive observation. These specifics are somewhat hard to record, and they are at least underlined by the several field notes from the interviews above.

These certainly are not the sole areas. Sanchez-Stockhammer concludes[51] that hybridization as a phenomenon occurs on all levels of language, as the following figure depicts:

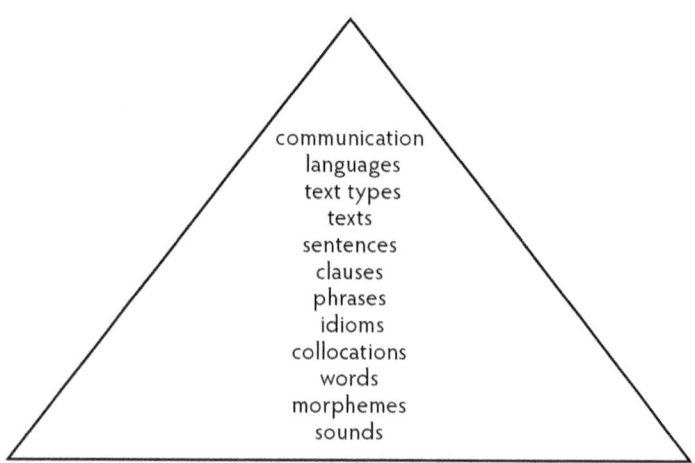

Figure 8: The levels of language[52]

In addition, there are elements of hybridization of standard versus colloquial Czech, dialect variations, or the presence of English vocabulary in the responses. Examples of other levels of languages in the figure could be found in the sample, but this is not the focus of this research. Nevertheless, there

---

51. Sanchez-Stockhammer, "Hybridization in Language," 153. This conclusion is applied for intra-lingual hybridization, yet may be extended to the inter-lingual hybridization as well; many studies exist on particular levels of languages comparing two foreign languages, see, for example, Volín and Poesová, "Perceptual Impact of Speech Melody," on English-Czech hybridization in intonation.

52. Sanchez-Stockhammer, 135.

is one more significant factor, related to the suppression of Czech language in relation to Czech identity and its suppression, and three more quotes on language suppression follow.

> I have learnt the dialects well, so people don't recognize by speaking that I am Czech. So, people can't tell by a first contact. The culture is almost closer to me than the Czech one, maybe not so anymore but during the time I was at school. And you know it by jokes, that you laugh more at Slovenian joke, than the Czech one. So, I completely merged with the southwestern Slovenian mentality.
>
> —Šimon, m, 20–30 years in Slovenia
>
> I have not succeeded for my children to speak fluent Czech. . . . Before the school, mum spoke Czech, dad Serbian, but when they started school, their vocabulary grew a lot, there were "dinosaurs, robots, extra-terrestrials" [in Serbian] . . . For years, we took care of one girl who was from a mother in an asylum centre. The child during the period of five years spending much time here, and a lot with my children, and that is one of the reasons why I went over to speak Serbian to my children.
>
> —Kristýna, f, 20–30 years in Serbia

The suppression of Czech during the long-term stay gets projected into missionaries' daily situations. The two extracts illustrate that one of the ways is through the missionaries' children, who grow up in the mission field and find themselves in more intense contact with the local language. Šimon's parents moved to Slovenia when he was little, he basically grew up there and completely mastered the local dialect. In contrast to Šimon, and other children of the missionaries in the sample, only Kristýna's children have a local dad. For Šimon, the suppression of Czech came naturally through school and spending more time with his Slovenian peers. Kristýna at first wilfully attempted to speak Czech to her children, yet has after several years became reconciled with the prevailing role of Serbian as a family language. It was not that one day she decided stop to speaking Czech; the change was gradual, yet she was aware of the process the whole time.

It seems that there are elements of both conscious and unconscious suppression of Czech which sometimes are intermingled, at least in Kristýna's case. The shift in language and the suppression of Czech as previously discussed (Patrik, Josef 1, Šimon, Kristýna) point to the unconscious element, while others, as documented by the analysis in the beginning of this sub-section, exemplify the rather conscious effort to suppress Czech language with the goal to learn the local language fast and fit in (Erika 1, Jonatán). Josef 1 adds another perspective on the intentionality:

> And the suppression of Czech identity was manifested specifically for example that we in public, in shops, in offices, wherever we were, we talked to each other in Croatian: "Speak Croatian," so that they don't hear Czech. Now it is not that constrained, still we try in public to speak Croatian, but it is without the constraint, we are free in that.
>
> —Josef 1, m, 20–30 years in Croatia

Josef 1 and his wife Klára initially suppressed their Czech language by conscious repetitive decisions to speak exclusively Croatian, even between themselves, and Josef 1 admitted it was partially motivated by the lack of acceptance. As already outlined, and as confirmed by Josef 1 here, Czech language is vital concerning Czech identity. This is an area when Czech identity suppression, and salience, become obvious. The evidence in this sub-section points to a partial finding that there is both unconscious and conscious factor in identity negotiation. And even though related to the language, it might prove momentous as it may apply in other areas where Czech identity may be situationally suppressed or salient.

5.3.3 Czech identity suppression in adjustment to the local culture

> Interviewer: Were there any moments when your "Czechness" is in the background, when you felt you merged with Slovenians?
>
> Ema 1: These are not moments, I perceive it is like this.
>
> —Ema 1, f, 20–30 years in Slovenia

There are external things that K. [our daughter] got married here and they have children. I have never planned I would have Slovenian grandsons, but that is our reality, our children grew up here. Also, the fact we bought the house, instead of renting, it was in line with the long-term calling and ministry.

—Patrik, m, 20–30 years in Slovenia

During those years we have gained in their eyes a different status. They see that we live here, we have goats, we work, we have children here, the children go to school and fluently speak their language. So, they have started to take us as their own. But the label that we are Czechs remains, and it will probably remain two generations after us.

—Josef 1, m, 20–30 years in Croatia

The family situation of Ema 1 and Patrik resembles their acquaintances Josef 1 and Klára in the nearby region in Croatia. Their "Czechness" is perceived as situationally suppressed, and they have settled for life and culturally adjusted in the two countries. Yet, no matter if they own a house, or a farm, have a local job, see children intermarry, they still are Czechs for their surroundings and in their own eyes. It must be noted that the respondents are usually not accustomed to think in terms of identity, and even less in "identity suppression" of their "Czechness." They prefer to consider the matters practically, in connection with their mission and cultural adjustment in the country.[53] The representatives of the three missionary families in Croatia respond to the adjustment and the national identity negotiation:

We made mistakes the first year or two that we kept saying: "Well, in our country it costs this and that." This sentence is to be forgotten by a missionary, there is no "in our country."

—Josef 1, m, 20–30 years in Croatia

We were led in the way that we should not export the culture, but the gospel, and that we are supposed to absorb their culture in the highest possible way. So, for my wife it was something

---

53. See Tennent, *Invitation to World Missions,* 352; Prince and Kikon, "Mission as Translation", 251.

> extremely hard, I can say almost impossible to fulfil. For me it was all right. But of course, it was a process, gradually. And we were led that the "Czechness" should not be pushed to the front.
>
> —Jonatán, m, 10–20 years in Croatia
>
> So, in a different culture you tend to get puzzled and ask yourself: What is right and what is not right? You get completely lost, compared to if you were in your own culture where you can simply address the issues. And the spiritual pressures are different.
>
> —Josef 2, m, 10–20 years in Croatia

While returning missionaries, due to the short nature of their stay and relatively low exposure to the local culture, did not seem to struggle with suppression of their national identity facet, or were in fact not competent to suppress it, it was typical for the long-term workers. It surely is more valid for the ladies who are less in contact with the local culture as they spend more time at home with children, yet these male respondents found it challenging as well. The missionaries' goal was absorbing[54] the local culture, and yet they were still closely associated with other Czech teammates.[55] They shared that this ambiguity, together with interpersonal issues, resulted in much confusion and was one of the factors leading to their burn-out.[56]

The effort of adjusting to the Croatian culture entailed pushing their "Czechness" to the background (Jonatán) and in a sense they forget about the Czech Republic (Josef 1). The identity negotiation of a missionary's adjustment is not without struggles (Josef 2), and it is a process (Jonatán) which is never finished – "it can never be a *fait accompli*."[57] Furthermore, it is followed by pitfalls of adjusting too little or too much. Missionaries find it

---

54. This goal, in their case, was urged by the sending mission agency and the local team leader.

55. Josef 1, Josef 2 and Jonatán were, together with a local person and an international worker, part of the same church eldership team.

56. Out of tactfulness and to honour sincerity of all respondents, it can be mentioned that the situation was complex, and the details are not essential for the purpose of this research on their Czech identity negotiation.

57. Bosch, *Transforming Mission*, 455.

difficult to discern what is cultural and what is supra-cultural.[58] Josef 1 in the initial phase adjusted too little, while Jonatán has seemingly adjusted too much. Josef 2 wrestled in his identity with what is biblical – Hiebert says that sociocultural and historical situations affect our faith and sharing of that faith: "As Christians, we are often unaware that we are shaped more by our contexts than the gospel. We take our Christianity as biblically based and normative for everyone."[59]

There is a creative tension in the engagement with culture, which includes a certain level of cultural adjustment – and Czech identity suppression. This section sought to thematically analyse Czech identity facet suppression in situations of interaction with other nationals, of language usage (the relation of Czech to English and Czech to local languages) and in connection with the missionaries' adjustment to the local culture. Berry and his co-authors say that "the course of change resulting from acculturation is highly variable, and depends on many characteristics."[60] It became clear from the evidence that the suppression of the Czech identity facet is (a.) never complete, (b.) it is situational, and (c.) it is connected to its salience. Therefore, the following section focuses on the concurrent moments of both suppression and salience of the Czech national identity facet.

5.4 Simultaneous salience and suppression of Czech missionaries' Czech identity facet

> I simply realize the Czech identity I have, but at the same time I don't want it to be a barrier and strictly hold onto it in order to develop an intercultural contact. . . . So, I can be proud of that, but at the same time be flexible and open.
>
> —Erika 1, f, 1 year in Bosnia and Herzegovina

> I think that was the first time I realized that it's someone who, and I think that was the Czech trade in her, she's like: "I want to get this done." And I think she was shocked, by us as a church

---

58. Hesselgrave, *Communicating Christ Cross-Culturally*, 104.
59. Hiebert, "Gospel in Human Contexts," 83.
60. Berry et al., *Cross-Cultural Psychology*, 352.

team, just in how, we were like: "No, let's keep this open." . . . She was a dutiful servant and at the same time she had her own ideas. Like, you have people who are servants that just go: "Tell me what to do" and then you have people: "This is what we'll do" and she was kind of a good mixture of them both.

—Bethany, f, teammate (Erika 1 Bosnia and Herzegovina)

Kristýna is not Czech, Kristýna is a bigger Serbian than I am. Really. She probably has more love for this country than I who have grown up here. You cannot notice in talking to her, in behaviour, that she is a Czech. You can a bit tell by her accent, but rarely. However, in behaviour, something we consider a thing of daily basis, which has always been like this and it will never change, Kristýna challenges that, for example something with children at school, when the child gets bullied, she goes and a Serb would say: "Ok, just punch him back or be silent and don't make problems." Kristýna goes and wants to talk to the educator. There you can see these differences.

—Miodrag, m, colleague (Kristýna Serbia)

While Erika 1 spoke more generally about her willingness to set aside the "Czechness," Bethany referred to some of the personality traits related to cultural differences regarding achievement and individualism, as discussed in the previous chapter. For both of them, "at the same time" seemed to be a key phrase. Miodrag affirmed Kristýna as Serbian, and added: "however." At first, he noticed Kristýna's apparent overwhelmingly suppressed "Czechness," yet as he developed his comment, he was reminded of a particular situation when she faced the Serbian education system and her Czech identity emerged. It has to be noted, again, that in instances of facing differing health or education systems, this might refer to a broader foreign identity, not solely to Czech. Miodrag and Bethany give evidence for the perception of the dynamics of their colleagues' Czech identity facet salience and suppression as an inevitable part of their everyday functioning within a team at work. Erika's response and the one of Radek below, nevertheless, indicate that the concurrence of the Czech identity coming to the foreground and to the background is part of the missionaries' introspection as well.

> Sometimes pride would sneak in that we are economically better, that I have a good car, even though it's a company car. So, the Czech facet protruded there . . . I have no problem when I go to the West, earlier we had the complex. Now we go often to Germany, you can buy their food, you can afford to go to a restaurant. On the other hand, when I go to Serbia I don't want to be full of myself that I am a Czech and I have a nice car, it can change very fast. They say: "We used to be up and you down, and now it's vice versa," and I say: "Well, for how long?" So, I am glad when we can have a sensitive heart and help financially and bring resources there. And I rejoice when we can give, it is better than to take. So, that's the balance, I am thankful to God for what I have, but I know it's from him.
>
> —Radek, m, returning to Serbia

During the interview, Radek multiple times mentioned the economic differences and that the Czech Republic is better off than Serbia.[61] Radek's statement records the initial feeling of national pride, based on a better functioning economy, which he almost immediately strove to replace by an effort to stay humble. Radek acknowledged his inner struggle as he was attempting to suppress his salient "Czechness" by a conscious effort.

> Vratislav: Yes. And I am saying: "That's what I want to keep." Really, there are some things that – "Yes, I will be gladly with you, I will be doing things that you are doing," but there are some things that I want to keep as a Czech. Perhaps the fact I don't learn perfect Croatian and maybe that I will go to bed on time or . . .
>
> Interviewer: Earlier, or?
>
> Vratislav: I usually go at half past nine, or at ten, that's my time. But I wake up at five am.
>
> —Vratislav, m, returning to Croatia

---

61. See World Bank, "GDP Per Capita." Moreover, the difference of urban vs. rural areas is present, as Radek keeps coming from the city of Olomouc to the provincial town Stara Pazova.

Some missionaries, like Vratislav, tend to be very principled. Vratislav was willing to suppress his "Czechness," which often became salient through his personality, yet there were areas where Vratislav refused to suppress his habits, including what he considered his Czech work rhythm and a complete giving up on speaking Czech. The preceding responses point towards the ambiguous nature of missionaries' self-identification as Czechs and their negotiation of the national identity facet. They in the context of mission seem to both aim for its suppression, putting their "Czechness" aside, and at the same time want to (consciously) or happen to (unconsciously) keep what they consider to be national identity traits.[62]

Based on the material above and on the identity dynamics already evidenced in (5.2) and (5.3), identity salience and identity suppression (of the Czech identity facet) functions rather unevenly, i.e. it is neither salience of "Czechness" nor its suppression, but both. Authors of "The Social Identity Perspective"[63] come to a point of reflection on multiple identity facets: "The question is whether identities are hydraulically related to one another, so that the more one identity prevails, the less others do. Or can multiple identities be simultaneously salient?"[64]

The answer would be to point to its complexity, as "never a final or settled matter"[65] of one's social identity, which is to be viewed in more dynamic terms. Instead of imagining the identity facets as pistons of an engine moving up and down in a regular fashion, two or more identity facets may become salient at the same time, with varying intensity. In other words, the standpoint that the more a particular identity facet is salient, the less other identity facets are suppressed may be quite limited – viewed through the lens of the simultaneous identity facet occurrence.

---

62. Going to bed earlier (Vratislav), differing state of economy (Radek), focus on achievement (Erika 1) and other attributes again, as in section 4.2.1, are certainly not specifically Czech cultural traits, yet to the missionaries they seem Czech in comparison to the relevant counterparts in cultures of the former Yugoslav nations.

63. Hogg et al., in their publication from 2004, focus in their research on small interactive groups (Hogg et al., "Social Identity Perspective").

64. Hogg et al., 268.

65. Jenkins, *Social Identity*, 4.

5.5 Chapter conclusions

Czech missionaries possess a particular dual social identity, since all missionaries belong both to the home society and the host society.[66] Their identity negotiation happens, as for everybody, in the context of interaction and conflict with others.[67] Depending on whether the differentiation connects to occupying a role or to group membership, two major versions of salience come to account: "salient" in the sense of coming to the surface in embodying a role – which fits identity theory – and "salient" over belonging to the other group – which fits social identity theory and social identity complexity.[68] The findings of this research based in missiology may partially refer to both, yet the focus is predominantly on the latter, as social identity complexity is addressed in chapters 7 and 8. This chapter 5 has started to answer the question, "How and in what circumstances does the Czech identity of Czech missionaries become salient or suppressed?", and the subsequent chapter 6 continues the quest. Still, based on the evidence retrieved from the primary data so far, this chapter can conclude with several points of partial findings regarding Czech identity salience and suppression:

1. Czech identity salience and suppression are situational. In certain situations, Czech missionaries tend to strengthen their Czech identity, while elsewhere they tend to suppress it and identify with former Yugoslavs. "Czechness" resides in missionaries at all times, and it can be highlighted or suppressed, yet never completely eliminated. These were the situations or patterns of the missionaries' situational strengthening and weakening of Czech identity facet, in interaction with the Bosnian, Croatian, Macedonian, Montenegrin, Serbian and Slovenian outgroup, which emerged from the data as themes:
    (a) Czech identity salience (1a.) in encountering artefacts, (2a.) in encountering other Czechs, Slovaks and other nationals.
    (b) Czech identity suppression, (1b.) in interaction with other nationals, in (2b.) Czech language suppression (to English, to local languages), (3b.) in the adjustment to the local culture.

---

66. Hiebert, *Anthropological Insights for Missionaries*, 239
67. Tajfel and Turner, "Social Identity Theory", 285.
68. See Roccas and Brewer, "Social Identity Complexity," 94.

2. Based on the findings of the situational simultaneous salience and suppression of "Czechness," it can be affirmed that identity facets occur simultaneously in an uneven fashion, rather than being inversely proportional.[69] Jenkins says that "identity is always a dialectic between similarity and difference,"[70] thus reminding that identity negotiation is enacted as a dynamic unsettled process, rather than supposing that identity construction resembles a settled entity of one's sum of identities which function in the manner that the more one identity facet is present, the less others are.
3. There is an internal and external aspect of identity salience and suppression. It differs in how the missionary perceives identity facets such as "Czechness" to himself or herself and how it appears to others. This was reported by the complementary sources in this research, such as, Miodrag and Vladan and their outside perspective of Kristýna in Serbia, or Eldina and Bethany with their external view of Erika 1 in Bosnia and Herzegovina. Circumstances and the level of salience and suppression of Czech identity vary with each missionary.
4. To deepen the internal aspect and focus on the identity carrier, setting aside for a moment the somewhat constrained terms of "salience" or "suppression," identity negotiation entails both unconscious and conscious factors. In certain situations, an identity facet (in this case the Czech national identity facet of Czech missionaries) becomes salient or suppressed unintentionally, while at other times it may be activated or deactivated intentionally. This is to some degree debatable, and the assertion will be further explored in the next chapter.
5. Negotiation of identity salience or suppression, and particularly of the simultaneous salience and suppression, proves to be significant for missionaries as persons and influences their mission practice. Missionaries seem to aim for the suppression of national identity, yet at the same time they do (unconsciously) or

---

69. Hogg et al., "Social Identity Perspective", 268.
70. Jenkins, *Rethinking Ethnicity*, 169.

desire to (consciously) keep components of this particular identity facet. This is also covered in the upcoming chapter. Jakub 1 provides a brief introduction to this connection of Czech identity negotiation to mission engagement:

> We had to somehow discover the Czech identity, what is it, how to use it, when it's good and when not. So, we have taken a look into the "Czechness" by the long-term stay abroad, by the eyes of other nations. If we value ourselves by staying here in the Czech basin, then at the end of our research we will say: "We are the best ones." (laugh) But when we look at it by the outside perspective, we can filter the "Czechness," sift it and perhaps even make it better ... Czech identity needs to be clarified somehow, maybe even built up, and paradoxically this can be done also by a stay abroad, especially the mission stay.

—Jakub 1, m, returning to Bosnia and Herzegovina

This personal stance of Jakub 1 refers to both salience and suppression of the Czech identity facet and actually corresponds with the starting point of social identity theory – the outgroup comparison is essential for the definition of the ingroup.[71] Departing from this, alongside the outgroup which forms the ingroup, the ingroup forms the outgroup (for whom it is the outgroup). There is a legitimate element of reciprocity in social identity. To employ this in my study, not only is identity negotiation (with its salience and its suppression) influential and decisive in mission, mission can also be decisive in informing one's identity. Chapter 6 follows up on this analysis and adds more specific missiological conclusions.

---

71. Tajfel, *Human Groups*.

CHAPTER 6

Discussion of Czech Identity in Mission in Former Yugoslav Countries

6.1 National identity in mission

Suppression of the national identity of the mission agent, as I explored it in the previous chapter is closely associated with "contextualization," "inculturation," or "translation" of mission, and is something desired, as a cursory glance into missiological literature reveals. Thomas Schirrmacher recognizes that "there should be no claim to superiority on the part of one's own culture above another culture."[1] I found that nearly any serious book on mission stresses the need of suppressing ethnocentrism.[2] The very concept of *missio Dei* entails the understanding that since the mission we participate in is God's, human agents and their identity, including the national identity, are not supposed to be the focus.[3] In other words, the attention is to be on other cultures, not on the missionary's own culture. Scott Klingsmith, who specialized in research on missions from Romania, Poland and Hungary, admitted the peril of ethnocentrism in mission which, according to him, can result either in

---

1. Schirrmacher, *Biblical Foundations*, 44.

2. Ethnocentrism can be defined as: "A suspicion of outsiders combined with a tendency to evaluate the culture of others in terms of one's own culture." (Giddens, *Sociology*, 673).

3. See Bosch, *Transforming Mission*, 392.

working with wrong motives or hindering Christians in initiating mission engagement altogether.[4]

On the other hand, missiological publications seem to encourage emerging missions from nations that begin to send workers across cultures, including those in the countries of Central and Eastern Europe, to emancipate themselves and to learn to perform missions in their authentic way. Klingsmith, towards the end of his thesis, exhorts intercultural workers "to discover the authentically Polish or Hungarian or Romanian way to do missions."[5] His colleague in the region, Anne-Marie Kool, agrees with this and calls for a mission paradigm for the Central and Eastern European countries using words such as "new," "innovative," or "emerging."[6] To clarify, this prompting occurs in the post-Communist region, in churches which are currently learning to send intercultural missionaries and which have, for a long time, held a general attitude of inferiority vis-à-vis the West.[7] In the perspective of these two authors, this salience of the national identity facet can, in this case, signify a means of self-identification, rather than involving ethnocentrism as such.

The theologian Christopher Wright argued from the Bible using Acts 17:26 and Deuteronomy 32:8: "National distinctives, then, are part of the kaleidoscopic diversity of creation at the human level, analogous to the wonderful prodigality of biodiversity at every other level of God's creation."[8] Viewed from the biblical perspective, God works with and through nations and ethnic groups – including Czechs. Despite having obtained a new primary identity marker, Christians retain these particularities[9] and according to missiologist Miriam Adeney, ethnic pride is not necessarily always negative:[10] "When ethnicity is treasured as a gift but not worshipped as an idol, God's world is

---

4. Missionaries, in his words, "begin to discover in themselves unconscious attitudes of superiority regarding culture, society or church life" (Klingsmith, *Missions Beyond the Wall*, 178). Compare this to the remarks on the Hungarian (Klingsmith, 83–84), Polish (Klingsmith, 129–130) and Romanian (Klingsmith, 159–161) ethnocentrism in mission.

5. Klingsmith, *Missions Beyond the Wall*, 192.

6. Kool, "Revolutions in European Mission," 22.

7. See Klingsmith, *Missions Beyond the Wall*, 178.

8. Wright, *Mission of God*, 456.

9. Campbell, *Paul and Christian Identity*, 156.

10. She compares ethnic pride to a joy parents feel at their child's graduation, where there are other parents with their children present. It is not bad in itself, only when exalted as though it were the highest good which can result in racism, feuds, wars and ethnic cleansing (Adeney, "Is God Colorblind," 417–418).

blessed, and we enjoy a foretaste of heaven."[11] To expand on this, the similes of ethnicity as a gift or idol surely do not imply that "ethnicity" should be treated as an object, they rather imply plural meanings. Similarly, this might be the case with "nationality" in the sense of national identity, including the national identity facet in the focus of this research. I am aware of the complexity when, avoiding the matter of ethnocentrism, I ask: "Could there be space for a healthy highlighting of one's national identity facet in mission?"

This chapter, therefore, concentrates on "Czech mission" – how the Czech missionaries' national identity might be utilized in their mission work and push it forward. One needs to bear in mind that, in fact, there may not be Czech or any other national mission by itself, as Bulgarian missiologist Kozhuharov reminds us: "Mission today is being done in a globalized world, and it cannot be purely 'Russian,' or 'Romanian,' or any other single cultural expression."[12] Besides the topic of (a.) Czech identity salience in mission (in 6.3), two other major areas arose from the data: (b.) Factors in favour of Czechs in former Yugoslav countries, both in 6.2 and 6.3, and (c.) several missiological implications of the significance of the differing perception of religious identity in the mutual intercultural encounter, in 6.4. In 6.5 the chapter is concluded, in the continuation of answering the original research sub-question number two, "How and in what circumstances does the Czech identity of Czech missionaries become salient or suppressed?", which intersect chapters 5 and 6.

Before the analysis itself, again, I include several technical notes. The respondents were requested to share about moments where Czech identity stepped to the foreground or to the background. Further, they were broadly asked to comment on their interaction as Czech missionaries in former Yugoslav countries. The only specific accompanying question was perhaps only: "Who do you think influences you as a Czech missionary?" Themes for this chapter emerged from the interaction with primary sources.

---

11. Adeney, 422.
12. Kozhuharov, "Christian Mission in Eastern Europe," 54.

6.2 Czechs and Westerners in mission in former Yugoslav countries

6.2.1 Czechs' ambiguous spatiality

> Josef 1: We came and there were missionaries from South Africa, from Korea, from Germany, from Scotland, from Finland, from America. So, we came here from Bohemia and we didn't experience a culture shock, but a "hara-kiri" culture shock.
>
> Klára: A multicultural shock.
>
> Josef 1: A multicultural "hara-kiri," because we became part of the team, a collective of people from different countries, and it's a mixture, a fireworks or cultures, that it was many times more difficult. If we came here and ended up among Croats, we have one culture.
>
> —Josef 1, m, 20–30 years in Croatia
>
> —Klára, f, 20–30 years in Croatia

All Czech missionaries in former Yugoslav countries at some point of their engagement come into cooperation with other missionaries, the majority from Western countries. Instead of one customary culture shock with the host culture (in their case Croatian), there was, in the rather expressive words of Josef 1, a "fireworks" of cultures, or "hara-kiri."[13] In contrast to more diverse societies in Western countries, Czechia with its population of slightly over ten million might be considered relatively monolithic, so it can create an even bigger culture shock for a missionary when he or she is found in such an environment.

> We don't have that much money to bring.
>
> —Josef 3, m, returning to Bosnia and Herzegovina
>
> They lived from their support, and it was not that type of Western missionaries that they would employ another five locals (laugh).
>
> —Matěj, m, leader of sending mission agency (Josef 1 Croatia)

---

13. This admittedly unusual comparison probably refers to the suicidal nature of missionary's dying to a person's own culture, or to the extremeness of the multicultural encounter.

Even though the Czech economic situation has changed favourably since the early 1990s, these two comments underline that Czechs have limited resources. The differentiation from the Western teammates is often in the realm of finances, which is connected to feelings of inferiority due to forty years of Communism which threw the country backwards, and to the label of Czech "Easterness."

Again,[14] the view that the Czech Republic is part of Eastern Europe is near to non-existent in Czech scholarship. Instead, two prevailing views are present: the Czech Republic as part of the "kidnapped" West[15] and the Czech Republic as part of Central Europe.[16] The latter self-perception of Czechs is often linked to the supposedly balanced central location between the cultural spheres of East and West.[17] Czechs' spatiality situation can be fittingly encapsulated as "no more Eastern, but not yet Western."[18] As was documented by the responses of Matěj and Josef 3, the first association with the West is often linked to the economic power, and in the comparison to their "clearly" Western colleagues from the USA, the United Kingdom or Germany, Czechs in this perspective are not Western.[19] On the other hand, not being that precisely defined as Westerners seems to play a role in the inculturation in non-Western contexts, which becomes clearer as the discussion proceeds.

> There is a difference in culture, yet with Czechs who come, with Czech youth, Czech missionaries, and visitors, the impressions are that they are very close. They have much better impact on our missionary work here than when English or some other foreigners who come. That is really interesting. So, we have young Englishmen who come, and they are much more lost because they live in a "culture bubble" [in English] in England. While the Eastern Europe, they come more relaxed and much better impact.
>
> —Vladan, m, pastor and team leader (Kristýna Serbia)

---

14. See section 1.2.4.1.
15. Slačálek, "Postcolonial Hypothesis Notes."
16. See Havel, *About Human Identity*.
17. Vlachová and Řeháková, "Identity of Non-Self-Evident Nation," 258.
18. Ieda, "Regional Identities," 62.
19. Still, it depends on the point of view, perhaps Czech missionaries and expatriate workers, including the countries of Central Asian former Soviet Union or elsewhere, could have been considered "Western."

> We make fun of you but perceive you Czechs as equals.
>
> —Diary notes-SN-2018-07 Sarajevo, Bosnia and Herzegovina

The two statements of the local pastors underline the subjective nature of perception in intercultural relationships. Vladan's response disclosed a sensitive matter of the sweet-and-sour issue of comparison of missionaries from different cultural backgrounds. He classified Czechs, together with Serbs, as Eastern Europeans, in opposition to English.[20] His statement that Englishmen are in a culture bubble is, nevertheless, highly questionable. Rather, Czechs are more prone to being in a "culture bubble," since their country is not that ethnically or religiously diverse.[21]

After talking to the pastors, I found they value missionaries who come as helpers from wherever. Among other things they certainly appreciate the resources and mission skills the Western workers bring, and at the same time, subjectively, positively evaluate those of more similar cultures. These are due to the historical connections discussed in the previous chapter, in this case Czechs are often perceived in a way as equals (Diary notes-SN) – which might lead to a significant impact in the mission engagement (Vladan).

6.2.2 Western – American?

> I think that the whole former Yugoslavia has a positive relationship to Czechs. So there has never been a moment when I would suppress it, rather opposed to that, when we as a church had teams from abroad, we have had English, Americans, but it is very specific when Czechs come, then you have a feeling that our people came, I mean from the Serbian side, because the cultures are very close.
>
> —Kristýna, f, 20–30 years in Serbia

> Serbs are in a strange schizophrenic situation, that on one hand they would like to go to the West, they like the Western money and the Western lifestyle. On the other hand, they

---

20. To be noted, Vladan is very familiar with English, since most returning and residing missionaries in the church he pastors are from England, and importantly, his wife is English.

21. Furthermore, if one thinks it through critically, we all function in some sort of a culture or sub-culture bubble.

hold an animosity towards the West and I am not surprised. If Americans bombed us, we probably would not have a warm relationship to them.

—Jakub 2, m, returning to Serbia

This perception, by the locals and by Czech missionaries themselves, of Czechs, is certainly subjective and to a high degree emotional. Based on the responses so far, it seems to be very positive, while the relationship to Westerners is ambiguous – both welcoming and reserved. To help underline this, there is one approach to someone coming from a similar culture: an equal and brother Slav; as opposed to a more pragmatic approach to someone coming from the West and making use of their resources, learning one's global language (e.g. English, French, German, Spanish, etc), and possibly going to work in the West.

As the analysis unfolds, when considering "the West," the respondents mostly mention the USA and Americans. Jakub 1 is referring, in connection with Americans, to the NATO bombing of Serbia in 1999. Perhaps the reason why Kristýna includes both Americans and English in one sentence is the presence of English missionaries in her church.

> I think that a Czech missionary will be more successful than an American missionary, because the way of thinking, the culture, the identity is much closer.
>
> —Daniel, m, returning to Slovenia

> I don't know, Americans sometimes have the connotation that they are the smartest ones who know how to do things the best and wherever they come. They bring their know-how, which is a prejudice, but it can raise the impression. So, I think Czechs don't have it.
>
> —Erika 1, f, 1 year in Bosnia and Herzegovina

> Another obstacle is that they [Czechs] believe American procedures, brochures and lectures, they have to create their own distinctive concept of mission within the communication between the two European (or even two Slavic) nations.
>
> —Jakub 1, m, returning to Bosnia and Herzegovina

"Western" certainly does not equal American, yet in minds of Czech missionaries, this often is the first association, perhaps thanks to their personal experience with other mission workers from the USA, who are proportionately quite numerous in the region, and as the result of narratives of the local people, who have had recent experiences with American nationals, mainly the peace keeping forces, during and after the recent war.

As is evident, the responses tend to turn into critique, which may be substantiated by the missionaries' negative intercultural experience or frustrations in their own work. In social competition, "the group members may seek positive distinctiveness through direct competition with the outgroup."[22] In the observation of the missionaries above, there are definitely elements of truth, yet simultaneously it is valid that, for the USA specifically, being a sending country for a longer time entails certain procedures of know-how and more self-confidence. While, on the other hand, Czechs might lack a clear idea of what to do. As a result, they sometimes become part of foreign mission paradigms.

As evidenced here, Czech missionaries (Daniel, Erika 1, Jakub 1) and local workers (earlier responses) tend to be at times critical of Western missionaries and optimistic about Czech missionaries, and this negotiating of the differences is an integral part of their self-identification in mission. Henry Tajfel wrote that the reason for evaluative differentiation is the need for the individuals to provide social meaning.[23] Czechs seem to favour themselves, opposed to the Western (and American) outgroup, yet the situation is rather complex and differs from person to person.

6.3 Czech identity salience in mission
6.3.1 Situational utilisation of Czech identity salience

> Earlier I would not tell you I feel like a Czech or that I don't care, I don't identify with anything, but gradually you realize that we have many positive features, in which one can take pride and that can actually enrich the work in the international context, so I simply realize the Czech identity I have, but at the same time

---

22. Tajfel and Turner, "Social Identity Theory," 285.
23. Tajfel, 276.

I don't want it to be a barrier and strictly hold onto it in order to develop an intercultural contact.

—Erika 1, f, 1 year in Bosnia and Herzegovina

This quote was already partially introduced when discussing the simultaneous salience and suppression of Czech identity in (5.4). This is experienced by many in an intercultural encounter: Erika 1 initially did not ponder her Czech identity, yet later, realized she can proactively utilize this identity facet for the advancement of the mission work. To expound on what Erika 1 talks about in general terms, this can be documented by a shared experience of Czech culture night (in the picture).

Photo diary-2014-04 Banja Luka, Bosnia and Herzegovina

In Banja Luka, where I worked, when a group from abroad came, they would go out to meet the people, starting conversations and inviting them to events, such as "culture nights" (in the picture). These were organized by the local church as both educational and outreach in their nature. At a particular Czech[24] culture night happening before Easter, the presenter had a brief speech about *beránek* (lamb), which is a Czech Easter cake in the shape of a lamb. He explained Czech Easter traditions and bridged it with a Gospel presentation, where the lamb represented Jesus. This is a clear example of the Czech identity facet being purposefully utilized in the mission work context.

> I think that whoever, missionary or Christian, because every Christian has a ministry, you always look for things that will connect you to people and you always look for a reason how to talk to people, and how to talk to them about God. So, if the "Czechness" fits there for me, I pull it out. . . . I am quite a visible person here, many people know me, because I am from Czechia, because of what we do.
>
> —Kristýna, f, 20–30 years in Serbia

Kristýna, while affirming the significance of her Czech identity, accentuates that she is ready to "pull out" other identity facets, and thus confirms the practice of intentionality in the utilisation of one's identity facets, including "Czechness." The perspective of intentional vs. unintentional usage of Czech identity in Czech missionaries' ministry relates to the findings of the preceding chapter, that there is an internal and external aspect of identity salience and suppression – whether a missionary perceives the Czech identity facet for himself or herself or whether it gets noticed by others.

Many times, therefore, there are unintentional situations of Czech identity salience in ministry emerging naturally. The picture below documents how a short-term Czech team drew attention from a national newspaper. Any positive media coverage helps the tiny Protestant community in Croatia, and the title reads, "Pastor Kreko, with asylum seekers, volunteers and Czechs builds the integration centre." The fact that the Czech team came to help with construction work, where Czechs were "volunteers" along with others, yet their national identity was depicted, helped draw the attention of the reporter who wrote the article.

---

24. The culture nights were numerous. Thai, Norwegian, English, American, Burkina Faso, Finnish and Costa Rican culture nights were also organized.

Discussion of Czech Identity in Mission in Former Yugoslav Countries 171

Photo diary-2018-09 Zagreb, Croatia

The next picture of the Czech short-term student team illustrates how Czechs, intentionally using their "Czechness," are making connections with the local students.

Photo diary-2016-04 Banja Luka, Bosnia and Herzegovina

The initial attraction for the Serbian students was certainly that they were foreigners, and thereafter that they, as foreigners, were Czechs. Still, as a result of the familiarity with Czechs and Slovaks with their partners in conversation, the recurring topic they had with local students was the break-up of Czechoslovakia as compared to the Yugoslav experience.

> Or one more Croatian, or commonly Balkan, problem comes to my mind that people are split and have disagreements and it's infiltrated the churches . . ., the non-Catholic churches are not numerous, but they keep splitting . . . I think that our missionaries were able to bring in a healthy emphasis, certain different approaches, and Josef 1 contributed to this a lot when he started to build relationships with other pastors in Istria, and for years he has been trying to bring them together and organize meetings and it has been more and more successful, and it's something I think very rare in Croatia, and because he's a Czech he could bring it in.
>
> —Matěj, m, leader of sending mission agency (Josef 1 Croatia)

For both Czechs and former Yugoslavs, history is important, and the themes of the recent fall of the regime and split of the countries keep coming to the surface. Matěj's response, which is rather subjective and biased in its criticism, points to how at certain times intentionally pushing to the front the Czech identity facet could prove to be counterproductive. Furthermore, there are several objections to the statement of Matěj: Firstly, this is a perspective of the organisation leader and it might be questionable to what extent the missionaries practised it. Secondly, Czechs and Slovaks are indeed considered by former Yugoslavs to be peaceful due to historical reasons, yet coming in advance with a peace-making agenda – this sort of intentional utilisation of a national identity facet – might actually create a barrier. Yet, if this happens unintentionally as a side effect or a connecting point, it could be beneficial.

In the missiological view there is a highly relevant affirmation of suppressing one's identity, including national identity, to identify with those the missionary serves. There is a legitimate danger of a nationalistic spirit being absorbed into missionary ideology. David Bosch warns against such excessive highlighting of the national identity: "Christians of a specific nation would develop the conviction that they had an exceptional role to play in the advancement of the kingdom of God through the missionary enterprise."[25] On the other hand, there are voices for active usage of one's national traits, calling for their engagement wherever advantageous.[26] Ralph Winter's conclusions for missions strategy as outlined by the E-scale suggest that the utilization of one's national identity facet in the sense of cultural proximity to the target culture can in fact prove advantageous to mission work.[27]

The evidence in this sub-section led to a partial conclusion that appropriate utilization of situational salience of the Czech identity facet could help advance the work of Czech missionaries in former Yugoslav countries. Besides that, it can be inferred that other missionaries may benefit from a positive utilisation of their national identity facet, as this is not restricted to Czechs.

6.3.2 Acceptance of Czechs by former Yugoslavs

> We were accepted well because we were Czechs. It was God's strategy. "Oh, you are Czechs, that's fine."
>
> —Ema 1, f, 20–30 years in Slovenia
>
> When we came there, Croats were talking about the war in Croatia, Bosnia and Kosovo, and that Czechs were the ones coming and saving tourism.
>
> —Josef 2, m, 10–20 years in Croatia
>
> I actually advised people to say, when you get into some misunderstanding, just say: "I am from Czechoslovakia," then everyone would forgive you and it will be OK. Then a friend came to me and said: "They almost beat me up in Bosnia." He got into a political discussion and the guys stood up to beat him up and he said: "I am from Czechoslovakia," "All right then," they sat down and continued the conversation.
>
> —Jakub 1, m, returning to Bosnia and Herzegovina
>
> In the work, in Serbia it plays a positive role that we are Slavs.
>
> —Jakub 2, m, returning to Serbia

---

25. Bosch, *Transforming Mission*, 299.
26. See Klingsmith, *Missions Beyond the Wall*; Kool, "Revolutions in European Mission."
27. Winter, "Frontier Mission Perspectives."

> Yes, when we say we are Czechs or from Bohemia, they approach it very positively, they tell us: "Brother, brother." Serbs they say to each other: "Brother, brother," or "bro bro," so they talk about us as Czechs. This is interesting because when we are in Bohemia, who has this thinking about these nations in this way?
>
> —Ema 2, f, 2–10 years in Serbia

This series of overwhelmingly positive utterances on the account of Czechs comes from missionaries who were present in Slovenia, in Croatia, in Bosnia and Herzegovina and in Serbia. It seems, due to cultural proximity, Czechs were accepted well across the former Yugoslav areas. Interestingly, Jakub 1 mentioned "Czechoslovakia" and not "the Czech Republic," as if alluding that Czechoslovakia entails an affirmative reputation due to the peaceful cohabitation of Czechs and Slovaks. Ema 1, while she considered being Czechs in Slovenia as "God's strategy," her husband responded more reservedly: "In general, we are accepted well as Czechs here" (Patrik, m, 20–30 years in Slovenia). Josef 2 recalled a positive reminiscence regarding Czechs and Slovaks from the local people on the coast – they were among the first ones who returned immediately after the war in the 1990s, and even kept coming for holidays even during the conflict.[28]

The matter of the acceptance of Czechs as Slavs is complex. The Slavic brotherhood, as Ema 2 suggested, might at times function only in one direction. This may again be connected to historical factors.[29] The political scientist Ondřej Slačálek stated: "Pan-Germanism and Pan-Slavism each contain specific elements of the colonial narrative, dominance and homogenization. They both offer assimilation into one version or another of imperial subjectivity and cultural identity."[30] Serbs are certainly more oriented towards Russia, also

---

28. Specifically, they kept coming to the Istria peninsula, which was not a war zone. Slovak social scientist Ivan Chorvát noted that in the early 1990s, "Czechs and Slovaks were the only tourists who dared to go there, helping again to revive and enhance local tourism" (Chorvát, "Czechs and Slovaks as Explorers," 8). This is significant and Croats value this, since the economy is highly dependent on the tourist industry.

29. Czechs of the nineteenth century, under the Habsburg dynasty rule, were oriented toward pan-Slavic ideas, yet often, after they visited tsarist Russia, were disillusioned (Slačálek, "Postcolonial Hypothesis Notes", 33).

30. Slačálek, "Postcolonial Hypothesis Notes," 31.

a majority Christian Orthodox country.[31] In addition, their country never bordered Russia or the Soviet Union. Czechs, with their twentieth century experiences of Russian intrusion (since 1945) and invasion (in 1968), tend to be more careful about pan-Slavic ideas, i.e. anything which savours Russian hegemony.[32] Instead, the notion of being Slavs, as situationally enhanced by Czech missionaries, functions more in the sense of a reference to the bilateral Czech – former Yugoslav dyad, based on the historical amity and mutual familiarity.

Up to this point, the acceptance of Czechs in connection with history has been discussed, yet the responses contained two instances of rejection:

> We were rejected only in one case and it was in Serbia concerning the legitimization of Kosovo's independence. Czechia has acknowledged the independent Kosovo, and Slovakia didn't. So, when we say we are from Czechoslovakia, they often hurry to ask: "Czechs or Slovaks?" "Czechs." "And you acknowledged Kosovo."
>
> —Jakub 1, m, returning to Bosnia and Herzegovina
>
> Croats despise us as Czechs. It could be seen in comparison to Americans, when Croats looked up to them and had them naturally as an authority. While we still were for them *Pemci* [pejorative for Czechs in Croatian, derived from the German *Böhmen*], even though Josef 1 was a pastor and Josef 2 was an elder.
>
> —Renata, f, 10–20 years in Croatia

The acknowledgement of the independence of Kosovo, the cradle of Serb culture, by the Czech government in 2008 still seems to re-emerge as an occasional stumbling block for individual Czechs in the region. Renata's response reflects the Croatian experience of contempt for Czechs whose buying power, especially in the 1990s when these missionaries arrived at the coast, was still lower, and they were not as attractive as missionaries from elsewhere.

---

31. To illustrate, Serbs have a saying: "There are three hundred million of us and Russians." ["*Nas i Rusa tristo miliona*"].

32. See Kubiš et al., "Czech Republic: Nation Formation", 140–144; Slačálek, "Postcolonial Hypothesis Notes", 33.

Next, when tackling the acceptance of Czechs, statements of non-Czechs should be consulted:

> I like when Czechs come here, they are automatically friends, part of the family immediately.
>
> —Miodrag, m, colleague (Kristýna Serbia)

> I will always remember you from the very first Czech team that came to Bihać in what, 2003 maybe? We were all amazed at what a good team it was, how you were such prayer warriors and how the language barrier was not a barrier at all. I think it was C. who said later that we could take Czech teams any time! And look what all has happened after that!
>
> —Diary notes-JP-2018-08 Tallin, Estonia

> I don't think that other missionaries are not useful . . . maybe it is in some way better to have Czech missionaries because of the similarities of the cultures, and because of the language and I think it is a big advantage.
>
> —Eldina, f, supervisor and team leader (Erika 1 Bosnia and Herzegovina)

> And I think, yeah, I can say that every single Czech team they were ready to do whatever needed to be done. They had an idea of what they wanted to do as well and they did it, but I think the people are hard-working, coming with a mission, wanting to get it done and willing to listen to us, which is always a big thing here with teams.
>
> —Bethany, f, teammate (Erika 1 Bosnia and Herzegovina)

This set of responses on the acceptance of Czech Protestant missionaries appears again rather idealistic. The evaluation of the Czech missionaries by co-workers (Serb, Bosnian, Estonian and South African) is useful, yet certain uncritical elements, caused by multiple factors, appear in the comments, since there are certainly negative elements of the Czech missionary endeavour. The first factor was the very fact that I, a Czech, performed the interview. Secondly, they all were favourable respondents, themselves Protestant believers. Thirdly,

Discussion of Czech Identity in Mission in Former Yugoslav Countries

there is a psychological factor: in one's reminiscences, positive experiences from the past usually tend to overshadow the negative ones.

In order to finalize the matter of Czech Protestant missionaries' acceptance and rejection, a broader research scale would be required. The following section continues the discussion on the practical outcomes for Czech mission in the former Yugoslav context.

6.3.3 Favourable factors for Czech missionaries in former Yugoslav countries

> Well, I think in general it's an advantage not only in Croatia but almost everywhere in the world to be a Czech missionary. I think as a nation we don't have tense relationships practically with any nation; mostly thanks to that, we didn't have colonies and didn't lead a war abroad. Many nations and countries in the world have tense relationships with someone else because of that, for example Americans have problems in many countries because they have led wars or supported an enemy from a different country. But Czechs are in this regard a blank slate and that's valid also in Croatia. No one has any reason to be biased and angry ahead of time.
>
> —Matěj, m, leader of sending mission agency (Josef 1 Croatia)
>
> The nations that have expanded, for example the French during Bonaparte or the Germans many times in history, or different armies, Turks, Polish, I don't know. The Czech have not expanded, Czechs have never led wars, they didn't have colonies. So, historically, we don't have anywhere a black shield with anyone.
>
> —Jakub 1, m, returning to Bosnia and Herzegovina

These responses, once more, are conditioned by affiliation and enthusiasm for Czech mission and need to be approached with some discernment. Czechs have not caused historical harm in former Yugoslavia and elsewhere, therefore they are likely to be received favourably. This claim arising from the preceding statements is certainly valid, yet calls for remarks to accompany it. Czechs might not have led wars, occupied a territory or colonized an underdeveloped country, nevertheless, an attitude of invaders might be reflected in the mission work of anyone who sets off with incorrect and contemptuous motives, regardless the place of origin. Moreover, Matěj and Jakub 1 are not precise in their judgement, since Czechs were in fact colonizers themselves in Carpathian Ruthenia[33] between 1918 and 1939 and were involved in the "development" of the Balkans in the time of Austria-Hungary.[34] Furthermore, as mentioned before, despite not being a typical Western formerly colonising country, the present-day Czech Republic by its import and export policies might share an indirect responsibility for unequal trade conditions.[35]

The above paragraphs again underline that history, often underestimated by Evangelicals, seems to play a significant role in acceptance of individual nationals. In spite of certain grey areas, elements in Czech history are beneficial for Czech missionaries. The following, so to say, benefit, is the perceived adjustability of Czechs in mission.

> I think we do have national pride, but we are cunningly ready to throw it off to gain something . . ., but on the other hand, we are able to subordinate and in mission we are able to come not as the ones who say "we know." And for me, it was very strange when I came to Poland and tried to speak in Polish, nobody was considering that I don't speak Polish and they didn't help me, not even so that they would try to use some Czech words to comfort me. When I come somewhere I always learn a couple of words, when I sat there they didn't behave in the way that I would understand them. It was shocking for me when I met, it was in Slovakia, with a Pole, I talked to him in Polish and he talked to me back in Polish. In a different country I tried to adjust to him

---

33. This part of today's Western Ukraine, formerly under the Austrian monarchy, was between 1918 and 1939 part of the newly created Czechoslovakia. Slačálek describes this turn of history as when the colonised Czechs became for period of time political and cultural colonisers (Slačálek, "Postcolonial Hypothesis Notes", 33). The present perfect tense is used for the ambiguous position of the ongoing economic ties and the use of cheap labour from this and from other parts of Ukraine.

34. Horký-Hlucháň and Profant, "Reflexion of the Global North", 19. My translation; original: "'*Rozvoj*' *Balkánu v době Rakousko-Uherska.*" The timeframe for Bosnia and Herzegovina would be from 1878 to 1918, and especially after the annexation in 1908. See also Holubec, *We Haven't Made It Yet*, 249.

35. This involves also manufacturing and the export of arms.

automatically. When I come to Slovakia I automatically try to use Slovak words to adjust to them. It is something in us Czechs, I don't know if it is brown-nosing.

—Josef 3, m, returning to Bosnia and Herzegovina

Roman 1: I know there are churches that send American missionaries, and I have seen the budget, it is written how many thousands of dollars for insurance, for this and that, incredible amounts. And then the Czech missionary or a Polish one, we can get modest . . . When I pray for food, I really thank. Because we have had a month when at the beginning you bought a chicken that you baked and the rest of month you were eating bread, not bread with ketchup, but bread.

Ema 2: But yes, there are some visitors, from America, they come and say: "This is cheap, this is cheap." And we have learnt to be quiet, because how do you keep explaining that it depends for whom it is cheap.

—Roman 1, m, 2–10 years in Serbia

—Ema 2, f, 2–10 years in Serbia

Roman 1, together with Ema 2, even though he recalls rather extreme situations of deficiency, finds more modest expectations in the living standard of Czechs[36] beneficial for mission.[37] When pondering adjustability, Josef 3 critiqued some aspects of Czech mentality and certainly, the four decades of communist rule (1948–1989) inevitably left marks on the Czech national character: "The Czech person was taught not to say too much, not to ask too much, not to care too much, not to be bold, creative, or innovative."[38] As the result, several characteristics seem to prevail: distrust of authorities and institutions,[39] distance from formalized religion,[40] a flawed work ethic and

---

36. This cannot be, according to him, affirmed on the whole, as there are exceptions of Western missionaries who are sensitive and adjust their lifestyle. On the contrary there certainly are Czech missionaries – they have not been encountered in this sample – who are not modest in material expectations when they adjust to local culture.

37. See Klingsmith, *Missions Beyond the Wall.*

38. Činčala, "Theoretical Proposal for Reaching," 123.

39. Hošek, *Gods Return*, 95.

40. Halík, "Catholic Church in the Czech Republic," 145.

personal character,[41] a poor approach to responsibility in public and private sectors,[42] cynical humour as a tool to oppose imposed dogmas,[43] and pessimism and feeble national self-confidence.[44]

This particular trait of Czech national character – their supposed inherent adjustability – may be caused by them being a nation of ten million which for long periods of its history was ruled by someone else. The two interview extracts above specifically mention two of its aspects: language adjustment and adjustment to the living standard. Roman 1 certainly finds deficiency negative, and Josef 3 finds this trait of yielding negative, as he speaks in terms of "cunning" and "brown-nosing," yet they both seem to affirm its usefulness in missions.

> The Balkans are an ideal mission field. First, historically, because within Austria-Hungary we were with some areas in one common state, or people have migrated, so Czechs have lived there. During the time of Communism, people would go there for holiday, Yugoslavs went here to study, so everyone knows something about Czechs, we are accepted well there. Also, for us it is accessible logistically. It is possible to go there and back for a long weekend. So, if you want to go to Indonesia, it requires time and money.
>
> —Jakub 1, m, returning to Bosnia and Herzegovina

Adding to what was already discussed, Jakub 1 mentioned geographical proximity: from south-eastern Moravia it is only three hundred kilometres to the Slovenian border, while from the western-most tip of Bohemia it is about one thousand seven hundred kilometres to the remotest part of North Macedonia. The journey to most places in former Yugoslav countries can be easily carried out from the Czech Republic by car in one day.

Whether the Balkans is an "ideal" mission field for Czechs, as Jakub 1 suggests, is questionable, nonetheless, founded on the preliminary conclusions in the preceding sub-section 6.3.2, together with the missionaries' remarks

---

41. Havel et al., *Briefly Please*, 243.
42. Havel, *Czech and European Identity*, 10.
43. Moyle, "Shadows of the Past," 19.
44. Drápal, *Will We Survive*, 13; Kvaček, "About Czech Self-Confidence," 163; Potůček, "Present Situation," 149.

and insights presented here (6.3.3), the following could be favourable factors for Czech missionaries in former Yugoslavia region:

- Slavic cultures and languages are close
- Equality factor: Czechs were historically economically poorer
- Familiarity with Czechs and a partial common history
- No historical harm
- Geographical proximity
- Czechs' presumed trait of adjustability

Before any conclusions are drawn it needs to be stressed that certainly, when discussing Czechs' advantages in mission, it always depends on individual missionaries' personal dispositions – character, commitment, talents and gifts, previous experiences and other factors. The starting position of being Czechs, i.e. their national identity, is only one aspect which to lesser or higher degrees influences missionary's predisposition for "effective"[45] mission in former Yugoslavia. The focus of this research is on broader identity, yet the list above, which surely is not exhaustive, points towards concomitant practical outcomes in supporting Czech mission in former Yugoslavia.

6.4 Religious identity facet and its missiological implications

Recently, following the war in the 1990s, former Yugoslav countries experienced two trends: growth of conversions to Protestantism and an influx of foreign missionaries.[46] Consequently, the newer churches, who make up a small minority, have often been looked upon with suspicion as a foreign threat and intrusion[47] or are labelled "sects."[48] This chapter section might not appear to concern "Czechness" per se, yet it is related since there are Czechs amongst these foreign Protestant missionaries and it concerns their religious

---

45. This is in quotation marks, since it is highly problematic, within a qualitative research and due to the nature of people-oriented mission work, to attempt to measure "effectiveness" or "success."
46. Compare with Milkov, "Roots of Proselytism," 99; and Magda and Wachsmuth, "Discerning the Body," 32.
47. Kuzmič, "Christianity in Eastern Europe," 27.
48. Mojzes, "Proselytism in the Successor States," 234.

identity negotiation.[49] This topic entails serious missiological outcomes and the respondents of this research were repeatedly returning to it, as the ethnoreligious[50] identity of former Yugoslavs is often the first or one of the first cultural traits Czech missionaries observe or are very soon informed about.

6.4.1 Challenges of ethnoreligious identity for Czech Protestant missionaries

> Interviewer: Do you recall any negative situations? When because you were Czechs, they were laughing, or?
>
> Roman 1: Yes, they were, not because of "Czechness," but because of Christianity. For example, when we were renting a space in a hotel and after a month and half they wrote us we are not allowed to go there, threatening us with a court appeal.
>
> —Roman 1, m, 2–10 years in Serbia

> I think that in general they were confused to meet a missionary from any other church than Orthodox church. In that area, "Christian" and "Orthodox" merge and if it's not an Orthodox, then it will logically be a Catholic – and they will look down on them. Yet all of a sudden they find out that it's something else and they will merge it with Mormons, Jehovah witnesses, Adventists, simply it will be something from these.
>
> —Jakub 3, m, sending parish priest (Erika 1 Bosnia and Herzegovina)

> In Croatia, a part of national identity is Catholicism, so a Christian who is not Catholic is strange, a member of a strange sect. So, Josef 1 said that when they got to know the locals, when they started to accept them or when they helped them with something, then they were saying: "Yes, they are from a sect, but from the good one." (laugh)
>
> —Matěj, m, leader of sending mission agency (Josef 1 Croatia)

---

49. They often aim to suppress their church affiliation and focus on the commonalities of Christian confession, such as the doctrine of Trinity, yet still they maintain particularities, such as the stress on the importance of Bible reading and a personal relationship with God.

50. That is, when religious communities are closely related to ethnic identities (Smith, *National Identity*, 7).

These responses lay out the evidence, which will be further widened and elaborated in this sub-section, of what Czech and other missionaries face as Protestants: (a.) unfamiliarity (Jakub 3), rejection (Roman 1), toleration, yet labelled a "sect" (Matěj).

The status of Protestants in the society of former Yugoslav countries differs from the one in the Czech context where it is a widely accepted form of Christianity and where more diverse views of religion prevail, given by the history of the Catholic-Protestant conflict[51] and a substantial atheist or non-religious matrix.[52] Peter Kuzmič explains that in the former Yugoslav countries, Protestant minorities are looked upon with suspicion as a radical movement which in the past divided Christendom and currently in its fragmented forms threatens national and religious identity and people's unity.[53] Muslim or Catholic and Orthodox Christian bodies are often unwilling to be open to alternative expressions of faith in their "canonical territory" due to the already discussed equation of religious and national identity.[54]

> Here, Orthodoxy is a national religion that everybody believes, even though it is Orthodoxy mixed with traditions, it is not only religion, but Serbian tradition. In Serbia, without the tradition, a person does not get born, does not get married, does not die, so it is in all spheres.
>
> —Kristýna, f, 20–30 years in Serbia

---

51. Hošek, *It Is Our Story.*
52. Nešpor, *Too Weak in Faith.*
53. Kuzmič, "Christianity in Eastern Europe," 27.
54. More in 2.4.4 "Religious identity in former Yugoslav countries." And see also Edženci, "Church Planting in Belgrade," 11.

Photo diary-2010-04 Laktaši, Bosnia and Herzegovina

Kristýna's statement clarifies the picture above of a billboard on a bus station in a town centre. It illustrates an example of a radical nationalist manifestation connected to the religion; it says: "Serb, do not forget. Christ is risen. Kosovo and Metohija has always been Serbia." The connection of the two identity facets is, it must be emphasized, certainly not something now overcome which only the older generation holds onto – a survey among youth in the Western Balkans recently confirmed that "ethnic and religious identities are almost completely overlapping."[55] Viewed in this way, Bosniaks are therefore Muslims, Croats are Catholic Christians, Macedonians are Orthodox Christians, Montenegrins are Orthodox Christians, Serbs are Orthodox Christians, and Slovenes are Catholic Christians.

---

55. Žeželj and Pratto, "What Identities", 167.

Discussion of Czech Identity in Mission in Former Yugoslav Countries

> Former Yugoslav countries are very religiously oriented. . . . Czech culture does not count on God. The Croatian does count on God, but not in the biblical sense, but in the sense of a traditional religion.
>
> —Josef 2, m, 10–20 years in Croatia

This, as Josef 2 noticed, is the specific challenge – that the religious identities, in the case of Christian identity, labelled as Catholic, Orthodox and Protestant,[56] in individual contexts usually signify ethnic, cultural and political orientations rather than being linked to the Christian gospel as such.[57] To note critically Josef's statement, Protestant Christians are often the ones who readily use the expression "biblical," in order to point out they are right, while others are not. They are known for their emphasis on the Scriptures, yet this does not imply the Bible is not held in high esteem and usage in the Catholic and Orthodox circles in former Yugoslav countries.

The two final extracts conclude this section on how ethnoreligious identity presents a genuine challenge for the work of Protestant, Czech and other, missionaries in former Yugoslav countries:

> Normal educated people, middle class, say: "This is in America, this is not in Europe, we have seen it in a film." The first contact was often a general misunderstanding: "Slovenes associated us with religious freaks, Jehovah witnesses, an American thing they know from films or something from Prekmurje." These are local specifics, I don't know how it is in other Balkan countries, it is complicated by national "slash" [in English] religious identity. When you are a Croat, you must be Catholic and so on, and here also: "We are all Christians."
>
> —Patrik, m, 20–30 years in Slovenia

---

56. This could apply to national minorities: "If you are not Lutheran, you are a sect. There is a strong Lutheran church where many people are, seventy percent are not born-again, thirty percent are. The priest is born-again and . . . he is deep in tradition, because he is paid by the members who would revolt" (Radek, m, returning to Serbia). Radek commented on something slightly different, which could be further explored and critiqued, yet the point here is that Vojvodina Slovaks delineate themselves from the majority Serb population, similarly based on religious-national identity.

57. Tennent, *Invitation to World Missions*, 39.

In spring, an article appeared in the local leading newspaper heading: "Jehovah's witnesses are again knocking on the door." One third of the article focused on our local Evangelical student movement, local branch of International Fellowship of Evangelical Students. Later in July, a state TV made an interview with myself and my colleagues about "various student movements in the town," I learnt the day it was broadcast it meant "the cults in the town."

Diary notes-DS-2013-07 Banja Luka, Bosnia and Herzegovina

Photo diary-2011-11 Banja Luka, Bosnia and Herzegovina

The picture of the newspaper article, entitled "Secret religious rituals in flats," documents the diary note above and the widespread generalizations in Bosnian Serb society, which is present across former Yugoslav countries. Peter, in his response, referred to the only Slovenian region influenced by the Reformation, which otherwise had little historical impact in the whole region.[58] Contemporary Protestant missionaries, therefore, consider themselves to be entitled to carry on the mission, which for the Evangelicals means proclaiming the gospel to all nations regardless of the jurisdiction. While on the other side, for the traditional ecclesial bodies, mission is rather focused on believers in diaspora and on preserving the national identity.[59] In former Yugoslavia, "Islam, Roman Catholicism, and Eastern Orthodoxy all consider this an auspicious time for the reactivating and re-education of the people traditionally in their spheres."[60] In this way, the institutionalized religion, like nationalism, has ambitions to supply "existential answers to individuals' quests for security, providing a picture of totality, unity and wholeness."[61]

The clash often occurs and, as evidenced in the sample of Czech Protestant missionaries, it represents certain challenges. Furthermore, it would be more precise to say that instead of speaking of specific challenges to be overcome, it is rather the general issues of unacquaintance, ignorance (Patrik) and antagonism (Diary notes-DS) that present the true obstacles to mission work. Patrik, who pastors a "megachurch" in the Slovenian context (fifty members) where the closest other Protestant church is one hundred kilometres away, kept returning to this theme throughout the interview. He emphasized the aforementioned:

> They are those who are the good ones, they have all the sacraments, they have done nothing wrong. . . . You are Christian because you got born here. So, this has been the biggest challenge for Protestant church planting and discipleship.
>
> Patrik, m, 20–30 years in Slovenia

Still, the Protestants themselves might have created other obstacles, which is the subject matter of the subsequent passage.

---

58. Mojzes, "Proselytism in the Successor States," 225.
59. Parushev, "Mission as Established Presence," 72.
60. Mojzes, "Proselytism in the Successor States," 236.
61. Kinnvall, "Globalization and Religious Nationalism," 759.

6.4.2 Protestants' challenge of contextualization

In Protestant churches in Bosnia and Herzegovina, missionaries from abroad comprise a substantial percentage of their membership.

Diary notes-DS-2008-10 Banja Luka, Bosnia and Herzegovina

I was attracted to see the situation similarly as in Ukraine, but the church functions on very different foundations than the church in Ukraine. The Ukrainian church comes from the roots, so it's very traditional, but here they sang the American worship songs and the American style, so I think that the influence of Christians from abroad and especially from the West was apparent there, so I felt a bit better in Ukraine, it was more genuine. Here it was excessively modern, but in the culture, where they lived it, it stood out like a sore thumb.

—Josef 3, m, returning to Bosnia and Herzegovina

The small size of Protestant churches in former Yugoslav countries[62] implies a higher proportion of foreign missionaries and, together with them, a natural influence from other cultures. This very issue drew the attention of Josef 3, as a pastor who plants churches across southern Moravia, and he kept returning to it, comparing this Bosnian experience with his previous trips to Ukraine.

Certainly, the thing that churches are small and weak there and for our small and weak churches it means that our influence is much bigger than we thought. If you come to Ukraine, we were supporting a pastor who had twenty thousand people under himself. When you come to Bosnia from a church of thirty to fifty people, then we are a megachurch. So that's perhaps the only country where I felt as a big pastor (laugh).

—Josef 3, m, returning to Bosnia and Herzegovina

It is one big problem of Serbian churches and churches around us that all of our training and philosophy of work, philosophy

---

62. Mojzes, "Proselytism in the Successor States," 225.

of church and approach to theology is Western, all Western, and that's a big reason why our churches are not big. And simply we don't know how to approach so that our people here understand it and we don't speak the language that they would understand.

—Vladan, m, pastor and team leader (Kristýna Serbia)

The picture below adds to the response on modernity (Josef 3), showing a poster inviting university students to a "Concert of Christian music" by a Czech short-term team. Many Serbian students, who were invited, avoided it as a cultic thing. They considered Christian music to be a choir music in a church building, not something accompanied by a bass guitar and drums in a concert club setting.

Photo diary-2011-11 Banja Luka, Bosnia and Herzegovina

It is rare to find a local Protestant pastor who would employ such self-critique, as Vladan (above), addressing the matter of a relatively poor embodiment of Protestant churches in an indigenous form. Many churches were established by the missionaries and in Kuzmič's words, they are frequently considered "a modernized Western faith, and thus a foreign intrusion."[63] As a result of that, these churches sometimes tend to become, under missionaries' influence, globalized (i.e. westernized), and indeed, "both missionaries and national church leaders often find their primary identity within the biculture."[64] Newer Protestant churches in the Balkans are often a unique meeting point of multiple cultures, when the feature of not being burdened by nationality is perceived as a positive contribution towards reciprocal reconciliation.[65] This diversity, as expressed by Schirrmacher, who says that Jesus's church "transcends all cultural and language barriers,"[66] might, on the other hand, appear to the local religious bodies to be a treacherous "transnational faith,"[67] a threat to the security of ethnoreligious identity.

Another challenge the respondents faced was connected to their emphasis on soteriological and ecclesiological approaches:

> Because here in the Orthodox churches, there is no God's word, there is liturgy in old Slavonic which is sung, smoke of the frankincense and the priest has his back turned to the people, so that he would not have his back to the altar and not be cursed by God. But the right perception is facing the people and telling them God's word.
>
> —Roman 1, m, 2–10 years in Serbia
>
> I never can tell who is saved, including our own local church, it is a relationship with God, if I find in Orthodox church someone and we start: "Do you believe in Father, Son –" we go from there, but it is not the case that you say at the beginning: "You don't believe, you are not a Christian."
>
> —Kristýna, f, 20–30 years in Serbia

---

63. Kuzmič, "Christianity in Eastern Europe," 27.
64. Hiebert, *Anthropological Insights for Missionaries*, 239
65. Milkov, "Roots of Proselytism," 101.
66. Schirrmacher, *Biblical Foundations*, 43.
67. The expression "transnational faith" is used in the case study from post-Communist Lithuania where traditional Catholic parents drink vodka at their children's wedding, who as converted Protestants consume Coca-Cola (Lankauskas, "On 'Modern' Christians"). The study's generalization is limited, yet it provides a point of documenting certain pro-Western orientations of Protestant churches in post-Communist European countries.

The context of the two missionaries, who both see the need of evangelism in formally Christian areas, is the same. Still, the more confrontational style of Roman 1, whose claims could certainly be challenged, does not leave much space for staying in one's church. On the other hand, Kristýna's response and her way of missions, in pointing to the relationship with God, does not necessarily entail converting from church to church.

In sum, multiple challenges, both external and internal, as viewed from these Protestant missionaries' perspectives, emerge in their mission work. In the next sub-section, the debate on ethnoreligious identity arrives at missiological conclusions for Czech Protestant missionaries and more generally for the two cultural contexts – former Yugoslav and Czech.

6.4.3 Towards a dialogue concerning ethnoreligious identity

> Everyone is proud about their nation, they look after their own, defend it and keep it, not willing to let go, it is hard to persuade about others/people about anything else. And as for religions, they would tell you, "We are Catholics, what will you tell me here, we are fine."
>
> —Daniel, m, returning to Slovenia
>
> When you are Serb, you are Orthodox, when you are Croat, you are Catholic, when you are Bosniak, you are Muslim. We don't have this mindset at all. And for evangelism it means that the treason of the ethnic religion is the treason of the whole ethnic group, which is a thing we don't have at all.
>
> —Josef 3, m, returning to Bosnia and Herzegovina

At first glance, as responses of the returning missionaries point to, the lines seem to be drawn. To choose for oneself and to embrace something different than the national mainstream religious belief is often considered a foreign concept, not compatible with the national historical pride (the response of Daniel). Moreover, there is a mentality of: "Why would we convert now in peace when we did not convert under the pressure of war?" and conversion to anything else can indeed be regarded treason to the nation itself (the response of Josef 3). This observed inclination seems not to be, nonetheless, a permanent state of affairs, as the statement from the south of Serbia, where only Orthodox Christianity and Islam have been widespread, documents:

> Until about five years ago, people thought: "cult," "West," "they take our Serbian ancestors from us." Traditions, simply nationalism. And all of sudden it has changed, people recognized we want good for people, for society, whether it is children's creative workshops, or music we do with youth. Nick Vujičić was in Niš and everyone knows it was through us. So, the environment has changed. Sometimes not on the personal level, but in general we experience a religious freedom.
>
> —Kristýna, f, 20–30 years in Serbia

Nick Vujičić is a world-known Australian motivational speaker and evangelist of Serbian origin. In places like Kristýna's town, one major side-effect of his ministry is positive public relations for Protestant churches. The way of thinking that, "If this great Serb can be a Protestant Christian, they are not that dangerous of a sect after all," is unfortunately not shared by everyone. Czech Protestant missionaries find themselves periodically struggling with the ethnoreligious identity of former Yugoslavs. On the other side, as the following set of statements evidence, they highly appreciated some of its elements:

> I think it is easier to talk about God. On one hand it's a disadvantage that they are all Orthodox here, on the other side there is advantage they have a notion of God, so if a person brings that topic, it is not completely off. They follow on that, we start to talk, and ask, and you are not a completely strange person. In Bohemia, we would be for some people totally off, what are we talking about.
>
> —Ema 2, f, 2–10 years in Serbia

> The kind of general awe of God, that's what we have recognized here. In Bohemia people boast about doing some fraud or immorality, not here.
>
> —Patrik, m, 20–30 years in Slovenia

What was positive, in Bohemia people lie, speak with vulgar words. The culture of religiousness influences fear, you can leave here unlocked cars, nothing gets lost. Not only the car, but things inside. And people, at least the older generations, lie less. The religiousness joins people together, and they try to live up to the rules. But the fact is that there is more safety of everything here.

—Ema 1, f, 20–30 years in Slovenia

I have seen the respect before God as in Ukraine. We don't experience this kind of respect, we take it for granted, but here with older people, you see this respect. Here in Croatia, it is in between Ukraine and us. And it comes to me that we should learn more, that we miss the respect and the humility, if you do it, then you are the legalist.

—Denisa, f, returning to Croatia

The widespread cultural Christianity and familiarity of most people with basic beliefs, due to the ethnoreligious environment, enables people to converse about God more openly, without the estrangement which is present in Czech society (Ema 2). Another element the respondents found favourable in this matter is the awe of God (Denisa), which, besides other things, influences for the better the level of moral matters, crime and safety (Patrik, Ema 1). To add to this, the response of Denisa is certainly conditioned by her limited experience in a Croatian provincial town in the Slavonia region (as opposed to more liberal areas like the Istria peninsula or the capital Zagreb). Also, Slovenia, counter to the rest of former Yugoslavia, is often considered to be a traditionally Catholic country, yet with strong secular humanism and a "liberal" anti-Catholic element in the society,[68] so the responses of Patrik and Ema 1 are perhaps based also more on the experiences in the region where they work, near the Italian border.

Nevertheless, as these interview extracts confirm, the religious situation in the Czech Republic, and in other former Yugoslav republics, differs significantly. In the European Values Study in 2017, the percentage of people who said religion was very or quite important in their lives was: Czech

---

68. Mojzes, "Proselytism in the Successor States," 238.

Republic 21.25, Slovenia 36.56, Croatia 64.29, and the results for other former Yugoslav countries were around eighty per-cent.[69] Only thirty-eight per cent of Czechs claimed they believed in God, while in Bosnia and Herzegovina and Montenegro it was about ninety-six percent.[70]

Looking closely at the two vastly different contexts, in the light of the evidence presented so far, two questions arise:[71]

1. How could former Yugoslavs be helped by Czechs, or by someone else, to step out of the ethnoreligious identity and to believe in what they personally prefer, simultaneously not betraying the national identity while constituting more genuinely national Protestant churches? In other words, can Czechs, who value equality and free choice in the sense of "You can be Czech and you can be anything – Christian (whichever), Buddhist, or Atheist," be of help to former Yugoslavs?

2. The other question is: How could, on the contrary, former Yugoslavs with their ethnoreligious identity inform those of majority non-religious background, such as Czechs, in a missional manner? Such engagement with ethnoreligious identity, in my understanding, does not by any means imply returning to pre-Christendom patterns in neo-paganism. It concerns Christian mission, and I am asking, even though my interviewees were all Czech missionaries, if mission is not also to be expected from the other direction? Could former Yugoslavs not be of help to Czechs also?

6.5 Chapter conclusions

I would like to summarize the findings of chapter 6 which built on chapter 5, on Czech identity salience and suppression. The current chapter aimed at the practical connection of the national identity facet negotiation to mission work

---

69. European Values Study, "EVALUE." This score for Czechs was the lowest in Europe, importance of God and belief in God, only Denmark and Sweden scored lower. Confidence in church was another lowest score Europe-wide (below eighteen per cent).

70. European Values Study, "EVALUE."

71. Answers to these questions are to be found on p. @@ under (a.) and (b.).

Discussion of Czech Identity in Mission in Former Yugoslav Countries 195

situations and continued to seek to answer, "How and in what circumstances does the Czech identity of Czech missionaries become salient or suppressed?" It became evident that the national identity is negotiated in comparison to other nationals, in situations of mission work, in the differing religious identity. Based on the evidence from the respondents and from diary notes, three partial conclusions in this chapter arose:

> 1. Czechs have several beneficial factors for mission in former Yugoslav countries.
>
> 2. Czech identity, when salient, at times can be useful for mission work.
>
> 3. Due to the nature of religious identity in both contexts, a twofold mission is possible.

In relation to 1. the Czechs' favourable factors in this E-2[72] context of former Yugoslav countries are:

- Slavic cultures and languages are close
- Equality factor: Czechs were historically poorer than former Yugoslavs
- Familiarity with Czechs and a partial common history
- No historical harm
- Geographic proximity
- Czechs' presumed trait of adjustability

These factors can serve as a fuel to unleash optimism for Czech mission:

> We are an ideal tool of God in former Yugoslav countries. God is calling Czechs and Slovaks[73] to missions – and we will be the first [in 1992].
>
> —Josef 1, m, 20–30 years in Croatia

Notwithstanding, this may at first glance appear to be a display of superiority, Josef 1 in his statement calmly recalled (i.e. not with a tone of mission triumphalism) their calling in the beginning of the 1990s when hardly

---

72. Referring to the E-scale – cultural proximity in evangelism (Winter, "Frontier Mission Perspectives").

73. Josef 1 included the Slovaks as a "brother" nation to Czechs (4.2.2), and it was in 1992 when it was still Czechoslovakia.

any international mission from Czechoslovakia existed. As a matter of fact, together with his wife, they are considered pioneers of Czech mission, and he is perhaps the best-known Czech missionary, respected all through Czech sending churches and in Croatia as well. Still, this sort of bold utterance seems somewhat Czecho- (Slovak-) centric and should be approached with caution. There needs to be a dose of caution on what he, and as well the other sources in (6.2) and (6.3), including the local respondents, stated on the beneficial factors for Czechs. The replies might have been conditioned by the sample selection and probably, Czech missionaries located elsewhere in the world would respond differently.[74]

In spite of the above, there are beneficial factors that the cultural proximity contributes to Czech mission in former Yugoslavia. The missiologist Clegg, writing about the Slavs, suggested: "The political, linguistic, cultural, mentality and lifestyle similarities create a window of opportunity for cross-cultural mission within the region, and make the natives of these countries specially suited to minister in other former communist, Slavic lands."[75] This corresponds with tools for strategizing cross-cultural mission. Recalling Ralph Winters' E-scale (missionary's distance to culture) and P-scale (distance to the church), it is according to him an "inherent waste of effort"[76] when the E number is larger than the P number, i.e. when missionaries are mobilized and trained in the West, crossing large cultural gaps, while workers can be found from cultures nearby.[77] This seems to be exactly the case for the mutual closeness of Czechs and former Yugoslavs who share historical traits, similarity in language and are mutually familiar. Czech missionaries can thus adjust faster among "brother Slavs" and be effective in the similar cultural context.[78]

In relation to 2. the evidence pointed to specific moments when "Czechness" came to the fore and I suggest that the situational salience of

---

74. For example, Czech missionaries in Central Asia would supposedly respond in favour of their workplace: These countries used to be part of the USSR, they are also post-Communist, living costs are acceptable. Czechs can easily learn Russian, which is still in use there, since it is a related Slavic language.

75. Clegg, "Understanding the Times," 62.

76. Winter, "Frontier Mission Perspectives," 64.

77. Tennent, *Invitation to World Missions*, 370.

78. It is not within the scope of this research, yet former Yugoslavs presumably dispose of similar beneficial factors for mission in the Czech context as well, including the familiarity with culture or similar language.

Czech national identity is useful for the advance of Czech mission work in former Yugoslav countries. While situational suppression of the national identity facet is in line with missiological literature on adjustment to local culture and a generally experienced mission practice, its situational salience appears more ambiguous due to the peril of ethnocentrism in mission. In this research, Czech identity is understood not in a nationalistic sense, but as a cultural heritage or background for the missionaries. To recall, Scott Klingsmith, one of the major missiologists who focused on the region, concluded his work by saying that leaders from Central and Eastern European countries are "eager to learn all they can from their more experienced colleagues in other parts of the world (not just the West), but they have to discover the authentically Polish or Hungarian or Romanian way to do missions."[79]

It was evident that Czech foreign mission is relatively new and emerging, and this material on the Czech identity facet displayed the search for an authentic Czech way to participate in global (worldwide) missions, while not merely adjusting to the Western-missionaries-dominated patterns in international teams. Admittedly, in asking for self-identification, "What does it mean to be Czech in missions?", a certain amount of potentially dangerous ethnocentrism is present. Still, I conclude that when handled properly as a situationally salient national identity facet, Czech (and possibly any other) national facet can serve as a beneficial asset for the advancement of mission work. The missionaries should be at least aware of it. Bodenhausen and Kang noticed that "the first step in successfully navigating 'the wholeness' of one's multiple identities is to recognize them."[80] The missionaries can often not consciously utilize it, yet at times it is intentional – and they need to learn how to operate with their national identity facet, when to suppress it and when to make it salient. In the endeavour, many factors are under question and the course of change is variable.[81] Unpredictable circumstances, such as the timeframe a missionary operates in, the political situation, people of influence, health, financial pressures, and others, often occur. Therefore "Czechness" is actually only one piece of a mosaic. National identity

---

79. Klingsmith, *Missions Beyond the Wall*, 192.
80. Bodenhausen and Kang, "Multiple Identities," 564.
81. See Berry et al., *Cross-Cultural Psychology*, 352.

negotiation in cultural adjustment for the advancement of mission work is, as I conclude, highly individual and changeable.

In relation to 3. the focus here is on Czech missionaries to former Yugoslavs, yet based on the material in (6.4) there are missiological conclusions for mission in both directions – from the Czech Republic to former Yugoslav countries, and from Bosnia and Herzegovina, Croatia, Kosovo, Montenegro, North Macedonia, Serbia, and Slovenia to the Czech Republic.

Viewed through the lens of the Protestant Evangelical perspective, there seems to be a genuine need for the Gospel message in "unreached nations."[82] Interestingly, these Central and Eastern European nations may, in some aspects, be described as "unreached." The definition of "unreached" differs, yet according to major Evangelical models, there needs to be at least five per cent Christians and at least two per cent Evangelicals, with a viable church, in order for a people group to be considered "reached."[83] Tennent exhorts, "missionary mobilization should focus on sending missionaries either to where there are no Christians or to where the church is not yet viable."[84] In former Yugoslav countries, the Evangelical church surely is less viable. There are areas with no Christians altogether and all Protestant churches are indeed tiny, perhaps with the exception of the Northern Serbian province of Vojvodina. Viewed comparatively,[85] the Czech Republic seems to be in a better position regarding access to the message of Christ. The Evangelical church, even though by no means gigantic, is more sizable and legitimate in society. From the Czech missionaries' point of view, they come from a place with a stronger Christian ethos and have something to offer. Nevertheless, it is the Czech Republic which usually is the number one country in prayer booklets on reaching the irreligious, "atheist world."[86]

---

82. Moreau, Corwin and McGee, *Introducing World Missions*, 154.

83. Two major statistics providers are Joshua Project and International Missions Board (IMB). For both, there needs to be at least two per cent Evangelicals in the population (Tennent, *Invitation to World Missions*, 364–368). Taken literally, this would mean both the Czech Republic and any former Yugoslav country are unreached. The statistics are precarious as they make strict differences between reached and unreached. The discussion on this and on the relationship of mission to evangelism could be expanded, yet it is outside the scope of this research.

84. Tennent, *Invitation to World Missions*, 372.

85. On the IMB scale of 0–7, when 0 means more unreached and seven more reached, the Czech Republic would score as three, while Bosnia and Herzegovina would score one and two (Global Research IMB, "Global Status").

86. See, Škrabal, "Religious Faith of Inhabitants," 5.

From this viewpoint, apart from those Protestant Evangelical missiologists who would agree that Muslims of former Yugoslavia need a chance to be presented with the Jesus in the Gospels, non-religious Czechs, with a distant conception of Christianity, need to be evangelized also, and formally Christian southern Slavs need to be evangelized, or re-evangelized, since their ethnoreligious identity often prevents them from clearly distinguishing what is Christian and what is part of their national tradition.

It is not the aim of this work to argue for the legitimacy of mission to nominal Christians[87] in this part of Europe, or to address the sensitive issue of whether Protestants should evangelize other Christians. Instead, it supposes that mission is being conducted from everywhere to everywhere: "The mission field is everywhere . . . wherever there is ignorance or rejection of the gospel of Jesus Christ."[88] This includes, among others, former Yugoslavs – and Czechs who could well be re-evangelized with the help of missionaries from either Protestant, Catholic, or Orthodox circles. Based on the evidence particularly on the nature of religious identity in both contexts, connected to the national identity facet, the partial findings led me to argue for a two-fold mission:

1. *Czechs can evangelize and inform the former Yugoslav ethnoreligious identity.* Freedom to change confession can be precarious in any culture, for family reasons, yet it seems that in the Czech Republic, it is more widespread. It is not merely connected to a more individualistic way of life, but as Newbigin accentuates, it in essence represents the Christian doctrine of freedom which "includes both the ability to hold vital convictions that lead to action and also the capacity to preserve for others the freedom to dissent."[89] This freedom can be linked to the social identity complexity concept. While in the predominantly ethnoreligious context of former Yugoslavia there is need for closure in high membership overlap – to be a good Croat you need

---

87. Peter Kuzmič points to nominal Christians as he sums up the discussion, "Nominalism Today" at the Lausanne Congress on World Evangelisation in Manila, which estimated seventy-five to eighty per cent of professing Christians to be nominal, falling into the following categories: "ethnic-religious identity" nominal, second-generation nominal, ritualistic nominal, and syncretistic nominal (Kuzmič, "Christian Mission in Europe," 22).

88. Wright, *Mission of God's People*, 27.

89. Newbigin, *Foolishness to Greeks*, 118.

to be Catholic,⁹⁰ Czechs have adopted a more liberal perspective of low membership overlap – you can be Czech and believe in anything. In connection to that, the Protestant church, unlike in the Czech Republic, tends to be viewed as a Western import. Similarly, a healthy self-identification process can be embarked upon by former Yugoslavs, who ask what it means to be, for example, a Serbian Protestant.

2. *Former Yugoslavs with their ethnoreligious identity can evangelize Czechs and inform Czech believers on their Christian identity.* My respondents highlighted in (6.4.3) prompting lower criminality and higher chastity in former Yugoslav countries, in contrast to the Czech Republic, yet this does not imply that immoralities do not occur to a similar degree there as well, they might only be more hidden or under the surface. Next, in former Yugoslav countries, the starting point that there is a God can be a huge step forward and an advantage. Most Czechs do not accept God's existence, even though they celebrate Christmas and Easter. Czechs could actually be informed about the meaning of these holidays and celebrate them properly. South Slavs are more festive and due to the glue of ethnoreligious identity the whole society is included in the preparation for holidays – for example, fasting, time of mourning before Easter Sunday, esteem for the saints of history, stress on the time family spends together. One cannot of course generalize for all Czechs, since many, especially those of Catholic tradition, do celebrate national holidays with their meanings.⁹¹ Still, most often, Czechs "celebrate" by merely appreciating a day off work.⁹²

This perception of twofold mission can be underlined by the final statement of Jakub 2:

---

90. Brewer used the example of Catholic and Italian: "Although these two groups do not objectively share all of their members (many Italians are not Catholic, and many Catholics are not Italian), some people may perceive them as highly overlapping: When they think about Italians they think about Catholics, and persons of different religious faith are not considered 'real' Italians. High perceived overlap in group memberships implies that the different ingroups are actually conceived as a single convergent social identity" (Brewer, "Social Identity Complexity and Acceptance," 18).

91. Apart from Christmas and Easter in the Czech Republic, there are single days of holiday linked with three Christian traditions: 5th July – Cyril and Methodius (Orthodox), 6th July – Burning at the Stake of Jan Hus (Protestant), 28th Sep – Czech Statehood Day (Catholic – St. Václav as a patron of the Czech nation).

92. Vlachová and Řeháková, "Identity of Non-Self-Evident Nation," 258.

I think the most important is, not only there, it is everywhere, to come and to listen, rather than to come and advise. I think that we Christians are guilty of that, we come and want to pass on something that no one needs.

—Jakub 2, m, returning to Serbia

The authors of, "Constants in Context: A Theology of Mission for Today," similarly, call in their conclusion for "a humble prophetic dialogue."[93] Therefore, within findings connected to practical outcomes for my research, it can be claimed that this sort of encounter of the representatives of the two culturally proximal contexts, accompanied by a learning attitude, might actually establish steps towards mission in two directions – Czechs blessing former Yugoslavs, and former Yugoslavs blessing Czechs.

To sum up, the role of chapter 6 was to discuss Czech mission in former Yugoslavia, in connection with the Czech national identity facet, and to aim towards partial missiological contributions. It built upon the material in chapter 4 on the cross-cultural comparison and the material in chapter 5 on Czech identity salience and suppression in the context of former Yugoslav countries. The following chapters 7 and 8 continue the discussion of the significance for missionaries to manage their national identity facet, namely how the Czech identity facet is interconnected with their other identity facets. It is viewed through the lens of the four interrelations within the social identity complexity concept, with the aim that the findings from the forthcoming data could (a.) help to further understand the negotiation of the Czech missionaries' identity in the former Yugoslav context and (b.) help inform the existing theoretical concept, reflected by this qualitative research.

---

93. Bevans and Schroeder, *Constants in Context*, 398.

CHAPTER 7

Czech Missionaries Negotiating Multiple Identity Facets

7.1 Introducing identity facets of Czech missionaries

Social identity, as already outlined, is complex and individuals are members of various groups at the same time.[1] Group membership, which can be categorized as ascribed or achieved[2] provides them with certain social identity. This identity is in scholarship sometimes classified as primary or secondary: "Apart from being human, which is a first unexpressed and anticipated component of self, primary identities are those connected to primary socialization processes in the early stages of life: gender, race/ethnicity and perhaps also disability."[3] It needs to be noticed that there can be no strictly delimited "primary" or "secondary" identities and single identities can be approached interchangeably, for example, family membership, class, or religion can in some societies be ascribed, while in others achieved. This seems to be valid for ethnic and national identity as well.[4]

Other social scientists, based in intercultural psychology, touch upon classifications of identity facets as well. Geert and Gert-Jan Hofstede, together

---

1. Roccas et al., "Toward a Unifying Model," 294.
2. Knifsend and Juvonen, "Role of Social Identity Complexity," 623.
3. Giddens, *Sociology*, 305.
4. See Barth, *Ethnic Groups and Boundaries*, 29.

with Michael Minkov in their book, "Cultures and Organizations: Software of the Mind,"[5] distinguish three specific layers:

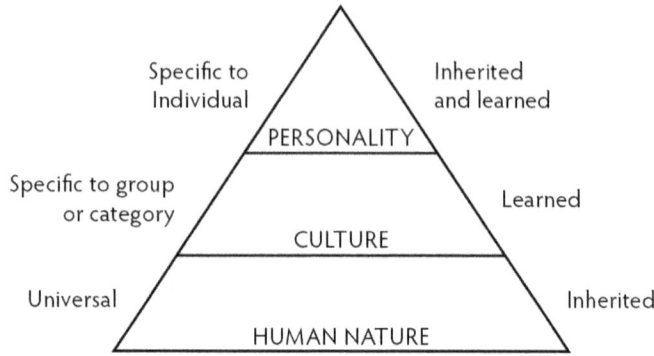

Figure 9: Three levels of uniqueness in mental programming.[6]

Even though the figure is quite self-explanatory, the authors admit that these "mental programmes" partially determine one's behaviour and only indicate what individuals' reactions are likely to be.[7] I found this Hofstede model of levels useful as a helpful grid to organize the material in this chapter, even though social identity seems to belong uniquely to the middle domain of "culture" which is specific for groups – it nevertheless overreaches and penetrates other levels. The analysis in chapter 7 comprises basic themes emerging from the data, primarily from responses of the interviewees. The thematical ordering is sorted here along the above Hofstede paradigm as: 7.2 human nature – 7.2.1 male or female, 7.2.2 family member; 7.3 personality – 7.3.1 personality traits holder, 7.3.2 interest group member, 7.3.3 worker; 7.4 culture[8] – 7.4.1 Christian, 7.4.2 missionary, 7.4.3 someone with regional or supraregional identity, 7.4.5 another national.

A cursory glance at such classification reveals its limits and calls for a brief clarification. First to note is that "Czechness" is not included, because it has

---

5. Hofstede G., Hofstede G. J. and Minkov, *Cultures and Organizations*.
6. Hofstede G., Hofstede G. J. and Minkov, 6.
7. Hofstede G., Hofstede G. J. and Minkov, 5.
8. Departing from the pyramid, my ordering would place the category "culture" last, due to the focus of this research on Czech national identity in the cultural proximity context of former Yugoslav countries.

already been addressed in chapters 5 and 6 and furthermore, the upcoming chapter 8 investigates precisely the interrelation of missionaries' Czech identity to their other identity facets. Second, these categories of identity facets by no means constitute a complete list. Other relevant categories did not emerge from the data of this research, yet they may be of significance as well: (a.) race, (b.) class, (c.) generation. (a.) The interviewees were all white. Czechs, and others in the former Communist "Eastern Europe," are to large extent racially uniform.[9] (b.) Hardly any differences were found in regard to class, all the sources came from the middle class; perhaps the only connection was the difference in city or village. (c.) There was no noticeable difference in the responses due to the age factor, most respondents were between thirty and fifty.

The goal of the current chapter is to provide introductory material for the subsequent one. One first needs to discover what these identity facets are in order to continue the discussion of how they interrelate with the Czech identity facet. Chapters 7 and 8 are therefore tightly connected, in addressing the third research sub-question, "How does the missionaries' 'Czechness' interact with their other identity facets?"

In order to ascertain findings on multiple identity facets in chapter 7 and on their interrelation with "Czechness" in chapter 8, the inquiry began by stating: "We have talked about being Czech as part of our identity. Now, could you tell me, what else is important that makes you who you are?" Other leading questions followed: "Do you strongly feel to be something or someone?", "Is membership in any group important for you?", "How do you perceive your 'Czechness' is related to the other parts of who you are?" This part of the interviewing process was the most demanding, as it was complicated to phrase an understandable question for respondents not used to pondering their identity regularly.

---

9. This might change in the future when Czech Vietnamese missionaries will be sent. By 30 September 2020, 616 659 foreigners have been registered with the Foreign Police, the majority came from Ukraine (158 300), Slovakia (123 266) and Vietnam (62 523) (Škrabal, "Religious Faith").

7.2 Human nature

7.2.1 Male or female

> Maybe only a reminiscence on when Erika was introducing the whole project, it was very interesting to follow the development of the congregation thinking. The first (laugh) reaction was that she has probably a boyfriend there, which was the idea that she wanted to marry and that's why she is going there.
>
> —Jakub 3, m, sending parish priest (Erika 1 Bosnia and Herzegovina)
>
> Only young girls apply for these trips. And guys are in the background in the church, because guys need to take risks. And people were calling me: "Where will we sleep?", "I don't know," "What will we eat?", "I don't know," "What and where?", "I don't know, God told us and we are going." "So, I am in." And suddenly, it was about fifteen people, and only three girls.
>
> —Jakub 1, m, returning to Bosnia and Herzegovina

The respondents did not explicitly address gender identity, yet they mentioned certain related situations. Erika 1 was my teammate and some of her sending church members drew their conclusions of a possible relationship due to the fact she was a single lady. Jakub 1, with a certain amount of sexism, complained during the interview that in Protestant circles he observed there were more women missionaries than men. Earlier in the interview, he critiqued mission trips in the form of visiting a partner church in Ukraine, where only "young girls applied for these trips." Instead, he strove to organize his mission trips to fit men, whom he considered to be more open to take risks. Such stereotyping might be disputable, yet what is important at this moment is that the respondents here recognized identity facets of Czech missionaries as male or as female.

> What crosses my mind is identity of a mother or a woman. I was the only one as a woman in the group and it certainly has an influence on the group. And I have been there only once, it was tense in his family, his marriage, so I don't know, hopefully it was good I was there, simply, I was able to have another

> perspective on things in the masculine group, women are sensitive to different things.
>
> —Erika 2, f, returning to Bosnia and Herzegovina
>
> For example, when you are a missionary lady, and mother, in a country where there is bad health care and you have to wait for it, then you experience it badly and you perceive it as a thorn.
>
> —Kristýna, f, 20–30 years in Serbia

To clarify, when Erika 2 mentioned "his family," she was referring to the local pastor the team went to help. Her experience counterbalances the statement of Jakub 1 on the otherwise generally recognized trend of more females than males in Protestant international mission. Her identity as woman became salient during these few days they spent travelling in the north of Bosnia with a group of men. Kristýna is similarly, with her husband and two sons, the only woman in the family, and she mentioned the gender identity facet in close connection to adjusting to the Serbian health care system. Interestingly, both Erika 2 and Kristýna mentioned identity as a woman and a mother. Gender identity is often tightly associated with being a family member which is analysed in the upcoming sub-section. These two identity facets, gender and family member, are something that all human beings have in common since this "human nature" is "something that determines our physical and basic psychological functioning."[10]

7.2.2 Family member

> Me personally, thanks to the fact we have children, I am a mother (laugh) and we do home schooling.
>
> —Ema 2, f, 2–10 years in Serbia
>
> Well, he is a parent also, and also a husband.
>
> —Matěj, m, leader of sending mission agency (Josef 1 Croatia)

The initial statements exemplify responses which were probably uttered as a reaction to the leading interview questions. Otherwise, the respondents

---

10. Hofstede G., Hofstede G. J. and Minkov, *Cultures and Organizations*, 6.

might not have referred to this rather apparent identity facet. Kristýna, again in connection with family and gender identity facet, gave it deeper thought:

> I look for "balance" [in Serbian] between being full-time in the church and at the same time I have children entrusted to me from God. I have children, I have a husband, I have a family, so these things need to function. Sometimes, I have a feeling that it is easier when a person is a dad, rather than when you are a mum. When a child is sick and the teacher calls you to pick him up, and you are leading a meeting, preparing a summer camp, which actually happened yesterday, you just say: "Ok, people, we are done," and then you go to the school.
>
> —Kristýna, f, 20–30 years in Serbia

It perhaps is not that evident in the West, yet in the society of southern Serbia, the roles are more clearly defined for women/mothers and for men/fathers. While Kristýna's husband is the main one responsible to bring home income, she takes care of the children's health and education. It becomes of course more complex when one is a Czech and a missionary. Later in the interview, Kristýna added to the reflection of these dynamics: "It is a search of a middle path so that family survives, and ministry survives. But a person does not have to be a missionary or Christian to face these matters." As she says, this tension truly is omnipresent and the debate on the issue could be broadened, yet at this point it will suffice to note that this very identity facet was the one the respondent repeatedly returned to throughout the interview.

> Kristýna is my best friend. Me and Kristýna are like born brother and sister. Since the first moment I came to church, Kristýna has been a mother, she is a mother to all. She is like an older sister. See, yesterday, and I am thirty-two years old, she brought me lunch. Not because I don't know how to cook anything, but she wanted to save my time. And when I became Christian, she has been bringing me food. When I became Christian, my whole family, mother, brother, sister, they disowned me.
>
> —Miodrag, m, colleague (Kristýna Serbia)

I see it positive, comparing to for example my family, that he is in touch with his family, with his dad, and that was the reason why he came back. He sensed that the family needs him, the father the most, and he came back before he goes somewhere else perhaps, but I don't know how much is this Czech because in our family this is not like that, so it's generally humane.

—Prokop, m, sending pastor (Marek Kosovo)

Being a mother, a wife and a lady seemed significant for Kristýna, based on her previous responses. And as could be seen from the statement of Miodrag, her surroundings perceived it strongly as well. Miodrag moved to Niš from a town about one hundred kilometres away and when he became a Protestant Christian, his Orthodox Christian family turned their backs on him. I am not aware whether the situation has improved, yet at that time, he acquired a new adoptive family, with pastor Vladan, Kristýna and other church members. The other responding supportive source, Prokop, opened up in the interview as well as he observed how Marek functions in certain elements in the family dynamics, and was inspired by that. For these respondents, perhaps due to their own previous family experiences, this particular identity facet of the missionary proved significant. It seems that identity is often redefined and renegotiated in terms of what people no longer are (Miodrag) or what they would like to be (Prokop).[11] As Miodrag's statement demonstrated, the family affiliation is connected with friendship and personality characteristics, which are the focus of the following section.

7.3 Personality

Hofstede and his co-authors describe "personality" as the third level of uniqueness in mental programming, as something not necessarily shared with any other human being: "It is based on traits that are partly inherited within the individual's unique set of genes and partly learned. Learned means modified by the influence of collective programming (culture) as well as by unique personal experiences."[12] The three-fold classification comes with

---

11. This resonates with what was asserted for the Czech identity construction in regard to history: Czechs no longer wish to be associated with Eastern Europe and see their place alongside the nations of Western Europe (Holý, *Little Czech*, 151), even though they have not reached the target yet (Ieda, "Regional Identities," 62).

12. Hofstede G., Hofstede G. J. and Minkov, *Cultures and Organizations*, 7.

limits, first of all, personality is arguably part of Hofstede's category "human nature" as well, and also some would argue that gender and family membership can be partly ascribed, yet achieved as well.[13]

7.3.1 Personality traits holder

> She is a "buddy" [in English]. A friend. I don't know what else to tell. All these people that lead the church, people who are in the team.
>
> —Vladan, m, pastor and team leader (Kristýna Serbia)
>
> Interviewer: What for you is important, what gets displayed in the mission work or, what else do you perceive yourselves to be?
>
> Roman 2: Identity of a gourmand, when I said my appreciation to the pastor's *ćevapi*, he was glad (laugh). Maybe the role of people of contentment [*pohodáři*], when you come there, you are at ease [*v pohodě*], you chat with him about all these things, you praise his car, his *ćevapi*, you say that they have a nice landscape, that they meet at a nice place, and you fill him with some kind of a positive vibe.
>
> —Roman 2, m, returning to Bosnia and Herzegovina

Vladan found a high value in having faithful and reliable friends on the team. While his approach, adding to what was said earlier by Kristýna, was rather contemplative and deeper in reflection, Roman 2 recalled the value of *pohoda*[14] and when pondering their identity facets, brought in humorous elements, which could otherwise be considered a digression from the topic. Personality traits could indeed relate to a wide realm of conceptions. To recall, they are defined by the protagonists of the Five-Factor model[15] as "dimensions of individual differences in tendencies to show consistent patterns of thoughts, feelings, and actions."[16] The level of consistency could be

---

13. A good example can be a child adoption.
14. For the value of *pohoda* – contentment – see section 4.4.
15. For a reminder, the organization of many specific traits in Five-Factor Model consists of: Neuroticism (N), Extraversion (E), Openness to Experience (O), Agreeableness (A), and Conscientiousness (C) (McCrae, "Cross-Cultural Research," 3).
16. McCrae and Costa, *Personality in Adulthood*, 25.

questioned and, it can be added, these personality traits can be subjectively perceived by the respondents. The two subsequent extracts exemplify this as they, as complementary sources, responded about the same missionary:

> "An authentic seeker," someone who was aware that truth is somewhere above her or in front of her and that it is desirable to approach it and reach for it, but she has definitely never had the feeling that she has grasped it. And she was very open in her evangelical piety. That means, she let others to look into her seeking, which I think, when she led youth group programmes, seemed to be a bit confusing because those people, who were a generation or about five years younger than her, expected finished answers. But she only let them take a look into her seeking.
>
> —Jakub 3, m, sending parish priest (Erika 1 Bosnia and Herzegovina)

> Like a busy bee in one way, you know bees are really nice and beautiful insects, they are so hard working and then produce honey, which is so sweet. I perceive her as a very quiet and a very strong person and a very hard-working person, also a prayer warrior, very faithful to the ministry where God called her, very loyal.
>
> —Eldina, f, supervisor and team leader (Erika 1 Bosnia and Herzegovina)

Erika 1 was referred to here as an "authentic seeker" and a "busy bee." While Jakub 3 included a critical element, Eldina was, on the other hand, favouring her former colleague and through the interview gave a very positive impression of Erika 1. They both, nevertheless, agreed on the missionary's timid temperament. This can be contrasted to temperaments of other Czechs:

> "Czechstrovert" is something between introvert and extrovert. He seems to be very silent here in Bosnia, but in the Czech Republic he appears to be the loudest person in the room.
>
> —Diary notes-JV 2012-07 Sarajevo, Bosnia and Herzegovina

> The local pastor's wife said about Kristýna: "She is like a dynamite."
>
> —Diary notes-DS-2019-06 Niš, Serbia (Kristýna)

> Some of the things in my character have changed, I used to be a silent and reserved person.

—Kristýna, f, 20–30 years in Serbia

It becomes evident that some missionaries, like Kristýna, have simultaneously brought from the Czech Republic their own predispositions and also have been influenced by the surrounding culture while working in the former Yugoslav context. The anonymous supporting source, a former colleague of myself in Bosnia and Herzegovina, added on this particular personality trait the facet of extraversion versus introversion. The responses above follow up on the findings in chapter 4 and the perceived "openness" and "closedness" of Czech and former Yugoslav cultures is here subjectively associated with a more silent vs. loud, or introvert vs. extrovert, behaviour. These, along with others, belong among the most commonly referred to personality traits and "they are familiar to laypersons, who use a huge vocabulary of trait descriptive adjectives (such as nervous, enthusiastic, original, accommodating, and careful) to describe themselves and others."[17]

> I ponder a lot on certain principles, I am an introvert in that and I need time to put my thoughts together. Then comes my extrovert part, after thinking it through, sometimes it is after two or three years, and I take it out and I teach because I think it can positively contribute to society.

—Daniel, m, returning to Slovenia

> The character is better than the experience. People like that grow fast, they are adaptable. . . . The gifting stays with you even when your character goes wrong. And they went to Jesus and said: "Did not we in your name . . . On the contrary, relying on the gifts, anointing, destroys the character. Character is more important than all of it, we all have gifts, Jesus was not stingy, he gave something to every person.

—Josef 1, m, 20–30 years in Croatia

To place these statements in context, Daniel here stepped aside from reflecting on himself as a Czech missionary and commented on self-identification in

---

17. McCrae, "Cross-Cultural Research," 3.

search of balance between his introversion and extraversion. Josef 1 responded in the context of pondering requirements for new potential Czech mission workers. The two final extracts of this sub-section are purposely set beside one another. Daniel, in line with the previous responses, focused on one's traits of personality – or character with distinguishing personal attributes. And Josef reflected on character in the sense of moral excellence and firmness.[18]

7.3.2 Interest group member

> He [Josef 2] got engaged there in the local club, Fontana Vrsar and became part of the young people. And he went with them play matches in Hungary or Slovenia and they could talk about God. They called him "Poborský,"[19] because he had long blond hair.
>
> —Renata, f, 10–20 years in Croatia
>
> He had more small communities of people who knew of him, the group you had the prayer group in the church, or in Počernice they have an ecumenical meeting once a month and now there is a community of prayers for Prague, from 7 to 7.30 am, so he goes there once a week.
>
> —Prokop, m, sending pastor (Marek Kosovo)
>
> I signed up for a course on Nordic walking. And many people despise it, some people do it . . . It was not because of this that I started to fit into the category of a Nordic walker.
>
> —Marek, m, 1 year in Kosovo

The responses reflect that group membership figures as one of the identity facets which contribute to missionaries' identity. Prokop only listed several groups that Marek was a member of. Marek, on the other hand, talked about a membership in a specific group in relation to his identity. He actually delineated himself from it, in a sense of refusing any labelling as "Nordic

---

18. See the definition in Meriam Webster, "Definition of Character."
19. Karel Poborský was a Czech national team player at that time. As a matter of fact, today, Josef 2 is bald and he jokingly admitted in the interview that he rather resembles another player, Jan Koller.

walker" – which in fact sounds rather odd when translated to Czech. Josef 2, as a player in the Fontana football club, hence part of the ingroup, was simultaneously part of an outgroup as the only Czech, and probably the only blond person on the team.

The previous theme and category of the identity facet revolved around personal attributes, while the current fits more precisely into the social identity theory of group membership, therefore the title "interest group member," when the interest may be represented by a sport, a hobby, church gathering or similar. I would like to suggest that the two are interconnected. John Turner, cautiously, says that "the possibility arises that social identity may on occasions function nearly to the exclusion of personal identity, i.e. that at certain times our salient self-images may be based solely or primarily on our group membership."[20] The statement is definitely valid, and as Turner admits, these are only certain circumstances when the group provides identity to the individual. Nevertheless, at the same time, personality is not always "lost" to the group, instead, it often is manifested in the group of shared interests, as Renata's response points out. Czech missionaries happen to be interest group members (as Prokop outlined), yet they do not seem to construct their identity around that. As Marek's example sets out, it often is an intentional refusal of categorization. Preferring rather a free association perhaps is connected to the Czechs' preference for evading memberships in any institutionalized groups.[21]

7.3.3 Worker

> I am a travelling salesman; my wife does finances.
>
> —Radek, m, returning to Serbia
>
> He also is a builder of a house and planter of various crops in the neighbouring estates, he has become a farmer there.
>
> —Matěj, m, leader of sending mission agency (Josef 1 Croatia)

---

20. Turner, "Towards Cognitive Redefinition," 19.
21. Hošek, *Gods Return*; Nešpor, *Too Weak in Faith*.

As church planters, that's how we perceive ourselves the most, it is what of course determines us the most.

—Patrik, m, 20–30 years in Slovenia

Because both of us are worship leaders, we play both piano and guitar, it was a certain means to get close to the people.

—Roman 2, m, returning to Bosnia and Herzegovina

In my thematic analysis, more elements are joined together in one collective category of a "worker" identity facet. It encompasses a variety of vocations, jobs and tasks. Furthermore, this includes both "secular" and "Christian" work, even though it is difficult to draw lines between the two. Also, while some mission work is a full-time job (Josef 1, Patrik), others have jobs in the Czech Republic and occasionally take on a missionary role (Radek, Roman 2). No matter how imperfect the category may appear, there is a purpose in this delineation, as will become clear when I connect it to the literature on social identity and on role related identity.

The first set of responses displays certainty in identification to a large extent. Radek described himself with his job providing him an identity and Matěj did similarly for Josef 1, who is himself a pastor and a counsellor. There, in the rural part of the Istrian peninsula in Croatia, in order to fit in the local tourism- and agriculture-based environment and to help support his family, Josef 1 with his city background found a new worker identity. In the context of mission work among southern Slavs, Roman 2 considered a significant part of who he and his wife Erika 2 were to be "worship leaders." This self-identification, and also even more so Patrik's perception of himself and his wife Ema 1 as primarily "church planters," was probably impacted by a pre-conditioned category, rooted in Protestant Evangelical missiology, based in ecclesiology.[22] The extract above manifests an unambiguous self-perception. Nonetheless, most interviewees displayed varied degree of hesitancy in affirming specific identity facets. They often moved from a hesitant approach to a gradual acceptance of it.

---

22. Bosch, *Transforming Mission*, 512.

> I don't feel myself set in any ministry, I am more of a person who likes to talk to people, who makes contacts with them. But to teach them, no, I am a chaotic, on the other side phlegmatic.
>
> —Denisa, f, returning to Croatia

> As a role, yes, I believe God has put in my life a calling, some wisdom perhaps, which, when someone wants to hear it, to pass on from it. But one thing I have learnt, I am not saying I do it for everyone . . . People that know me, they trust me, they ask me: "What do you think about it?", not because they will do it the way I am saying, but they will think about it. It is my kind of approach to ministry, to come, be a friend, and see if someone has an interest. So, an unofficial level of being a friend, rather than being an advisor. You would have to study for it.
>
> —Jakub 2, m, returning to Serbia

> Ema 2: We do home schooling.
>
> Interviewer: So, you are a teacher?
>
> Ema 2: I don't see myself as a teacher, but that's what I am. So, this takes a lot of time for me, and it is an area where God is working in me a lot, so, I would definitely adhere to this identity.
>
> —Ema 2, f, 2–10 years in Serbia

These interview extracts, again like the response of Marek in (7.3.1), depict an unease about being categorized as someone or something. The work of both Denisa and Jakub 2 is based on relationships, yet while for Denisa it is a genuinely unspecified work of multitasking in its nature, the mission work of Jakub 2 has all the features of a supporting mentor and a Christian counsellor. He performs the work, and still rejects being called "counsellor" or "advisor." Next, Ema 2 initially claimed that she did not identify with being a teacher, yet she then embraced the newly obtained identity facet – interestingly, this turn happened during the interview, which might have had a therapeutic effect on the reality. The following focus group record with a missionary couple continues this hesitant tone, and again, it moves towards an affirmative condition:

Josef 1: People were telling me: "You are a spiritual father." And I was always rejecting it, they take me like that, I don't. So, for many years, I rejected to play this role, even though I was playing it and people, even those who were much older than me, I could be their biological son, they were saying to me that I was their spiritual father. I was afraid of that. "Why?" I was afraid to fail them as dad . . . I try to be more of a friend. But they don't say that: "You are our spiritual father," because here in Croatia it is a sensitive word.

—Klára: The spiritual father, the pope.

Josef 1: But it is clear to me that I do play that role and I don't avoid it and I realized the responsibility, especially now when I minister to the pastors.

. . . Klára: (Laugh). No, I don't perceive myself as a mother.

Josef 1: She is in the phase of denial, but who knows Káťa, he knows she is a mum.

Klára: Yes.

—Josef 1: Of your children.

Klára: That thing yes.

Josef 1: But she is a mum, she has the heart. We have in the church a girl who is in tough situation, they took children, they put them in the orphanage and Káťa would cry over that the child: "I might take it home." She is like that, she has a mother heart.

—Josef 1, m, 20–30 years in Croatia

—Klára, f, 20–30 years in Croatia

To help understand the particular situation, Josef 1 was a long-term team leader and a role model for the other two Czech missionaries, and he worked for about twenty years as a senior pastor in the church. He recently passed on the church leadership to a local person and retreated to the ministry of supporting pastors in the region. The conversation on spiritual parenthood of Josef 1 and Klára, who themselves have three children, marks the move from denial to recognition of one's identity. It may be noticed that the further the analysis in this sub-section proceeded, the greater the difference with the preceding sub-section on group membership as a basis of identity could be observed. I came to conclude that the reason may rest in the dissimilar basis of one's identity. Looking critically at the category of "personality" as outlined by Hofstede and the collective of authors[23] through this lens, the matter turns out to be truly complex. Social psychologists Burke and Stets differentiate between personal, social and role identities, which all have a different base:

> While role identities are based on the different social structural positions individuals hold, such as spouse, worker, and parent, social identities are based on individuals' memberships in certain groups as in persons being Democrat, Latino, or Catholic. Person identities are based on a view of the person as a unique entity, distinct from other individuals.[24]

The findings on Czech missionaries, with the identity facet categories in (7.3), seem to align to this generally accepted perception, where (7.3.1) "personality traits holder" corresponds to personal identity, based on individual self-concept;[25] (7.3.2) "interest group member" agrees to social identity, where memberships imply an ingroup and an outgroup, and, correspondingly, a sense of "us" versus "them";[26] and (7.3.3) "worker" is in accordance with role identity in identity theory (IT) which is tied to social position that helps guide people's attitudes and behaviour. Last-mentioned role identity is defined as "the internalized meanings of a role that individuals apply to themselves"[27] and these meanings are, in the responses of the Czech missionaries sample, for example, spiritual father, church planter, Christian, missionary.

Coming back to social identity theory, its basic claim about social competition is that "the group members may seek positive distinctiveness through direct competition with the outgroup."[28] This would apply to 7.3.2, yet in the initial sub-section of 7.3.1 and in the current one, identity is negotiated as the

---

23. Hofstede G., Hofstede G. J. and Minkov, *Cultures and Organizations*, 6.
24. Burke and Stets, *Identity Theory*, 129.
25. Burke and Stets, 129.
26. Burke and Stets, 118.
27. Burke and Stets, 114.
28. Tajfel and Turner, "Social Identity Theory," 285.

result of a personal self-identification quest or of a search of self-identification in a role. This triple aspect of one's complex identity is reflected also in the following section, where the identity facets related especially to social and role-based identity.

7.4 Culture

The beginning of this section requires a brief explanation. The titles "Christian," "missionary," and other identity facets in (7.4) relate to the "culture" category in the sense of a collective learned phenomenon as outlined by Hofstede and others.[29] According to them, culture is "at least partly shared with people who live or lived within the same social environment, which is where it was learned. Culture consists of the unwritten rules of the social game."[30] What is significant for this analysis is the communal, shared, social, aspect, and again, bearing in mind it touches upon an aspect of identity as understood by both social identity theory and identity theory.

7.4.1 Christian

> Interviewer: Do you perceive yourself as something else, as identity or role? Anything comes to your mind?
>
> Jakub 2: As a child of God perhaps.
>
> —Jakub 2, m, returning to Serbia
>
> Certainly, what Roman [her husband] has said earlier, the identity in Christ.
>
> —Ema 2, f, 2-10 years in Serbia

When asked very broadly about what else, apart from being Czechs, the missionaries perceive themselves to be, they often referred first to their

---

29. Hofstede G., Hofstede G. J. and Minkov, *Cultures and Organizations*.

30. Hofstede G., Hofstede G. J. and Minkov, 6. They further say that "culture as 'collective programming of the mind' resembles the concept of habitus proposed by the French sociologist Pierre Bourdieu" (1930–2002): "Certain conditions of existence produce a habitus, a system of permanent and transferable dispositions. A habitus ... functions as the basis for practices and images ... which can be collectively orchestrated without an actual conductor" (Hofstede G., Hofstede G. J. and Minkov, quoted from Bourdieu 1980: 88–89; translation Geert Hofstede).

identity facet as Christians. This was the most reoccurring and accentuated identity facet among the respondents.[31]

Brief comments of Jakub 2 and Ema 2 introduce the issue, while others engaged with it within the interview in a deeper manner:

> Mission trip participants get confronted with their "Czechness" and with their Christianity, because you go there to spread Christian faith. You have a Christian faith, but which one? And when you start to present it, it goes through a correction or confrontation. The Bible says: "Give and it will be given to you." . . . So, you want to pass on a right faith and suddenly you realize where you had a crooked view and you get corrected. You want to stress a Christian value and to present it to people and in fact you realize the value in a different light or you notice another value which you yourself can accept and identify with. . . . And when you are in contact with the representatives of other cultures, then your own culture gets tested, right? You have to examine it.
>
> —Jakub 1, m, returning to Bosnia and Herzegovina

> I think a much bigger influence on him was Anglo-American Christianity, the strongest his stay in England. But after he believed, he was getting to know his family history, which was connected to Brethren Church, that his great grandfather was a pastor in Brethren Church.
>
> —Prokop, m, sending pastor (Marek Kosovo)

> I know Erika 1 as a parishioner, as a church member, participant in the youth group, a person who has been relatively for a long time looking for her role, her position of what she should as a Christian be doing. And at this point, I think she is still in search for it in the position of a missionary. . . . It was absolutely obvious that she changed in prayer. Only that she started to address God differently, the diction, the formulations, when the expression

---

31. More respondents agreed that, in their view, Christian identity exceeds other identity facets, including their Czech identity – and precisely this relation of Christian and Czech identity facets is further discussed in (8.3) on the social identity theory category of dominance.

"Lord," she changed to "Father" and also the style of prayer, it has changed distinctly, you could tell by the first glance which testifies about a spiritual move towards somewhere, according to me, noticeably towards good.

—Jakub 3, m, sending parish priest (Erika 1 Bosnia and Herzegovina)

Perceptions of the "Christian" identity facet by the responding Czech Protestant missionaries certainly correspond with their own definition of what it means to be Christian. This can be connected to belonging to and practices of a particular church or denomination (one's "Christianity" as an institutionalized faith), or the Christian identity facet can mean relationship to God (one's "Christianity" supposedly affecting each aspect of one's life). The latter is in line with William Campbell's understanding of a Christ-follower identity,[32] as introduced in (2.2.5) and it seems it is in focus here for Czech missionaries, according to their responses.

Each respondent above approaches the Christian identity facet from a different angle. In the continuation of the preceding discussion on varying aspects of what Christian identity means, Jakub 1 asks: "Which Christian?" To put the statement in context, Protestant Christians of various denominations, whom he takes with him on his mission trips, often pressure themselves, due to their limited days off work, hopping from place to place, to pass on the Christian message. According to Jakub 1, the challenges with aspects of religious devotion in the "receiving" side, which the participants faced, could actually turn towards helping evaluate and reform their own Christian, and national, identity facets. This confirms what the missiologist Samuel Escobar, who referred to this as "mission in reverse," said: "They went to serve and to learn, and they brought back insights and perspectives that enriched the life of their home churches."[33]

Prokop perceived two aspects of Marek's Christian identity facet. An original – foreign, when he became a believer, and the complementary – local. Both of these have, according to Marek's pastor, who knows him very well, supposedly contributed to informing Marek's identity as a Christian. It

---

32. Campbell, *Paul and Christian Identity*, 12.
33. Escobar, *New Global Mission*, 162.

needs to be admitted that technically there can be no differentiation between "foreign" and "local," since both are foreign and both are local, it depends on perspective. Still, what played a role for Marek surely was a collective expression of Christian faith, in two culturally diverse Protestant contexts, in the United Kingdom where he lived for several years, and in the Czech Republic, after his return. Campbell points out that collectiveness is actually a major feature of Christian identity – Christians are not "isolated individuals individually adhering to Christ but a corporate entity in which individuals together grow and develop in one body."[34]

The final insight into yet another aspect of what the Christian identity facet may look like is the perception by Jakub 3 of Erika 1's progress towards a higher intimacy with God. This is yet another aspect of Christian identity – it is essentially relational which entails that Christians relate to God, to fellow believers and to other people – believers are in the world, yet they are not of the world.[35] Jakub 3 initially regarded her as a church member with certain roles in local ministry and a relationship with God on her own. Furthermore, after the one-year experience in Bosnia and Herzegovina, he observed certain positive changes in the shift in intimacy in her relationship with God.

Based on the responses, it can be seen that the Christian identity facet is certainly not monolithic and that it is subject to varying degree of nuance.

7.4.2 Missionary

> Roman 1: We were there as pioneering missionaries. We know there are churches, but you know every church has a different emphasis on different things and teachings, that's why we chose the church where God leads us.
>
> Roman 1: There was a market and Ema said to me: "I would like this string of beads." And I started to get upset inside, we are missionaries –
>
> Ema 2: You took me to the wrong place (laugh).

---

34. Campbell, *Paul and Christian Identity*, 154.
35. Tanner, *Theories of Culture*, 115–116.

> Roman 1: We don't have money, why does she have this wish?
>
> —Roman 1, m, 2–10 years in Serbia
>
> —Ema 2, f, 2–10 years in Serbia

The missionary identity facet is a bit ambivalent and ambiguous. Perceived broadly, these are communicators of the gospel of Jesus Christ in intercultural settings.[36] And while most respondents in the sample expressed varying levels of disassociating from being a "missionary," some seemed to identify with it. Roman 1, in accordance with the church planting policy of their sending denomination, considered themselves, both in Zagreb (Croatia) and Belgrade (Serbia) as "pioneering missionaries." This was interestingly despite the fact other churches, including Protestant Evangelicals, were present in the area. In the second response, a notion of modesty and comparatively low budget stood out for Roman 1 as an attribute of being a missionary.[37] Other responses document missionaries' uneasy self-identification.

> Because she got married young, she didn't have her own identity. So, she said: "I am not a missionary, I went to follow my husband, but I have no calling to mission." And she started to work in tourism: "I am a missionary's wife and that's all, I don't care about the church, I will come to church on Sunday and leave, as anybody else." ... So, she started to work in tourism, employed by Czechs, but of course she got into contacts with Croats, in various levels, from cooks, waiters and so on. And they wondered why we live there, and we could share, it was a way to people.
>
> —Jonatán, m, 10–20 years in Croatia

It is a bit problematic when Jonatán responds on behalf of his wife, who was the only long-term Czech missionary not involved in this research, as he retrospectively evaluated the experience in Croatia. He was the missionary and she, not that excited about the move from the Czech Republic, rejected any association with it – both with the missionary label and function. And

---

36. Hiebert, *Anthropological Insights for Missionaries*, 28.
37. This issue of missionaries' limited economic resources also came to the surface in the interviews with Josef 2 and Renata (7.4.3) Marek (4.3), and several others.

she served in the church in her free time, alongside the tourist guide job. It nevertheless seems that gradually they both managed to soften the sharp edges of their initial identity delineation. Jonatán also has started to work in tourism, and instead of typical "missionaries," they pursued radiating the Gospel of Christ while working with people interculturally. Patrik's processing is somewhat similar:

> Today I am thinking, theoretically, I think we followed God's lead, but I am thinking that it might have been better to come to a context like this as a non-missionary. To say: "We like Slovenia, we want to make a business here." But in this way, we came with a stamp in our forehead: "Protestant missionary," "We came to convert you." And it brought some sort of cautiousness.
>
> —Patrik, m, 20–30 years in Slovenia

The "missionary" facet surely appears inappropriate in lands with Christian heritage. This re-evaluating of Patrik and the assessment of businessman identity, along with, or instead of the missionary identity, depicts well what most missionaries in former Yugoslavia go through: they negotiate their status and usually there are one or more elements that not only legitimize their stay in the eyes of many local people, but allow them to develop their gifts and abilities and to serve the community in a practical way. Later in the interview, Patrik added:

> We are primarily not missionaries, understand, of course we do belong to that category, on ground of that we went from one country to another, yes, but it was not for us: "Now we'll be missionaries." The Lord God gave us on our heart Jablonec [in northern Bohemia], so we went to Jablonec and planted the church. And it was mission too, even though it was mission in our own culture – and then it is not called mission, but it is the same.
>
> —Patrik, m, 20–30 years in Slovenia

Patrik refused to be categorized as missionary in a way and referred to the artificial geographical division between evangelism and "mission."[38] He has

---

38. Tennent, *Invitation to World Missions*, 24; Wright, *Mission of God's People*, 26.

been seriously reconsidering the approach to the missionary identity and so did others, who have spent over twenty years in a former Yugoslav country:

> Josef 1: I feel certainly Czech, a Czech who has accepted Croatia as his country. I definitely don't perceive myself as being on a visit here. I am here as at home, this is my home. I perceive it. Even though I am a Czech and I will remain a Czech ... We didn't say we are missionaries here, we are immigrants.
>
> —Josef 1, m, 20–30 years in Croatia
>
> I have come to mission to serve God here and I am God's servant. When you say "missionary" it is kind of cold.
>
> —Kristýna, f, 20–30 years in Serbia

Both Josef 1 and Kristýna explicitly disidentified with being "missionaries." Their "immigrant" identity, in the words of Josef 1, i.e. their rootedness in Croatia and Serbia, yet still with ties to his home country and to other Czechs, reflects how missionaries are "transcultural people – insiders and outsiders at the same time."[39] According to missiologist Paul Hiebert, missionaries "acquire an international perspective and the ability to adapt to more than one culture, but at the price of being fully adjusted to none of them."[40] As Josef 1, Kristýna and Patrik expressed, there is an internal struggle and a push towards leaving the missionary identity behind and becoming more local – which can never be fully complete.[41]

It can be concluded that the longer the missionary spends in the country, the less a "missionary" remains in his identity. It seems as if the self-identification shifts from a missionary identity of those who visit regularly or spend their first years in the country (represented by Roman 1 and Ema 2) to a more non-missionary identity, as supported by the latter parts of the responses in this sub-section.

---

39. Hiebert, "Gospel in Human Contexts," 29.
40. Hiebert, *Cultural Anthropology*, 40.
41. Missionaries can never, as Hiebert says, "go native" and they need to affirm both cultures and the bicultural identity within them (See Hiebert, *Anthropological Insights for Missionaries*, 105–106).

7.4.3 Someone with regional or supranational identity

7.4.3.1 Someone with regional identity

> I really think that the Czech identity moved into the background, that we were not there in a role of, I don't know how to say, some Moravians, who are proud of the piece of the field they have.
>
> —Roman 2, m, returning to Bosnia and Herzegovina

> For me it is more complicated with DNA, because I have Hungarian ancestors, and Germans in the family and so, but these are genetic matters, because I feel Moravian.= . . . I don't like the differentiation; Prague people say how we Moravians are great, but many not so great people live here. I have got to know many nice Prague people. More so, here we are becoming more like Prague people than Olomouc, the southern Moravia is different, now the villages are dying out, these are myths, I think, that this idea that Moravians are better people is not true.
>
> —Radek, m, returning to Serbia

> One of my strongest experiences was when Brazilians came here and when they found out we were Moravians, they went to their knees and almost kissed our feet. And I was shocked. They said they wanted us to pray for them but when they prayed for us, a big respect. . . . I think they started to exist to a big extent through Moravian brothers and the revival they have now is due to the work of Moravian brothers. And when they came here and realised they were in Moravia and that we are descendants of Moravians, then they had a big respect that they almost bowed down to us. It was very unpleasant for us.
>
> —Josef 3, m, returning to Bosnia and Herzegovina

Zooming in on the regional identity facet first, Moravia, the historical Czech Republic region was highlighted in the interviews with those from Moravia. While Roman 2 in his responses referred interchangeably to his "Czechness" and "Moravianness," Radek stated clearly that he feels like a Moravian, yet he denied that Moravians are better[42] people (a common ste-

---

42. "Better" in the sense of more authentic, sincere and cordial (than Bohemians).

reotype in the Czech Republic). Josef 3 was reminded of his Moravian identity facet when a group of foreign visitors to his church wanted him to pray for them, and they knelt down, showing respect and thankfulness for the Moravian brothers' mission. Identity, thus, often emerges in connection with historical factors. Interestingly, Bohemian identity was not mentioned by any respondent, while the Moravian part came to the surface multiple times, perhaps due to this eastern region's moresdistinguished folklore and tendencies for emancipation. Recent NEO-PI-R research on Czech regional stereotypes concluded that they correlate a lot,[43] yet in comparison to Bohemians, Moravians were distinguished by slightly more extraversion and cordiality.[44]

Another aspect within this particular identity negotiation my interviewees disclosed was the dynamic of city vs. country:

> Because we come from the village . . . when we were at the mission field, we needed less money than [the other two Czech families in the location] because their living standard was higher. And it comes in handy in mission when you don't have much money. [Others] did, praise God, but we were surviving from month to month. So, the fact we came from poorer conditions came in handy, that we could live with little and improvise and survive with little.
>
> —Renata, f, 10–20 years in Croatia

These missionaries, Josef 2 and Renata from southern Bohemia, sensed a contributive significance of their identity as "villagers" in contrast to their teammates in Croatia who came from Czech towns. They found their starting point helpful during the later years, which were economically demanding for them. This identity facet is not limited to Czech regional identity:

---

43. Cholastová, "Regional Stereotypes," 87.

44. Cholastová, 48. After obtaining data from participants of all the three historical regions, the author in her Master thesis in psychology claimed that "Silesians and especially Moravians seem to be, in contrast to Czechs, ['Czechs' are used here, meaning 'Bohemians'; my clarification note] much more amiable. Typical Moravians are, as opposed to Bohemians and Silesians, considered as less neurotic and more extrovert." (Cholastová, 87) My translation; original: "*Slezané a zvláště Moravané se pak vůči Čechům jeví jako mnohem více přívětivější. Typičtí Moravané jsou respondenty oproti Čechům a Slezanům posuzováni jako méně neurotičtí a více extravertní.*"

> It is hard to say, we don't know Croatian culture as such, Slavonians are different, people in the continent, but I would say that the similarities are in that we are people with a warm heart, Slavs, that we like company, "fellowship" [he said it in Croatian], relationships are important for us.
>
> —Josef 1, m, 20–30 years in Croatia

Josef 1 and Klára have been working in the Istrian peninsula, which differs from the rest of Croatian coast – which again differs from various regions of the interior. The Croatian regional differences in its five major regions were recently examined by applying the Hofstede Model.[45] The results, nevertheless, showed relatively small differences and the authors came to the conclusion that Croatia is, with respect to Hofstede's dimensions of national culture, quite homogenous.[46]

It seems that when approached with quantitative methods,[47] the results for either are not that geographically diverse for the Czech Republic or for Croatia[48] – they do not substantially vary, in line with the relatively small size of the countries. Nonetheless, both studies call for qualitative approaches. The respondents of my research perceive that the region they come from is significant for their identity formation. And scholars suggest that these regional elements are arguably not going to decrease in their importance in the face of rising globalization.[49]

7.4.3.2 Someone with supranational identity

> Me and my wife [Jaromíra] are different in this because what has helped us a lot that we could get to know people from different cultures. A black man lived here for a while and in our

---

45. Rajh, Budak and Anić, "Hofstede's Culture Value Survey."

46. Rajh, Budak and Anić, 323. Authors of the paper stated on the Hofstede dimensions of culture: "The results show that Croatia scores lower on power distance, is a moderately high individualistic country, has a tendency towards 'feminine' culture and has a lower level of long-term orientation" (Rajh, Budak and Anić, 309).

47. See charts in Cholastová, "Regional Stereotypes," 87; Rajh, Budak and Anić, "Hofstede's Culture Value Survey, 318.

48. It is to be noted that Croatia is due to its shape and historical development perhaps the most diverse in regional differences of all former Yugoslav countries

49. Jenkins, *Rethinking Ethnicity*, 45; Kuecker, "Ethnicity and Social Identity", 59.

family there are some racists and some of them terrible, they hate black people, and I had to slow them down, because they were calling him a [racist remark] and my mother-in-law would proudly say: "I am a racist," she is not ashamed, even though she is an educated person.

—Radek, m, returning to Serbia

This response sheds a bit of light on the rather sensitive matter of prejudices within the predominantly homogenous Czech society.[50] The debate on this could be expanded[51] yet it suffices to say that this extract only reveals how Radek and Jaromíra negotiated their Czech identity in terms of appreciating being enriched and informed by those different from them. It is as if they attempted to revolt against the constrained thinking of their relatives in adhering to a more "global identity" which is not fixed to a particular ethnic group.

I identify myself with certain European identity. The way of thinking we have that comes from Christian and Greek thinking is very different from the one in other parts of the world. So, I would fit myself into that.

—Erika 1, f, 1 year in Bosnia and Herzegovina

Zooming out from the Czech identity facet, the next most obvious is the European, which can sometimes be interlinked or supplemented by the European Union identity facet. The picture above was taken during the existence of transit refugee camps in Croatia in 2015, where people mostly from the Middle East and Afghanistan were streaming to the EU countries. Volunteers from across Europe and North America came to help and so did our group from Bosnia and Herzegovina. At those moments the European or the EU identity became salient for me as a Czech missionary for the reason that instead of being surrounded by Bosnian students and American teammates, as was my daily routine, I found myself working alongside French, Germans and other Europeans.

---

50. The Czech Republic is a country with a majority single ethnic group, at times referred to as "nation-state" (Eriksen, *Ethnicity and Nationalism*, 119).

51. See Fawn, "Czech Attitudes Towards the Roma"; Burjanek, "Xenophobia among the Czech Population."

Erika 1 referred to herself as European as a first reference which came to her mind in answer to, "What else, apart from yourself being Czech, can you think of?" Being aware of her personal journey, I noticed that this response might have been conditioned by the recent one-year experience of life in south Asia. As her statement depicts, indeed, the ability to compare to the outgroup, which leads towards forming social identity,[52] may result in one's realisation that the ingroup is broader than originally visualized. This illustrates, as some have already critiqued,[53] that there may be a problem with the social identity theory focus on intergroup processes, when the reality of nested elements within identity, and simultaneous belonging to intergroups and intragroups, is much more complex.

Photo diary-2015-10 Slavonski Brod, Croatia

7.4.4 Another national

Renata: When we lived there for about ten years, it was in Poreč, a man came and asked us to pay a bill for electricity, Jirka [Josef

---

52. Tajfel, *Human Groups.*
53. Esler, "Outline of Social Identity Theory," 22.

2] told him: "I am a Czech." And he said: "No, you are not a Czech, you a Bosnian." (laugh)

Josef 2: I told him I would not pay, I am not [Croatian] citizen, so why should I pay, charge the local people. He said: "You are no foreigner, you are Bosnian."

—Renata, f, 10–20 years in Croatia

—Josef 2, m, 10–20 years in Croatia

Ivica said: "Jozo, I have to tell you something," I was "Jozo."

—Josef 2, m, 10–20 years in Croatia

In the course of the adjustment process, people around Josef 2 started to call him, instead of the Czech version of Joseph (*Josef*) the Croatian variant (*Jozo*). The anecdote Renata and Josef 2 shared above discloses how being associated with one of the former Yugoslav nationals, connected with a long-term stay, was considered advantageous. To be considered Bosnian or Slovenian in Croatia is a compliment, it means that the missionary has moved towards being more local. This was evident by Josef's fluency in Croatian and this adjustment is furthermore evident in missionaries' adapted usage of Czech language.[54] The following national identity facet, apart from former Yugoslav, Czech missionaries pointed to was Slovak.

> I feel well in the Balkan temperament. It works better for me with my temperament than in Bohemia. I have Slovak roots, Slovak genes, Slovaks are much closer to me. So, de facto if I would describe Croats, they are Slovaks blended by the Balkans, in a way.

—Jonatán, m, 10–20 years in Croatia

> In fact, they perceive us practically as Slovaks because we speak Slovak and you walk in the street and fifty per cent of people are Slovaks, the streets have Slovak names; other towns are Hungarian.

—Radek, m, returning to Serbia

---

54. The analysis of accent, vocabulary and syntax of Czech missionaries in former Yugoslav countries can be found in chapter sub-section 5.3.2.

To follow up on chapter 1 when the Czech and Slovak environment was introduced, in most Czechs' perception, due to the common past, the language similarity, and the current political, commercial and cultural ties, Slovakia is in a sense not a foreign country.[55] Czechs generally understand Slovak, yet Radek has learned to speak it actively, in order to be more effective in his work. As the result of that, his Czech identity facet was replaced by the Slovak when local people, of course the non-Slovak population, perceived them as Slovaks. Jonatán, with his family heritage in Slovakia, found this national identity facet beneficial for his contextualization in the southern Slavic context.

> Kristýna: We all live in a pseudo-Serbian culture, all around us English.
>
> Vladan: Yes, I am a minority here.
>
> Kristýna: He is a minority, him and I are the only Serbs. So, we have many English, many foreigners.
>
> —Kristýna, f, 20–30 years in Serbia
>
> —Vladan, m, pastor and team leader (Serbia)

The reality of tiny Protestant communities in many former Yugoslav contexts, such as the church in southern Serbia pastored by Vladan, working in international teams when both the local workers and Czech missionaries find themselves adopting elements of the cultures of their Western teammates. For Kristýna, this means situational identifying with English colleagues. For me as a missionary in Bosnia and Herzegovina it meant a situational disassociating from my "Czechness" and becoming somewhat Americanized. The picture below documents one of the instances of having been exposed to American culture, an occasional presence at the Easter egg hunt. The identification with Americans was more multi-levelled. Apart from it being often manifested in the way of performing mission work,[56] it was evident also in the change of my diet when I have started to eat peanut butter, maple syrup and tortillas.

---

55. Chalániová, "Cultural Diplomacy and Stereotypes", 27.
56. This is discussed earlier in section 6.2.2.

Photo diary-2009-04 Zenica, Bosnia and Herzegovina

The last discussed identity facet in this chapter, belonging to another nation, emerged as a subjective self-perception or perception by others in this research. For Czech missionaries, these other nationals were either (a.) former Yugoslavs, (b.) Slovaks, or (c.) other foreign, usually Western, nationals. During the investigation, yet another phenomenon occurred.

> When I am in Bohemia and I hear someone speaking Croatian, it is strange (laugh), I hear someone very close to me, it is interesting. But, when I digress from the topic, there is lot of Ukrainians, and I like to talk to them too, with minorities, we feel very close to those people.
>
> —Klára, f, 20–30 years in Croatia

I was a part of a group of Bosnian students who came to volunteer at an event in Prague (in the picture volunteers wear read hoodies). During this short-term mission trip to the Czech Republic, which took place after six years of living in Bosnia and Herzegovina, I, in a way, identified with the team as we represented the southern Slavic[57] other, rather than "Czech" being my primary national identity. Klára, as a Czech in Croatia, shared her experience of not being indifferent when she changed the environment and visited the Czech Republic – her Croatian, or more broadly Slavic, identity situationally activated.

Photo diary-2014-11 Prague, Czech Republic

When I am not here and I pray for things, my prayers always aim at Slovenia. People, Slovenia, the area, and where my heart, my spirit is, it is here. . . . So, I would say that I feel more Slovenian than anything else, also because of this.

—Šimon, m, 20–30 years in Slovenia

I always say that I am a half-Czech and a half-Croat and my heart is on the Croatian side, which gets obvious when there are some football matches and Croatia plays the Czech Republic. I unequivocally support Croatia. But when you watch the film

---

57. The Slavic part is mentioned to encapsulate all Bosniak, Croat and Serb students joined in.

Pelíšky and hear the Czech anthem it is a heart issue and I identify with that nation and with that identity, and in that case, I am a Czech.

—Daniel, m, returning to Slovenia

As Klára's response already initiated, the perspective of a spatial (Šimon) or a situational (Daniel) context seems to be highly significant. Identity negotiation is certainly produced and reproduced in relation to location and situation.[58] Šimon, while in Slovenia, perceived his Czech identity.[59] On the contrary, while he was away from the country where he has spent almost his whole life, his Slovenian identity facet became salient. He admitted the emotional connection that he feels, being more Slovenian than Czech. This resembles Daniel, who only differs in this matter as his father is a Croat from Dalmatia. For Šimon and Klára, one national identity facet becomes salient, depending on a location. For Daniel it probably is not dissimilar, yet in this extract which one of his two national identity facets becomes salient, depended on a particular situation.

7.5 Chapter conclusions

Both identity theory and social identity theory protagonists agree that the overall self or one's identity is organized into multiple identities or identity facets, "each of which is tied to aspects of the social structure."[60] The sum of these multiple "social identifications," according to John Turner, describes one's overall social identity. The exact quotation reads: "The sum total of the social identifications used by a person to define him- or herself will be described as his or her social identity."[61] It is a useful definition, yet firstly, as this chapter disclosed, it must be noted that it could be problematic to "describe" the identity. A more useful phrasing could be "shape" or "contribute towards forming." Secondly, arguably there cannot be a definite sum of multiple identifications, or identities, or of identity facets. Instead, and

---

58. Jenkins, *Rethinking Ethnicity*, 49.
59. Compare to Šimon's response in (5.2.2).
60. Stets and Burke, "Sociological Approach to Self," 132.
61. Turner, "Towards Cognitive Redefinition," 18.

in accordance with the social identity complexity concept,[62] it is the matter of an intricate process of interrelation of multiple identity facets, which are furthermore subjectively represented.

To summarize chapter 7, scholars propose multiple bases to one's identity: individual self-concept for personal identity, expectations tied to social positions for role-based identity, social group membership for social identity.[63] In my analysis, these were recognized and distinguished, yet also somewhat joined all together. This intermingled, or even to say straightforwardly, messy feature of one's identity referred to its complexity.

Based on my research, these were the tentative categories discovered, apart from their Czech national identity facet: male or female, family member, personality traits holder, interest group member, worker, Christian worker, Christian, missionary, someone with regional or supranational identity, and the identity facet of other national. This arrangement emerged by employing thematic analysis on the case study of Czech Protestant missionaries, who were interviewed between 2018 and 2019, and admittedly this list cannot be considered definite and complete. Rather, it serves as a starting point for the purpose of this research, as it helped prepare material for the subsequent analysis in chapter 8. The identity facets were repeated with varying frequency, and some did in a bigger scale interact with missionaries' "Czechness." The next chapter analyses this very phenomenon in the light of four social identity complexity interrelations: intersection, dominance, compartmentalization and merger.[64]

---

62. Roccas and Brewer, "Social Identity Complexity."
63. Burke and Stets, *Identity Theory*.
64. Roccas and Brewer, "Social Identity Complexity."

CHAPTER 8

Interrelations of "Czechness" with Other Identity Facets: Discussion of Social Identity Complexity

8.1 The four social identity complexity interrelations as the analysis framework

Basic themes in the preceding chapter served as reference points to which the analysis in this chapter ascribes "Czechness," as it focuses on the subjective representation of the multiple ingroup identities of social identity complexity – intersection, dominance, compartmentalization and merger. As already outlined in chapter 2, social identity complexity delineates four basic forms of such interrelations: (a.) intersection as an outcome of larger categories from which it is derived and distinct from, (b.) dominance as a subordination of other identities to one primary group identity, (c.) compartmentalization as a situational realization of one's identity facet in the process of differentiation, and (d.) merger as the sum of all combined ingroup identities.[1]

---

1. Roccas and Brewer, "Social Identity Complexity," 88–89.

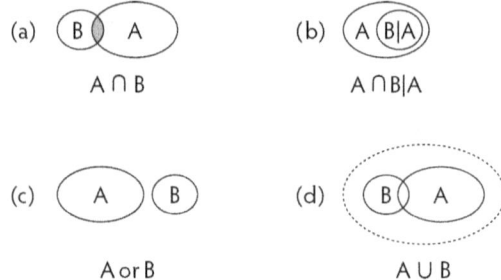

Figure 10: Multiple ingroup representations[2]

To add to the diagram, intersection and dominance are assigned to a relatively low-complexity, and compartmentalization and merger to relatively high-complexity.[3] The architects of the theoretical concept present their expectation: "Complexity of the social identity may help individuals successfully confront the affective implications of negative events related to their social identity."[4] What they have in mind is aiming at higher social identity complexity in order to help reduce ingroup favouritism[5] and increase outgroup tolerance.[6] In 2.2.3 I laid out that the social identity complexity protagonists focused mainly on the multicultural contexts, utilizing the theoretical construct as a tool for peaceful cohabitation and reducing prejudice in diversified societies such as in the USA or Israel.[7] Still, social identity complexity has been used more widely and applied to other stratified samples.[8] It is therefore highly valid to use it as a lens through which to look at Czech

---

2. Roccas and Brewer, 90.

3. Roccas and Brewer, 93.

4. Roccas and Brewer, "Social Identity Complexity," 102. The social psychologist Bodenhausen agrees with social identity complexity when he concludes that a more complex self-understanding contributes towards better functioning in various group environments (Bodenhausen, 12).

5. Tajfel and Turner say that "mere awareness of an ingroup is sufficient to stimulate in-group favouritism" (Tajfel and Turner, , "Social Identity Theory", 284).

6. The social identity complexity research aims to set a "foundation of a social psychologically informed approach to social identity, tolerance, and prejudice reduction" (Brewer and Pierce, "Social Identity Complexity and Outgroup," 436).

7. Roccas and Brewer, "Social Identity Complexity"; Brewer, "Social Identity Complexity and Acceptance."

8. Kok, "Social Identity Complexity Theory"; Meyer, "Social Identity Complexity and Sports"; Xin, Xin and Lin, "Effect of Trustors", 206.

missionaries in the intercultural encounter and to investigate their social identity complexity.[9] In the light of this, some of these questions and further issues can be considered and addressed:[10]

- Which of the four interrelations of identity facets fit the Czech missionaries the most? Or can each one of them be taken under consideration and to what degree?
- Is it possible that conclusions on low versus high social identity complexity can be drawn from this case study of Czech missionaries? Do they possess low or high complexity?
- Would higher complexity lead to better missionary adjustment in South Slavic cultures, contribute to lowering mutual outgroup prejudices and having positive effects on missionaries' work?

Answers to the above may not be the only missiological implications inferred from the research sub-question, "How does the missionaries' 'Czechness' interact with their other identity facets?" Notwithstanding the significance of possible outcomes for mission practitioners in negotiating their identity situationally in their cross-cultural encounters, chapter 8 focuses primarily on theoretical contributions concerning social identity complexity. This research implies the following potential contributions to social identity complexity:

(a) This is qualitative research. Roccas, Brewer and most of the other authors who followed in their footsteps, employ quantitative analysis, based on large scale surveys. To my knowledge, in-depth interviews in connection to social identity complexity have been utilized by only a few article authors.[11]

(b) This is not the typically Western-based research. Even though several studies utilizing the social identity complexity concept have recently appeared in non-Western contexts, for example,

---

9. In fact, social identity complexity can also be used by engaging a more unified sample, while carefully investigating multiple levels of high or low social identity complexity, as exemplified by the study, "Quest for Ethnic Identity in the Modern World: The Georgian Case" by Vladimer Gamsakhurdia.

10. The first set of questions below is answered in 8.6.1, and those of the latter two bullet points in 8.6.2.

11. O'Connor et al., "Sense of Community"; Gamsakhurdia, "Quest for Ethnic Identity."

in China,[12] in Georgia[13] and interestingly partially also in Serbia,[14] the majority of them are performed in the comparatively multicultural and multi-ethnic societies of the West which differ from contexts in the former Communist European countries.

(c) The focus of this research is on the four multiple ingroup memberships or identity facet interrelations of social identity complexity.[15] Scholars across various disciplines predominantly focus on the negotiation of low versus high complexity. In accordance with the original social identity complexity thesis that "awareness of ingroup diversity provides an effective formula for reducing intergroup prejudice,"[16] they aim to confirm that high social identity complexity relates to positive intergroup attitudes. These are conclusions of migrant studies in Italy,[17] in Germany and in the UK,[18] child and adolescent studies in the USA.[19] This research, in contrast, attempts to examine these four in detail in order to provide insight into how to utilize social identity complexity in an innovative way.

Based on what is stated under (c.), the four social identity complexity interrelations of missionaries' "Czechness" with their other identity facets constitute organizing themes in this chapter. They are arranged in ascending order from lowest to highest complexity, as originally outlined by Roccas and Brewer.[20] The data in 8.2, 8.3, 8.4, and 8.5 display evidence of the Czech identity facet interrelating with one of the other identity facets, in the light of

---

12. Xin, Xin and Lin, "Effect of Trustors."
13. Gamsakhurdia, "Quest for Ethnic Identity."
14. Levy et al., "Complex Social Identities."
15. Intersection, dominance, compartmentalization and merger are, according to social identity complexity, "four alternative forms of identity structure that reflect different ways in which the relationships among multiple ingroups can be subjectively represented" (Roccas and Brewer, "Social Identity Complexity," 89–90). Again, being aware of the differentiation of social identity theory and identity theory perception of what defines one's identity (Burke and Stets, 129), most of the time I prefer to use the term "identity facet," which probably diverges from the social identity complexity group membership delineation, and bridges to identity theory.
16. Roccas and Brewer, "Social Identity Complexity," 104.
17. Prati et al., "Encouraging Majority Support," 429.
18. Schmid, Hewstone and Al Ramiah, "Neighborhood Diversity," 141.
19. Knifsend and Juvonen, "Role of Social Identity Complexity," 623.
20. Roccas and Brewer, "Social Identity Complexity," 89–91..

social identity complexity, and the chapter ends in 8.6.1 by critiquing aspects of the theoretical concept.

Before commencing the analysis proper, it can be pointed out that the current analysis often correlates with that of the preceding chapters. Identification of self and others in cultural similarities and differences, in chapter 4, and situational Czech identity salience and suppression, in chapter 5, are – as the brief set of responses below demonstrates – interlinked with the multiple ingroup memberships (or identity facets) interrelation categories of social identity complexity.

> Interviewer: According to you, how to you perceive Czech and Croatian culture?
>
> Vratislav: A big difference . . . Their traditions are hard, firstly to understand why they mean it this way as they say it or simply to understand some things, it has been a problem to me. *But we are getting into it, we are becoming some kind of Croats* [emphasis added].
>
> —Vratislav, m, returning to Croatia

> We very strongly intended that I do not bring Czech culture there. I am persuaded that Serbs, Croats and Bosniaks *do not need Czech culture, they need Christ* [emphasis added]. Of course, it is very hard to eliminate it when you are used to something. For example, with American missionaries it is more apparent, because the cultures are more distant, our culture and Serbian culture is not so distant, because they are Slavic cultures.
>
> —Jakub 2, m, returning to Serbia

> Daniel: In Bosnia, there were moments *I was ashamed I was a Czech* [emphasis added], sincerely (laugh). These are the differences in mentality, I know it, when Czechs come to the coast, they are categorized somehow and I know about it and know it and now I am like that as well, so it was a bit strange, because I adjust to the mentality and behave like the locals. But *Czechs behave as Czechs and at the times I am with them, I was almost ashamed* [emphasis added].

Interviewer: What were the moments?

Daniel: I do not know, Czechs have their individual demands, in Croatia people adjust to how it works there, for example to pay the bill or to order something, it is how it is done, that is how everybody does it. But Czechs have their individual demands.

—Daniel, m, returning to Slovenia

In the realm of placing the two cultural contexts side by side, Vratislav, a bit judgementally, responded on the differing traditions, Daniel recalled the differences in behaviour, and Jakub 2 focused rather on the similar traits in the two Slavic areas. As for identity salience and suppression, all three interviewees realize the need to suppress their Czech identity facet in order to fit into the local culture, in accordance with the mission work requirements.[21] Emphases were added to help locate the parts of the responses which relate to the present area of interest, addressing the multiple identity facets.

When Vratislav says they are "becoming some kind of Croats," this could relate to the social identity complexity category of intersection when they might find themselves somewhere in the middle – they let go of some of their "Czechness" and obtain elements of Croatian culture, to a certain degree. Next, Jakub 2 is presenting an example of the Christian identity facet dominating the other facets. Finally, the response of Daniel is linked with compartmentalization and, furthermore, it seems a bit disordered: He says: "I was ashamed I was a Czech," and later on: "When I was with Czechs, I was almost ashamed." This simultaneous realization comes from his background of being both Czech and Croat, and one of the double national identity facet is situationally salient.

All three responses would well classify within chapters 4, 5, and 6, and this only emphasizes the complexity of the analysis which follows.

---

21. To be precise, within this interview section, they were all aware of it, yet other places in their interview transcripts record that they at times struggled with suppressing "Czechness." Daniel, moreover, witnessed the salient "Czechness" in a situation of a visiting short-term mission team when, "off-duty" and ordering food in the restaurant, they showed no attempts to adjust.

8.2 Intersection

Intersection, i.e. applying diverse group identities into a single intersected social identity,[22] of two differing national identity facets, was found by some respondents to be disorienting and problematic:

> After some time, we blended. It is stupid somehow, you do not feel you are a Czech, at the same time you are not a Croat, and you are *something in between* [emphasis added]. That is a very odd feeling. And when we came back we noticed some faults of the Czech culture because the Croatian culture is far ahead in some things and you feel unpleasant in your own culture and you are ashamed of it, but you have to live here now.
>
> —Renata, f, 10–20 years in Croatia
>
> Crisis of identity (laugh).
>
> —Ema 1, f, 20–30 years in Slovenia
>
> Crisis of identity, what else can I tell you (laugh), you don't know who you are. We can talk about it with humour, but it is hard, in many areas we have reached the edge . . . We will always remain Czechs, no matter whether we stay here or we go for retirement back to Bohemia.
>
> —Patrik, m, 20–30 years in Slovenia

"Crisis of identity," referring to the position in between two identity facets might be deemed a cliché, due to the excessive usage of this syntagma. Still, interestingly both of the missionaries worded it this way independently.[23] Jenkins argued that identification matters as a cognitive mechanism that humans use to sort themselves and others,[24] yet maintained that these classificatory models are "multidimensional, unlikely to be internally consistent, and may not easily map on to each other."[25] The missionaries, indeed, often struggle in the identification process and a certain crisis or clash within a

---

22. Roccas and Brewer, "Social Identity Complexity," 91.
23. Patrik referred to crisis of identity during the interview in December 2018 and Ema 1 in July 2019, with Patrik and their son Šimon present.
24. Jenkins, *Social Identity*, 13.
25. Jenkins, 6.

person might occur, as these responses document. The third respondent admitted she no longer felt Czech but not yet Croatian and used the words "something in between" which suitably describe the social identity complexity category of intersection.

> And within me it is colliding, things I have brought from the Balkans.... In thinking and in manners of behaviour and I am glad, sincerely, that I came out of it.
>
> —Daniel, m, returning to Slovenia
>
> And here it is perhaps too "free" [in English] in some areas. And when you have some values, Christian or other values, you don't jump too much into the Czech "free." And I'm in search of a balance between the conservative and the free and I think it's good.
>
> —Daniel, m, returning to Slovenia

Daniel's response reflects his unique identity as Czech-Croat or Croat-Czech. His experience is not dissimilar to the children of Kristýna (Kristýna, f, 20–30 years in Serbia), who have obtained both Czech and Serbian identity facet, since Kristýna's husband is a Serb. As the two responses demonstrate, Daniel finds this conflicting for himself as well, yet he has gradually been learning to reconcile the two and acknowledge this intersection position. For the harmony Daniel and many others in-between two cultures attempt to achieve, Roccas and Brewer specify a term "integrated biculturalism" which, according to them, unlike compartmentalization, where different cultural experiences are incompatible, acknowledges multiple cultural identities simultaneously.[26] I would add that it is also dissimilar to intersection as outlined and that it might more fittingly be classified as the social identity complexity category of merger.

To add to the discussion of these in-between positions, it gets more complicated by the presence of more, in this case national, identity facets.[27] These multidimensional intersections, which consist of not only two units, assuredly

---

26. Roccas and Brewer, "Social Identity Complexity," 93.

27. More people can identify as both one of the former Yugoslav nations and as Slovak or other, or even some form of supranational identity. Czech missionaries' international teammates, visiting teams from other countries, conferences abroad – it all contributes to the complexity of such intersection.

are demanding to define and vary substantially with each missionary. Identity theorists say: "Identities do not always operate in isolation, but they interact with other identities in particular situations."[28] Following this brief introductory analysis, intersection will be further explored in the later section related to merger 8.5 and particularly in 8.6.1 where this social identity complexity interrelation is linked to the relevant literature and critiqued.

8.3 Dominance

Dominance is another form of interrelation of identity facets or ingroup memberships when inconsistencies are suppressed, and the social world is divided along a single ingroup-outgroup categorization.[29] In the case of Czech missionaries' "Czechness," it can either situationally dominate or be dominated.

> After four or five years I did not feel Czech anymore, then you have dreams in Croatian, you get into that stage that you do not translate. . . . For me the reverse culture shock was worse, it was more difficult for me. Firstly, I was in a much worse condition, I was returning as a wretch. And secondly, I wasn't aware how I have changed during that time, how I found myself in the Croatian culture. In contradiction, I am more like fish in water there, while in Czech culture I feel that I need to pretend more.
>
> —Jonatán, m, 10–20 years in Croatia

In Jonatán's perception, within the process of adjustment in his family's long term stay in Croatia, and upon return to Czechia, it was the situational dominance of another national identity over the Czech one. Such a strong statement was solitary; the vast majority of respondents did not consider any of the former Yugoslav identities becoming that dominant. The most significant theme for social identity complexity interrelation of dominance, nevertheless, was the superiority of the Christian identity facet in this matter. Before discussing the dominance of being Christian over being Czech, I will briefly address two following responses:

---

28. Burke and Stets, *Identity Theory*, 130.
29. Roccas and Brewer, "Social Identity Complexity," 91.

> In Bohemia there are many churches, many different denominations and groups and even within a denomination there are differences. And the teams, our participants, they were from different churches. . . . I mixed the people up and I said that these are some local habits, but Christ is bigger, God's kingdom is something more than what the church in your village says to be right. . . . So, I told them to act like Christ's followers during the mission – and not like members of this and that church. Because then, instead of mission, it is propagation of one's denomination.
>
> —Jakub 1, m, returning to Bosnia and Herzegovina
>
> The spiritual answer is that we are God's children because when we stress anything else, then it falls apart. I think Lord God is repeatedly returning us to that we are God's children and God's friends, Jesus calls us friends somewhere. And if we stress more some other identity: "I am a worship leader, I am a children worker, I lead music workshop" [in Serbian], I think we have lost the focus of who we are.
>
> —Kristýna, f, 20–30 years in Serbia

What matters most, in this perspective, is to be Christians, i.e. Christ's followers (in Jakub's words), God's children or God's friends (in Kristýna's words). Jakub 1 perceives church denomination ingroup as inferior to a wider Christian ingroup, it is not only in the realm of perception for him, yet he imprints his beliefs and instils this particular dominant Christian identity facet in participants of mission trips he organizes. Kristýna, when asked about her identity in general, the first thing that came to her mind was being God's children (i.e. her Christian identity facet). She considered all other facets, including Christian worker identities, as subsidiary.

The dominant Christian identity is in accordance with what William Campbell concluded for the principal first-century missionary: "Paul shares with gentiles in Christ the primary identity-marker which in faith is Christ."[30] This identity facet emerged for Czech missionaries in encounters with other nationals, within the context of common times of worship and prayer:

---

30. Campbell, *Paul and Christian Identity*, 157.

> Prayers, I experienced, as Jesus said in the Bible that he came to destroy barriers dividing us, I have experienced when we prayed and the Holy Spirit came there was unity and peace, or when saw the Scripture the same way. I experience these things through God somehow, not that much through the culture. . . . When I experience the unity with them, it is in prayers.
>
> —Radek, m, returning to Serbia
>
> We played a worship song which has a very simple text, practically it is only one word "hallelujah" which gets repeated with a certain melody, and it is a very nice melody, and the people joined in singing and it was there, the merging on the spiritual line. And then you realize that it does not matter when one is a Croat, one Serb, one who knows what, and we all are God's.
>
> —Roman 2, m, returning to Bosnia and Herzegovina

Both Radek and Roman 2 realized that it did not matter where they were from, that they were Czechs and others were outgroup – in those moments of experiencing spirituality together they all were ingroup, uniting in the dominant overreaching Christian identity. Other respondents were very explicit about how they perceived the interrelation of being Czech and being Christian at the same time:

> Christian identity is the one that reaches over all and gives the opportunity not to lift up the Czech and European as something primary.
>
> —Erika 1, f, 1 year in Bosnia and Herzegovina
>
> Not our "Czechness" but our Christianity, so that we would behave biblically and not in a Czech way. Because we present biblical values, not the Czech culture. Of course, somehow it will come out in the contact, in the conversation, that we are also Czechs. But first of all, we are citizens of the Heavenly Kingdom – and that's where we should have the centre of gravity.
>
> —Jakub 1, m, returning to Bosnia and Herzegovina

Jakub 1 verbalizes the priority of Christian identity facet as something "we should have" and Erika 1 says that it gives the opportunity to not elevate the

Czech identity as something primary. These responses show that missionaries consider the suppression of "Czechness," below the dominant Christian identity, to be the desired goal, i.e. not as something already happening and taken for granted.

> See, we search the identity in Christ. I know it might sound like a Christian cliché, but this is how it is. We have never tried to bring our culture . . . Personally, I don't refer to us being Czechs, I don't search for identity in that, certainly we have nothing to be ashamed of, because we have history, sometimes I say, look at Moravian brothers, what it was, the biggest mission movement worldwide, we have things to be proud about in this matter. What do I have to offer to people as a Czech?
>
> —Roman 1, m, 2–10 years in Serbia

Roman 1, on the other hand, professes that this is precisely what their practice is – the dominant Christian identity facet, and the Czech one as secondary. The only moment he claims his "Czechness" is in connection with Christian history, as in his perspective of Moravian brothers as part of the Czech nation's historical legacy.[31] The matter of setting aside altogether the Czech identity facet is, nevertheless, highly problematic, no matter how wishful and purposeful a missionary's practice is. Lesslie Newbigin, as a former missionary to India, at first considered his evaluations of Hindu beliefs and practices to be based on God's revelation in Christ, yet later realized it was conditioned by his home culture.[32] This unsettled issue is underlined by the following response.

> From my point of view, what we are solving is not if we are Czechs or perceive ourselves as Czechs, but rather where God is calling us, the future steps, how to give a structure to the church and how to pass on the relay to a next generation, so that a wider group of, from our perspective, young generation which would be able to manage the church . . . That's what we are solving now, rather than being Czechs, or being in Bohemia, or Slovenians,

---

31. See Tennent, *Invitation to World Missions*, 248.
32. Newbigin, *Foolishness to Greeks*, 21.

but where God's calling leads us, how to finish the race so that the fruit remains.

—Patrik, m, 20–30 years in Slovenia

Patrik and his wife Ema 1 were not able to completely delineate themselves from the national identity facet, yet Patrik's perspective is that for them this identity facet is not top in the list of priorities. For him there are more urgent identities they focus on in everyday situations of mission work, such as being a Christian, being a pastor, being a church planter. In addition to that, during the interview, Patrik gave indications of mild irritation at my recurring questions on Czech identity while, instead, he seemed to have preferred talking more of mission work.[33]

The missionaries' statements in this section revealed a certain dominance of Christian identity. It can be noted that it is "dominance" in the sense of transcending, not replacing national (or other) identity facets. The theologian J. Daniel Hays, with the goal of helping put down ethnic differences as a base of reconciliation,[34] argued for the new identity in Christ replacing the old.[35] He claimed that early Christians' "new self-identity (ethnicity) 'in Christ' replaces their old ethnic identity"[36] and referred to Paul exhorting believers in his letter to the Philippians to imitate him. Just as Paul cast off his old identity as a Hebrew as "rubbish," so they too should cast off their old identity.[37] The question arises, nevertheless, how justifiable it is to hold that Paul ceased to be a Jew, a learned Pharisee, a Roman citizen, etc. The view of Hays conflicts with Campbell, who also reads Paul in the context of ethnic identity and says that "despite the fact that Christian identity is a Christ-defined identity, to be in Christ is to retain one's particularity whether as a Jew or as a gentile."[38] Paul's intention, according to him, was not to blur the boundaries of ethnicity,

---

33. This response originates from the second interview with Patrik (first took place in December 2018, second in July 2019) and he might have felt we have addressed the "Czechness" sufficiently. Furthermore, Patrik's church in Slovenia and my home church have been involved in common projects lately.

34. Hays, "Paul and the Multi-Ethnic," 87.

35. He based his argument by naming and discussing biblical motifs: being baptized into Christ, being clothed "in Christ," becoming a citizen of heaven, obtaining new kinship – getting adopted into the family of God with the common ancestor Abraham (Hays, 84–86).

36. Hays, 78.

37. Hays, 86.

38. Campbell, *Paul and Christian Identity*, 156.

but rather to reconfigure the relationship between people who, even though united in Christ, remain different.[39]

Together with Campbell, and grounded in the missionaries' responses, it appears more legitimate to view the dominating Christian identity as not cancelling, but rather, transcending all other identities. To complement this partial finding that the Christian identity facet overarches the Czech national identity, based on the material above, it can be affirmed that such dominance is often situational. Furthermore, even though some individuals evince signs of dominance as their prevailing identity facet interrelation, missionaries' identity complexity might probably score, according to social identity complexity, higher as merger, yet when particular issues are in focus, related to matters of the Christian identity facet, the interrelation of dominance comes forward.

8.4 Compartmentalization

Compartmentalization implies dividing identity facets into single compartments which occasionally come to the foreground. According to Roccas and Brewer, these social identities are "context specific or situation specific."[40] In their understanding, situations relate to moments of expressing certain types of behaviour in social contacts, such as stress or in-group threat.[41] The contexts are viewed as specific environments, as locations, and the authors give an example of social identities at the office.[42] Still, "context" can certainly be perceived more widely; it can refer to various historical, cultural and religious contexts,[43] and to personal relationships since as humans "we live in particular contexts: our family, our neighbourhood, our town, our country."[44] The term "context" could, therefore, instead of distinguishing between context and situation,[45] serve more as an umbrella term for the context of setting (broader location in time and space) and of situation (particular

---

39. Campbell, 8.
40. Roccas and Brewer, "Social Identity Complexity," 90.
41. Roccas and Brewer, 98–99.
42. Roccas and Brewer, 91.
43. Bevans and Schroeder, *Constants in Context*, 205.
44. Hiebert, "Gospel in Human Contexts," 82.
45. Roccas and Brewer, "Social Identity Complexity," 90.

Interrelations of "Czechness" with Other Identity Facets

circumstances). In my utilization, as already outlined in (5.1), for Czech missionaries this broader context is after 1989 in one of former Yugoslav countries, and the situations Czech missionaries find themselves in at times refer to their particular relational, social, historical, geo-political, contexts. This delineation is the reason I do not refer to "contextual," but rather "situational" identity salience in connection to compartmentalization, which is in line with the social identity complexity terminology.

> I am proud of Czech identity, but it is because I live in Serbia. If I lived in Czechia, I would feel more Serbian identity which I have in me, because of the family reasons. My grandfather is a Serb or because simply I have been living there the last thirty years and more, so I evidently do have the Serbian identity.
>
> —Miroslav, m, acquaintance and director of Czech minority association in Belgrade Serbia (Kristýna Serbia)

> Klára: But concerning our perception of "Czechness," it is strange because when we are in Bohemia we long for Croatia as for our home, and when we are here and something is happening in Bohemia politically or with someone close to us, then again we experience it from the position of a Czech, they are ours, that is our country, so we are some kind of –
>
> Josef 1: Outcasts.
>
> Klára: Neither here, nor there, or more so both, or I don't know, heavenly citizens.
>
> Josef 1: No place on earth, like the Son of God. Your home is in heavens and when you focus on heaven, when you are here you look forward to there, when you are there you look forward here. But definitely we are rooted more here.
>
> Klára: We are at home here. But at the same time, we love Bohemia . . . Yet, if I am to go back to Bohemia, which could happen, I would be sad after Croatia and I would miss it.
>
> —Klára, f, 20–30 years in Croatia
>
> —Josef 1, m, 20–30 years in Croatia

Compartmentalization refers to identity salience – while one or more identity facets are activated, others are muted, yet not completely abolished. Miroslav, depending on the location, lives out his Czech identity when in Serbia and his Serbian identity when in the Czech Republic. Klára and Josef 1, even though professing the dominant Christian identity,[46] and prioritizing Croatia, perceive it similarly to Miroslav. For them, the context of their current location determines that the other national identity facet becomes activated, the one not present. I record in my diaries, that in the context of an international conference where I came from Zagreb with a group from Croatia, I identified with Croats and with other students from former Yugoslav countries. There was a Czech group present as well, yet I hardly spent any time with them; the picture below documents a reunion gathering of delegates from former Yugoslav countries.

Probably not all the cases, yet Miroslav's situations might relate to the principle of hypodescent in racial studies[47] which holds that people with a mixed racial heritage are usually assigned a monoracial identity based on their distinctive features which are unfamiliar in majority society.[48] This principle refers more to external perceptions, yet is not completely dissimilar from the self-perception of multiple identity facets described here, where for example, Miroslav, his minority identity facet (Czech/Serbian) becomes salient in a majority environment (in Serbia/in the Czech Republic).

---

46. It is not the focus of this passage, yet it seems useful to comment that this sort of perspective on Christian identity might depend on respondents' eschatological perception of heaven.

47. Bodenhausen and Kang, "Multiple Identities," 552–553.

48. Bodenhausen and Kang say that "these distinctive features tend to capture more selective attention, leading subsequently encountered ambiguous or multiracial people who have these features to be categorized according to minority group membership" (Bodenhausen and Kang, 553) and add examples of black/white biracial people in the USA who would be considered black, or of Chinese/white people who would be considered Chinese in New Zealand, or white in China (Bodenhausen and Kang, 553).

Photo diary-2004-04 Györ, Hungary

Josef 1 above expressed that at times they have tended to view themselves as "outcasts." The response of Jonatán below evinces similar, yet perhaps more detrimental, clashes of self-perception in salience of social identities:

> I was writing reports to Bohemia, for Czechs, I was writing reports to Japan, because for one half we were supported by Japanese, so I was writing for Japanese in a Japanese way. And then I was writing reports to America, for Baptists, in an American way. It was like three people were writing it. But I was the one writing it, so that everyone would be satisfied, I agreed with the church expectations, it's a schizophrenia. I sold myself for money actually, for God's work. "Money for God's work" – you excuse everything to yourself then.
>
> —Jonatán, m, 10–20 years in Croatia

Jonatán used to write his prayer update or newsletter, in Czech for Czechs and then in English with one version for his American and the other for his Japanese supporters. Retrospectively, he viewed this very negatively and for such a compartmented way of missionary practice used the word "schizophrenia." This discrepancy in the situational identity salience was one of many factors that led to Jonatán's burn out, which he admitted in the interview.[49]

> Josef 2: I am not able to go and speak in shorts. And I consider it good.
>
> Renata: We lift up the clothing culture in Czechia. It strikes your eyes.
>
> —Josef 2, m, 10–20 years in Croatia
>
> —Renata, f, 10–20 years in Croatia
>
> Well, in general, the Bosnian way suited me (laugh), so, I got into it, it is more spontaneous. And I think the "Czechness" I left for myself for the personal time when I went for a trip or so.
>
> —Erika 1, f, 1 year in Bosnia and Herzegovina
>
> My friend from Zenica and I led a group (short-term mission team) of Czechs to a nature park in the south of Herzegovina. The gatekeepers charged them, yet when they overheard the two of us speaking to each other in the local language, they declared: "It is free for you, you are their guides."
>
> —Diary notes-DS-2015-06 Kravica Falls, Bosnia and Herzegovina

Josef 2 and Renata share many experiences with Jonatán with whom they worked at the same location. One particular issue they struggled with was in situations related to clothing. They have gradually adopted the Croatian standard and presently back in the Czech Republic, it is the manner their "Croatianness" becomes salient. Erika 1 when in society with other people strove to adjust and comply, in her private time, her Czech identity facet manifested through individual hiking trips or similar activities. Her response is quite open ended, yet it points out that she compartmentalized the Bosnian Serb and Czech identities, depending on whether she was with people or alone. The third response from personal diaries recalls a specific situation

---

49. Due to the discretion entrusted to me as the interviewer, I cannot address the burnout in detail. Still, it can surely be added that multiple identity negotiations can be listed among the factors, in its connection to expectations and requirements of outsiders – who were coming from diverse cultural backgrounds.

in a particular location – national park entrance gate cashier – when I, as a Czech missionary was, in contrast to the other Czechs, considered a local. The preceding data excerpts have indicated that compartmentalization of a single identity facet can be considered both beneficial and demanding, depending on the missionaries' condition and state of affairs. Compartmentalization is classified as "relatively high complexity,"[50] yet it does not mean it is unproblematic. The responses point towards the challenge to balance multiple social identities which are situation dependent. Furthermore, hardly ever do only two distinguished identity facets figure in a situation of compartmentalization. Roccas and Brewer mention that "there may be situations in which more than one categorization is relevant and salient."[51] This brings me to the last and most complex social identity complexity interrelation in the upcoming section.

8.5 Merger

Merger as the last subjective representation of identity facet interrelations resembles compartmentalization, nevertheless the conjunction "or" is replaced with "and," for the reason that "differences are recognized and embraced in their most inclusive form."[52] It is the highest possible representation of how one's ingroup memberships or identity facets interact, and often appear to transcend single categorical divisions.

One of the respondents, when asked about moments when he suppressed his "Czechness," answered:

> I did it most of the time. *I did not perceive that I am a Czech and they are from another culture* [emphasis added]. I was always trying to speak their language, to use the thing they use, eat the same food they eat.
>
> —Marek, m, 1 year in Kosovo

This missionary in Kosovo seemed to embrace his identity facets in their most inclusive form, as he viewed his national identity with blurred edges.

---

50. Roccas and Brewer, "Social Identity Complexity," 93.
51. Roccas and Brewer, 91.
52. Roccas and Brewer, 91.

He did not perceive he was Czech, and they were Kosovo Albanians or Serbs. That does not mean that he was not aware of it at all, yet he avoided categorizations if not necessary. As Marek's following response demonstrates, he thinks like this concerning his other identity facets as well; others expressed their reflection on this matter in a similar way:

> Interviewer: And what else, what for you are other groups that you belong? Your nationality is Czech, how else do you see yourself, are you, for example, a member of a group?
>
> Marek: Well, I think I don't have it set in that way, I don't deal with it at all (laugh).
>
> —Marek, m, 1 year in Kosovo
>
> Interviewer: Do you feel as a Czech, Slovenian, do you have any dash, any percentage?
>
> Šimon: I don't know whose I am, my mum's and dad's (laugh).
>
> Ema 1: And mum and dad don't know whose they are (laugh). So, it is hard for him.
>
> Šimon: I would say that this broadens my cultural spectre, so I understand how people function, because in every country, every nation is limited and has certain problems and some pluses.
>
> —Šimon, m, 20–30 years in Slovenia
>
> —Ema 1, f, 20–30 years in Slovenia
>
> I am somehow without identity, or I don't know how I should call myself. I am a Czech, but I probably don't mind where I live, I do not insist on having deep roots, to get rooted somewhere.
>
> —Denisa, f, returning to Croatia

Again, Marek avoids claiming for himself any categories of identity, he perceives he is who he is in a rather integrated way. This does not concern him, and he seems to have it sorted out. Jenkins says on identification that classification implies evaluation and that we "humans are generally not disinterested classifiers."[53] The peril of passing judgements could be one reason

---

53. Jenkins, *Social Identity*, 6.

for the avoidance, perhaps connected to Marek. Šimon, on the other hand, admits that he does not know whose he is. Instead of being assigned to Czech or Slovenian identity, he jokingly suggests his identity is derived from his parents. This can either be a sign of insecurity in both Šimon and Eva, who joined in the response, or it can also mean that they embrace all identities and do not occupy themselves with the necessity of categorization. Denisa likewise alleges her lack of knowledge in this matter, and even though she considers herself Czech, she does not insist on it and perceives herself as someone without a set identity.

These responses point to both insecurity and refusal of Czech missionaries to think in the categories of individual identity facets. Merger, by its definition "preserves both differentiation and integration in an inclusive social identity."[54] and there are signs of avoiding the differentiation part in some of the responses. Nevertheless, they all subjectively perceive their identities as somewhat integrated, and this in its highly inclusive form is linked to the social identity complexity interrelation of merger. Brewer says that complex social identity lessens the possibility of obtaining firm unequivocal answers, so "consequently, there is no definite answer to questions such as 'is this person one of us or one of them?'"[55]

Merger as a category of high complexity is truly complex and the remaining responses in this section point towards the realization that there is often a reciprocal relation of merger to other social identity complexity interrelations.

> Unfortunately, in the census in Serbia it is not possible to register as both, Serb and Czech. But according to me that should be possible, because in essence I am both Czech and Serb, at least partially.
>
> —Miroslav, m, acquaintance and director of Czech minority association in Belgrade Serbia (Kristýna Serbia)

Miroslav, similar to Daniel,[56] who found himself in-between two national identities, would technically belong to the same category (intersection). Yet his response here reveals that internally he perceives himself more integrated

---

54. Roccas and Brewer, "Social Identity Complexity," 92.
55. Brewer, "Social Identity Complexity and Acceptance," 20.
56. This is discussed earlier in 8.2.

as Serb and Czech (merger), and on the official level he is obliged to declare himself as either Serb or Czech (compartmentalization).

> At the beginning when we were here I wanted to be a Croat to Croats, based on the word that Paul[57] says: Czech to Czechs, Croat to Croats, Jew to Jews, Greek to Greeks. And inside of me I was setting apart from the Czech culture, therefore I was learning the language, this is *a moment when you start forgetting your language and you don't know the local yet* [emphasis added].... At that time, I was going through a desire to be accepted by the culture, accepted by the local people, that they accept us as their own, I really was putting a lot of stress on that, but it was not good in this degree. It is good when one adjusts, I think that Paul means this when he is speaking about it, that you adjust, but that you are aware of that identity of yours, not trying to remake it, because it is as it is and it will stay that way. But I went into extreme in this and that was one of the factors why later I burnt out, because they will not accept you, based on that you are attempting to be a Croat to Croats, that you start behaving like them, speaking like them.
>
> —Josef 1, m, 20–30 years in Croatia

This comparatively lengthy excerpt from an interview underlines well how merger emerges from intersection. Josef 1 desired his primary national identity to be switched from Czech to Croatian, but he found himself in the place of intersection (emphasized). Gradually, he became more confused, and it was even one of the factors leading to his burn out. Josef 1 eventually realized it is useful to adapt to the local environment, yet still realized that elements of his original identity can be kept and held in a healthy balance.

> I was on one hand trying to adjust to the nations, but it is not completely possible, because you need to have some of your own identity, otherwise you would erase the intercultural dialogue of it, you would become a member of the other culture and the mission would die.
>
> —Jakub 1, m, returning to Bosnia and Herzegovina

---

57. He is referring to the biblical text 1 Corinthians 9:20, written by the apostle Paul.

Jakub 1 added to the aspect of the reality lived by Josef 1, which he himself experienced in only a limited way, perhaps due to the short-term nature of the sojourns. Jakub 1 emphasized that keeping national identity is important in order not to erase the intercultural dialogue. Understanding of "mission" in his statement is seemingly influenced by comprehension of mission as international mission,[58] meaning the possibility of cessation of the intercultural aspect of the work.

> I think that, as a missionary, you have the advantage to take from each culture the good things. And you try to change the wrong, and hope that God changes situations around you and people around you. And our country is really the heaven, inhabitants of heaven, so you asked me how I perceive it, so I think we are "inhabitants of God's kingdom" [in Serbian].
>
> —Kristýna, f, 20–30 years in Serbia

Kristýna, in her response, expresses a rather typical spiritual viewpoint, when Christian identity facets dominate, yet to supplement it, she aims for her own national or cultural identity to integrate all the benefit from others. The extract from the interview with Eldina resonates with that:

> I do not see it is a clash for her but in some way it complements her. But also, my opinion is that all of us who experience different cultures and live in different cultures we are none of the cultures anymore. . . . You cannot be 100 per cent Czech if you have lived in Bosnia for some time, I cannot be 100 per cent Bosnian if I have lived in America for five years, you know. I am not 100 per cent American and I will never be, but that is again for me positive because it tells me that we belong to a different kingdom anyway. . . . I think we are building an identity in Christ. We cannot be anymore 100 per cent of anything.
>
> —Eldina, f, supervisor and team leader (Erika 1 Bosnia and Herzegovina)

Eldina left Bosnia and has been living for a while in the USA and can therefore partially identify with Erika 1 about whom she gives evidence.

---

58. Bosch, *Transforming Mission*, 10; Tennent, *Invitation to World Missions*, 24.

She, similar to Kristýna, finds Christian identity to be principal and all other identity facets to be complementary. In Eldina's words she cannot be 100 per cent of anything and the reality of a stay abroad, in contact with foreign culture, removes 100 per cent of one's cultural or national identity.[59] What transcends is exactly the Christian identity facet.

To sum up, it has proved to be the case with most Czech missionaries in this research that the social identity complexity interrelation of their identity facets often appears to be as intersection or compartmentalization, yet the ideal they aim at is merger, and dominance plays a significant role. For Marek, Šimon, Ema 1 and Denisa, merger is the outcome of thinking in wider and more integrated categories of identity. For Miroslav, merger is a desired identity interrelation, arising from intersection and compartmentalization. For Josef 1, merger is an arrival point he reaches after struggling with national identity facets. For Kristýna and Eldina, merger seems to be the state of affairs, with an overarching Christian identity.

The interpretation in this section leads to the finding that for Czech missionaries in former Yugoslavia, and apparently for others as well, their multiple identity facets interrelation is, or is supposed to be merger, with an attached dominance of the Christian identity facet.

8.6 Chapter conclusions

8.6.1 Critical evaluation of social identity complexity concept

This concluding section which looks at Czech Protestant mission through the lens of social identity complexity provides a space to explore how aspects of the social identity complexity concept can be validated and critiqued by this qualitative research. The social identity complexity multiple ingroup interrelations proved to function well as a grid in the preceding four sections, where each type was documented by the responses, and often more than one social identity complexity interrelation was retrieved within individual extracted statements. This qualitative study, based on in-depth interviews and personal

---

59. See Lingenfelter and Mayers, *Ministering Cross-Culturally*, 114. It has to be added that the degree of such change depends on cultural distance (where does a person go) and on time (how long has a person spent in the given place).

diary, largely affirms the social identity complexity findings. An individual (Czech missionary) possesses multiple ingroup memberships or identity facets, which interrelate and can be generally sorted on a continuum from lower to higher.[60] For Czech missionaries in the sample, there was no single interrelation which would prevail; these were the connections related to the single social identity complexity interrelations:

- intersection – being disjointed in-between the two national identities
- dominance – domination of the Christian identity facet
- compartmentalization – in settings and situations of Czech identity salience
- merger – integrating the differences in cultural adjustment

The proposers of social identity complexity by their careful wording acknowledge that the concept is not clear-cut: "Complexity of social identities may *vary* within and between the four types . . . intersection and dominance can, *in general*, be classified as *relatively* low-complexity representations."[61] In spite of its generally excepted validity and wide usage across scholarly disciplines, the theory needs to be approached critically. Based on the evidence of this qualitative research, with its selection of primary sources, and by adopting missiological insights, I make the following claims which may help to inform aspects of social identity complexity:

1. The difference between internal and external perception of social identity complexity is underestimated and should be considered a significant factor.
2. Intersection as a category of low identity complexity is more complex than a unique set of identity, which is set in place in-between two or between more identity facets.
3. High social identity complexity does not necessarily equal low outgroup prejudice.

(1.) There is a difference in the internal vs. external perspective of one's identity facet interrelations and the two perspectives call for correlation. Both one's social identity (category-based) and identity (role-based) are

---

60. Roccas and Brewer, "Social Identity Complexity," 89–90.
61. Roccas and Brewer, 93. Emphasis added.

accompanied by internal and external aspects. Stryker and Burke notice that role identity entails a duality: "Role is external; it is linked to social positions within the social structure. Identity is internal, consisted of internalized meanings and expectations associated with a role."[62] This differentiation is certainly useful – one's identity (internal perspective) is linked with one's role (external perspective). I argue that one's social identity, as well, carries the internal-external dimension and it depends on who is the agent of perception. What proved beneficial in this research was the inclusion of both Czech missionaries themselves (internal perceivers) and supplementary primary sources (external perceivers).

To be specific, the evidence showed, in relation to differentiating between internal and external manifestation, that a Czech missionaries' identity facet interrelation was often perceived as dominance or compartmentalization by the outside observers, while the identity carrier himself or herself subjectively perceived it as intersection or merger. The external perspective usually focused on one distinguished visible feature which became prominent, yet the internal perspective or the missionary was able to reveal the untidiness of the interrelation combination of single identity facets. The internal-external perspective proved to be the key element to shed light on the functioning of the four interrelations. This perhaps seems self-evident, yet it usually is not included in the largely quantitative works on social identity complexity, when respondents are asked in surveys how they perceive themselves. I am aware that the authors of the social identity complexity concept deliberately focus on one's own subjective representation of multiple identity facets, as a response to previous research that predominantly focused on perceptions from other persons,[63] yet adding the element of how a person is perceived by others might help to grasp a more integrated perspective. A step further within the internal perception would be to investigate the self-conscious versus the unconscious perception of one's identity facets interrelation, yet it is beyond the scope of this research.

(2.) The social identity complexity lowest identity complexity category "intersection," outlined as a "single social identity with one consolidated

---

62. Stryker and Burke, "Past, Present, and Future," 289.

63. Roccas and Brewer, "Social Identity Complexity," 88; Brewer, "Social Identity Complexity and Acceptance," 14.

ingroup,"[64] is in reality very complex. The authors of social identity complexity do mention in their work that "complexity of social identities may vary within and between the four types,"[65] yet as they focus on describing intersection, it gives the impression that it is in between two or more identity facets, being unique and unchangeable. A more plausible variant is that in the process of identification, this identity continues evolving, and it is aware of larger units out of which it was derived, continuously opened to these outgroups and drawing from them. There seems to be a very thin line between intersection, compartmentalization, dominance and merger, especially in moments of identity salience, as demonstrated by the evidence regarding the Czech identity facet salience.

Intersection is not an unequivocal unit. In the last quoted response, Eldina declares about herself: "I cannot be 100 per cent Bosnian if I have lived in America for five years. I am not 100 per cent American and I will never be." In her eyes, there is no clear-cut Bosnian American or American Bosnian. Malcolm McFee in his article, "The 150% Man, a Product of Blackfeet Acculturation" (1968), concluded that American indigenous people have added to their cultural repertoire and became bicultural. Lingenfelter and Mayers added a missiological perspective on contextualization aligned to McFee's anthropological finding: "Like these Native Americans, people committed to effective cross-cultural ministry will never become one-hundred percent insiders in another culture or subculture."[66] Missionaries do not, strictly speaking, belong to the "intersection" category of social identity complexity, otherwise they would not be suitable for the nature of their task and get involved with people who are outgroup. Hiebert says that missionaries become part of "biculture," which, even though made up of elements of both cultures, is rather an interaction, not a synthesis.[67] Their intersection of the biculture (or multiculture) entails higher complexity and is never settled and is accompanied by inner stress.[68]

---

64. Roccas and Brewer, "Social Identity Complexity," 90.
65. Roccas and Brewer, 93.
66. Lingenfelter and Mayers, *Ministering Cross-Culturally*, 12.
67. Hiebert, *Anthropological Insights for Missionaries*, 228.
68. Lingenfelter and Mayers, *Ministering Cross-Culturally*, 111–112.

Even though the evidence of Czech missionaries' identity negotiation confirms that there are no sharp edges to the social identity complexity categories, which often overlap, there is a substantiated differentiation between intersection and other categories of interrelations as presented by the social identity complexity concept. It can be, nevertheless, noticed that not all scholars share this view. While some do not attempt to arrange the interrelations on a scale from lowest to highest,[69] others, like Bodenhausen, work with only three categories. For him the social identity complexity categories of "intersection" and "merger" are incorporated into "integration" as a fused categorical identity.[70] He does work with higher and lower identity interrelations, yet omits intersection as such, which suggests that he perceives its actual complexity. These references are mentioned at this point in order to support the assertion that intersection is to be avoided as "low identity complexity."

(3.) High social identity complexity does not automatically entail low outgroup prejudice. Undoubtedly, a more complex identity is beneficial, and scholars agree that high social identity complexity and ingroup diversity helps reduce intergroup prejudice.[71] The findings of this research on Czech missionaries' identity negotiation affirmed that less complex forms of identity facets interrelations, which function more as a fixed singular identity, could be potentially detrimental for the mission agents and people they are influencing. And in connection with that, when a missionary is opened to higher identity complexity, to learn, to change and to adjust, that is generally when the intergroup prejudice lowers.

On the other hand, I conclude that outgroup tolerance or intolerance is not linked solely to a person's high or low identity complexity but is also dependent on their character.[72] As argued above, intersection can indeed be complex and as such, it might not necessarily lead towards outgroup prejudice more than dominance or compartmentalization. Employing this logic of argumentation, the matter of exhibiting signs of, for example merger, does not make one prone to less prejudice *per se*. Instead, it is dependent on the approach taken by the very person who might incline to either of the social

---

69. See Graham, Sorell and Montgomery, "Role-Related Identity," who list five categories.
70. Bodenhausen, "Diversity," 7.
71. Roccas and Brewer, "Social Identity Complexity," 104; Bodenhausen, "Diversity," 12.
72. That is, character defined in as moral excellence and firmness (Merriam Webster, "Definition of Character").

identity complexity interrelations in a particular setting or situation. One of the respondents, Josef 1, was quoted earlier: "Character is more important than all of it, we all have gifts."[73] Character traits such as humility, learning attitude, respect for others, readiness to embrace new ideas – all these can be vital factors in play, yet precarious to address by quantitative research which is mainly performed by social identity complexity studies. This conclusion correlates with the statement of Bodenhausen and Kang:

> Although high social identity complexity is associated with more favourable intergroup attitudes, there are many social and psychological factors that limit its development, including high need for closure, desire to maintain the status quo, high stress, or cognitive load, and living in a monocultural or stratified society.[74]

Czech missionaries' ability to embrace the differing cultural elements of former Yugoslavs and to manage the situational salience of "Czechness" thus seems to depend more on personal predispositions, such as character traits, rather than solely on a skill in interrelation multiple identity facets he or she holds. It needs to be admitted that the humble stance of an integrated (merger-like) identity of a missionary is an ideal which is not always present. The ideals that "missions must flow out of mission, which means we have no missional authority apart from the mission of the triune God"[75] and that mission is supposed to be a "humble prophetic dialogue"[76] are truly not always embodied. Notwithstanding this consideration, this section pointed out this is yet another aspect in which the social identity complexity concept could be supplemented and be explored more in future studies, based perhaps more on in-depth interviewing, or on biographical, evaluative or action research.

This chapter has sought to respond to the research question, "How is the identity of contemporary Protestant Czech missionaries negotiated in their interaction with Slavs in former Yugoslavia?", with its particular sub-question, "How does the missionaries' 'Czechness' interact with their other identity facets?" This missiological qualitative case study of Czech missionaries in former Yugoslav countries argued for innovative ways to complement the

---

73. See section 7.3.1.
74. Bodenhausen and Kang, "Multiple Identities", 559.
75. Tennent, *Invitation to World Missions*, 67.
76. Bevans and Schroeder, *Constants in Context*, 398.

social identity complexity theoretical construct, which is largely based in quantitative research. I claimed (1.) that internal and external perceptions of identity interrelations should be correlated, (2.) that the "intersection" category can be challenged as a low identity complexity, and (3.) that high complexity often means low intergroup prejudice, but not always, since there are intrapersonal factors involved.

8.6.2 Missiological implications of social identity complexity

Finally, along the suggested modifications to the elements of social identity complexity, I would like to enclose brief implications for mission practitioners. I propose that missionaries themselves can benefit from their self-understanding and from reflection on their social identity, in terms of ingroups and outgroups, and on their role-related identity. In a missiological perspective, similarly to the social identity complexity concept, a more integrative treatment of one's identity facets is a desired goal and suitable for intercultural work. Paul Hiebert in the mid-1980's used similar terminology to that introduced by Roccas and Brewer in 2002 for the identity of missionaries who live in-between their own and their local culture:[77] (a.) rejection, i.e. either staying in the original or "going native" (which corresponds to the dominance of social identity complexity); (b.) compartmentalization, i.e. certain duplicity of switching between the two (social identity complexity labels it compartmentalization as well); (c.) integration, i.e. a healthy acceptance of cultural variance (not dissimilar to the social identity complexity category of merger). He critiqued both rejection[78] and compartmentalization[79] and encouraged integration[80] as the most suitable model for identity negotiation.

With regard to this and grounded in the evidence from Czech missions in former Yugoslav countries, I conclude that high social complexity functions are better for the Czech missionaries: "Czechness" as one of many identity parts becomes salient in certain contexts (compartmentalization) or is

---

77. Hiebert, *Anthropological Insights for Missionaries*, 105–108.

78. "Try as we may, the people will always know we are foreigners." (Hiebert, 105)

79. "We may be accused of hypocrisy and duplicity . . . this can lead to confusion and insecurity and, in the extreme, to an identity crisis and cultural schizophrenia." (Hiebert, 107)

80. "In the long run and at the deepest levels, we need to work toward an integration between the two cultures within us." (Hiebert, 107)

included in the whole (merger). On the other hand, the less complex forms of identity interrelations, functioning more as a fixed "identity," could be potentially harmful for the mission work. Intersection could imply an unwillingness to be changed by the mission field experience and by the non-Czech outgroup. Dominance could be even more harmful when a situational threat of Czech ethnocentrism might become a barrier for the missionary work. In conclusion, the more singular forms of identity could be potentially detrimental for the mission work and higher identity complexity, when the missionary is open to adjust and learn, it can be beneficial for the advancement of missions. Therefore, I conclude that Czech missionaries do not possess either low or high complexity, yet the identity facet interrelation that the missionaries should settle is to be merger, with dominance or, in other words, with the transcending element of the Christian identity facet.

Based on the findings of my research, the answer to the question whether higher complexity would lead toward better missionary adjustment, together with lowering outgroup prejudice and a positive effect on their work, was found to be affirmative. The central thesis of the social identity complexity concept is: "Awareness of ingroup diversity provides an effective formula for reducing intergroup prejudice."[81] Based on the evidence of this research, this can be modified and utilized as follows. My thesis is that awareness of the (Czech) national identity facet and its proper situational utilization provides a tool for reducing missionaries' prejudice in their effective contextualization (in former Yugoslav countries).

---

81. Roccas and Brewer, "Social Identity Complexity," 104.

CHAPTER 9

Conclusion

9.1 Introduction

9.1.1 Thesis summary

In the thesis, I began the exploration with an overview of where this research entitled, "Czech Mission: Identity of Czech Protestant Missionaries in Their Interaction with Slavs in former Yugoslav countries," was located. After introducing the geopolitical space and the basic terminology in chapter 1, I established the theoretical framework in chapter 2, with its social psychological, intercultural psychological, and missiological concepts. In chapter 3, the methodological approach was laid out. I used predominantly semi-structured interviews with Czech Protestant missionaries and complementary primary sources, in former Yugoslav countries, after 1989. This data was augmented by the personal diaries of several missionaries, including my own, in the form of diary notes and photos. In the analysis chapters, my investigative scope was intentionally limited by the predominant themes that emerged from the evidence, extracted from the respondents. The thematic analysis employed a specific grid for every chapter, according to themes in line with individual research questions:

In chapter 4 I used the Trompenaars and Hampden-Turner model of cultural dimensions,[1] in a concise cross-cultural comparison of Czechs and former Yugoslavs: 4.2 rules vs. people orientation, 4.3 achievement vs. ascription, 4.4 individual vs. communitarian, 4.5 openness vs. closeness,

---

1. Trompenaars and Hampden-Turner, *Riding the Waves of Culture*.

4.6 temperament differences. Chapter 5 was organized along the key of 5.2 Czech identity salience, 5.3 Czech identity suppression, and 5.4 simultaneous salience and suppression of Czech missionaries' Czech identity facet. Chapter 6 expanded on Czech identity salience in mission (in 6.3), and besides that, it was in its missiological conclusions rather thematically fragmented. In chapter 7 I thematically arranged the material, engaging Hofstede's model of the three levels of uniqueness of mental programming,[2] in dialogue with identity as understood by identity theory and social identity theory.[3] I extracted the following categories for Czech missionaries, apart from their national identity facet: male or female, family member, personality traits holder, interest group member, worker, Christian worker, Christian, missionary, someone with regional or supranational identity, and identity facet of other national. The approach in the final analysis chapter 8 was to analyse the responses thematically according to the four social identity complexity interrelations of multiple ingroup representations: intersection, dominance, compartmentalization and merger.[4]

The final chapter 9 aims to review research questions this thesis addressed, the findings and the central argument that developed from its findings. I assess how each chapter advanced and contributed towards the goal and finally, the concluding section presents ideas for further research.

9.1.2 Returning to research questions

In the quest of providing a direction for my investigation I asked the central research question, "How is the identity of contemporary Czech missionaries negotiated in their interaction with Slavs in former Yugoslavia?" Having been aware at the commencement that answering might be complex and multifaceted, I employed three leading sub-questions.[5] The findings of chapter 4 for research question 1, chapters 5 and 6 for research question 2, and chapters

---

2. Hofstede G., Hofstede G. J. and Minkov, *Cultures and Organizations*.
3. Burke and Stets, *Identity Theory*.
4. Roccas and Brewer, "Social Identity Complexity."
5. Research question 1: "To what extent can the Slavic Czech missionaries working with the fellow-Slavs in former Yugoslav countries be considered to be cross-cultural?"; Research question 2: "How and in what circumstances does the Czech identity of Czech missionaries become salient or suppressed?"; Research question 3: "How does the missionaries' 'Czechness' interact with their other identity facets?"

7 and 8 for research question 3, led me to particular assertions, as summed up here as answers to the three questions:

Research question 1: "To what extent is the Slavic Czech missionaries working with the fellow-Slavs in former Yugoslav countries cross-cultural?" My research found that Czechs are in some respects culturally similar to Bosniaks, Croats, Macedonians, Montenegrins, Serbs and Slovenes. Yet, their cultures differ. To expand on this, they share several common historical epochs; they speak related Slavic, yet distinct, languages; their appearance is similar, they dress like average Europeans; they eat, drink and use similar products. They resemble, yet significantly differ in values and behaviour, including the areas of orientation to rules vs. relationships 4.2, achievement vs. ascription 4.3, individual vs. communitarian way of life 4.4, being "open" or "closed" 4.5, and in their national temperament 4.6. Such cultural proximity is to be placed as E-2 on Ralph Winter's E-scale.[6] Regarding the Slavic element in the leading question, the findings demonstrated that it concerns mainly language, historical amity and mutual familiarity of Czechs and southern Slavs. Namely, it signifies something of a bilateral Czech and former Yugoslav dyad, rather than a pan-Slavic sentiment. To add to answering research question 1, a broader alternative response would be that Czechs perceive the cross-cultural factor to the extent in which their Czech identity becomes activated and salient over their other identity facets. This spans to answering the following research sub-question.

Research question 2: "How and in what circumstances does the Czech identity of Czech missionaries become salient or suppressed?" I proceeded to demonstrate that Czech missionaries' Czech identity becomes (a.) salient, (b.) suppressed, or (c.) simultaneously salient and suppressed. The evidence of Czech missionaries showed that their national identity negotiation is a dynamic and unsettled process which has an internal and external aspect of its salience and suppression. Namely, it differs whether the missionaries perceive identity facets such as "Czechness" for themselves or whether others evaluate how it appears to them. Furthermore, the Czech identity facet in certain situations becomes salient or suppressed unintentionally, while at other times it may be activated or deactivated intentionally. These themes, which certainly are not absolute, emerged from the data regarding circumstances

---

6. Winter, "Frontier Mission Perspectives," 64.

of identity salience and suppression: Czech identity facet salience in encountering artefacts, in encountering other Czechs, Slovaks and other nationals; Czech identity facet suppression in interaction with other nationals, in Czech language suppression (to English, to local languages), in the adjustment to the local culture.

Research question 3: "How does the missionaries' "Czechness" interact with their other identity facets?" The most complex question entailed the most complex answer. To help answer it, I applied the four social identity complexity interrelations of multiple ingroup memberships in my research. These encompassed more broadly both identity facets or single identities as outlined by social identity theory (identity based on group membership) and the corresponding categories as outlined by identity theory (role-based identity). As a result, the Czech national identity facet of Czech missionaries was proven to relate to other parts of who they are within all categories, intersection, dominance, compartmentalization, merger.[7] After a careful examination of these four categories, I concluded that their social identity complexity interrelation often appears to be intersection or compartmentalization, yet the ideal they aim at is merger – which as the most inclusive social identity embraces, yet recognizes, the differences.[8] Also, dominance plays a significant role, since my findings pointed at Christian identity, the goal of which is to take precedence over the Czech national one. My results as a response to the third research question were that the missionaries' – Czechs in former Yugoslavia, yet possibly others as well – multiple identity negotiation is, or is supposed to be, merger with an attached dominance of the Christian identity facet.

9.2 Contribution to knowledge

Starting from the main research question, "How is the identity of contemporary Czech missionaries negotiated in their interaction with Slavs in former Yugoslavia?", I came to realize the complexity of the task in responding to it. In my research I focused on several aspects – similarity and difference of the two culturally proximal contexts, situational salience and suppression of

---

7. Roccas and Brewer, "Social Identity Complexity."
8. Roccas and Brewer, "Social Identity Complexity," 91.

the Czech identity facet, the interaction of missionaries' "Czechness" with their other identity facets. To help maintain focus, I aimed at one specific contribution, the aspect connected to social identity complexity, and it is addressed here in 9.2. I investigated how my qualitative research could affirm or critique elements of the social identity complexity concept. Through the research process, I have become aware of other partial contributions informing literature on mission. These are addressed further in 9.3 in the section which considers possible overlap with mission practice.

In accordance with literature on identity,[9] the evidence of this research confirmed the notion of identity with blurred edges: In chapter 5, I found that salience and suppression of single identity facets operate rather unevenly. Rather than being inversely proportional in the manner that when the more one identity facet is present, the less others are, the evidence showed that Czech missionaries function in a more organic way when multiple identities can be simultaneously salient.[10]

Next, my findings confirmed that the line between social identity theory and identity theory is not that thick. In chapter 7 I outlined several categories of personal, social and role-based identity, which were manifestly interrelated. Therefore, these findings confirmed the identity theorists' stance who call for a more integrative look on social identity theory and identity theory.[11] For the identity carriers themselves, various types of self-identifications are often blended. This perhaps seems to conflict with the classical outline of social identity theory,[12] yet it is in line with those identity theorists, such as Stets and Burke, who hold a more unifying approach, in claiming that the processes of self-categorization into groups (social identity theory) and identification into roles (identity theory) are analogous.[13] The evidence suggested that even though Czech missionaries happen to be group members, they often did not seem to construct their identity around that and intentionally refused the categorization. This might be connected to specific characteristics of Czechs

---

9. Tajfel, *Human Groups*; Holmberg, "Understanding Christian Identity"; Jenkins, *Social Identity*.
10. Hogg et al., "Social Identity Perspective," 268.
11. Stryker and Burke, "Past, Present, and Future," 289.
12. Tajfel, *Human Groups*; Turner, "Towards Cognitive Redefinition"; Tajfel and Turner, "Social Identity Theory."
13. Stets and Burke, "Sociological Approach to Self," 145.

who tend to evade memberships in any institutionalized groups,[14] or it more probably points out weaknesses in social identity theory and its focus on intergroup processes[15] when, instead, the reality of nested elements within identity and simultaneous belonging to intergroups and intragroups is much more complex.

The complexity of one's identity in societal behaviour is the focus of the social identity complexity concept.[16] My qualitative study, based on in-depth interviews and personal diary, largely affirmed the findings of quantitative studies on social identity complexity. An individual (Czech missionary) possesses multiple ingroup memberships or identity facets, which interrelate and could be sorted on a continuum from lower to higher complexity.[17] My research results assigned the following social identity complexity interrelations to Czech missionaries:

- intersection – being disjointed in-between two national identities
- dominance – domination of the Christian identity facet
- compartmentalization – in settings and situations of Czech identity salience
- merger – integrating the differences in cultural adjustment

The proposers of social identity complexity acknowledge that the concept is not clear-cut: "Complexity of social identities may *vary* within and between the four types . . . intersection and dominance can, *in general*, be classified as *relatively* low-complexity representations."[18] Social identity complexity has become accepted in the academy and widely used across scholarly disciplines, yet it can still be approached critically. In my qualitative research with its missiological perspective, I made these claims which may help inform social identity complexity:

1. The distinction between internal and external perception of multiple identity interrelations is underestimated and should be considered to be a significant factor.

---

14. Hošek, *Gods Return*; Nešpor, *Too Weak in Faith*, 187.
15. Esler, "Outline of Social Identity Theory," 22.
16. Roccas and Brewer, "Social Identity Complexity."
17. Roccas and Brewer, 89–90.
18. Roccas and Brewer, "Social Identity Complexity." Emphasis added.

2. Intersection as a category of low identity complexity is more complex than a unique set of identities, which is between two or more identity facets.
3. High social identity complexity does not necessarily equal low outgroup prejudice.

First, I conclude that there was a defining moment in the internal vs. external perspective of one's identity facet interrelations. Both one's social identity (category-based) and identity (role-based) are accompanied by internal and external aspects. Stryker and Burke noticed that role identity entails a duality: "Role is external; it is linked to social positions within the social structure. Identity is internal, consisting of internalized meanings and expectations associated with a role."[19] I argued that one's social identity also carries the internal-external dimension, and it depends on who is the agent of perception. To be specific, an identity facet interrelation was often perceived as dominance or compartmentalization by the outside observers, while the identity carrier (Czech missionary) himself or herself subjectively perceived it as intersection or merger. The external perspective usually focused on one distinguished visible feature which became prominent, yet the internal perspective revealed the untidiness of the interrelation combination. I acknowledge the deliberate social identity complexity limitation and the focus on subjective self-perception of multiple identity interrelations,[20] yet my evidence showed that it is necessary to add the element of how a person is perceived by others in order to achieve a more integrated perspective. Correlation of internal and external perception can be a step forward for further social identity complexity research.

Second, the social identity complexity lowest identity complexity category "intersection," outlined as "single social identity with one consolidated ingroup,"[21] was proved to be very complex in reality. The authors of social identity complexity do mention in their work that "complexity of social identities may vary within and between the four types."[22] Yet the description of

---

19. Stryker and Burke, "Past, Present, and Future," 289.
20. Roccas and Brewer, "Social Identity Complexity," 88; Brewer, "Social Identity Complexity and Acceptance," 14.
21. Roccas and Brewer, "Social Identity Complexity."
22. Roccas and Brewer, 93.

intersection gives the impression that it resides between two or more identity facets, being very unique and unchangeable. A more plausible option is that in the process of identification, this identity continues evolving, it is aware of larger units out of which it was derived and is continuously open to these outgroups and drawing from them. Some scholars do not attempt to arrange the interrelations on a scale from lowest to highest at all,[23] while others do – Bodenhausen works with less categories and incorporates the social identity complexity categories of "intersection" and "merger" into "integration" as a fused categorical identity,[24] which may point towards the actual complexity of intersection.

Furthermore, with regard to the possible application in mission studies, intersection does not seem to fit the category of "low identity complexity." Missionaries are required to engage the outgroup, therefore they cannot belong to the "intersection" category of social identity complexity.

Their intersection entails higher complexity, and rather than a synthesis, it is an interaction, accompanied by tension.[25] Even though the evidence of Czech missionaries' Czech identity facet interrelations (a.) led to the conclusion of avoiding intersection as low complexity, and (b.) emphasized that there are no sharp edges to the social identity complexity categories which often overlap, it did not find itself in conflict with the substantiated differentiation between intersection and other categories of interrelations as presented by the social identity complexity concept.

Third, my research highlighted that high social identity complexity does not necessarily entail low outgroup prejudice. The findings on Czech missionaries affirmed that when a missionary departs a certain single identity and is opened to higher identity complexity, when he or she is willing to change and adjust, that is supposedly when the intergroup prejudice lowers.[26] On the other hand, as manifested above, intersection can indeed be complex and as such, it might not necessarily lead towards outgroup prejudice more

---

23. See Graham, Sorell and Montgomery, "Role-Related Identity," who enlist five categories.

24. Bodenhausen, "Diversity," 7.

25. Hiebert, *Anthropological Insights for Missionaries*, 228; Lingenfelter and Mayers, *Ministering Cross-Culturally*, 111–112.

26. See Roccas and Brewer, "Social Identity Complexity," 104; Bodenhausen, "Diversity," 12.

than dominance or compartmentalization. Similarly, the matter of exhibiting signs of, for example, merger does not make one prone to less prejudice *per se*. Instead, it is dependent on the approach taken by the very person who might incline to either of the social identity complexity interrelations in a particular setting or situation. These personal predispositions, such as character traits, including humility, learning attitude, respect for others, and readiness to embrace new ideas, are precarious to address by the quantitative research which is mainly performed by social identity complexity studies.

A final reflection, in light of the three claims above, it is becoming obvious that social identity complexity as a theoretical framework for my research is to some degree both adequate and inadequate. On one hand, social identity complexity by its methodological delineation and understanding of terminology does not involve some of the aspects which I addressed, and it focuses chiefly on policy making in multicultural societies.[27] On the other hand, nevertheless, it also serves to help individuals navigate "real life" with their cross-cultural identities.[28] Therefore I suggested it to be supplemented by the relevant elements, summed up in (9.2). And even though the context of the empirical material of the original social identity complexity study, among students in the USA and Israel, differs from my focus on Czechs in former Yugoslav countries, I found social identity complexity very pertinent for this qualitative research.

9.3 Missiological findings and implications for mission practice

9.3.1 Central argument

The social identity complexity concept thesis is: "Awareness of ingroup diversity provides an effective formula for reducing intergroup prejudice."[29] Based on the evidence of this research, I modified it and devised the following utilisation. My thesis is that awareness of the (Czech) national identity facet and its appropriate situational utilization provides a tool for reducing missionaries' prejudice in their effective contextualization (in former Yugoslav countries).

---

27. Brewer, "Social Identity Complexity and Acceptance," 28.
28. Roccas and Brewer, "Social Identity Complexity," 103–104.
29. Roccas and Brewer, 104.

Like the social identity complexity concept findings, in mission studies, a more integrative treatment of a person's identity facets is a desired aim and is suitable for intercultural work. The missiologist Hiebert critiqued "rejection" and "compartmentalization," and advanced the approach of "integration," similar to the category of merger in social identity complexity, as the most suitable model for a missionary's identity negotiation.[30] In social identity complexity terms, intersection could imply an unwillingness to be changed by the mission field experience and by the non-Czech outgroup. Dominance could be even more harmful when a situational threat of Czech ethnocentrism might become a barrier for the missionary work. I concluded that the interrelation of identities missionaries should arrive at is to be merger, with dominance, or with a transcending element, of the Christian identity facet.

My interview-based research established that any categories, including the four social identity complexity delineations, have their limitations. To outline an exact delineation and a degree of how "high" an identity complexity can score is indeed not easy, and the social identity complexity proponents themselves admit the perils of such an effort.[31] Still, the evidence of Czech missions in former Yugoslav countries, reflecting the missiological literature, led me to conclude that in ideal situations high social complexity signifies prerequisites for better adjustment and functioning of missionaries, as it contributes to lowering mutual outgroup prejudices and positively effects the missionaries' work. On the other hand, the less complex forms of identity interrelations, or the more singular forms of identity, could be potentially harmful for the mission work. In (7.4.2) I documented the significant element of negotiating the missionary identity facet. This very facet seemed to appear on many occasions inappropriate in lands with Christian heritage. It was evidenced for Czech Protestant missionaries that the longer they stayed in one of the former Yugoslav countries the more they refused to be categorized as missionaries. With these missionaries, a certain shift towards more effective adjustment took place, and it was expounded by the missionaries' more comprehensive self-perception – and a more complex social identity complexity.

---

30. Hiebert, *Anthropological Insights for Missionaries*, 105–108.
31. Roccas and Brewer, "Social Identity Complexity," 93.

9.3.2 Implications for "Czechness" in mission in former Yugoslav countries

I clearly documented in this research that Czech missionaries, or alternatively other foreign missionaries, are to be attentive to their national identity facet, due to the impact which relates to their conduct in a foreign environment, which they seek to influence missionally. This can help them immensely, to prepare for mission work in an intercultural context, to function daily on the mission field, and to experience a healthy return to their sending country, which is often a problem as mission practice confirms. The awareness and apt negotiation of the national identity facet can be crucial in periods of acculturative stress and the adjustment to local culture (or to cultures of others in international teams). In my work I argued that missionaries need to consider their situational national identity salience for two reasons: (a.) They can evade it in the process of adjusting in the local culture, (b.) they can learn how to profit from it – utilize it for the advancement of the mission work.

(a.) Czech missionaries should avoid salience of the Czech national identity facet. All missionaries, not excluding Czechs, have a tendency towards ethnocentrism and towards a culturally conditioned export of Christianity.[32] The tension in the engagement with culture of the "other" is something unavoidable and in essence very human,[33] yet missiologists would agree that it is something missionaries are supposed to fight against, in the process of cultural adjustment, no matter how difficult the discernment of what is cultural and what is supra-cultural might prove.[34] My findings confirmed that this effort to a great extent entails suppression of missionaries' national identity. I discovered that for Czech missionaries, major areas of its occurrence are in their behaviour in interaction with other nationals and in their language utilisation. Furthermore, the evidence on suppression of the Czech identity facet led me to affirm that it is never a complete process – missionaries ideally aim to suppress their national identity, yet at the same time they do (unconsciously), or desire to (consciously), keep components of this particular identity facet.

---

32. Newbigin, *Foolishness to Greeks*, 3; Hiebert, "Gospel in Human Contexts," 83.
33. Tajfel and Turner, "Social Identity Theory," 285.
34. See Hesselgrave, *Communicating Christ Cross-Culturally*, 104; Lingenfelter and Mayers, *Ministering Cross-Culturally*, 112.

(b.) Czech missionaries should benefit from situational salience of the Czech national identity facet. My findings revealed this could be done on two levels: first, on the one level valid for Czech Protestant missionaries in former Yugoslav countries, and second, on the broader level applied to the emerging Czech mission movement, as a modest contribution to global mission.

First, my research demonstrated that adequate management of situational salience of the Czech identity helps advance the work of Czech missionaries in former Yugoslav countries. Grounded in evidence by Czech missionaries and supplementary sources I argued that Czech missionaries possess these favourable factors in what was assigned as an E-2 culturally proximal context:[35]

- Slavic cultures and languages are close
- Equality factor: Czechs were historically economically poorer than former Yugoslavs
- Familiarity with Czechs and a partial common history
- No historical harm
- Geographic proximity
- Czechs presumed trait of adjustability

This list, which is certainly not exhaustive, is substantiated with evidence from my primary sources. It must be admitted that its main weakness is the subjective factor of personal perspective, based on outgroup comparison.[36] I noticed that Czechs seem to favour themselves, and so did southern Slavs, in opposition to their Western missionary colleagues, yet the situation in reality is rather complex and differs in individual cases.

These findings, nonetheless, were in harmony with missiological literature propounding mission in culturally proximal contexts and tools for strategizing cross-cultural mission.[37] Ralph Winter's conclusion in relation to the E-scale involved the utilization of one's national identity in the sense of cultural proximity to the target culture, which can prove advantageous to mission work, since workers from cultures nearby do not need to cross large cultural gaps.[38]

---

35. Winter, "Frontier Mission Perspectives."
36. Tajfel and Turner, "Social Identity Theory," 287.
37. Clegg, "Understanding the Times", 62; Winter, "New Macedonia," 357.
38. Winter, "Frontier Mission Perspectives," 64.

Second, my research demonstrated that applicable and apt situational salience of "Czechness" can become advantageous for self-identification in Czech missions. Now, this does not comprise of a Czech identity in a nationalistic sense, but as a cultural heritage or background of the missionaries, in connection to what the scholars point to as emancipation of new missionary-sending post-Communist countries.[39] Voices calling for more active usage of one's national predispositions are supposedly not to conflict with the widely recognized need for national identity suppression in contextualization, as explained earlier. Rather, the salient Czech, or Hungarian, or Romanian, or any other relevant, national identity, can be an expression of a search for an authentic way to participate in global missions, while not merely adjusting to the Western missionary dominated patterns in international teams. These teams were, in most cases for Czech Protestant missionaries in former Yugoslav countries, influenced or led by Americans and the team language was English, which set the parameters for the mission performance dynamics.[40] For Czechs this meant a double cultural adjustment and two languages to learn. Yet it additionally implied that Czechs, who objectively are not that experienced in contemporary cross-cultural mission work, have started to ask for self-identification – "What does it mean to be a Czech in missions?"

To sum up, in the missiological view, there is a highly relevant orientation in suppressing one's identity, including national identity, to identify with those the missionary serves. There is a legitimate danger of a nationalistic spirit being absorbed into missionary ideology, as David Bosch warns: "Christians of a specific nation would develop the conviction that they had an exceptional role to play in the advancement of the kingdom of God through the missionary enterprise."[41] Still, even though an amount of perilous ethnocentrism might be potentially present, I concluded that when treated correctly as a situationally salient national identity facet, Czech (and possibly any other) national facet can serve as a beneficial asset for the advancement of the mission work. My research revealed many positives of missionaries' "Czechness" in the context of former Yugoslav countries and exhibited the Czechs' self-identification process, which is still developing in newly emerging

---

39. Klingsmith, *Missions Beyond the Wall*; Kool, "Revolutions in European Mission."
40. See Newbigin, *Foolishness to Greeks*, 9.
41. Bosch, *Transforming Mission*, 299.

missionary-sending nations, contributing with its small, yet proportionately significant, share in the mosaic of global Christian mission.

9.3.3 Mission to former Yugoslavs and to Czechs

In continuation of the preceding missiological implications, my conclusions involved legitimate reasons for justification of mission to both former Yugoslavs and to Czechs. This was grounded in literature on religious identity in the two culturally proximal, yet non-uniform,[42] contexts and in the evidence of my qualitative research. I argued for a twofold mission:

- Czechs can evangelize former Yugoslavs and inform their ethnoreligious identity. Freedom of choice to change confession[43] should be validated, with the capacity to preserve traits of national identity. Former Yugoslavs were found to possess high perceived overlap in group membership, therefore having low social identity complexity, due to the strong ties of national and religious identity.[44] In section 6.5 I portrayed the example used by Brewer of the link between being Italian and being Catholic, when some might perceive Italians of other religious faiths as not "real" Italians.[45] This high membership overlap refers to low social identity complexity, which as evidenced by my findings on ethnoreligious identity, is present also in the Western Balkans. This should be taken into consideration by Czechs or any other missionaries. When saying "taking into consideration" I refer to the ambiguous on-field situation[46] that while some contemporary Czech Protestant missionaries might focus on revitalizing the existing church bodies, others, who would be in a majority, lean towards a more conversionist approach. In the effort to "proclaim the gospel," and encouraging the members of ethnoreligious communities towards diversity, they might be, perhaps even

---

42. This refers preliminarily to the diversified region of former Yugoslavia, with its Christian Catholic, Christian Orthodox, and Muslim majority population.
43. Newbigin, *Foolishness to Greeks*, 118.
44. Brewer, "Social Identity Complexity and Acceptance," 18.
45. Brewer, 18.
46. See (6.4.2)

unconsciously, stimulating higher social identity complexity within the societies of former Yugoslav countries. In connection with this, unlike in the Czech Republic, the Protestant church is often viewed as a Western import in countries of former Yugoslavia. This could change due to the commencement, or deepening, of the already initiated self-identification process of former Yugoslav Protestants.

- Former Yugoslavs, with their ethnoreligious identity, could evangelize irreligious Czechs and inform Czech believers about their Christian identity. Firstly, most Czechs are "believers in something,"[47] and they do not share the former Yugoslavs' general awe of God which influences their morals. Second, Czech evangelical believers can be reminded of matters of Christian tradition, namely observance of Christian holidays and perhaps learn to collectively celebrate them.

These conclusions are in accordance with the notion, heavily supported by missiological literature,[48] that the mission field is omnipresent. The focus of my research was Czech mission agents and their identity, yet this mission from everywhere to everywhere involves mission both to former Yugoslavs, and to Czechs. The former Yugoslavs, due to their ethnoreligous identity, are considered by Czechs (Protestant Evangelical missionaries, as documented in this research) in need of the Christian gospel and they develop their mission effort to them. And the paradoxical finding was that Czech could themselves be evangelized, or re-evangelized, by former Yugoslavs.

Based on the findings on national identity negotiation in relation to religious identity in both cultural spheres, I concluded that evangelism or re-evangelism is required, and intercultural mission could be performed in both directions – Czechs (from whichever church affiliation) to former Yugoslavs, and former Yugoslavs (from either Protestant, Catholic, or Orthodox circles) to Czechs. Such mission endeavour, appropriately accompanied by mission reflection, could significantly contribute to global Christian mission.

---

47. Halík and Hošek, *Czech Perspective on Faith*; Hošek, "Discerning the Signs."
48. Kuzmič, "Christian Mission in Europe"; Volf, "Fishing in the Neighbor's Pond"; Escobar, *New Global Mission*; Wright, *Mission of God's People*.

9.4 Further research

Notwithstanding the contributions of the present research, its limitations concern multiple levels:[49]

(a.) The research approach itself, as a multiple case study, where more elements of narrative inquiry and biographical research could be involved.

(b.) The focus of the study on Czech Protestant missionaries working with Slavs in former Yugoslav countries since 1989, when only thirty-one respondents participated. Furthermore, there are more elements of Czech identity than those related to the social identity complexity four multiple ingroup representations, which were in focus here.

(c.) My personal bias as a researcher in the qualitative nature of the investigation.

This research was interdisciplinary, and it is expected that this would be so for many future scholarly endeavours as well. The results are therefore proportionately limited and, with this in mind, I suggest the following areas of possible further research. Due to clarity, I arrange the areas of possible further research according to disciplines: (1.) social psychology, (2.) intercultural psychology, (3.) missiology.

(1.) Roccas, Brewer and other authors who followed them, employ quantitative analysis, based on large scale surveys, and there are only a few qualitative approaches.[50] My findings suggest that more qualitative studies of social identity complexity are needed. The situational salience of "Czechness" was found to often depend more on personal predispositions, such as character traits, rather than on a skill in the interrelation of multiple identity facets he or she holds. This was merely one particular aspect in which the social identity complexity concept could be supplemented and explored more in future studies, also based more on in-depth interviewing, or on evaluative or action research.

Another aspect for exploration is the internal and external dynamics of social identity complexity. Instead of a survey on how the respondents perceive themselves, another agent of subjective perception could be added, namely, how others perceive the respondents might help to grasp a more

---

49. For (a.) see section 3.1.2, for (b.) see section 3.2.1, for (c.) see section 3.3.1.

50. See O'Connor et al., "Sense of Community"; Gamsakhurdia, "Quest for Ethnic Identity."

integrated perspective. A step further within the internal perception would be to investigate the self-conscious versus the unconscious perception of one's identity facets interrelation, which is an even more intricate exercise.

In addition, as depicted, one of the limitations of this research was looking closely at only one aspect of social identity complexity. Nevertheless, instead of addressing only the four interrelations of identity facets, new research could focus on antecedents of social identity complexity – experiential factors, situational factors, and personal attributes.[51] These could be tracked in-depth for each respondent individually.

(2.) Along with more qualitative studies on social identity complexity, I also advocate for more qualitative studies of cultural differences. When approached quantitatively, intercultural psychologists find that the results do not substantially vary,[52] yet evidence of my primary sources indicated that identity trait nuances in cross-cultural comparison can be found. Next, I found that, due to historical factors, self-identification in spatiality is of significance, and seems somewhat understudied. In spite of their differences, Czechs and former Yugoslavs share similar traits in self-identification in spatiality – in (a.) negotiation of establishing themselves geopolitically within Europe and in (b.) negotiation of naming their countries. To explore more how this particular spatial self-identification functions could be interesting for intercultural and management studies, and there is space for similar research in other corresponding contexts. It might also seem useful to address mutual perception more deeply and spatial identification, instead of merely self-identification. Certainly, more field-based studies of Czechs and former Yugoslavs could emerge.

(3.) While more qualitative studies of the topic would be welcome in mission studies as well, in this area there is more space to explore how to utilize quantitative methods. These methods, such as assessment tools for measuring efficiency in culturally proximal or distant mission,[53] due to their obvious limitations when it comes to human agents of mission, seem to be often omitted. Nonetheless, it might be useful if further studies consider

---

51. Roccas and Brewer, "Social Identity Complexity," 96–99.

52. Cholastová, "Regional Stereotypes"; Rajh, Budak and Anić, "Hofstede's Culture Value Survey."

53. Winter, "Frontier Mission Perspectives"; Hesselgrave, *Communicating Christ Cross-Culturally*.

the measurement models of cultural dimensions, such as Hofstede model, NEO-PI-3, GLOBE, or Trompenaars and Hampden-Turner model of cultural dimensions, and attempt to develop strategic tools in missiology.

Next, further research on the interconnectedness of mission to religious, non-religious, and ethnoreligious identity would be highly recommended. The topics of national identity of the missionaries, of patriotism and nationalism in mission, and of negotiating other national cultures on the team, are in my perspective comparatively undervalued by contemporary scholars. Perhaps the reason I consider theologizing on mission in these matters as beneficial is due to my own perspective as a Czech mission scholar and practitioner, i.e. as someone from a relatively small nation with a limited mission force, in a self-identification process. Next, it would be helpful to find similar, and more extensive, studies in cross-cultural contexts, as "sending countries" and "mission fields" continue to evolve. In connection with that, there is room for more research on mission from the Czech Republic and from former Yugoslav countries.

There is room for initial research on Protestant (and perhaps other Christian) mission from former Yugoslav countries. Former Yugoslavs presumably share similar beneficial factors for mission to similar contexts with Czechs, including familiarity with culture or similar language. No matter how small the emerging Protestant mission from former Yugoslav countries is, it could still be addressed in missiological literature. The phenomenon of sending individual missionaries from Vojvodina province to the southern parts of Serbia and to Montenegro, and also other "internal" missionaries from Croatia and from Serbia to Bosnia and Herzegovina after 1991 is familiar (despite the lack of missiological literature discussing).[54] During the course of this research, nevertheless, I have witnessed new former Yugoslav missionaries leaving for another non-former Yugoslav countries as full-time missionaries, continuous missions to the Roma, and the rise of missions to the refugees who have been traversing the Balkans since 2015.

There is room for on-going research on Czech mission. It seems remarkable that there is a growing international Czech mission, despite the rather

---

54. This note relates to pastors of Protestant churches, who moved from Croatia and Serbia to start or lead churches in Sarajevo, Banja Luka, Mostar, and other locations in Bosnia and Herzegovina, and many of them still were active in the region at the time of completing the thesis.

unfavourable religious situation and domestic needs.[55] Still, as has been demonstrated, literature on international mission from the Czech Protestant churches (and other churches to varying degrees) is meagre and needs to be enhanced. My thesis is a pioneering work in a sense, yet it focused on one aspect (national identity) in one specific area (former Yugoslav countries). Other topics could be: the mission theology basis on which Czech churches send and support intercultural missionaries; contemporary mission to Czechs and to foreigners in the Czech Republic; Czech missionaries' identity in other culturally proximal contexts, such as in former Soviet republics. In general, the appearance of more publications on mission in connection to identity would be useful, as is highlighted by one of my respondents:

> Czech identity needs to be clarified, or perhaps even built up. Paradoxically, this will be helped by a sojourn abroad, and especially the mission stay.
>
> —Jakub 1, m, returning to Bosnia and Herzegovina

Jenkins says that "identity is produced and reproduced during interaction, and interaction is always situated in context."[56] Jakub 1 highlighted that one such context can be intercultural mission. I would correct him and say that it cannot be completely "clarified" or "built up," but instead it is being constantly renegotiated, since this search for self-identification is continuous.[57] This similarly is valid for me when I retrospectively reflect on the PhD process.

Even though this research journey began in 2016 when at OCMS, the more I learned the more I realized that even with the thesis finished, the research of such a topic signifies limitations and a need for continuation. That is the reason why the scope of possible further research was portrayed so widely. I suggested research endeavours to be pursued in the fields of social psychology, intercultural psychology, and missiology. On the other hand, my recommendations are not exhaustive. The potential the topic entails will hopefully spark fresh engagement by scholars and reflective practitioners in the future.

---

55. Činčala, "Theoretical Proposal for Reaching"; Novák, "Critical Examination of Mission"; Fajfr, "Critical and Evaluative Study."

56. Jenkins, *Rethinking Ethnicity*, 65.

57. Jenkins, *Being Danish*, 3; Bauman and Raud, *Practices of Selfhood*, 55.

Appendices

Appendix A

Interviewees' Detailed Profiles

Name	Interview date	Gender	Age	Czech region of origin	Location, country code	Timeframe or location	Ministry/Relation to missionary
Primary sources: Czech residing missionaries							
Erika 1	06 Jun 2018	f	20–30	Central Bohemia	Banja Luka, Bosnia and Herzegovina	1 year (2010–2011)	Student evangelism and discipleship
Marek	18 Oct 2018	m	30–40	Prague	Priština, Kosovo	1 year (2017–2018)	English teacher, prayer group, church
Josef 2	06 Nov 2018	m	40–50	Southern Bohemia	Rovinj, Croatia	10–20 years (1997–2001)	Teaching, preaching, evangelism
Renata	06 Nov 2018	f	40–50	Southern Bohemia	Rovinj, Croatia	10–20 years (1997–2001)	Worship, small groups
Patrik	01 Nov 2018	m	50–60	Prague/Northern Bohemia	Nova Gorica, Slovenia	20–30 years (since 2000)	Pastor, work with drug addicts, business
Kristýna	06 Jun 2019	f	40–50	Western Bohemia	Niš, Serbia	20–30 years (since 1998)	Youth work, worship, church ministry
Roman 1	08 Jun 2019	m	30–40	Prague	Beograd, Serbia	2–10 years (since 2016)	Pastor, teaching, evangelism
Ema 2	08 Jun 2019	f	30–40	Central Moravia/ Prague	Beograd, Serbia	2–10 years (since 2016)	Evangelism
Josef 1	19 Jul 2019	m	40–50	Northern Moravia/ Prague	Rovinj, Croatia	20–30 years (since 1996)	Pastor, counselling

Interviewees' Detailed Profiles

Name	Interview date	Gender	Age	Czech region of origin	Location, country code	Timeframe or location	Ministry/Relation to missionary
Klára	19 Jul 2019	f	40–50	Prague	Rovinj, Croatia	20–30 years (since 1996)	Worship, evangelism, small groups
Ema 1	23 Jul 2019	f	50–60	Prague/Northern Bohemia	Nova Gorica, Slovenia	20–30 years (since 2000)	Work with drug addicts, teaching music
Šimon	23 Jul 2019	m	20–30	Slovenia/Northern Bohemia	Nova Gorica, Slovenia	20–30 years (since 2000)	Youth work
Jonatán	12 Sep 2019	m	40–50	Prague	Rovinj, Croatia	10–20 years (1999–2009)	Evangelism, church work
Primary sources: Czech periodically returning missionaries							
Jakub 1	23 Nov 2018	m	30–40	Central Bohemia	Bihać, Bosnia and Herzegovina	To Bosnia and Herzegovina (and to Serbia and North Macedonia)	Working with refugees, evangelism
Josef 3	04 Dec 2018	m	40–50	Central Moravia	Sanski Most, Bosnia and Herzegovina	To Sanski Most, Bosnia and Herzegovina	Local church support, evangelism
Radek	05 Dec 2018	m	50–60	Central Moravia	Stara Pazova, Serbia	To Stara Pazova, Serbia (and to Montenegro)	Local church support

Name	Interview date	Gender	Age	Czech region of origin	Location, country code	Timeframe or location	Ministry/Relation to missionary
Vratislav	30 Jul 2019	m	50–60	Silesia	Daruvar, Croatia	To Daruvar, Croatia, moving in 2021	Local church support, youth work
Denisa	30 Jul 2019	f	50–60	Silesia	Daruvar, Croatia	To Daruvar, Croatia, moving in 2021	Local church support, evangelism
Jakub 2	25 Sep 2019	m	40–50	Central Moravia	Silbaš, Serbia	To Stara Pazova, Serbia	Local church support
Daniel	12 Nov 2019	m	30–40	Croatia / Prague	Nova Gorica, Slovenia	To Nova Gorica, Slovenia, to Bosnia and Herzegovina, to Croatia	Teaching, church support
Roman 2	28 Dec 2019	m	30–40	Southern Moravia	Banja Luka, Bosnia and Herzegovina	To Banja Luka, Bosnia and Herzegovina	Local church support
Erika 2	28 Dec 2019	f	30–40	Southern Moravia	Banja Luka, Bosnia and Herzegovina	To Banja Luka, Bosnia and Herzegovina	Local church support

Interviewees' Detailed Profiles 295

Name	Interview date	Gender	Age	Czech region of origin	Location, country code	Timeframe or location	Ministry/Relation to missionary
				Supporting primary sources			
Jakub 3	08 Nov 2018	m	50–60	Prague	Prague	Parish priest	(Erika 1)
Eldina	16 Nov 2018	f	40–50	Bosnia and Herzegovina	USA	Team leader and supervisor	(Erika 1)
Prokop	19 Nov 2018	m	40–50	Prague	Prague	Sending pastor	(Marek)
Matěj	21 Nov 2018	m	50–60	Prague	Prague	Leader of sending mission agency	(Josef 1, Klára, Josef 2, Renata, Jonatán)
Miodrag	07 Jun 2019	m	20–30	Serbia	Serbia	Colleague in church team	(Kristýna)
Vladan	07 Jun 2019	m	50–60	Serbia	Serbia	Local church pastor and team leader	(Kristýna)
Miroslav	10 Jun 2019	m	30–40	Serbia/Prague	Serbia	Director of Czech minority association in Belgrade, Serbia	(Kristýna)
Stojan	19 Jul 2019	m	40–50	Bosnia and Herzegovina/ Serbia	Serbia	Husband	(Kristýna)
Bethany	28 Oct 2019	f	40–50	South Africa	Bosnia and Herzegovina	Teammate	(Erika 1)

Appendix B

Informed Consent for Research

About this research:
This research focuses on Czech missionaries in the countries of former Yugoslavia since 1989. I would like to better understand how missionaries handle their identity in their interactions with Slavs in Bosnia and Herzegovina, Croatia, Kosovo, North Macedonia, Montenegro, Serbia and Slovenia and how this is reflected in their ministry.

What this research involves:
I would like to address all Czechs who have been active in some way in cross-cultural work with Slavs in former Yugoslavia. If you agree to take part in this research, I will perform an audio recorded interview approximately forty-five minutes long. Also, if the situation permits, I would like to interview people connected to missionaries on the sending and the receiving side.

Possible risks of your participation:
The risks are minimal, but there is a possibility that some of the questions might make you uncomfortable. However, I do not want you to feel

uncomfortable and you do not have to answer any question if it concerns personal matters that you prefer to keep for yourself.

Possible benefits of your participation:

There might be no direct benefits for you, but your participation will likely help contribute towards further development of mission from the Czech Republic.

Maintaining your privacy:

Audio records will be stored safely in my computer and only my two supervisors and I will have access to them. When I finish my studies, I will delete them. Your personal data will be handled with care according to the EU directive about data protection (GDPR). The research about Czech missionaries in former Yugoslavia cannot be in its nature wholly anonymous, but a certain level of anonymity is granted.

What if I decide to withdraw from the research?

Participation is completely voluntary. You have the right to step away at any time from the interview and the data provided will not be used.

What if I have an additional question, concern or complaint?

The research results might be published in an academic journal or a scientific-popular literature. You have the possibility to request the text before its publishing, read it through and approve it. You can always contact me at symonuv@gmail.com or you can turn (in English) to OCMS: ocms@ocms.ac.uk.

I _____ consent to participate in the study by David Symon "Identity of Czech missionaries in the former Yugoslav countries." I have read the foregoing information or it has been read to me. I have had the opportunity to ask additional questions and to get satisfactory answers. My participation in this research is completely voluntary. I have received a copy of the Informed consent for research.

Date _____ Signature _____

I, David Symon, as the researcher have witnessed that the research participant has read the Informed consent for research and has made him- or herself familiar with the interview. The participant has had the opportunity to ask questions and I answered them to the best of my ability. The participant has received from me a copy of Informed consent for research.

Date _____ Signature _____

Appendix C

List of Semi-structured Interview Questions

Primary sources – Czech missionaries

0. Background information
   (a.) Could you tell me something about yourself and how you got involved in mission work in [one of the countries of former Yugoslavia]?
   (b.)
   - What is your name and how old are you?
   - Where do you come from (town, region)?
   - What is your church affiliation?
   - Where do you work and for how long (place, ministry type, role in the team, partner church or mission organisation)?

1. Research question: "To what extent are the Slavic Czechs working with their fellow-Slavs in former Yugoslav countries cross-cultural?"
   (a.) In your opinion as a Czech, to what degree can work with Slavs in former Yugoslavia be considered cross-cultural?
   (b.)
   - How do you perceive the differences and similarities between the Czech and [former Yugoslav] culture?

- How do [former Yugoslavs] respond to you as a Czech missionary?
- Could you recall a moment when they accepted you and listened to you because of that, or when they rejected you, or when they were indifferent?

2. Research question: "How and in what circumstances does the Czech identity of Czech missionaries become salient or suppressed?"
   (a.) Could you tell me about how important it is for you to be Czech in . . .?
   (b.)
   - To what extent do you feel Czech?
   - Were there any situations where you really felt very Czech?
   - How did you feel, were you happy, proud or was it embarrassing?
   - Were there any situations where you abandoned your "Czechness" and you identified more with former Yugoslavs? What was it like?

3. Research question: "How does the missionaries' 'Czechness' interact with their other identity facets?"
   (a.) We have talked about being Czech as part of our identity. Now, could you tell me, what else is important that makes you who you are?
   (b.)
   - Do you feel strongly as something or someone?
   - Is membership in any groups important for you?
   - Who do you think influences you as a Czech missionary?
   - How do you perceive your "Czechness" is related to the other parts of who you are?

Primary sources – other respondents

0. Background information
   (a.) Could you tell me something about yourself and how you know [the missionary's name]?

(b.)
- What is your background (name, age, town, region, church denomination, mission organisation)?
- For how long have you known the missionary? Could you tell me something about his/her ministry and what is his/her role in the mission task?

1. "To what extent are the Slavic Czechs working with their fellow-Slavs in former Yugoslav countries cross-cultural?"
    (a.) In your opinion as a Czech, to what degree can work with Slavs in former Yugoslavia be considered cross-cultural?
    (b.)
    - How do you perceive the differences and similarities between the Czech and [former Yugoslav] culture?
    - How do you find [former Yugoslavs] accept a Czech missionary?
    - Could you recall a moment when they accepted [missionary's name] and listened to him/her because of that, or when they rejected him/her, or when they were indifferent?

2. "How and in what circumstances does the Czech identity of Czech missionaries become salient or suppressed?"
    (a.) To what degree do you experience [the missionary's name] as Czech?
    (b.)
    - Do you see him/her more as a foreigner or a local?
    - Were there any situations when he/she felt like a local or when he/she felt like a complete foreigner?

3. "How does the missionaries' 'Czechness' interact with their other identity facets?"
    (a.) We have talked about [the missionary's name] as being Czech. Now, could you tell me, how else do you perceive this person?
    (b.)
    - Is he/she a member in any group?
    - How does he/she handle the various roles/responsibilities he/she has at the same time?

- How does he/she, according to you, perceive the relationship of being Czech to the other parts of who he/she is?

Appendix D

Interview Transcript Example

Date: 2019-07-19
Interviewee: Josef 1, Klára
Location: Rovinj, Croatia, their house
Notes:
- These are two records – informal chat (18 min), scheduled interview (59 min)
- Circumstances: first, the informal chat was loud (children having breakfast), the second at times interrupted, for a part of the interview I needed to rock the baby.
- Josef has a rich Czech vocabulary.
- In 1993 they started coming, two months or four months at a time, then since 1996 they live here.
- One day before the interview I participated in a home group, led by Josef, the topic from the Bible was on not being judgemental.
- Off the record comment: Cultural differences: In Croatia people work more on black market and avoid taxes.
- Off the record comment: Cultural similarities: Slavs have an opinion on everything; people here ask directly about finances (how much you earn, spend on a car, or for rent).

(Record number 2)
(Time: 9:16–13:25)

Josef 1: . . . I was shocked the most, positively, when together with pastors from Istria and Kvarner region we were planning a Bible training school for leaders. They were appointing among themselves who will teach the subjects and said: "We don't want foreigners to keep coming here to teach that, experts from the West, from abroad." And then, the guy who was saying that looked at me and realized that I was myself a foreigner (children interrupted) and he looked at me and said: "You've been for long ours" (laugh). So, this positively shocked me.

Klára: But concerning our perception of "Czechness" it is strange because when we are in Bohemia we long for Croatia as for our home. And when we are here and something is happening in Bohemia politically or with some of our friends, then again we experience it from the position of a Czech, they are ours, that is our country, so we are some kind of . . .

Josef 1: Outcasts.

Klára: Neither here, nor there, or more so both, or I don't know, heavenly citizens.

Josef 1: No place on earth, like the Son of God. Your home is in heavens and when you focus on heaven, when you are here you look forward to there, when you are there you look forward here. But definitely we are rooted more here.

Klára: We are at home here. But at the same time, we love Bohemia.

Interviewer: You have mentioned the meeting of pastors, when you merged with the locals. Do you recall any other situations, anything else when "Czechness" was suppressed, when you were one of Croats, or when you yourselves suppressed it?

Josef 1: At the beginning when we were here I wanted to be a Croat to Croats, based on the word that Paul says: Czech to Czechs, Croat to Croats, Jew to Jews, Greek to Greeks. And inside of me, I was setting apart from the Czech culture, it was because of that that I was learning the language. This is a moment when you start forgetting your language and you don't know the local yet. It is like you had a stroke and you start learning to speak again and to formulate thoughts. So, your IQ falls down to the level of a ten-year-old boy, you don't know how to express yourself, it is very weird. And at that time, I was going through a desire to be accepted by the culture, accepted by the local people, that they accept us as their own. I really was putting a lot of stress on that, but it was not good in this degree. It is good when one strives to adjust, I think that Paul means this when he is speaking about it, that you adjust, but that you are aware of that identity of yours, not trying to remake it, because it is as it is, and it will stay that way. But I went into extreme in this and that was one of the factors why later I burnt out, because they will not accept you, based on that you are attempting to be a Croat to Croats, that you start behaving like one of them, speaking like them.

Bibliography

Primary Sources

Interview sources: for a detailed explanation see Appendix A
- Czech Protestant missionaries in former Yugoslav countries

Daniel, m, returning to Slovenia
Denisa, f, returning to Croatia
Ema 1, f, 20–30 years in Slovenia
Ema 2, f, 2–10 years in Serbia
Erika 1, f, 1 year in Bosnia and Herzegovina
Erika 2, f, returning to Bosnia and Herzegovina
Jakub 1, m, returning to Bosnia and Herzegovina
Jakub 2, m, returning to Serbia
Jonatán, m, 10–20 years in Croatia
Josef 1, m, 20–30 years in Croatia
Josef 2, m, 10–20 years in Croatia
Josef 3, m, returning to Bosnia and Herzegovina
Klára, f, 20–30 years in Croatia
Kristýna, f, 20–30 years in Serbia
Marek, m, 1 year in Kosovo
Patrik, m, 20–30 years in Slovenia
Radek, m, returning to Serbia
Renata, f, 10–20 years in Croatia
Roman 1, m, 2–10 years in Serbia
Roman 2, m, returning to Bosnia and Herzegovina

Šimon, m, 20–30 years in Slovenia
Vratislav, m, returning to Croatia

- Supplementary sources related to individual missionaries

Bethany, f, teammate (Erika 1 Bosnia and Herzegovina)
Eldina, f, supervisor and team leader (Erika 1 Bosnia and Herzegovina)
Jakub 3, m, sending parish priest (Erika 1 Bosnia and Herzegovina)
Matěj, m, leader of sending mission agency (Josef 1 Croatia)
Miodrag, m, colleague (Kristýna Serbia)
Miroslav, m, acquaintance and director of Czech minority association in Belgrade, Serbia (Kristýna Serbia)
Prokop, m, sending pastor (Marek Kosovo)
Stojan, m, husband (Kristýna Serbia)
Vladan, m, pastor and team leader (Kristýna Serbia)

Field notes from the interviews

- Field notes-DS-2018-10 Prague, Czech Republic (Marek Kosovo)
- Field notes-DS-2019-06 Niš, Serbia (Kristýna Serbia)
- Field notes-DS-2019-07 Velika Gorica, Croatia (Patrik Slovenia)
- Field notes-DS-2019-07 Velika Gorica, Croatia (Josef 1 Croatia)

Personal diaries

- Diary notes (2008–2019)

Diary notes-DS-2008-10 Banja Luka, Bosnia and Herzegovina
Diary notes-DS-2013-07 Banja Luka, Bosnia and Herzegovina
Diary notes-DS-2015-06 Bar Montenegro
Diary notes-DS-2015-06 Kravica Falls, Bosnia and Herzegovina
Diary notes-JV-2012-07 Sarajevo, Bosnia and Herzegovina
Diary notes-JV-2018-07 Sarajevo, Bosnia and Herzegovina
Diary notes-SN-2018-07 Sarajevo, Bosnia and Herzegovina
Diary notes-JP-2018-08 Tallin, Estonia

- Photo diary (2003–2018)

Photo diary-2003-08 Struga, North Macedonia

Photo diary-2004-04 Györ, Hungary

Photo diary-2007-07 Gojbulja, Kosovo

Photo diary-2009-03 Sarajevo, Bosnia and Herzegovina

Photo diary-2009-04 Zenica, Bosnia and Herzegovina

Photo diary-2009-01 Mostar, Bosnia and Herzegovina

Bibliography

Photo diary-2009-04 Banja Luka, Bosnia and Herzegovina

Photo diary-2010-04 Laktaši, Bosnia and Herzegovina

Photo diary-2011-11 Banja Luka, Bosnia and Herzegovina

Photo diary-2012-09 Novo Čiče, Croatia

Photo diary-2014-11 Prague, Czech Republic

Bibliography

Photo diary-2016-04 Banja Luka, Bosnia and Herzegovina

Photo diary-2011-11 Banja Luka, Bosnia and Herzegovina

Photo diary-2014-04 Banja Luka, Bosnia and Herzegovina

Photo diary-2015-10 Slavonski Brod, Croatia

Photo diary-2017-05 Prijedor, Bosnia and Herzegovina

Photo diary-2018-09 Zagreb, Croatia

Photo diary-2018-07 Sarajevo, Bosnia and Herzegovina

Secondary Sources

Adeney, Miriam. "Is God Colorblind or Colorful?: The Gospel, Globalization and Ethnicity." In *Perspectives on the World Christian Movement: Reader*, edited by Ralph D. Winter and Steven C. Hawthorne, 415–22. Pasadena: William Carey Library, 2009.

Allik, Jüri, A. Timothy Church, and Fernando A. Ortiz. "Mean Profiles of the NEO Personality Inventory." *Journal of Cross-Cultural Psychology* 48, no. 1 (2017): 1–9.

Anderson, Benedict. *Imagined Communities: Reflection on the Origin and Spread of Nationalism*. 2nd ed. London: Verso, 1991.

Auer, Stefan. "After 1989, Who Are the Czechs?" *Nationalism and Ethnic Politics* 12, no. 3–4 (2006): 411–30. https://doi.org/10.1080/13537110600882627.

Augoustinos, Martha, and Stephanie De Garis. "Too Black or Not Black Enough: Social Identity Complexity in the Political Rhetoric of Barack Obama." *European Journal of Social Psychology* 42, no. 5 (2012): 564–77. https://doi.org/10.1002/ejsp.1868.

Balík, Stanislav. *Christianizace Českých Zemí ve Středoevropské Perspektivě [Christianization from the Czech Lands in the Central European Perspective]*. Brno: Matice moravská, 2011. https://www.muni.cz/vyzkum/publikace/961062.

Bargár, Pavol. "Mission in the Czech Republic: An Ecumenical Perspective." In *Mission in Central and Eastern Europe: Realities, Perspectives, Trends*, edited by Corneliu Constantineanu, Marcel Macelaru, Anne-Marie Kool, and Mihai Himcinschi, Constantineanu Corneliu et al., 270–91. Oxford: Regnum Books International, 2017.

Barnett, Mike, and Robin Martin, eds. *Discovering the Mission of God: Best Missional Practices for the 21st Century*. Downers Grove: InterVarsity Press, 2012.

Barth, Fredrik. *Ethnic Groups and Boundaries: The Social Organization of Culture Difference*. Bergen; Oslo: Universitetsforlaget; London: George Allen & Unwin, 1969.

Bauman, Zygmunt, and Tim May. *Thinking Sociologically*. 2nd ed. Ebook Central. Malden: Blackwell Publishing Ltd, 2004. https://ezproxy-prd.bodleian.ox.ac.uk/login?url=http://ebookcentral.proquest.com/lib/oxford/detail.action?docID=1811104.

Bauman, Zygmunt, and Rein Raud. *Practices of Selfhood*. 1st ed. Cambridge: Polity, 2015.

Bekus, Nelly. *Struggle over Identity: The Official and the Alternative "Belarusianness."* Budapest: Central European University Press, 2010.

Bellamy, Alex J. *The Formation of Croatian National Identity: A Centuries-Old Dream*. Europe in Change. Manchester: Manchester University Press, 2003.

Berg, Bruce L. *Qualitative Research Methods for the Social Sciences*. 7th ed. Upper Saddle River: Pearson, 2009.

Berry, John W, Ype H Poortinga, Segall H Marshall, and Pierre R Dasen. *Cross-Cultural Psychology*. Cambridge: Cambridge University Press, 2002.

Bevans, Stephen B., and Roger Schroeder. *Constants in Context: A Theology of Mission for Today*. American Society of Missiology Series; No. 30. Maryknoll: Orbis, 2004.

Blaive, Muriel. "The Czechs and Their Communism, Past and Present." In *Inquiries into Past and Present*, edited by Deanna Gard, Izabella Main, Oliver Martyn, and James Wood, Vol. 17. Vienna: IWM Junior Visiting Fellows' Conferences, 2005. http://www.iwm.at/publications/5-junior-visiting-fellows-conferences/vol-xvii/muriel-blaive/.

Bodenhausen, Galen V. "Diversity in the Person, Diversity in the Group: Challenges of Identity Complexity for Social Perception and Social Interaction." *European Journal of Social Psychology* 40, no. 1 (2010): 1–16.

Bodenhausen, Galen V., and Sonia K. Kang. "Multiple Identities in Social Perception and Interaction: Challenges and Opportunities." *Annual Review of Psychology* 66, no. 1 (2015): 547–74.

Bosch, David J. *Transforming Mission: Paradigm Shifts in Theology of Mission*. American Society of Missiology Series; no. 16. Maryknoll: Orbis Books, 1991.

Bourdieu, Paul. *Le Sens Pratique [The Practical Sense]*. Paris: Editions de Minuit, 1980.

Brewer, Marilynn B. "Social Identity Complexity and Acceptance of Diversity." In *The Psychology of Social and Cultural Diversity*, edited by Richard J. Crisp, 11–33. Chichester: Blackwell Publishing Ltd, 2010.

Brewer, Marilynn B., and Ya-Ru Chen. "Where (Who) Are Collectives in Collectivism? Toward Conceptual Clarification of Individualism and Collectivism." *Psychological Review* 114, no. 1 (2007): 133–51.

Brewer, Marilynn B., and Kathleen P. Pierce. "Social Identity Complexity and Outgroup Tolerance." *Personality and Social Psychology Bulletin* 31, no. 3 (2005): 428–37. https://doi.org/10.1177/0146167204271710.

Britannica, "Kosovo: Self-Declared Independent Country," https://www.britannica.com/place/Kosovo.

British Educational Research Association, "Ethical Guidelines for Educational Research." https://www.bera.ac.uk/publication/ethical-guidelines-for-educational-research-2018.

Brodnjak, Vladimir. *Rječnik Razlika Između Hrvatskoga i Srpskoga Jezika [The Dictionary of the Difference between Serbian and Croatian Language]*. Zagreb: Školske novine, 1992.

Brodský, Jiří. "Czech Identity and Returning to Europe," *Sien Quarterly* 1–2 (2003–2004): 9–22.

Bryman, Alan. *Social Research Methods*. 5th ed. Oxford: Oxford University Press, 2016.
Burjanek, Ales. "Xenophobia among the Czech Population in the Context of Post-Communist Countries and Western Europe." *Sociologický Časopis/Czech Sociological Review* 9, no. 1 (2001): 53–67.
Burke, Peter J., and Jan E. Stets. *Identity Theory*. Oxford: Oxford University Press, 2009. http://www.oxfordscholarship.com/view/10.1093/acprof:o so/9780195388275.001.0001/acprof-9780195388275.
Cambridge Dictionary, "Context." https://dictionary.cambridge.org/dictionary/english/context.
Campbell, William S. *Paul and the Creation of Christian Identity*. T&T Clark Library of Biblical Studies. London: T&T Clark, 2006. https://www.bloomsburycollections.com/book/paul-and-the-creation-of-christian-identity/.
Castells, Manuel. "Globalisation and Identity: A Comparative Perspective." *Transfer*, no. 1 (2006): 56–66.
Černý, Pavel. "A Response to Paul Negrut." *Transformation* 16, no. 1 (1999): 24–26.
———. "Jeden Pán, jedna víra a současné eklesiologické hledání [One Lord, One Faith and Contemporary Ecclesiological Searching]." *Studia theologica* 17, no. 3 (2015): 155–70.
———. *Kristovo dílo spásy jako základ a imperativ misie: aktivity Světové rady církví* [*Christ's Work of Salvation as a Foundation and Imperative for Mission: Activities of World Council of Churches*]. 1st ed. Pontes pragenses 41. Brno: L. Marek, 2006a.
———. "Misijní Podoba Církve Dnes: Hledání Podoby Misijní Církve pro 21. Století [Mission Form of Contemporary Church: Searching for the Missional Church for 21st Century]," 1–12. Praha, 24–25.11. 2006b. https://pavel.onesim.net/system/attachments/blobs/000/000/005/original/Misijn%C3%AD_podoba_c%C3%ADrkve_dnes-116-06.pdf?1359022212.
———. "Mission in the Czech Republic: A Search for a Relevant Mission Theology in a Post-Secular Environment." In *Mission in Central and Eastern Europe: Realities, Perspectives, Trends*, edited by Corneliu Constantineanu, Marcel Macelaru, Anne-Marie Kool, and Mihai Himcinschi, 603–18. Oxford: Regnum Books International, 2017.
———. "Mission of the Contemporary Church: A Meditation on the Missionary Practice of the Gospel in the Secular Environment of the Czech Republic." Edited by Zuzana Jurechová, Pavol Bargár, and Dalibor Vik. *Central European Missiological Forum*, 2011, 48–54.
———. "Praxe Dialogu Křesťanů s Příslušníky Jiných Náboženství [Practice of Christians' Dialogue with Members of Other Religions]." In *Křesťané a Jiná Náboženství* [*Christians and Other Religions*], edited by Karel Taschner and

Pavel Hošek, 1st ed., 137–51. Evangelikální Fórum: Sborník Evangelikálních Teologů 4/2004. Praha: SET, 2004.

———. "Vztah Teologie a Misiologie: Misijní Hermeneutika [Relationship of Theology and Missiology: Mission Hermeneutics]." Praha: Středoevropské centrum misijních studií, 2007. http://pavel.onesim.net/system/attachments/blobs/000/000/004/original/Misijni_hermeneutika_Cerny.pdf?1359022038.

Český Statistický Úřad [Czech Statistical Office], "Náboženská víra obyvatel podle výsledků sčítání lidu – 2011 [Religious Faith of Inhabitants According to the 2011 Census]." https://www.czso.cz/csu/czso/nabozenska-vira-obyvatel-podle-vysledku-scitani-lidu-2011-61wegp46fl.

Chalániová, Daniela. "Cultural Diplomacy and Stereotypes in Present-Day Czecho-Slovak Relations: Breaking with the Past? Heterostereotypes of Czechs and Slovaks Twenty Years from the Velvet Divorce." Edited by Martina Topić and Siniša Rodin. *Cultural Diplomacy and Cultural Imperialism: European Perspective(s)*, 2012, 161–88.

Chmiliar, Linda. "Multiple-Case Designs." In *Encyclopedia of Case Study Research*, edited by Albert J. Mills, Gabrielle Durepos, and Elden Wiebe, 582–83. Los Angeles: SAGE, 2010.

Cholastová, Eva. "Regional Stereotypes: Perception of Personality Traits in the Typical Czech, Moravian and Silesian [Posuzování Regionálních Stereotypů: Percepce Osobnostních Rysů Typického Čecha, Moravana a Slezana]." MA Thesis, Masyrykova univerzita Brno, 2010. https://is.muni.cz/th/yonxw/Diplomova_prace_Eva_Cholastova.pdf.

Chorvát, Ivan. "Czechs and Slovaks as Explorers of the Yugoslavian Adriatic Coast," 1–9. Blackpool, United Kingdom, 2009.

Činčala, Petr. "A Theoretical Proposal for Reaching Irreligious Czech People through a Mission Revitalization Movement." Thesis, Andrews University, 2002. http://digitalcommons.andrews.edu/cgi/viewcontent.cgi?article=1023&context=dissertations.

Čižmárová, Libuše. "History of and Popular Attitudes towards Names for the Czech-Speaking Territory." *AUC Geographica* 50, no. 1 (2015): 7–22.

Clandinin, D. Jean. *Handbook of Narrative Inquiry: Mapping a Methodology*. Thousand Oaks: Sage Publications, 2007. http://www.loc.gov/catdir/enhancements/fy0661/2006020694-t.html.

Clegg, Malcolm. "Understanding the Times – Research into the Impact and Direction of Christian Mission in Post-Communist Central and Eastern Europe at the Turn of the Century." MA Thesis, University of Sheffield, 2001.

Comrie, Bernard, ed. *The World's Major Languages*. 2nd ed. London: Routledge, 2009.

Constantineanu, Corneliu, Marcel V. Măcelaru, Anne-Marie Kool, and Mihai Himcinschi, eds. *Mission in Central and Eastern Europe: Realities, Perspectives, Trends*. Oxford: Regnum Books International, 2017.

De Mesa, José M.: "Mission and Inculturation." In *A Century of Catholic Mission: Roman Catholic Missiology 1910 to the Present*, edited by Stephen B. Bevans, 224–231. Oxford: Regnum Books International, 2013.

DeRoche, John Estano, and Constance DeRoche. "Ethics." In *Encyclopedia of Case Study Research*, edited by Albert J. Mills, Gabrielle Durepos, and Elden Wiebe, 337–344. Los Angeles: SAGE, 2010.

Dolista, Josef. *Misijní Úsilí Církve [Mission Effort of the Church]*. Teologie, sv. 17. Kostelní Vydří: Karmelitánské nakladatelství, 2001.

Drápal, Dan. *Problémy Sytých: Česko a Evropa v Dnešním Světě [The Problems of the Full: Czechia and Europe in the Contemporary World]*. 1st ed. Praha: KMS, 2008.

———. *Will We Survive Western Missionaries?: Reflections of a Czech Pastor on Meeting the Western Missionaries*. 2nd ed. Praha: Ampelos, 1997.

Drbohlav, Dušan, Lenka Lachmanová-Medová, Zdeněk Čermák, Eva Janská, Dita Čermáková, and Dagmara Dzúrová. "The Czech Republic: On Its Way from Emigration to Immigration Country," 2009. https://www.researchgate.net/publication/268427876_The_Czech_Republic_on_its_way_from_emigration_to_immigration_country.

Dumetz, Jerome, and Eva Gáboríková. "The Czech and Slovak Republics: A Cross-Cultural Comparison." *Marketing Science & Inspirations* 11 (2016): 2–13.

Durkheim, Emile. *The Elementary Forms of the Religious Life*. London: George Allen and Unwin Ltd., 1971.

Edženci, Slavko. "Church Planting in Belgrade." *Acta Missiologiae* 2011, no. 1 (2011): 7–32.

Eisenhardt, Kathleen M. "Building Theories from Case Study Research." *The Academy of Management Review* 14, no. 4 (1989): 532–50. https://doi.org/10.2307/258557.

Eriksen, Thomas Hylland. *Ethnicity and Nationalism: Anthropological Perspectives*. 3rd ed. Anthropology, Culture, and Society. London: Pluto Press; Palgrave Macmillan, 2010. https://ezproxy-prd.bodleian.ox.ac.uk/login?url=http://ebookcentral.proquest.com/lib/oxford/detail.action?docID=3386255.

Escobar, Samuel. *The New Global Mission: The Gospel from Everywhere to Everyone*. Downers Grove: IVP Academic, 2003.

Esler, Philip F. "An Outline of Social Identity Theory." In *T&T Clark Handbook to Social Identity in the New Testament*, edited by Brian J. Tucker and Coleman A. Stohl, 13–39. London: Bloomsbury T&T Clark, 2016. https://doi.org/10.5040/9780567669865.

European Values Study. "EVALUE – European Values in Education," https://www.atlasofeuropeanvalues.eu/maptool.html.

Fajfr, Daniel. "A Critical and Evaluative Study of the Roles and Partnership of Expatriate Christian Workers and Czech Evangelicals." MA Thesis, International Baptist Theological Seminary, 2005.

Fawn, Rick. "Czech Attitudes Towards the Roma: 'Expecting More of Havel's Country?'" *Europe-Asia Studies* 53, no. 8 (2001): 1193–1219. https://doi.org/10.1080/09668130120093192.

Foteva, Ana. *Do the Balkans Begin in Vienna?: The Geopolitical and Imaginary Borders between the Balkans and Europe*. Austrian Culture; Vol. 47. New York: Peter Lang, 2014. https://ezproxy-prd.bodleian.ox.ac.uk/login?url=http://ebookcentral.proquest.com/lib/oxford/detail.action?docID=1689203.

Gamsakhurdia, Vladimer. "Quest for Ethnic Identity in the Modern World: The Georgian Case." *Cogent Social Sciences* 3, no. 1 (2017): 1–14.

Geertz, Clifford. *The Interpretations of Cultures*. New York: Basic Books, 1973.

Gellner, Ernest. *Nations and Nationalism*. 1st ed. Oxford: Blackwell Publishing Ltd, 1983.

———. *Thought and Change*. Nature of Human Society Series. London: Weidenfeld and Nicolson, 1964.

Giddens, Anthony. *Sociology*. 8th ed. Cambridge: Polity Press, 2017.

Gilbert, Marvin, Alan R. Johnson, and Paul W. Lewis, eds. *Missiological Research: Interdisciplinary Foundations, Methods and Integration*. Pasadena: William Carey Library, 2018.

Gilliland, Dean S. "Contextual Theology as Incarnational Mission." In *The Word Among Us: Contextualizing Theology for Mission Today*, edited by Dean S. Gilliland, 9–31. Eugene: Wipf and Stock Publishers, 2002.

Global Research IMB, "Global Status of Evangelical Christianity," https://grd.imb.org/research-data/.

Globe Project, "An overview of the 2004 study: Understanding the Relationship Between National Culture, Societal Effectiveness and Desirable Leadership Attributes." GLOBE 2020. https://globeproject.com/study_2004_2007.

Golubović, Jelena, and Charlotte Gooskens. "Mutual Intelligibility between West and South Slavic Languages." *Russian Linguistics* 39, no. 3 (2015): 351–373. https://doi.org/10.1007/s11185-015-9150-9.

Gomm, Roger, Martyn Hammersley, and Peter Foster, eds. *Case Study Method: Key Issues, Key Texts*. Los Angeles: SAGE, 2000: repr. 2011.

Goodwin, Stephen R. *Fractured Land, Healing Nations: A Contextual Analysis of the Role of Religious Faith Sodalities Towards Peace-Building in Bosnia-Herzegovina*. 1st ed. Frankfurt am Main: Peter Lang AG, 2006.

Graham, Carolyn W., Gwendolyn T. Sorell, and Marilyn J. Montgomery. "Role-Related Identity Structure in Adult Women." *An International Journal of Theory and Research* 4, no. 3 (2004): 251–71.

Grant, Beth. "Interdisciplinary Research: Challenges and Pitfalls." In *Missiological Research: Interdisciplinary Foundations, Methods and Integration*, edited by Marvin Gilbert, 21–26. Pasadena: William Carey Library, 2018.

Greenberg, Robert D. *Language and Identity in the Balkans: Serbo-Croatian and Its Disintegration*. Oxford: Oxford University Press, 2004.

Halík, Tomáš. "Katolická Církev v České Republice Po Roce 1989 [Catholic Church in the Czech Republic after 1989]." In *Společnost v Přerodu. Češi ve 20. Století. Sborník Referátů z Cyklické Konference Demokracie 2000*, edited by Vratislav Doubek, 144–158. Praha: Masarykův ústav AV ČR, 2000.

Halík, Tomáš, and Pavel Hošek, eds. *A Czech Perspective on Faith in a Secular Age*. 1st ed. Cultural Heritage and Contemporary Change. Series IVA, Eastern and Central European Philosophical Studies, volume 51. Washington, DC: The Council for Research in Values and Philosophy, 2015.

Hamel, Jacques, Stéphane Dufour, and Dominic Fortin. "Conflict of Methods." In *Case Study Methods*, 19–28. Qualitative Research Methods; v. 32. Newbury Park: SAGE, 1993. https://ezproxy-prd.bodleian.ox.ac.uk/login?url=http://methods.sagepub.com/book/case-study-methods.

Hamplová, Dana, and Zdeněk Nešpor. "Invisible Religion in a 'Non-Believing' Country: The Case of the Czech Republic." *Social Compass - SOC COMPASS* 56, no. 4 (2009): 581–597. https://doi.org/10.1177/0037768609345975.

Haney, Richard L. "Mapping Mission as Translation with Reference to Michael Polanyi's Heuristic Philosophy." Thesis, Middlesex University, 2014.

Hašek, Jaroslav. *The Good Soldier Švejk and His Fortunes in the World War*. Penguin Classics. London: Penguin, 2000.

Hatzopoulos, Pavlos. *The Balkans beyond Nationalism and Identity: International Relations and Ideology*. London: I.B. Tauris, 2008.

Havel, Václav. *Česká a Evropská Identita [Czech and European Identity]*. Praha: Knihovna Václava Havla, 2013.

———. "Český Úděl? [Czech Destiny?]." In *O Lidskou Identitu: Úvahy, Fejetony, Protesty, Polemiky, Prohlášení a Rozhovory z Let 1969–1979 [About Human Identity: Essays, Columns, Protests, Disputations, Declarations and Interviews, 1969–1979]*, by Václav Havel, 193–200. edited by Vilém Prečan and Alexander Tomský, 3rd ed. Praha: Rozmluvy, 1990. http://www.ucl.cas.cz/edicee/data/antologie/zdejin/3/havel-1.pdf.

———. *O Lidskou Identitu: Úvahy, Fejetony, Protesty, Polemiky, Prohlášení a Rozhovory z Let 1969–1979 [About Human Identity: Essays, Columns, Protests, Disputations, Declarations and Interviews, 1969–1979]*. Edited by Alexander Tomský and Vilém Prečan. 3rd ed. Praha: Rozmluvy, 1990.

Havel, Václav, Karel Hvížďala, Joska Skalník, and Karel Cudlín. *Prosím Stručně: Rozhovor s Karlem Hvížďalou, Poznámky, Dokumenty [Briefly Please: An Interview with Karel Hvížďala, Notes, Documents]*. 1st ed. Praha: Gallery, 2006.

Hays, Daniel J. "Paul and the Multi-Ethnic First-Century World: Ethnicity and Christian Identity." In *Paul as Missionary: Identity, Activity, Theology, and Practice*, edited by Trevor J. Burke and Brian S. Rosner, 76–87. London: Bloomsbury T&T Clark, 2011. https://doi.org/10.5040/9780567661104.

Hesselgrave, David J. *Communicating Christ Cross-Culturally: An Introduction to Missionary Communication*. Grand Rapids: Zondervan, 1991.

———. *Contextualization: Meanings, Methods, and Models*. Grand Rapids: Baker Book House, 1989.

Hiebert, Paul G. *Anthropological Insights for Missionaries*. Grand Rapids: Baker Book House, 1985.

———. *Cultural Anthropology*. Grand Rapids: Baker Book House, 1983.

———. "The Gospel in Human Contexts: Changing Perceptions of Contextualization." In *MissionShift: Global Mission Issues in the Third Millennium*, edited by David J. Hesselgrave and Ed Stetzer, 82–102. Nashville: B&H Publishing Group, 2010.

Hofstede, Geert, Gert Jan Hofstede, and Michael Minkov. *Cultures and Organizations: Software of the Mind*. New York: McGraw Hill, 2010.

Hofstede Insights. "Hofstede Insights – Country Comparison," https://www.hofstede-insights.com/country-comparison/croatia,czech-republic,serbia,slovenia/.

Hofstede Insights. "The Six Dimensions of National Culture," https://hi.hofstede-insights.com/national-culture.

Hogg, Michael A., Dominic Abrams, Sabine Otten, and Hinkle. "The Social Identity Perspective: Intergroup Relations, Self-Conception and Small Groups." *Small Group Research* 35, no. 3 (2004), 246–76. https://www.researchgate.net/publication/44279493_The_Social_Identity_Perspective.

Hogg, Michael A., Deborah J. Terry, and Katherine M. White. "A Tale of Two Theories: A Critical Comparison of Identity Theory with Social Identity Theory." *Social Psychology Quarterly* 58, no. 4 (1995): 255–69. https://doi.org/10.2307/2787127.

Holmberg, Bengt. "Understanding Christian Identity." In *Exploring Early Christian Identity*, edited by Frey, Jörg, Friedrich Avemarie, Judith Gundry-Volf, and Hans-Josef Klauck, 1–32. Wissenschaftliche Untersuchungen Zum Neuen Testament. 226. Tübingen: Mohr Siebeck, 2008.

Holubec, Stanislav. *We Haven't Made It yet: Images of the Other and Historical Memory during the Post-Communist Transformation [Ještě Nejsme Za Vodou: Obrazy Druhých a Historická Paměť v Období Postkomunistické Transformace]*. Praha: Scriptorium, 2015.

Holý, Ladislav. *The Little Czech and the Great Czech Nation: National Identity and the Post-Communist Transformation of Society*. Cambridge Studies in Social and Cultural Anthropology; 103. Cambridge: Cambridge University Press, 1996.

Horký-Hlucháň, Ondřej, and Tomáš Profant. "Reflexe Globálního Severu a Jihu Mezi Východem a Západem [Reflexion of the Global North and South between East and West]." In *Mimo Sever a Jih: Rozumět Globálním Nerovnostem a Rozmanitosti [Beyond North and South. Understanding Global Inequalities and Diversity]*, 9–36. Praha: Ústav mezinárodních vztahů, 2015.

Horrell, David G. "'Becoming Christian': Solidifying Christian Identity and Content." In *Handbook of Early Christianity: Social Science Approaches*, edited by Blasi, Anthony J., Paul-André Turcotte, and Jean Duhaime, 309–36. Walnut Creek: Rowman Altamira, 2014. https://www.researchgate.net/profile/David_Horrell/publication/29811796_Becoming_Christian_solidifying_Christian_identity_and_content/links/0deec53970c9148534000000.pdf.

Hošek, Pavel. *A Bohové Se Vracejí: Proměny Náboženství v Postmoderní Době [Gods Return: Religious Changes in the Postmodern Time]*. Jihlava: Mlýn, 2012.

———. "Discerning the Signs of the Times in Post-Communist Czech Republic: A Historical, Sociological and Missiological Analysis of Contemporary Czech Culture." In *A Czech Perspective on Faith in a Secular Age*, edited by Tomáš Halík and Pavel Hošek, 13–42. Washington, DC: The Council for Research in Values and Philosophy, 2015a.

———. *Islám Jako Výzva pro Křesťany [Islam as a Challenge for Christians]*. 1st ed. Praha: Návrat domů, 2016.

———. *Je to Náš Příběh: Teologický Esej o Vlastenectví a Křesťanských Hodnotách České Kultury [It Is Our Story: A Theological Essay on Patriotism and Christian Values in Czech Culture]*. Brno: Centrum pro studium demokracie a kultury, 2018.

———. "Towards a Kenotic Hermeneutics of Contemporary Czech Culture." In *A Czech Perspective on Faith in a Secular Age*, edited by Tomáš Halík and Pavel Hošek, 1–12. Washington, DC: The Council for Research in Values and Philosophy, 2015.

Hroch, Miroslav. *Social Preconditions of National Revival in Europe: A Comparative Analysis of the Social Composition of Patriotic Groups among the Smaller European Nations*. Translated by Ben Fowkes. New York: Columbia University Press, 2000.

Ieda, Osamu. "Regional Identities and Meso-Mega Area Dynamics in Slavic Eurasia: Focused on Eastern Europe." *Regio - Minorities, Politics, Society - English Edition* VII, no. 1 (2004): 3–22.

Jarjabka, Akos. "Organizational Culture in the Light of Central and Eastern European Cultural Similarities and Differences." *Közgazdász Fórum – Forum on Economics and Business* 17, no. 6 (2014): 8–40.

Jenkins, Richard. *Being Danish: Paradoxes of Identity in Everyday Life*. Copenhagen: Museum Tusculanum, 2011.

———. *Rethinking Ethnicity: Arguments and Explorations*. 2nd ed. Los Angeles: Sage, 2008.

———. *Social Identity*. 4th ed. Key Ideas. London: Routledge, Taylor & Francis Group, 2014.

Johansson, Rolf. "Case Study Methodology," 1–14. Stockholm, 2003. http://www.psyking.net/htmlobj-3839/case_study_methodology-_rolf_johansson_ver_2.pdf.

Johnson, Alan R. "Case Studies." In *Missiological Research: Interdisciplinary Foundations, Methods and Integration*, edited by Marvin Gilbert, 123–126. Pasadena: William Carey Library, 2018.

Jørgensen, Knud. "Introduction: Mission as Learning." In *A Learning Missional Church Reflections from Young Missiologists*, edited by Beate Fagerli, Rolv Olsen, Kari S. Haug, Knut Tveitereid, and Knud Jørgensen, 3–14. Oxford: Regnum Books International, 2012.

Jović, Dejan. "Communist Yugoslavia and Its 'Others.'" In *Ideologies and National Identities: The Case of Twentieth-Century Southeastern Europe*, edited by John Lampe and Mark Mazower, 277–302. Budapest: Central European University Press, 2006. http://books.openedition.org/ceup/2438.

Kenney, Padraic. *The Burdens of Freedom: Eastern Europe since 1989*. Global History of the Present. Black Point: Fernwood Publishing Ltd., 2006.

Kinnvall, Catarina. "Globalization and Religious Nationalism: Self, Identity, and the Search for Ontological Security." *Political Psychology* 25, no. 5 (2004): 741–67. https://doi.org/10.1111/j.1467-9221.2004.00396.x.

Klingsmith, Scott. *Missions Beyond the Wall: Factors in the Rise of Missionary Sending Movements in East-Central Europe*. Nürnberg, Bonn: VTR Publications, 2012.

Kłoczowski, Jerzy. *East-Central Europe's Position within Europe: Between East and West – L'Europe Du Centre-Est Dans l'espace Européen: Entre l'Est et l'Ouest*. Edited by Jerzy Kłoczowski. Lublin: Instytut Europy Środkowo-Wschodniej, 2004.

Kluckhohn, Florence Rockwood, and Fred L. Strodtbeck. *Variations in Value Orientations*. Westport: Greenwood Press, 1961.

Knifsend, Casey A., and Jaana Juvonen. "The Role of Social Identity Complexity in Inter-Group Attitudes Among Young Adolescents." *Social Development* 22, no. 3 (2013): 623–640. https://doi.org/10.1111/j.1467-9507.2012.00672.x.

Koeshall, Anita L. "Focus Group Interviews." In *Missiological Research: Interdisciplinary Foundations, Methods and Integration*, edited by Marvin Gilbert, 144–148. Pasadena: William Carey Library, 2018.

Kok, Jacobus. "Social Identity Complexity Theory as Heuristic Tool in New Testament Studies." *HTS Teologiese Studies/Theological Studies* 70, no. 1 (2014): 1–9. https://doi.org/10.4102/hts.v70i1.2708.

Komlosy, Andrea, and Hannes Hofbauer. "Identity Construction in the Balkan Region – Austrian Interests and Involvement in a Historical Perspective." In *Cultural Transitions in Southeastern Europe: Cultural Identity Politics in the (Post-)Transitional Societies*, 11–30. Zagreb: Institute for International Relations, 2011.

Kool, Anne-Marie. "A Missiologist's Look at the Future: A Missiological Manifesto for the 21st Century." In *Mission in Central and Eastern Europe: Realities, Perspectives, Trends*, edited by Corneliu Constantineanu, Marcel Macelaru, Anne-Marie Kool, and Mihai Himcinschi, 694–710. Oxford: Regnum Books International, 2017.

———. "Revolutions in European Mission – What Has Been Achieved in 25 Years of Eastern European Mission?" In *ResearchGate*. Bucharest, 2014. https://www.researchgate.net/publication/304213062_Revolutions_in_European_mission_What_has_been_achieved_in_25_years_of_Eastern_European_Mission.

Kozhuharov, Valentin. "Christian Mission in Eastern Europe." *Acta Missiologiae* 4, no. 1 (2015): 45–55.

Krejčí, Jaroslav. *O Češství a Evropanství: O Českém Národním Charakteru. 2. Díl [Czechness and Europeanness: About Czech National Character. Part 2]*. 1st ed. Dědictví Komenského, sv. 2. Ostrava: Amosium servis, 1995.

Krejčí, Pavel. "Don't Be Afraid of Czechia, It Needs Your Help." *Klaudyán: Internet Journal of Historical Geography and Environmental History* 5, no. 1 (2008): 30–37.

Křesťanská misijní společnost [Christian Mission Society]. "Život Víry [Life of Faith]." https://zivotviry.cz.

Kubiš, Karel, Vlasta Kubišová, Karolína Růžičková, and Michael Voříšek. "Czech Republic: Nation Formation and Europe." In *Entangled Identities: Nations and Europe [Electronic Resource]*, edited by Atsuko Ichijo and Willfried Spohn. Ebook Central. London: Routledge, 2005. https://ezproxy-prd.bodleian.ox.ac.uk/login?url=http://ebookcentral.proquest.com/lib/oxford/detail.action?docID=4758221.

Kučerová, Stanislava. "Konec České Národní Identity? [The End of Czech Identity]." In *Česká a Slovenská Otázka v Soudobém Světě: Základy Naší Hodnotové Orientace v Době Rozšiřování a Reforem EU [Czech and Slovak Question in the Contemporary World: The Basics of Our Value Orientation in the Time of EU's Broadening and Reforms]*, edited by Stanislava Kučerová, 220-27. Brno: Konvoj, 2002.

Kuecker, Aaron. "Ethnicity and Social Identity." In *T&T Clark Handbook to Social Identity in the New Testament*, edited by Brian J. Tucker and Coleman A. Stohl, 59-78. London: Bloomsbury T&T Clark, 2016. https://doi.org/10.5040/9780567669865.

Kundera, Milan. "Český Úděl [Czech Destiny]." In *O Lidskou Identitu: Úvahy, Fejetony, Protesty, Polemiky, Prohlášení a Rozhovory z Let 1969-1979 [About Human Identity: Essays, Columns, Protests, Disputations, Declarations and Interviews, 1969-1979]*, by Václav Havel, 3rd ed. edited by Vilém Prečan and Alexander Tomský, 187-93. Praha: Rozmluvy, 1990. https://is.muni.cz/el/1423/jaro2011/SOC403/um/Cesky_udel.pdf.

Kuzmič, Peter. "Christian Mission in Europe." *Themelios* 18, no. 1 (1992): 21-25.

———. "Christianity in Eastern Europe: A Story of Pain, Glory, Persecution and Freedom." In *Mission in Central and Eastern Europe: Realities, Perspectives, Trends*, edited by Corneliu Constantineanu, Marcel Macelaru, Anne-Marie Kool, and Mihai Himcinschi, 13-29. Oxford: Regnum Books International, 2017.

———. "The Journey from War to Peace in Bosnia: A Contextual Reflection of an Active Participant." In *Mission as Ministry of Reconciliation*, edited by Knud Jørgensen and Robert Schreiter, 223-30. Regnum Edinburgh Centenary Series. Oxford: Regnum Books International, 2013.

Kvaček, Robert. "O Českém Sebevědomí [About Czech Self-Confidence]." In *Česká a Slovenská Otázka v Soudobém Světě: Základy Naší Hodnotové Orientace v Době Rozšiřování a Reforem EU [Czech and Slovak Question in the Contemporary World: The Basics of Our Value Orientation in the Time of EU's Broadening and Reforms]*, edited by Stanislava Kučerová, 162-65. Brno: Konvoj, 2002.

Lankauskas, Gediminas. "On 'Modern' Christians, Consumption, and the Value of National Identity in Post-Soviet Lithuania." *Ethnos* 67, no. 3 (2002): 320-44. https://doi.org/10.1080/0014184022000031.

Lapadat, Judith C. "Thematic Analysis." In *Encyclopedia of Case Study Research*, edited by Albert J. Mills, Gabrielle Durepos, and Elden Wiebe, 926-27. Los Angeles: SAGE, 2010.

Levy, Aharon, Iris Žeželj, Marija Branković, Srdjan Dusanic, Martijn Van Zomeren, Tamar Saguy, and Eran Halperin. "Complex Social Identities and Intergroup Relations: Gateway Groups in the Western Balkans." *Social Psychology* 50, no. 3 (2019): 201-6.

Lieu, Judith. *Neither Jew nor Greek?: Constructing Early Christianity*. London: Bloomsbury T&T Clark, 2016. https://doi.org/10.5040/9780567665430.

Lingenfelter, Sherwood G, and Marvin K. Mayers. *Ministering Cross-Culturally: An Incarnational Model for Personal Relationships*. 3rd ed. Grand Rapids: Baker Academic, 2016.

Magda, Ksenija, and Melody J. Wachsmuth. "'Discerning the Body' in Cross-Cultural Relationships: A Critical Analysis of Missional Partnership in Southeastern Europe." *Kairos: Evangelical Journal of Theology* 8, no. 1 (2014): 23–43.

Malesevic, Siniša. *Identity as Ideology: Understanding Ethnicity and Nationalism*. Basingstoke: Palgrave Macmillan, 2006.

Maloku, Edona, Colette van Laar, Belle Derks, and Naomi Ellemerks. "Stimulating Interethnic Contact in Kosovo: The Role of Social Identity Complexity and Distinctiveness Threat." *Group Processes and Intergroup Relations* 22, no. 7 (2018): 1039–58.

Marshburn, Christopher K., and Eric D. Knowles. "White Out of Mind: Identity Suppression as a Coping Strategy Among Whites Anticipating Racially Charged Interactions." *Group Processes And Intergroup Relations* 21, no. 6 (2018): 874–892.

Masaryk, Tomáš Garrigue. *Česká Otázka; Naše Nynější Krize; Jan Hus [Czech Question; Our Contemporary Crisis; Jan Hus]*. Česká otázka 8. vyd., Naše nynější krize 7.vyd., Jan Hus 9. vyd. Spisy T.G. Masaryka, sv. 6. Praha: Masarykův ústav AV ČR, 2000.

May, Tim. *Social Research: Issues, Methods and Process*. 4th ed. Maidenhead: McGraw Hill, 2011. http://www.ebrary.com/landing/site/bodleian/index-bodleian.jsp?Docid=10481018.

McCabe, Kira O., and William Fleeson. "Are Traits Useful? Explaining Trait Manifestations as Tools in the Pursuit of Goals." *Journal of Personality and Social Psychology* 110, no. 2 (2016): 287–301.

McCrae, Robert R. "Cross-Cultural Research on the Five-Factor Model of Personality." *Online Readings in Psychology and Culture* 4, no. 4 (2002): 1–12.

McCrae, Robert R., and Paul Costa. *Personality in Adulthood: A Five-Factor Theory Perspective*. 2nd ed. New York: Guilford Press, 2003.

McCrae, Robert R., Paul Costa, and Thomas A. Martin. "The NEO-PI-3: A More Readable Revised NEO Personality Inventory." *Journal of Personality Assessment* 84, no. 3 (2005): 261–270.

McFee, Malcolm. "The 150% Man, a Product of Blackfeet Acculturation." *American Anthropologist* 70, no. 6 (1968): 1096–1107.

McIntosh, John A. "Missio Dei," in *Evangelical Dictionary of World Missions*, edited by Moreau, A. Scott, Harold A. Netland, Charles Edward van Engen, and David Burnett. Baker Reference Library. Grand Rapids: Baker Books, 2000.

Merriam Webster Dictionary. "Definition of Character," https://www.merriam-webster.com/dictionary/character.

Meyer, Dirk. "Social Identity Complexity and Sports Fans." MA Thesis, University of Pretoria, 2014. http://repository.up.ac.za/handle/2263/45021.

Milkov, Kosta. "The Roots of Proselytism: Ecclesiology and Atonement Theology." In *The Mission of God: Studies in Orthodox and Evangelical Mission*, edited by Mark Oxbrow and Tim Grass, 99–109. Regnum Studies in Mission. Oxford: Regnum Books International, 2015.

Miller, Kevin P., Marilynn B. Brewer, and Nathan L. Arbuckle. "Social Identity Complexity: Its Correlates and Antecedents." *Group Processes & Intergroup Relations* 12, no. 1 (2009): 79–94. https://doi.org/10.1177/1368430208098778.

Miłosz, Czesław. *Rodná Evropa [Native Realm: A Search for Self-Definition]*. Translated by Helena Stachová. Velká řada. Olomouc: Votobia, 1997.

Mojzes, Paul. "Proselytism in the Successor States of the Former Yugoslavia." *Journal of Ecumenical Studies* 36, no. 1–2 (1999): 221–43.

Moreau, A. Scott. *Contextualization in World Missions: Mapping and Assessing Evangelical Models*. Grand Rapids: Kregel Publications, 2012.

Moreau, A. Scott, Gary Corwin, and Gary B. McGee, eds. *Introducing World Missions: A Biblical, Historical, and Practical Survey*. Grand Rapids: Baker Academic, 2020.

Moreau, A. Scott. "Mission and Missions." In *Evangelical Dictionary of World Missions*, edited by Moreau, A. Scott, Harold A. Netland, Charles Edward van Engen, and David Burnett. Baker Reference Library. Grand Rapids: Baker Books, 2000.

Moriceau, John Estano. "Generalizability." In *Encyclopedia of Case Study Research*, edited by Albert J. Mills, Gabrielle Durepos, and Elden Wiebe, 337–344. Los Angeles: SAGE, 2010.

Morris, Alan. *A Practical Introduction to In-Depth Interviewing*. Los Angeles: SAGE, 2015.

Moyle, Marsh. "Shadows of the Past: The Lingering Effects of the Communist Mindset in the Church and Society." *Transformation: An International Journal of Holistic Mission Studies* 16, no. 1 (1999): 17–20. https://doi.org/10.1177/026537889901600106.

Nadační Fond Nehemia [Endowment Fund Nehemia], "Časopis Nehemia Info [Nehemia Info Magazine]." https://nehemia.cz/?page_id=7863.

Neill, Stephen. *A History of Christian Missions*. Harmondsworth: Penguin Books, 1986.

———. *Creative Tension*. Edinburgh: Edinburgh House Press, 1959.

Nešpor, Zdeněk R. *Příliš Slábi ve Víře: Česká Ne/Religiozita v Evropském Kontextu [Too Weak in Faith: The Czech (Non)Religiosity in the European Context]*. 1st ed. Praha: Kalich, 2010.

Nešpor, Zdeněk R., and Zdeněk Vojtíšek. *Encyklopedie menších křesťanských církví v České republice [Encyclopedia of Small Christian Denominations in the Czech Republic]*. 1st ed. Praha: Karolinum, 2015.

Newbigin, Lesslie. *Foolishness to the Greeks: The Gospel and Western Culture*. London: SPCK, 1986.

Niebuhr, H. Richard. *Christ and Culture*. New York: Harper & Brothers Publishers, 1951.

Novák, David. "A Critical Examination of Mission in Czech Evangelical Churches: Context, Reality, Roots, and Vision." MA Thesis, International Baptist Theological Seminary, 2004. ftp://ftp.marl.iastate.edu/Warren-2/Czech/2008/Czech%20research%20by%20Novak.pdf.

O'Connor, Coilin. "Jara Cimrman – The 'Greatest Ever' Czech?" Radio Prague International. https://english.radio.cz/jara-cimrman-greatest-ever-czech-8095952.

O'Connor, Erin L., Huon Longman, Katherine M. White, and Patricia L. Obst. "Sense of Community, Social Identity and Social Support Among Players of Massively Multiplayer Online Games (MMOGs): A Qualitative Analysis." *Journal of Community & Applied Social Psychology* 25, no. 6 (2015): 459–473. https://doi.org/10.1002/casp.2224.

Pabian, Petr. "Czech Christianity in a Post-Christian Society." *Communio Viatorum*, no. 1 (2015): 77–89.

Pamir, Peri. "Nationalism, Ethnicity and Democracy: Contemporary Manifestations." *The International Journal of Peace Studies* 2, no. 2 (1997). http://www.gmu.edu/programs/icar/ijps/vol2_2/pamir.htm.

Parushev, Parush R. "Mission as Established Presence and Prophetic Witness in Culturally Orthodox Contexts." In *Evangelical Mission in the Eastern European Orthodox Contexts: Bulgaria, Romania, Moldova and Ukraine*, edited by Mihai Malancea, 57–112. Chisinau: Universitatea Divitia Gratiae, 2013.

Patočka, Jan. "Filosofie Českých Dějin: Přednáška Pronesená Dne 23. 4. 1969 v Rámci Cyklu 'Česká Otázka' v Klubu Socialistické Akademie [The Philosophy of Czech History: Lecture Held on 23rd April 1969 during the Cycle 'Czech Question' in the Socialistic Academy Club]." *Sociologický Časopis/Czech Sociological Review* 5, no. 5 (1969): 457–72.

Pekař, Josef. *Smysl Českých Dějin: O Nový Názor Na České Dějiny [The Meaning of Czech History: About a New Opinion on Czech History]*. 2nd ed. Praha: Historický klub, 1929.

Peters, George W. *A Biblical Theology of Missions*. Chicago: Moody Press, 1972.

Phillips, Estelle. *How to Get a PhD: A Handbook for Students and Their Supervisors*. 5th ed. Maidenhead: Open University Press, 2010.

Plecitá, Klára. *Národní identita a vztah k Evropské unii: Česká republika v západo- a středoevropském srovnání [National Identity and the Relationship to European*

Union: *The Czech Republic in the Western- and Central European Comparison]*. Studie Národohospodářského ústavu Josefa Hlávky 1/2012. Praha: Národohospodářský ústav Josefa Hlávky, 2012.

Potůček, Martin. *Jak Jsme Na Tom a Co Dál?: Strategický Audit České Republiky [Present Situation and What Next?: Strategic Audit of the Czech Republic]*. 1st ed. Praha: Sociologické nakladatelství (SLON), 2005.

Prašnikar, Janez, Marko Pahor, and Jasna Vidmar Svetlik. "Are National Cultures Still Important in International Business? Russia, Serbia and Slovenia in Comparison." *Management: Journal of Contemporary Management* 13, no. 2 (2008): 1–26.

Prati, Francesca, Richard J. Crisp, Felicia Pratto, and Monica Rubini. "Encouraging Majority Support for Immigrant Access to Health Services: Multiple Categorization and Social Identity Complexity as Antecedents of Health Equality." *Group Processes & Intergroup Relations* 19, no. 4 (2016): 426–38. https://doi.org/10.1177/1368430216629814.

Prince, Brainerd, and Benrilo Kikon. "Mission as Translation: A Fusion of Three Horizons." *Transformation* 35, no. 4 (2018): 251–63.

Publications Office of the European Union. "EU Vocabularies," https://op.europa.eu/en/web/eu-vocabularies/th-concept/-/resource/eurovoc/5781.

Pynsent, Robert B. *Questions of Identity: Czech and Slovak Ideas of Nationality and Personality*. Budapest: Central European University Press, 1994.

Radosta, Pavel. *Společné Století [Czech and Slovak Century]*. Praha: Česká centrála cestovního ruchu – Czech Tourism, 2017.

Rajh, Edo, Jelena Budak, and Ivan-Damir Anić. "Hofstede's Culture Value Survey in Croatia: Examining Regional Differences." *Journal for General Social Issues* 25, no. 3 (2016): 309–27.

Rattay, Petr. "Atheism in the Czech Republic: Are Czechs Atheists?" MA Thesis, University of Chester, 2013. http://docplayer.net/23186437-Atheism-in-the-czech-republic.html.

Rițișan, Gheorghe, and Corneliu Constantineanu. "APME – A Case Study in Cross-Cultural Mission Originating from Eastern Europe." In *Mission in Central and Eastern Europe: Realities, Perspectives, Trends*, edited by Corneliu Constantineanu, Marcel Macelaru, Anne-Marie Kool, and Mihai Himcinschi, 345–62. Oxford: Regnum Books International, 2017.

Roberts, Brian. *Biographical Research*. Understanding Social Research. Buckingham: Open University Press, 2002.

Roccas, Sonia, and Marilynn B. Brewer. "Social Identity Complexity." *Personality and Social Psychology Review* 6, no. 2 (2002): 88–106. https://doi.org/10.1207/S15327957PSPR0602_01.

Roccas, Sonia, Lilach Sagiv, Shalom Schwartz, Nir Halevy, and Roy Eidelson. "Toward a Unifying Model of Identification with Groups: Integrating

Theoretical Perspectives." *Personality and Social Psychology Review* 12, no. 3 (2008): 280–306. https://doi.org/10.1177/1088868308319225.

Samuel, Vinay, and Chris Sugden. *Mission as Transformation: A Theology of the Whole Gospel*. Eugene: Wipf & Stock, 2009.

Sanchez-Stockhammer, Christina. "Hybridization in Language." In *Conceptualizing Cultural Hybridization: A Transdisciplinary Approach – Heidelberg Studies on Asia and Europe in a Global Context*, edited by Philipp Wolfgang Stockhammer, 133–57. Berlin: Springer-Verlag, 2012.

Sanneh, Lamin. *Translating the Message: The Missionary Impact on Culture*. Maryknoll: Orbis Books, 2008.

Schirrmacher, Thomas. *Biblical Foundations for 21st Century World Mission: 69 Theses Toward an Ongoing Global Reformation*. Bonn: Verlag für Kultur und Wissenschaft, 2018.

Schmid, Katharina, Miles Hewstone, and Ananthi Al Ramiah. "Neighborhood Diversity and Social Identity Complexity: Implications for Intergroup Relations." *Social Psychological and Personality Science* 4, no. 2 (2013): 135–42. https://doi.org/10.1177/1948550612446972.

Schreiter, Robert J. "Communication and Interpretation across Cultures: Problems and Prospects." *International Review of Mission* 85, no. 337 (1996): 227–39.

Seidman, Irving. *Interviewing as Qualitative Research: A Guide for Researchers in Education and the Social Sciences*. New York: Teachers College Press, 2006.

Skoko, Božo. *Hrvatska i Susjedi: Kako Hrvatsku Doživljavaju Građani i Mediji u Bosni i Hercegovini, Crnoj Gori, Makedoniji, Sloveniji i Srbiji [Croatia and Its Neighbours – How Is Croatia Perceived in Bosnia and Herzegovina, Montenegro, Macedonia, Slovenia and Serbia]*. Hrvatski Identitet. Zagreb: AGM; Novelti millenium, 2010.

Škrabal, Josef. "Náboženská Víra Obyvatel Podle Výsledků Sčítání Lidu [Religious Faith of Inhabitants According to the Census Results]." Lidé a Společnost. Praha: Český statistický úřad, https://www.czso.cz/documents/10180/20551795/17022014.pdf/c533e33c-79c4-4a1b-8494-e45e41c5da18?version=1.0.

Slačálek, Ondřej. "The Postcolonial Hypothesis Notes on the Czech 'Central European' Identity." *ALPPI Annual of Language & Politics and Politics of Identity*, 2016, 27–44.

Smith, Anthony D. *National Identity*. Reno: University of Nevada Press, 1991.

Stets, Jan E., and Peter J. Burke. "A Sociological Approach to Self and Identity." In *Handbook of Self and Identity*, edited by Mark R. Leary and June Price Tangney, 128–152. New York: Guilford Press, 2003.

———. "Identity Theory and Social Identity Theory." *Social Psychology Quarterly* 63, no. 3 (2000): 224–237. https://doi.org/10.2307/2695870.

Storm, Ingrid. "Secular Christianity as National Identity: Religion, Nationality and Attitudes to Immigration in Western Europe." Thesis, University of Manchester, 2011.

Stryker, Sheldon, and Peter J. Burke. "The Past, Present, and Future of an Identity Theory." *Social Psychology Quarterly* 63, no. 4 (2000): 284–97. https://doi.org/10.2307/2695840.

Svatoň, Robert. "Jednota a poslání: Podněty k reflexi o vztahu mezi ekumenismem a misijním působením církve [Unity and Mission: Impulses for Reflection on the Relationship between Ecumenism and the Mission Activity of the Church]." *Studia theologica* 16, no. 3 (2014): 72–86.

Švob-Đokić, Nada. "Balkans Versus Southeastern Europe." In *Redefining Cultural Identities: Southeastern Europe*, edited by Nada Švob-Đokić, 35–41. Zagreb: Institute for International Relations, 2001.

Symon, David. "Studie Současného Studentského Slangu v Banja Luce [Studies of Contemporary Student Slang in Banja Luka]." MA Thesis, Charles University in Prague, 2008.

Tajfel, Henri. *Human Groups and Social Categories: Studies in Social Psychology*. 1st ed. Cambridge: Cambridge University Press, 1981.

Tajfel, Henri, and John C. Turner. "The Social Identity Theory of Intergroup Behavior." In *Political Psychology: Key Readings*, edited by J. T. Jost and J. Sidanius, 276–293. New York: Psychology Press, 2004.

Tanner, Kathryn. *Theories of Culture: A New Agenda for Theology*. Guides to Theological Inquiry. Minneapolis: Fortress Press, 1997.

Tennent, Timothy C. *Invitation to World Missions: The Trinitarian Theology for the Twenty-First Century*. Grand Rapids: Kregel Publications, 2010.

Teponen, Kati Ellen. "The Czech Destiny as a Space Inbetween?: Victimhood and Fate in the Dissident Thought of Milan Kundera and Václav Havel 1968–1989." MA Thesis, University of Helsinki, 2014. https://helda.helsinki.fi/bitstream/handle/10138/42816/Thesis%20Kati%20Temonen.pdf?sequence=1.

"The Cape Town Commitment: A Confession of Faith and a Call to Action." *International Bulletin of Missionary Research* 35, no. 2 (2011): 59–80. https://doi.org/10.1177/239693931103500202.

The World Bank, "GDP Per Capita," https://data.worldbank.org/indicator/NY.GDP.PCAP.CD.

Thomas, Gary. *How to Do Your Research Project: A Guide for Students in Education and Applied Social Sciences*. Los Angeles: Sage, 2009.

THT Consulting. "Trompenaars Hampden-Turner – Culture for Business," https://www2.thtconsulting.com.

Thurmond, Veronica A. "The Point of Triangulation." *Journal of Nursing Scholarship* 33, no. 3 (2001): 253–258. https://doi.org/10.1111/j.1547-5069.2001.00253.x.

Todorova, Maria. *Balkan Identities: Nation and Memory*. London: Hurst & Company, 2004.

———. *Imagining the Balkans*. Oxford: Oxford University Press, 2009. https://ezproxy-prd.bodleian.ox.ac.uk/login?url=http://oxford.eblib.com/patron/FullRecord.aspx?p=431330.

Tomić, Đorđe. "From 'Yugoslavism' to (Post)Yugoslav Nationalisms: Understanding Yugoslav 'Identities.'" In *European National Identities: Elements, Transitions, Conflicts*, edited by Roland Vogt, Wayne Cristaudo, and Andreas Leutzsch, 271–292. Piscataway: Transaction Publishers, 2014.

Toró, Tibor. "Compatibilities and Incompatibilities in the Political Doctrines of Communism and Nationalism." *Acta Universitatis Sapientiae. European and Regional Studies* 1 (2010): 33–58.

Trompenaars, Fons, and Charles Hampden-Turner. *Riding the Waves of Culture: Understanding Diversity in Global Business*. London: Nicholas Brealey Publishing, 2012.

Turner, John C. *Rediscovering the Social Group: A Self-Categorization Theory*. Cambridge: Basil Blackwell, 1987.

———. "Towards a Cognitive Redefinition of the Social Group." *Cahiers de Psychologie Cognitive/Current Psychology of Cognition* 1, no. 2 (1981): 93–118.

Uherek, Zdeněk, and Ana Bryson. "Ladislav Holý and Ernest Gellner: Representatives of Two Incompatible Approaches to the Study of Central European Society?" *Czech Sociological Review* 9, no. 2 (2001): 247–57.

Václavík, David. *Náboženství a Moderní Česká Společnost [Religion and Modern Czech Society]*. 1st ed. Praha: Grada, 2010.

Verkuyten, Maykel, and Borja Martinovic. "Social Identity Complexity and Immigrants' Attitude Toward the Host Nation: The Intersection of Ethnic and Religious Group Identification." *Personality and Social Psychology Bulletin* 38, no. 9 (2012): 1165–77. https://doi.org/10.1177/0146167212446164.

Vlachová, Klára. "Significant Others and the Importance of Ancestry for Czech National Identity." *National Identities*, Taylor & Francis Online, 1–16. https://doi.org/10.1080/14608944.2017.1362378.

Vlachová, Klára, and Blanka Řeháková. "Identity of Non-Self-Evident Nation: Czech National Identity after the Break-up of Czechoslovakia and before Accession to the European Union." *Nations and Nationalism* 15, no. 2 (2009): 254–279.

Vlasin, Alexandru. "Twenty-Five Years of Mission Movement in Central and Eastern Europe: An Indigenous Perspective." In *Mission in Central and Eastern Europe: Realities, Perspectives, Trends*, edited by Corneliu Constantineanu, Marcel Macelaru, Anne-Marie Kool, and Mihai Himcinschi, 56–66. Oxford: Regnum Books International, 2017.

Volf, Miroslav. *Exclusion and Embrace: A Theological Exploration of Identity, Otherness, and Reconciliation*. Nashville: Abingdon Press, 1996. http://www.ebrary.com/landing/site/bodleian/index-bodleian.jsp?Docid=10430631.

———. "Fishing in the Neighbor's Pond: Mission and Proselytism in Eastern Europe." *International Bulletin of Missionary Research* 20, no. 1 (1996): 26–31.

Volín, Jan, and Kristýna Poesová. "Perceptual Impact of Speech Melody Hybridization: English and Czech English." *Research in Language*, 14, no. 1 (2016): 31–41.

Wachsmuth, Melody J. "Missional Insights: Exploring the Foundations of Mission in the Southeastern European Context." *Kairos* 7, no. 1 (2013): 69–78.

Webster, Leonard, and Patricie Mertova. *Using Narrative Inquiry as a Research Method: An Introduction to Using Critical Event Narrative Analysis in Research on Learning and Teaching*. Abingdon: Routledge, 2007.

Wijsen, Frans. "Intercultural Theology and the Mission of the Church." *Exchange* 30, no. 1 (2001): 218–228.

Winter, Ralph D. "Frontier Mission Perspectives." In *Seeds of Promise: World Consultation on Frontier Missions, Edinburgh 80*, edited by Allan Starling, 45–124. Pasadena: William Carey Library, 1981.

———. "The New Macedonia: A Revolutionary New Era in Mission Begins." In *Perspectives on the World Christian Movement: Reader*, edited by Ralph D. Winter and Steven C. Hawthorne, 4th ed., 347–60. Pasadena: William Carey Library, 2009.

Winter, Ralph D., and Bruce A. Koch. "Finishing the Task: The Unreached Peoples Challenge." In *Perspectives on the World Christian Movement: Reader*, edited by Ralph D. Winter and Steven C. Hawthorne, 4th ed., 531–546. Pasadena: William Carey Library, 2009. https://joshuaproject.net/assets/media/articles/finishing-the-task.pdf.

Wheeler, Ray. "The Legacy of Shoki Coe." *International Bulletin of Missionary Research* 26, no. 2 (2002): 77–80.

Wright, Christopher J. H. *The Mission of God: Unlocking the Bible's Grand Narrative*. Nottingham: InterVarsity Press, 2006.

———. *The Mission of God's People: A Biblical Theology of the Church's Mission*. Grand Rapids: Zondervan, 2010.

Xin, Sufei, Ziqiang Xin, and Chongde Lin. "Effects of Trustors' Social Identity Complexity on Interpersonal and Intergroup Trust." *European Journal of Social Psychology* 46, no. 4 (2016): 428–440. https://doi.org/10.1002/ejsp.2156.

Yin, Robert K. *Case Study Research: Design and Methods,* 3rd ed. Thousand Oaks: SAGE Publications, Inc, 2002.

Ysseldyk, Renate, Kimberly Matheson, and Hymie Anisman. "Religiosity as Identity: Toward an Understanding of Religion From a Social Identity

Perspective." *Personality and Social Psychology Review* 14, no. 1 (2010): 60–71. https://doi.org/10.1177/1088868309349693.

Yu, Carver T. "Culture from an Evangelical Perspective." *Transformation* 17, no. 3 (2000): 82–85.

Žeželj, Iris, and Felicia Pratto. "What Identities in the Present May Mean for the Future of the Westen Balkans." In *Shaping Social Identities After Violent Conflict: Youth in the Western Balkans*, edited by Felicia Pratto, 159–188. Basingstoke: Palgrave Macmillan, 2017.

Zrinščak, Siniša. "Anonymous Believers as a Sociological Challenge: Religions and Religions Changes in Post-Yugoslav States." In *Religions, Churches and Religiosity in Post-Communist Europe*, edited by Irena Borowik, 68–80. Krakow: Zakład Wydawniczy "NOMOS," 2006. http://www.sinisazrinscak.com/wp-content/uploads/2012/12/Zrinscak-in-Barker-book-2006.pdf.

Langham Literature, with its publishing work, is a ministry of Langham Partnership.

Langham Partnership is a global fellowship working in pursuit of the vision God entrusted to its founder John Stott –

> *to facilitate the growth of the church in maturity and Christ-likeness through raising the standards of biblical preaching and teaching.*

Our vision is to see churches in the Majority World equipped for mission and growing to maturity in Christ through the ministry of pastors and leaders who believe, teach and live by the word of God.

Our mission is to strengthen the ministry of the word of God through:
- nurturing national movements for biblical preaching
- fostering the creation and distribution of evangelical literature
- enhancing evangelical theological education

especially in countries where churches are under-resourced.

Our ministry

Langham Preaching partners with national leaders to nurture indigenous biblical preaching movements for pastors and lay preachers all around the world. With the support of a team of trainers from many countries, a multi-level programme of seminars provides practical training, and is followed by a programme for training local facilitators. Local preachers' groups and national and regional networks ensure continuity and ongoing development, seeking to build vigorous movements committed to Bible exposition.

Langham Literature provides Majority World preachers, scholars and seminary libraries with evangelical books and electronic resources through publishing and distribution, grants and discounts. The programme also fosters the creation of indigenous evangelical books in many languages, through writer's grants, strengthening local evangelical publishing houses, and investment in major regional literature projects, such as one volume Bible commentaries like the *Africa Bible Commentary* and the *South Asia Bible Commentary*.

Langham Scholars provides financial support for evangelical doctoral students from the Majority World so that, when they return home, they may train pastors and other Christian leaders with sound, biblical and theological teaching. This programme equips those who equip others. Langham Scholars also works in partnership with Majority World seminaries in strengthening evangelical theological education. A growing number of Langham Scholars study in high quality doctoral programmes in the Majority World itself. As well as teaching the next generation of pastors, graduated Langham Scholars exercise significant influence through their writing and leadership.

To learn more about Langham Partnership and the work we do visit **langham.org**

www.ingramcontent.com/pod-product-compliance
Lightning Source LLC
Chambersburg PA
CBHW052012290426
44112CB00014B/2208